EVOLUTIONARY INNOVATIONS

Evolutionary Innovations

The Business of Biotechnology

Maureen D. McKelvey

OXFORD

UNIVERSITY PRESS

OXFORD

UNIVERSITY PRESS

Great Clarendon Street, Oxford OX2 6DP

Oxford University Press is a department of the University of Oxford.
It furthers the University's objective of excellence in research, scholarship,
and education by publishing worldwide in

Oxford New York

Athens Auckland Bangkok Bogotá Buenos Aires Calcutta
Cape Town Chennai Dar es Salaam Delhi Florence Hong Kong Istanbul
Karachi Kuala Lumpur Madrid Melbourne Mexico City Mumbai
Nairobi Paris São Paulo Singapore Taipei Tokyo Toronto Warsaw
and associated companies in Berlin Ibadan

Oxford is a registered trade mark of Oxford University Press
in the UK and in certain other countries

Published in the United States
by Oxford University Press Inc., New York

© Maureen McKelvey 1996

The moral rights of the author have been asserted
Database right Oxford University Press (maker)

First published 1996

First published in paperback 2000

British Library Cataloguing in Publication Data

Data available

Library of Congress Cataloging in Publication Data
McKelvey, Maureen D.
Evolutionary innovations: genetic engineering for human growth hormone and
insulin/Maureen D. McKelvey.
Includes bibliographical references and index.
1. Genetic engineering.   2. Biotechnology industries—United States.   3. Biotechnology
industries—Sweden.   4. Recombinant human insulin.   5. Recombinant human
somatotropin.   I. Title.
TP248.6.M38   1996   660'.65—dc20   95–49174
ISBN 0–19–828996–0
ISBN 0–19–829724–6 (pbk.)

1 3 5 7 9 10 8 6 4 2

Typeset by J&L Composition Ltd., Filey, North Yorkshire
Printed in Great Britain
on acid-free paper by
Biddles Ltd., Guildford & King's Lynn

Acknowledgements

This book is intended for a rather diverse audience which shares an interest in the relationships between science and technology and in research- and development-intensive industries like pharmaceuticals. More specifically, the book analyses, both theoretically and historically, early commercial uses of genetic engineering as developed to make human growth hormone and, to some extent, insulin.

The book has been developed on the basis of my Ph.D. dissertation, defended in June 1994 at the Department of Technology and Social Change, Linköping University, Sweden (McKelvey 1994b). The research project, 'Transforming Genetic Engineering from Science into an Industrial Tool', was supported by the Swedish Council for Planning and Coordination of Research (Forskningsrådsnämnden, FRN) under the Teknik och samhälle research programme.

This book is the result of a stimulating intellectual adventure, where many have participated. I would particularly like to acknowledge intellectual support from our research programme in Linköping, particularly by Professor Charles Edquist and Dr Mark Elam. They have given generously of their time, interest, and friendship. I would also especially like to thank Professor Richard Nelson for being the discussant at my Ph.D. defence and to members of the grading committee. Many thanks to the persons whom I interviewed who were involved in these early commercial uses of genetic engineering. They have generously contributed by giving of their time in interviews as well as by writing lengthy comments on an earlier draft. Despite all the comments, I, of course, bear the responsibility for all remaining errors of logic and substance.

Permission to reproduce quotes from archival material has been granted by the University of California, San Francisco library, and the Massachusetts Institute of Technology library. Melbourne University Press, and Professors Nossal and Coppel, have also given permission to reproduce the diagrams reproduced in Chapter 4.

As to the references, they are divided into three sections—Bibliography; Archival and Unpublished Material; and Interviews and Personal Communication. Moreover, the three Swedish letters 'å', 'ä', and 'ö' are used in the text, but in the references, they can be found under the English letters 'a', 'a'and 'o', respectively.

Having and creating academic visions truly depends on having friends and family. My husband Tomas, my parents, Michaelyn

McKelvey and Hamilton C. McKelvey, and the rest of our families have given me more love, more encouragement, and more hopes than words can express.

May 1995
Vikingstad

Contents

List of Figures

List of Abbreviations

cDNA	complementary DNA
DNA	deoxyribonucleic acid
DsU	Departementsserie/Utbildningsdepartementet (Ministry Series/Ministry of Education)
FAST	forecasting and assessment in science and technology
FDA	Food and Drug Administration
GMAC	Genetic Manipulation Advisory Group Committee
hGH	human growth hormone
HPLC	high pressure liquid chromotography
Kabi	KabiVitrum
KMN	Koncessionsnämnden för miljöskydd (The Swedish Board on Public Health)
LIF	Läkemedelsindustriföreningen (the Swedish Pharmaceutical Industry Association)
LO/TCO	Landsorganisationen/Tjänstemännens Centralorganisation (Trade Unions)
met hGH	human growth hormone with an extra methionine (192 amino acid)
met-less hGH	human growth hormone (191 amino acid)
MIT	Massachusetts Institute of Technology
mRNA	messenger RNA
NIH	National Institutes of Health
NPA	National Pituitary Agency (later, National Pituitary and Hormone Agency)
OECD	Organization for Economic Co-operation and Development
OTA	Office of Technology Assessment
pit hGH	human growth hormone extracted from human pituitary glands
R & D	research and development
rDNA	recombinant DNA
rDNA hGH	human growth hormone made with recombinant DNA techniques
SOU	Statens offentliga utredningar (the Swedish State's Official Investigations)

STU   Styrelsen för Teknisk Utveckling
                 (The Swedish Board of Technical Development)
trp   trytophan (a promoter)
UCSF   University of California, San Francisco
USDA   United States Department of Agriculture

Preface to Paperback Edition

Internationally, the development and use of new knowledge and innovations is increasingly recognized as one of the crucial explanations for modern economic growth. Basic science, national innovation systems, new growth theory, management of innovation, and so forth are concepts used to understand how and why firms and other organizations develop and use knowledge of economic value. Their decisions and actions hence decide the pace and direction of innovations. Firms try to develop and use new knowledge in their daily activities as they react to, implement, and change market and technical conditions. They are increasingly interested in innovations, alongside traditional concerns of costs, time, and quality. Academics and policy-makers try to analyse and explain the underlying processes of innovations as important phenomena in their own right and in order to propose appropriate guidelines for firms and public policy.

In fact, the intervening period between the original hardback edition of this book and this new paperback edition has been a period where the central themes developed here have been recognized as increasingly important. This book is one contribution to a much larger debate on the knowledge economy, on Schumpeterian economics, and on the management of innovation in firms, in addition to the specific topic of the business of biotechnology.

The tale found in this book is one of how two quite different firms struggle to manage their knowledge-seeking activities, and it gives a good insight into research and development during radical change. It provides case studies for both management and engineering students. At the time of original publication the genetic engineering techniques analysed here were very new and untried in many dimensions; it was new basic research, new biological processes to control, new government regulation, new business applications, etc. Although the recombinant DNA techniques themselves are quite well established today, the process by which they were improved, implemented, tried, and rejected gives insights into radical innovation processes with other genetic engineering techniques, as well as with other types of knowledge.

Rather than just following established procedure, the engineers, scientists, and managers in the firms described here try to understand and manage changes in technology and knowledge during a period where many dimensions are being called into question. Two dichotomies are useful in order to understand their conflicting perceptions and incentive structures—science vs. technology, and market vs. government.

During the two decades analysed here, public opinion swings from potential fear of the monsters of genetic engineering to acceptance of it for pharmaceuticals. New regulations and tests have to be developed, discussed, and agreed upon in order to set what are considered acceptable standards of safety, efficacy, and so forth. Standards are a process of negotiation. Existing physical processing equipment and methods of assessing pharmaceuticals are found to be deficient and hence new ideas—as well as new sources of ideas—are necessary to solve unexpected challenges. The market expands much quicker than expected, partly as a result of a ban of substitute products, and partly as a result of new and unexpected uses of the product. In other words, from the perspective of management of innovation and of engineering in firms, this book provides exciting case studies of how and why certain firms did, or did not, make a quick move into use and development of new knowledge with high economic value.

Although drawn from the early history of modern biotechnology (e.g. the 1970s) to the early 1990s, the story told here is by no means passé or even finished. The controversies continue for this specific case, and in reflection of larger issues for the biotechnology community in specific and for new knowledge in general. Some particular issues of interest are:

1. The continuing fortunes of these two firms, with implications for the dynamics of knowledge-based firms;
2. Disputes over intellectual property rights, with implications for knowledge spill-overs and the university's role in the knowledge-based society;
3. Management issues for knowledge-intensive sectors like biotechnology.

The firms and organizations involved here, as well as the larger issues they represent, continue to be current issues for all firms in environments characterized by turbulence in technology, knowledge, and markets.

Genentech, the dedicated biotechnology firm analysed here, is generally considered the first dedicated biotech firm, and one of the few American start-ups which developed into a significant independent firm. And yet even they were bought up by a large European chemical-pharmaceutical company (Hoffman-LaRoche; Roche AG), in return for injections of capital. Roche purchased 60 per cent in February 1990, then after another injection of capital in 1995, it was given an option to buy the rest by June 1999. In early June 1999, Roche excercised that option to buy out 100 per cent of Genentech, but immediately said that they would sell 19 per cent in an IPO. The biotech firm could have been bought up and merged into the larger corporation, but will instead continue to have a degree of independence.

In this longer-term relationship between two quite different firms, there have been continuing conflicts of ideas and interests over what to do with a specialized knowledge-producer within the concerns and goals of a large established multinational company. The questions have circled around how to integrate the small into the larger and how to leverage the specialized scientific knowledge in order to make money in other products. Genentech is still a symbol of the American dream of entrepreneurship as well as of overall developments in the biotechnology sector, and yet it also symbolizes the complex, global division of labour within genetic engineering for pharmaceuticals.

In the 1970s, Kabi was a small company in the global pharmaceutical industry—although large in this specific product market for human growth hormone (hGH). It was owned by the Swedish state and was fighting for survival. Kabi signed one of the very first R&D contracts for the biotechnology industry—a contract with Genentech to produce human growth hormone through recombinant DNA techniques. Kabi was later merged into a larger Swedish pharmaceutical company named Pharmacia, and the Swedish state sold its remaining share in a wave of privatization in the mid-1990s. After becoming a publicly-traded company, Pharmacia then merged with the American pharmaceutical company Upjohn to become Pharmacia & Upjohn. The company is no longer particularly Swedish nor has special ties to the Swedish state. P&U is instead more of a major contender in the global pharmaceutical market and reflects continuing trends towards mergers in pharmaceuticals and in industry in general. Human growth hormone is still one of its major products.

Thus, the firms analysed here reflect larger issues related to entrepreneurship and mergers, to specialized division of knowledge production, and to the relative importance of the national context vs. globalization. Without giving definitive answers, this book provides a structure and content which allows a discussion of the modern dynamics of high-tech sectors. In doing so, it goes beyond the firm *per se* to see the relative importance of other factors such as university science and regulation, and also goes beyond the American context to the global one.

A second very important issue involves disputes over intellectual property rights. Making claims of ownership through patenting, licensing, and the like is one means of capturing economic benefits from new knowledge. In this book, the issue is the development of new scientific knowledge in relation to ownership and commercial exploitation of that knowledge. Conflicts over intellectual property rights involve an established pharmaceutical company, Eli Lilly; a prestigious medical research university, the University of California San Francisco (UCSF); and the first dedicated biotechnology firm, Genentech. The two firms and one university have had complex relationships related to ownership of knowledge, and have been embroiled in legal disputes for many years at a cost of millions of dollars.

Between the three, there were early licensing agreements, flows of personnel, and flows of money. Disagreements are focused around the limits of patenting and licensing agreements related to genetic engineering, but are relevant to all knowledge-intensive sectors which are changing rapidly. As detailed in the book, Eli Lilly bought techniques and knowledge relevant for their primary product, insulin, as well as for hGH. They had agreements with both UCSF and Genentech. UCSF has had a prestigious scientific name in the relevant basic science, and the university was also early in patenting research results. Genentech was started by a venture capitalist and by a leading UCSF scientist who continued working at the university. Genentech hired a number of researchers from UCSF.

The University of California spent nine years and $20 million trying to prove that Genentech had used their rDNA material and infringed on their patent. UCSF filed a patent in 1977 (patent continuation in 1982; US Patent No. 4,363,877) with three co-authors. It provides human growth hormone sequeces (rDNA transfer vectors). As detailed in the book, one of the three UCSF scientists then moved to Genentech after having conflicts with the two senior scientists at UCSF, taking some cell material with him. The material contained sequence information vital for Genentech's success with a scientific experiment and in fulfilling an R&D agreement, but using it would constitute patent infringement. Genentech has always claimed to have sequenced the human growth hormone independently—and differently. Claims of patent infringement and breach of licensing agreements have linked all three.

The strongest claim for the UCSF patent infringement case in 1999 has been the testimony of the researcher who moved from UCSF to Genentech. He had carried out similar experiments at UCSF and had taken the material with him. He is currently head of a major research unit in Germany. He now testifies that he and the other Genentech scientists faked their data and used the university material instead. Genentech and some press articles insinuate that it is somewhat strange that this case comes to the fore two decades later. Why is he willing to testify now for UCSF? When under oath, he has testified previously that they never used the material. Was he finally tired of the lies and the 'secret pact' to cover it up? Did he fall for the temptation of being eligible for 17 per cent of any royalties (e.g. several million dollars) to be paid to UCSF in case of patent infringement, since he was co-author of the original UCSF patent? If they did use the university material, then this is grounds for patent infringement today—and hence implies that the firm would be liable to pay royalties of 3 to 12 per cent on Genentech's $1.2 billion sales over almost twenty years, plus punitive damages. The lawsuit between UCSF and Genentech continued to June 1999 with the jury not being able to decide whether the evidence proved stealing or not. As it was a hung jury, this has meant that UCSF has not won a victory—unless they want to go to the courts again to appeal the decision.

Thus, there are major issues here about ownership of knowledge which are relevant to the entire biotechnology sector as well as to other highly knowledge-intensive sectors. One of the first obvious issues is the difficulty of defining and maintaining ownership rights at a time when the very boundaries and definitions of what is patentable are being questioned—and where scientific knowledge is developing very quickly. The question for managers, engineers, and scientists is how to determine which knowledge has economic value and whom has ownership claims over it. By granting ownership over novelty through intellectual property rights, the government hopes to increase incentives to innovate. Being able to trade rights in the market may also enable, and encourage, transfer of new knowledge and techniques compared to a counter case of keeping them secret. It might, however, prevent diffusion, thereby reducing the collective benefits. Going beyond the economists' trade-off lies the question of our understanding of knowledge, of what can be sold in a market, as well as the limits and boundaries of intellectual property rights. Along with software, biotechnology has been the centre of many disputes over which techniques and knowledge are, and should be, patentable. This is an on-going discussion, and one which has challenged the existing agreements over intellectual property rights. How does new knowledge of economic value develop? Who has a claim in contributing to the development of such knowledge and what do conflicts tell us about the overall process?

Another issue relates to the value of scientific integrity and reputation, both to research scientists and to firms dependent on selling specialized knowledge. This is relevant to all knowledge-producing firms dependent on having a good reputation for scientific work in order to sell to other firms. In this case Genentech has always claimed that it did its own research in a way that did not infringe on the university's patent claims which cover knowledge which could not have produced practical results. They did so at the last moment under strong pressures to fulfil the external research contract. The biotech firm claims to have done so mainly due to the efforts of a second scientist from a different university, who worked closely with university researchers from yet another university.

Although synthesizing the gene may not seem to be such a major issue to the uninitiated—or even to today's scientific researchers or their students—at the time, doing so successfully was a major scientific accomplishment. It gave this new and untried biotech firm scientific prestige and reputation; a necessary and perhaps sufficient condition in order to sell their specialized scientific knowledge in directions relevant for other firms. Failing to synthesize it would not only have meant that the biotech firm would fail to fulfil their R&D contract for this particular project, it would also have meant not getting a reputation for selling high quality science. This in turn would have reduced their chances of receiving additional R&D alliances from other firms. The value of their knowledge would have been considered lower. Note that it was not scientific knowledge in itself that was valuable; it was the combination of basic scientific knowledge and techniques with other knowledge and techniques in order to do something of value to firms. Thus, if Genentech did not in fact independently do the experiments and research they claimed to have done, then this would be a form of intellectual dishonesty—what the university and press would call stealing. This would also mean that the firm misrepresented their abilities to future buyers.

However, Genentech is so concerned about their reputation and/or so sure of their case that they made photocopies of their lab notebooks, with details of all the experiments, open for inspection for all viewers on their website. They want scientists to have direct access to the facts and be able to judge by themselves. They claim their evidence proves that their experiments were different and that since the experiments were succeeding, there were no motivations to 'cheat/steal' at the last moment. They also published a short version of their arguments in *Nature*, the leading scientific journal where the original article was published. Scientific reputation is clearly important to this biotech firm and is reflected in the fact that they have published over 4000 articles between 1978 and 1999.

The rather complex conflicts over intellectual property rights as detailed in the book also lead us to re-examine the role of the university. Today, many argue that the university has a crucial role to play in stimulating regional economic growth and development. One way of doing so is through spin-off companies. Although opening a start-up firm is currently applauded as scientific entrepreneurship, at the start of the biotechnology revolution, basic scientists who started a company (and who also remained at the university) created many controversies, as discussed in later chapters. This was a breach of the traditional view of the scientist working for other types of intellectual rewards. Obviously, however, there were strong incentives to start firms, as basically all the senior scientists at UCSF with economically-valuable knowledge about gene synthesis were quickly allied with firms.

The current discussion seems to increasingly view stimulating growth as synonymous with creating spin-off companies. In that case, stimulating growth is not a process of the diffuse spill-over of the benefits of knowledge from the university to the surrounding area and society. It is a very specific one, where intellectual property rights play a prominent role. Someone has to have scientific knowledge which has economic value. In this situation, ownership over knowledge, techniques, etc. are crucial for reaping private economic benefits—for individuals, universities, firms, and so forth. In the meantime, governments world-wide have either flattened out, or else cut, in real terms the funding for basic science, leaving many universities to view patenting, start-ups, and the like as one form of making up lost revenue. However, in addition to focusing on direct revenue and direct linkages, the university can contribute to regional economic development through many direct and less direct ways, not least through stimulating basic research. Empirical research has indicated that although firms will generally not list direct contacts with universities as the source of specific innovations, the firms do recognize the importance of the general development of knowledge.

In this particular case, the university is claiming ownership over knowledge and techniques developed there. Although this practice is accepted and increasingly encouraged today, this book details an early case where an American university took a large step away from the post-World War II view that the university creates knowledge which is a public good and usable by all. By taking a patent, the university stood to benefit directly. If the university only fulfils that role of developing knowledge as a public good, then there would be no conflicts and lawsuits. If the firm takes knowledge and techniques developed by a university and translates that into a product or process innovation of economic value, then that is what is supposed to happen. Here, however, there is a conflict because the university is clearly trying to assert its claims of ownership. The university can then no longer claim a special distinction as an organization which develops knowledge as a public good, because it is actually acting in the same way as a firm.

In fact, the reason that some American universities have successful 'technology transfer offices' is that they hold a few patents of high economic value. It can be a lucrative business. UCSF and Stanford hold a joint patent by Professors Cohen and Boyer on recombinant DNA cloning technology, and this patent is easily Stanford's most valuable one. From financial year 1975 to financial year 1997, this patent grossed royalties of $221 million. By way of comparison, the next best patent for the period has grossed $22 million, or one tenth that amount. By implication, they hold many patents that are of medium to no value. That the value of patents can vary greatly is a fundamental point that many universities worldwide seen to have missed when they try to imitate what they think is the American model. Having a technology transfer office is not enough. Technology transfer offices generate money for the university when they manage a portfolio of patents to sell those of higher economic value. Doing so implies a trade-off, because it may be increasingly difficult to justify government expenditures for the university as a producer of general knowledge. The demands start shifting towards producing knowledge which is immediately useful, rather than knowledge which may or may not have a longer-term benefit for society and the economy.

Thus, the case discussed cannot be thought of as an accusation of a minor theft. The universities and researchers involved can make millions through a handful of specific patents, or else spend money on monitoring and taking out patents but without returns. Currently, biotechnology and software patents are important for creating revenue for American universities, and worldwide, the idea of patenting scientific research is particularly popular in a time of decreasing government funding for universities. The question remains, however, as to what demands governments will increasingly try to put on research at universities and research institutes.

This case, and its continuing saga, brings to the fore a number of other questions directly relevant to those wishing to start-up—and/or deal with—firms in knowledge-intensive sectors. One of the obvious issues facing engineers, scientists, and management is how to determine the economic value of your own, and others', knowledge. This comes into play, for example, when deciding whether or not to engage in joint ventures, collaborative alliances, and the like. The problem is how to evaluate the uncertainty about the actual content of the others' knowledge, about its economic value, about the enforceability of any ownership claims, and so forth. Patents, conflicts, lawsuits, and changes of testimony can happen many years and many millions of dollars later. After all, Kabi/Pharmacia & Upjohn are similarly being sued for patent infringement, through their association with Genentech. This lawsuit will undoubtedly cost more than the original R&D contract. Even for a short-term contract, there is a longer-term risk of getting hit by lawsuits which cost lots to fight—and even more if you lose. Engaging in an alliance and/or licensing agreement must be a question of making sure that the person you are buying from actually has reasonable ownership claims over the knowledge and/or techniques he or she is purporting to sell you exclusively. Engaging in agreements means facing the additional uncertainty that the legal system is under pressure to change, and different parts of the world may have very different intellectual property rights. Such differences are rapidly becoming one of the key issues in international trade.

Balancing potential risks and opportunities under uncertainty is, however, a reality for firms. The option of not doing anything is generally not a real option for firms engaged in fast-moving environments and products. Not doing anything means being left behind and out of business. These are challenges that have to be addressed by all firms which are selling or buying intangibles. The picture becomes more complicated when the knowledge being developed is done partly through public funding and partly through private.

A final point on the implications of this case for management of innovation addresses the question of true uncertainty. Knowledge which has economic value in a narrow application may not be as broadly useful as initially thought. Finding out requires trying out as well as explicit strategies to decide where to go next. In fact, the use of genetic engineering detailed here is one of the minor uses in pharmaceuticals today. Initially, it was thought to be a major trajectory for developing new pharmaceuticals. Partly, however, due to the high costs of production, using genetic engineering to make human proteins is currently seen to be a minor use in pharmaceuticals. The major use of genetic engineering is to improve the efficiency of the drug discovery process, in combination with a better understanding of the workings of the body. Combining that knowledge implies that pharmaceuticals can be more directly designed to do certain things. In the last few decades, the pharmaceutical industry has increasingly put money into research and development, only to see a decreasing efficiency of results in terms of new block-buster drugs. Genetic engineering has been put to good use to try to again improve the efficiency of the drug discovery process. Production through recombinant DNA still faces significant problems in terms of costs, and delivery and process control. Thus, genetic engineering for pharmaceuticals has seen a branching-off of knowledge towards new innovation opportunities and towards dead-ends over time.

In closing, I would like to thank the International Joseph A. Schumpeter Society and Wirtschaftswoche for awarding this book the 1996 International Joseph A. Schumpeter Society Prize for the best scientific work in the field of 'Learning, Entrepreneurship and the Dynamics of the Firm'. The prize committee was made up of an international group of acclaimed academics, and their motivation follows.

'This study represents a highly original and careful application of evolutionary ideas to biotechnology, tracing the history of the technology and the roles played by various individual actors, especially the interaction of an American and a Swedish firm, both early leaders in the field. It is an impressive piece of empirical work, which provides a good balance between theory, empirical analysis and policy relevance. It also spans the potential gap between micro and macro and brings into the analysis a thorough understanding of the technology underlying the dynamics of evolving industry and firm structure.'

I am proud to acknowledge this prize as a reflection of the growing importance of research about innovations for firms and economic change. The future offers interesting possibilities to combine case studies and quantitative work in order to develop our theoretical and analytical understanding of the relationships between firm innovations, development of knowledge, and economic growth.

September 1999

1

Introduction

Arguments about the importance of 'market pull' versus 'technology push' are in this sense artificial, since each market need entering the innovation cycle leads in time to a new design, and every successful new design, in time, leads to new market conditions.[1]

Overview

This book arises from a conviction that technological changes, or innovations, are crucial processes underlying dynamic change in advanced market economies. They lead to changes in productivity and to economic growth for firms and for national economies. For example, the development and diffusion of agricultural machinery has replaced many manual jobs in agriculture but has instead created jobs in the design and production of those machines and in other newly created sectors. Seen in a longer perspective, economic growth and increased social welfare usually involve major upheavals, including changing patterns of productivity and job creation in different industrial and service sectors. Technological innovation processes are important because they introduce dynamics into economic growth and impact the wider society. It is therefore important to study such processes explicitly, as it is done in this book.

Innovations are novelties which add economic value and may be technological, market, and/or organizational in orientation. Innovations may take the form of a new machine, a new way of doing things, or they may involve redesigning an existing product for a niche market or changing how work is carried out in an organization. Technological innovations can thus add economic value as some combination of changes in goods and services, including production processes and organization. By adding novelty to the economy, innovations thereby change the conditions of competition for firms and often open up room for further technical improvements and profits. Firms in sectors with rapidly changing technologies and dynamic competition have to make continuous improvements and learn.

The resulting technical changes may lead to dramatic changes in the

---

[1] Kline and Rosenberg (1986: 289–90).

economy, and eventually in individuals' daily lives, or to relatively insignificant changes. The car and surrounding road system has radically changed how modern societies are organized and the structure of production (what is produced), but there are also insignificant changes such as yearly improvements to existing car models. In other words, innovation processes can result in changes which are somewhere between radical and incremental. A few technologies like genetic engineering and information technology are considered more radical than others because they can affect many different aspects of the economy and society.

This book specifically analyses technological innovation processes, that is, how technical novelties of economic value are created. It examines early commercial uses of genetic engineering to see how and why individuals and organizations were able to innovate. The story is much more complex than firms simply imitating what scientists have done. Telling it helps us learn about how and why agents can develop technological innovations. How can they change their vision of a radical innovation into a form useful in the economic sphere? How do they deal with the challenges of developing new science and technology which are in a very fluid phase of change?

The focus here is on innovations which combine economic and technical dimensions in novelty. According to an old dispute, the economic dimension can be seen as 'market pull', which is the idea that innovators make technical improvements in response to perceived market demand. They identify an innovation which is likely to sell and then design a technology to fit what the market will demand. 'Technological push' is the idea that innovators think in technical terms and see obvious opportunities for technical improvements.[2] As the chapter epigraph indicates, this dispute about which is more important is *passé* in modern innovation theory and hence in this book. Economic and technical dimensions are intertwined in technological innovation processes. A technical improvement will change the structure and size of market demand, and the development of an idea based on market demand relies on a series of technical improvements. Economic and technical dimensions directly and irreversibly influence each other in innovations.

Thus, the emphasis here is not on innovations as objects but on the processes whereby innovations are conceived, improved, modified, and used in an economy. Generating such novelty fundamentally depends on knowledge-seeking activities by agents. Agents must conceptualize both economic and technical dimensions. They identify the opportunities and challenges necessary for succeeding with the innovation and try to direct their knowledge-seeking activities to meet them. For radical technologi-

---

[2] See Mowery and Rosenberg (1982) for a discussion of this debate of how market pull and technology push are both necessary for innovations.

cal changes, many individuals and many organizations contribute. They respond to, and act in anticipation of, a changing environment. Their decisions about where to search for novelty are influenced by market forces, technical opportunities and technical dead ends, and social institutions, among others. Technological change thus depends on the actions of individual agents as well as social interactions among different agents in a socio-economic context.

This book describes parallel technological innovation processes enabling firms to use genetic engineering for the production of pharmaceuticals.[3] More specifically, historical case studies focus on knowledge-seeking activities by firms, universities, and others to develop relevant knowledge and techniques. The following chapters show how and why firms interacted with other agents and informal institutions to develop genetic engineering for the pharmaceutical human growth hormone (hGH). The innovation processes so described centre around two firms which moved into genetic engineering very early—namely the Swedish pharmaceutical firm Kabi and the American biotech firm Genentech. The book thus also deals with innovation processes in two different national contexts.

On the one hand, this book presents original historical material about the challenges and opportunities of commercial uses of genetic engineering in the 1970s and 1980s. This history has been sorely missing in scholarly and popular discussions, which have mostly focused on basic scientists or on venture capitalists. The specific challenges of identifying, modifying, and developing relevant knowledge and techniques within firms has not previously been dealt with in detail. These case studies are thus interesting in themselves but are also indicative of broader trends in the modern biotech industry. The challenges and opportunities facing these firms were often very specific, but they also represent more general categories of problems facing all agents trying to use genetic engineering this way.

So, on the other hand, this book draws upon theoretical approaches to analyse technological innovation processes. It has a multi-disciplinary approach, including perspectives focusing on technological change from a variety of scientific traditions. Each has something to offer. This book thereby opens up new paths and questions for later research and should contribute to ongoing theoretical discussions about technological change and innovations. The argument presented here is that this multi-disciplinary approach clearly illustrates how knowledge, institutions, and

---

[3] Although a distinction is made between the scientific techniques of genetic engineering and the biotech industry *per se*, the terms 'genetic engineering' and 'biotech' are here used synonymously, following common praxis in English. 'Genetic engineering' refers to a set of techniques involving controlled changes to DNA, while the term 'biotechnology' refers to a broad category of biological processes, including beer- and bread-making. Despite this broad definition, the terms 'biotech industry' and 'modern biotechnology' refer to biological processes which are based on the scientific techniques of genetic engineering. See further Chapter 4.

agents coevolve during processes of radical technological change. This interaction underlies—or causes—the pattern here identified as evolutionary. It is important to point out that the concept 'evolution' as used here is explicitly defined in relation to theoretical principles from biology as discussed in Chapter 2. This book provides a fresh approach to understanding the dynamics of technological changes.

Understanding the general characteristics of innovation processes as proposed in this book should benefit both scholars interested in economic and technical change and practitioners involved in actually developing technology. Researchers in various academic disciplines should be interested in the generalizable evolutionary patterns and theoretical arguments in relation to ongoing debates about how to understand technological change. Practitioners involved in developing actual technologies should also be interested but for different reasons. Whether managers of firms, scientific or engineering researchers, or government policy-makers, practitioners can learn about the challenges and opportunities with which others have had to deal. Using the evolutionary metaphor, they can think of the world in terms of individuals and environments, in terms of generation of novelty, retention, and selection. This can help structure their understanding of the opportunities and challenges they face. The conceptual relationships between science and technology (in relation to this evolutionary metaphor) should, for example, help analyse why certain activities are more successful in certain environments than in others.

By focusing on the contributions of multiple individuals and organizations which enabled early commercial uses of genetic engineering, this book provides insights about the complex world in which we live as well as about theoretical discussions of technological change in the economy. It provides a new way of conceptualizing innovation, not as a final object or outcome but as a complex process involving many agents responding to, and creating, environmental conditions.

Situating the Research Questions

This book thus specifically analyses technological innovation processes. The particular importance of innovations to modern market economies was recognized in the early part of the twentieth century by the Austrian economist Joseph Schumpeter. Although often ignored within orthodox economics, Schumpeter's writings have subsequently stimulated many researchers to specify the importance and role of innovations to successful competition in firms and economic growth. Related bodies of work claiming some inspiration from Schumpeter can be found in many scientific fields including evolutionary and institutional economics, geography, management, and history of technology, among others. Schumpeter therefore provides an interesting starting point for analysing the importance of technological change for economic change.

According to the Schumpeterian economist Frederic Scherer (1984: vii), Schumpeter's three major propositions about the relationships between innovations and the economy can be summarized as follows:

1. Innovations, in particular technological innovations, give capitalist economies their dynamic character through the process of 'creative destruction'. Due to major technological changes, old industries and old firms are replaced by new ones. The economic structure is not static; it is in flux.

2. Technological progress in business is one of the most important factors explaining gains in real income per capita. Technological change gives opportunities for productivity gains and is thus one motor of economic development. In this process of stimulating technical change, large firms play a particularly important role.

3. The possibility of capturing a temporary monopoly position stimulates agents to develop technological innovations. Firms have the potential of getting short-term but abnormally high profits if their innovation succeeds. Because the innovator is ahead of the others, s/he gains a temporary monopoly position by increasing price or productivity and hence can capture entrepreneurial returns. Others imitate, driving down prices. The process of innovation drives further economic and technical change. This contrasts sharply with the notion of continuous, perfect market competition. Temporary monopolies reached through innovations create and necessitate disequilibrium situations.

These three propositions will not be tested here. They are instead presented as an introduction to the neo-Schumpeterian perspective found in this broader multi-disciplinary approach to the economics of technical change. Even though much of evolutionary economics has been founded in his name, the extent to which Schumpeter's theory is specifically evolutionary is up for interpretation.[4]

---

[4] For example, two recent books differ greatly on this issue. Andersen (1994: ch. 1) argues that Schumpeter was indeed an evolutionary economist because of his emphasis on dynamics. In a major review and reinterpretation of the history of economic thought, Hodgson (1993: ch. 10) argues that Schumpeter's view of economic evolution differed greatly from the pattern of change identified in biological evolution and that therefore Schumpeter's theory was not evolutionary. Hodgson argues that Veblen has more specifically evolutionary notions to offer modern economists than Schumpeter (Hodgson 1993: ch. 9). Hodgson (1993: 150) argues that 'despite their current diplomatic convenience and positive ambience, the "Schumpeterian" or "neo-Schumpeterian" [Nelson and Winter 1982: 39] labels are . . . inappropriate for theoretical work of this type.' Hodgson argues that whereas modern evolutionary economists include some analogy for natural selection, Schumpeter saw evolution as development along a given path—as did Marx. This is an 'ultimately unsatisfactory way to reconcile general equilibrium theory with notions of variety of change' (Hodgson 1993: 150).

Whether or not his theories fulfil the criteria for being called evolutionary economics, Schumpeter's perspective stresses dynamic, qualitative change in the economy as well as the importance of major technological innovations. These two propositions are of central importance to the subject addressed in the current book. Genetic engineering has involved traumatic economic change as well as radical technical and scientific novelty.

Although the earlier writings of Schumpeter identified the key role of individual entrepreneurs in introducing major innovations, his later writings stressed that firms automated the generation of novelty by bringing research and development (R & D) in-house, into the firm. R & D departments brought science into firms and helped institutionalize processes for introducing novelty into the economy. That novelty is the basis for future competition. This is why large firms are seen to be particularly important. In more recent interpretations, Christopher Freeman (1982) has emphasized that major upswings in business cycles are caused by the exploitation of the productive potential of major new technologies. Radical new technologies offer more opportunities for improvements, which increase productivity. Many of these major technologies originate from deliberate activities of searching for novelty, whether they were specifically scientific or not.

Schumpeterian and evolutionary economics contribute to a wider body of research on innovations and technical change. One of the major questions which has been addressed during the past thirty years in this literature is the relationship between science and technology. It is an important question quite simply because of the possibility of basic science to indicate the productive potential of major new technologies and because of the similarities between search activities in universities, research institutes, and corporate R. & D. Related questions about the relationships between science and technology involve the respective roles of markets and government.

There has been renewed academic discussion to develop an understanding of what science and technology are and how practitioners in each go about creating novelty. What are science and technology? Do different organizations tend to specialize in one or the other type of activity? To what extent do practitioners who utilize these two respective bodies of knowledge interact? What are the cognitive relationships between these different bodies of knowledge? How do the communities communicate? Some of this discussion will be taken up below and in Chapter 3 in relation to the respective roles of firms and governments in supporting the two communities of researchers.

Another reason for interest in this question has to do with changes in society. In particular, there has been a massive expansion of government support for basic research and for universities after World War II. Basic science performed by universities and research institutes has long been seen as the origin of major technical changes affecting the rest of society. Many scientists have argued, and policy makers assumed, that government support of science, especially basic research, at non-firm organizations will generate benefits for society in the long run. Medicine is an example where governments support research on diseases in return for new knowledge and treatments which are supposed to benefit the population as a whole. If the potential for profit exists, firms are then assumed to translate science into technology and products. All benefit. Government support of science has often been justified by referring to the indirect but important long-term benefits to society.

The economic arguments for a division of labour between government supporting basic research and firms paying for further technical development has been based on the idea of market failure, especially the difficulties of making a market for information work. According to two early and influential articles by the economists Richard Nelson (1959) and Kenneth Arrow (1962), firms underinvest in long-term research because they have difficulties in evaluating new information and technology. Firms and others face true uncertainty about what will be discovered through R & D activities and about the economic value of that information. Uncertainty means that firms have difficulties in evaluating options, and so firms have difficulties in calculating potential returns on investments in search activities. They must make informed guesses. They also face problems with selling information in a market because it can be difficult to get the buyer to pay for information without disclosing the very information the producer wants to sell. Once the buyer has that information, s/he no longer needs to buy it. The market for information thus differs from markets for commodities.

In addition to the market failure argument, governments are often assumed to have special reasons for being interested in basic research. The results of basic research are assumed to be a public good and, in fact, a special kind of public good where the creation and diffusion of information will lead to significant future benefits to society (the economy).[5] Science produces more benefits for society than for any one individual because information can be used by many without diminishing its value. A physical law like gravity will not change because many utilize it in calculations, but on the contrary, many can benefit from utilizing this physical law in order to design functioning technologies. Because social returns are greater than individual returns, firms will therefore underinvest in the creation of long-term knowledge, e.g. that

[5] Bernal (1967) and Bush (1945) both emphasize the long-term benefits of science, albeit from the different perspectives of scientists believing, respectively, in communism and in the ideals of independent basic science.

which is not applicable to fairly immediate problems. Governments therefore ought to support basic research. This division of labour between what governments ought to do and what firms ought to do has often been summarized as science versus technology.

However, both in practice and in theory, it has been shown that it is difficult for firms to develop radically new technologies, even after basic scientific results have been obtained. Radical technologies pose new challenges for firms as they try to translate theory or information into economic practice. Therefore, another reason for this increased interest in the relationships between science and technology is the changing and complex challenges facing firms, particularly strategic and R & D managers and researchers. There is the realization that in many industries, novelty is necessary to survive. At the same time, generating and using novelty is difficult, even when it does not directly entail science. Research has shown that firms' technological innovations often do not directly draw upon contemporary basic science.[6] The division of labour can therefore be not so clear-cut, and corporate knowledge-seeking activities can be challenging.

Even when firms do not directly rely on basic science, interactions between university science and the commercial development of technologies are often important. If nothing else, firms develop and draw upon internal and external bodies of knowledge and techniques to carry out search activities in-house, better known as R & D. Basic scientific research has helped develop, systematize, and pass on such knowledge although other knowledge is specific for the sector, even the firm. Firms are particularly interested in the application of general knowledge and techniques to specific questions, problems, and challenges. Developing such applications may require the development of new types of knowledge, where the firms can work on very different types of challenges from those of university scientists.

Whether or not contemporary basic science is used, major innovations have often been based on previous scientific research or aided by development of new generalizable knowledge. To deal with complexity, firms may therefore need to be able to monitor and understand external scientific research in order to identify opportunities and threats. Doing so often requires special corporate competences. In order to have the capacity to absorb scientific or technical information developed elsewhere, Cohen and Levinthal (1989) have argued that firms must do some research themselves. This may be one explanation for why, in the past century, firms have organized systematic engineering and searching activities.[7] R & D enables firms to access new knowledge

---

[6] Faulkner and Senker (1994).
[7] See Schumpeter (1968), Schmookler (1966), and Freeman (1982).

and to develop longer term strategies and competences beyond the day-to-day running of the firm. Science often indicates future trends, or future technical challenges facing firms. This is often valuable information for making strategic management decisions about the future of the firm. Strategic management decisions must see beyond the present, even though choices will often be based on guesses and visions rather than rational calculations. Corporate R & D also modifies external and internal information into a form useful for the specific context of the firm.

In short, managers and researchers involved with R & D continually have to ask how best to deal with existing and new knowledge in a quickly changing, complex environment. This is a difficult question to answer in general terms because the actions and responses will depend upon firms' own capabilities as well as on local environmental conditions. Firms will have quite different strategies, competences, and abilities to adapt to innovative challenges, including both economic and technical aspects. In different types of industrial and service sectors, managers have begun to recognize the need to be able to incorporate strategies to monitor and carry out technological change as part of the overall firm strategy.

In more recent years, governments have also become increasingly interested in actively aiding the competitive position of national firms. It is argued, for example, that the government should help build up the technical competences of firms in, say, information technologies, in order better to compete in the international market. Technological change has been identified as a key asset in this race. In order to fulfil this goal, governments have been demanding more immediate returns on investment in new knowledge creation.[8] They want to see a return in the form of new jobs; knowledge transformed into new products; competitive positions of firms and economic growth; and so forth. So in addition to basic science, governments have been increasingly interested in providing more direct support for technical development, including joint R & D consortia, specified technical procurement, and encouraging firms to learn to learn. Science no longer reigns supreme over technology; both are expected to deliver benefits. This change in emphasis in government science and technology policy has occurred in parallel with more nuanced academic conceptions of what science and technology are and how they interact.

There are thus many reasons for being interested in relationships between science and technology in connection with questions about firms' innovations, about government policy, and about national economic change. In particular, this perspective opens up research questions

[8] See Tyson (1992) for a more theoretical argument about why governments ought to invest in supporting R & D-intensive industries.

about the relationships between innovations and economic change, including the respective roles of markets and governments. Based on this perspective, we can analyse the relative roles of university researchers, of firms, of government agencies, and so forth, in contributing to an innovation process.

Early Commercial Uses of Genetic Engineering

Genetic engineering is one of the most modern, controversial, and dynamic of the science based technologies. Genetic engineering is not an object; it is instead a set of techniques, or way of doing things. The development of these techniques from the 1970s and onwards illustrates changing relationships between research oriented towards science and research towards commercial uses, and between universities and firms. Over time, these two types of activities have been relatively closer or further apart. When activities are relatively closer together, the research itself may be quite similar, and it is easier for individuals to communicate and to move between organizations.

As recently as the early 1970s, scientific research fields like molecular biology and biochemistry, from which genetic engineering techniques were developed, were still considered research mainly of interest within the university world. By the late 1970s and early 1980s, these scientific disciplines were shown to generate knowledge and techniques with potential market value. At this point, there was a small distance between basic university research and economically interesting research and development. This distance was small in the sense that very similar activities could be carried out in universities and in firms, although with different goals in mind.

As will be shown in this book, the distance between different types of activities can change over time. Genetic engineering was initially perceived as important for basic science and far from environments involving market forces. Later, the distance was perceived to be quite small for some activities and further away for others. Luigi Orsenigo (1989) has argued, however, that the main core of university science and of industrial applications in biotechnology quickly developed along divergent paths. Even so, we shall see that firms engaged in scientific activities and university scientists engaged in technological activities, even after divergent trajectories had emerged. The distance between different environments is thus more a matter of perception, e.g. perceptions of scientific, technological, and economic opportunities, than a matter of objective differences.

This book uses comparative case study methodology in order to gather and organize historical material about specific processes of technological innovations. The focus is on knowledge-seeking activities enabling early commercial uses of genetic engineering, specifically for production of hGH and to some extent insulin. Following closely after insulin, human growth hormone was the second commercial application of genetic engineering as the basis of production. This book is a tale of the pharmaceutical firm Kabi of Sweden and to some extent Eli Lilly of the USA, which acted very early to access this alternative production technology. It was early relative to the nascent state of basic scientific research. Both contacted the American biotech firm Genentech to carry out industrially directed scientific research, although Lilly had other strategies as well. After a time, Genentech also decided to produce hGH made this way, and so this book is also a tale of Genentech's parallel activities and their relations with university science. The technological innovation processes involving Kabi and Genentech in interactions with others thus form the core empirical material.

Because the technology was so novel scientifically and technically in the 1970s, early commercial uses of genetic engineering to make pharmaceuticals like insulin and hGH presented scientific, technical, and economic challenges to the innovating agents. Initially, both university scientists and corporate researchers and management had common goals in modifying bacteria to build the human protein hGH. Researchers at universities soon moved on to other projects, whereas firms concentrated on solving the challenges of designing an economical and technically functioning production system.

The knowledge-seeking activities of these firms are therefore placed in relation to scientific research, starting with a description of events in the early 1970s. The firms' involvement includes in particular the transformation of knowledge and techniques into products, from funding two published scientific papers in 1979 to approval of recombinant DNA hGH with an extra amino acid (met hGH) in 1985 and then approval of met-less hGH after 1987. This is the period in which genetic engineering techniques became commercially viable because firms invested significant resources in developing technically and economically functioning production processes. After this period, the focus has been on sales, with a world-wide market for hGH of approximately $1 billion.

Although these innovation processes were largely organized within firms, the case studies cannot, in fact, be said to concentrate only on the strategies of specific firms. Instead, a contribution of this particular study is that the innovative activities of firms are placed in relation to other agents' knowledge-seeking activities—whether those agents were involved in basic science or in economic activities—and in relation to changes in the public context. Emphasis is thus placed on how and why different agents, sometimes responding to different environmental conditions, contributed to, accessed, and further developed the knowl⌐

and techniques necessary for this commercial use of what were initially scientific techniques. Such interactions are a key theme of the book, in the theoretical as well as the empirical chapters.

The challenges and opportunities of commercial use were more evident in the early cases described here than in later cases of genetic engineering. Early applications of genetic engineering can thus provide a useful 'window' to view how radical changes in science and technology are developed and absorbed into firms and nations. Initially, in both the pharmaceutical industry and in basic medical research, only a small number of individuals and organizations used genetic engineering techniques. These were the ones who perceived the potential benefits of engaging in these activities and had competences and resources to develop them. As genetic engineering techniques were developed and proved their worth, more and more people used them, to the point that many are today routinized tools.[9] Therefore, as commercial uses of genetic engineering have become more common, the challenges of innovation have become less obvious.

Gathering this historical but relatively contemporary material about technological innovation processes has involved gathering information which is potentially of economic value to the firms. They may want to use research results and technical specifications in the future to gain competitive advantages, thereby giving them incentives to keep such information secret. A number of interviewees have mentioned that very detailed specifications were secret. Nevertheless, the general course of events and level of detail recorded in subsequent chapters are based on interviews and public information. In fact the firms have also published a number of scientific articles in various scientific and engineering fields. They have incentives to publish such material in order to be seen as participating in scientific communities. This appears particularly relevant for communities of researchers working on technologies close to university research and also for new firms dedicated to commercial use of scientific techniques. Secrecy may thus be balanced by incentives for scientific disclosure, although the level of detail differs.

The degree of secrecy associated with corporate material about technological innovations differs by industry and by whether the technology will be used as a final product or as part of a production process. According to the Yale survey, a large American survey of this question, the amount of secrecy involved depends on how well the firm can safeguard its innovation.[10] Safeguarding means protecting one's own potential economic benefits by trying to prevent competitors from imitating without paying. Protection of the innovating firms' interests can take various forms. Some are directly regulated and embodied in

---

[9] See Clarke and Fujimura (eds. 1992).   [10] Nelson (1990: 201).

institutions such as the patent system, whereas other protection involves a firm's actions relative to competitors. Particularly important are the advantages of moving first, which gives firms the possibility of learning quickly to make a technology more efficient (a steep learning curve) and to gain lead time into the market, which can increase market share. The first-moving firms start developing and using a technology before others and so learn how to use it more efficiently and sell it before others.

The Yale survey indicates that R & D-intensive industries, which include pharmaceuticals, tend to rate patents as more effective in preventing duplication of products relative to other industries. Within the R & D-intensive industries, patents are easier to obtain when 'the composition of the product is relatively easy to define and limit' as in pharmaceutical formulas, in contrast to other R & D-intensive but complex system technologies like aeroplanes.[11] Patents give legal ownership but also require that previously secret information become public knowledge. However, for production process innovations, all industries rated secrecy as more important than patents or the first mover advantages. The pharmaceutical industry rates patents as important for both product and process innovations, but clearly rates patents as more effective for products than for processes.[12]

As this book focuses on developing genetic engineering to manufacture hGH and not on the search process leading to hGH as an effective pharmaceutical, the focus is on new process technologies. The Levin *et al.* survey (1987) indicates that firms would want to keep this type of information secret. In addition to activities to integrate genetic engineering into production, the book also addresses scientific activities to develop genetic engineering and medical knowledge about uses and markets.

Moreover, secrecy in production processes is often used to gain immediate advantages over competitors. For example, secrecy can be used when firms try to develop a product quickly and get it to the market and thereby gain early mover advantages. Secrecy did play a role here when, for example, the firms switched to a new bacteria construction (a new set of genetic engineering techniques and biological materials). In these examples, the information was more valuable to the

---

[11] Levin *et al.* (1987: 800). Nelson draws out the implications of secrecy and relates firms' responses to empirical data, which shows that the bulk of industrial R. & D. is oriented towards product innovations and not process innovations. In many industries, process innovations are done by upstream firms or suppliers. Nelson argues that the finding is consistent with Eric von Hippel's proposition 'that the locus of inventive activity is determined, in part at least, by where the ability to appropriate returns is greatest' (Nelson 1990: 202). Pavitt (1984) more systematically relates the locus of innovative activity in the economy to ability to appropriate returns. This results in his classification of different types of industries by innovative potential.

[12] Levin *et al.* (1987: 797).

firm immediately when developed, but in that this book describes a historical process, these secrets are less valuable to the firms now. Secrecy can also be an important way to continue protecting production process methods over time, when improvements to the techniques have reduced costs and increased quality. The technical details kept secret in these case studies were deemed to be so specific that they were not essential to understanding the broader processes of technological innovation.

There has also been a major patent dispute relating to genetic engineering to produce insulin and hGH. This patent dispute included the main early agents in the United States, i.e. Genentech, the American pharmaceutical firm Eli Lilly, and the University of California, and involved 'numerous contracts and patents that relate to human growth hormone'.[13] This raises an additional methodological problem about the interview material. The firms and this university—and hence to some extent the researchers and managers interviewed or described in written material—have had a current interest in giving a particular version of the history before settlement. Giving a particular version could help them win the patent lawsuit. This is not intended to insinuate that the interviewees construct a new fable, but it does indicate the difficulties of weighing different accounts of the same course of events. Attempts were therefore made to determine the interests and motives of individuals giving information, and hence the reliability of different sources.[14] Multiple sources of information were also used where possible. Different strategies were thus used to attempt to deal with the general problem of investigating technological innovation processes of value for firms.

Reflections on Ensuing Chapters

Chapter 2 explores and develops a theoretical perspective about technological innovation from an evolutionary perspective, while Chapter 3 addresses this question by examining the relationships between science and technology. These two chapters introduce the main outlines of the theoretical world within which this book contributes. That theoretical world contains the partially overlapping contributions of heterodox evolutionary and institutional economics, management, sociology, and history of science and technology. The particular perspective developed

[13] Raines (1992). Genentech and Eli Lilly settled the eight-year conflict out of court in January 1995. Eli Lilly agreed to pay '$145 million to settle all claims and counter-claims' (*Financial Times* 1995: 17).

[14] Historical source criticism provides three pertinent questions. These are: whether the source is accurate, whether it is relevant, and whether it is representative. See Nilsson (1973: 179).

here is of coevolutionary innovation for science based technology, and it is a new combination of theoretical contributions.

In the type of detailed case study work used here, introducing the technology is an important task to help the reader through the historical twists and turns. Chapter 4 therefore provides a layperson's explanation of the use of genetic engineering techniques to make human growth hormone, the scientific basics of these techniques, and how this particular use relates to the larger public debate over genetic engineering. This chapter forms a bridge to move from the highly abstract, theoretical arguments about science, technology, and evolutionary innovation to a very specific, and empirically rich discussion of the historical technological innovation processes involving recombinant DNA techniques to produce human growth hormone.

The detailed historical descriptions in Chapters 5, 6, 7, and 8 chronologically recount the history of these commercial uses of science from the early 1970s to the mid-1980s. Particular emphasis is placed upon knowledge-seeking activities in relation to four environments which influence how and why agents pursue knowledge-seeking activities. For, along with an empirical contribution to our understanding of the internal commercial history of these technical developments, these four chapters also contribute to a further development and discussion of the theoretical issues. Chapters 9 and 10 therefore contain conclusions about innovation processes in relation to an evolutionary perspective on economic change and in relation to science and technology.

2

Evolutionary Innovations

Natural selection made us and it works on us still, as it does for other species, but its force is as nothing compared with the changes in our abilities wrought by *cultural evolution*—the transmission of knowledge, skills, and behavior by teaching and tradition.[1]

Introduction

This book analyses parallel historical technological innovation processes in order to develop more general theories and comments about technological change in modern market economies. Competing technological innovation processes involving genetic engineering are thus at the centre of description and analysis in subsequent chapters.

A technological innovation process means the process whereby agents act to transform new knowledge, inventions, and/or scientific techniques into economic value, often through products, production processes, and/or changes to the organization. The focus here is thus not on why a product is successful in a market nor why a technology functions; it is instead on the scientific, technological, and other knowledge-seeking activities enabling technical change. Although innovations eventually result in economic value in the market, studying processes of technological innovation means concentrating on the process of searching for new knowledge, artefacts, and techniques.

It is here argued that innovation processes are constituted by many knowledge-seeking activities, whereby agents' perceptions and actions are translated into practice. These result in a pattern of evolutionary innovation. 'Evolution' means neither of two common definitions, namely, only incremental change or progress towards a higher goal. Evolution is instead here described as a theory about a pattern of change. 'Evolutionary innovation' refers to a pattern of change defined by four principles, and the changes are the result of interactions among individuals, populations, and environments over time. An evolutionary pattern of technical change is here defined to include generation of novelty leading to diversity, retention and transmission of characteris-

---

[1] Luria *et al.* (1981: 596) emphasis in original.

tics over time within the population which innovates, social selection, and an assumption of non-optimization. Coevolutionary innovation refers to mutual dependencies between knowledge, institutions, and agents.

This perspective also contributes to theoretical discussions about the relationships between science and technology by defining different environments for innovation in Chapter 3. It is argued that activities of seeking for knowledge are carried out in response to some combination of scientific or technological orientation and of market forces or government influence. This helps structure our understanding of how science and technology do or do not interact.

This chapter first compares and contrasts biological and socio-economic evolution theories in order to specify how the evolutionary metaphor can be made relevant for understanding technological innovation. It cannot be used directly but must be modified for use. The evolutionary analogy is useful because innovations involve the development and diffusion of information, as well as novelty and selection among alternatives. The next section then goes further to analyse how specific technological innovation processes can be described as evolutionary. This discussion draws upon a broad range of existing research, from which four principles underlying evolutionary innovation are proposed. This concept is closely related to the heterodox tradition of evolutionary economics, so the subsequent section reviews the general epistemological assumptions of this tradition in order to indicate how and why analyses of technical and economic change can be integrated. This culminates in an elaboration of three issues of particular interest, namely (1) firms' competences and perceptions, (2) lock-in and trajectories, and (3) radical versus incremental change.

Biological and Socio-Economic Evolution

In this book, the proposition of evolutionary innovation is based on an explicit reinterpretation of biological theories in order to make them relevant for socio-economic phenomena like technical change.[2] There are

---

[2] The discussion of biological theories of evolution mainly relies upon a reputable university textbook, namely Luria *et al.* (1981). This textbook has been used for several reasons. One is that given the rather rudimentary state of theories about socio-economic evolution, it is better to develop first a solid understanding of the basics of biological evolutionary theory before going into all the contemporary debates. Nevertheless, another reason for using this textbook is that Gould, in particular, is active in the current debates about the pace of evolution.

important differences between the two realms of evolutionary theory, with significant implications for the mode of evolution described in this book. This section also clarifies why an evolutionary metaphor is appropriate for analysing technical and economic change. One of the most important reasons is the ability to focus on change as a process of accumulating and transferring information within a population.[3]

To elaborate on the similarities and differences between biological and socio-economic evolution, it is interesting first to spend a few paragraphs discussing three relatively radical philosophical implications of the biological evolutionary theory proposed by Charles Darwin in *The Origin of Species* in 1859. Darwin's theory of natural selection has important consequences for traditional notions that change has purpose and that progress is positive, and for our understanding of the relationship between humans and nature, specifically human superiority over nature.[4] Mentioning the following philosophical implications will reduce the risk that readers will make incorrect assumptions about the perspective of evolutionary innovation proposed here.

What, then, was philosophically radical about Darwin's theory of natural selection? First, in contrast to the traditional Western philosophical tradition of separating mind and spirit from matter and body, Darwin believed that matter is the basis of existence. One philosophical implication is that both spirit and mind arise from the body and brain. Humans do not, therefore, have a privileged position, one step above nature and closer to God, due to their mental capabilities. Humans are instead part of nature.

Nevertheless, evolutionary biologists do discuss a type of evolution specific to humans, called 'cultural evolution'. In cultural evolution, learning, traditions, behaviour, and the like influence how the human race changes at least as much as biological evolution based on genes. We must distinguish between the cultural evolution of the human race and socio-economic evolution of knowledge developed by humans. Only the latter socio-economic evolution involving knowledge concerns us here. When the evolutionary- metaphor is used to describe socio-economic phenomena like innovation processes, then learned knowledge is the most important mode of evolution.

Second, Darwin argued that there is no higher purpose or principle underlying the existing state of nature or influencing its direction of change. Darwin contradicted the notion of divine intervention, or pur-

---

[3] Hodgson (1993: ch. 3) gives a coherent overview of different conceptions of evolution as used by economists. In particular, Hodgson distinguishes between using evolution to mean 'development' or 'progress' and how it is defined in modern theories in biology. In particular, evolutionary theory in biology discusses phylogenetic evolution, where there is no ultimate goal to variety generation and selection, and where equilibrium may be a temporary phenomenon.   [4] This discussion is based on Luria *et al.* (1981: 584–7).

pose, where everything has its preordained place in a harmonious nature. In contrast, Darwin argued that this apparent 'higher purpose' is simply the outcome of the struggle of individuals to survive and procreate.[5] The evolutionary principles of competition, transmission over time, and selection thus results in an outcome of apparent order.

Finally, Darwin argued that evolution is not inherently progressive; it does not inevitably lead to improvements. It does not lead to 'absolute progress' or necessarily to a gradual movement from less to more complex organisms. Improvements must instead be defined in relation to the environment, the context. What is important is understanding the relationships and mutual influences between organisms and environments. In the sense that organisms which are better adapted to an environment tend to become more common over time, natural selection does act creatively to adapt populations of organisms to local environments.

These three philosophical implications indicate that Darwinian evolutionary theory in biology develops explanations based on historical events. This differs from the strictly deterministic and predictive natural laws as found in traditional physics. Biological evolutionary theory does not try to identify optimal or equilibrium states valid across all periods and places, nor does it try to identify physical laws valid under all conditions. Instead, biological evolutionary theory emphasizes historical contingencies, and broad principles and patterns of change. Neither does absolute progress occur: selection of favoured traits is related to local environmental conditions.[6]

This implies, on the one hand, that unique events are important, and on the other hand, that these unique, micro-level events and diversity still add up to an aggregate, identifiable pattern. This pattern is dynamic, based on qualitative change. Due to these two simultaneous levels of analysis, evolutionary theory can provide a useful metaphor of change for social and economic phenomena.

A specific comparison of the two types of evolution—biological and cultural—by the noted palaeontologist Stephen Gould can help guide our thinking here. Gould applauds, and yet warns against, using evolutionary metaphors for understanding technological change by pointing

[5] See McKelvey (1992) for the argument that popular accounts of evolution neglect reproduction and care of the young and instead emphasize 'survival of the fittest'. Evolution is as much about procreation as it is about selection. McKelvey argues that procreation has been neglected largely because it is interpreted as women's work (children; offspring; reproduction) whereas the second represents characteristics attributed to men (fighting; survival; production).

[6] Physical laws have been the basis of explanation in neo-classical economics, as argued by Mirowski (1989). The dynamic, historical nature of evolutionary biological theory is an important reason for its appeal to economists. See Hodgson (1993) for a thorough discussion of the influence of evolutionary theory on the history of ideas in economics.

to three caveats about applying biological theories to the social sciences. Gould's reservations about transferring this metaphor are that:

First, cultural evolution can be faster by orders of magnitude than biological change at its maximal Darwinian rate—and questions of timing are of the essence in evolutionary arguments. Second, cultural evolution is direct and Lamarckian in form: the achievements of one generation are passed by education and publications directly to descendants, thus producing the great potential speed of cultural change. Biological evolution is indirect and Darwinian, as favourable traits do not descend to the next generation unless, by good fortune, they arise as products of genetic change. Third, the basic topologies of biological and cultural change are completely different. Biological evolution is a system of constant divergences without any subsequent joining of branches. Lineages once distinct, are separate forever. In human history, transmission across lineages is, perhaps, the major source of cultural change. Europeans learned about corn and potatoes from Native Americans and gave them smallpox in return.[7]

Gould thus points to potential blunders of analogy when transferring evolutionary metaphors from biology to human events, and particularly to problems which arise when the analogy is too simplistic.

Moreover, the three potential problems which Gould identifies cannot be ignored, because they touch the essence of what is interesting in technical change—respectively, its close dependence on social change, the importance of learning and transmission of knowledge, and the role of stimulus.[8] For example, Gould notes the importance of learning and of transmission of diseases between groups of geographically separated humans. Such stimuli in the sense of learning, imitation, and inspiration are very relevant for technical change. The biological metaphor cannot be directly applied to socio-economic phenomena. Instead, doing so involves specific modifications relevant for human knowledge processes.

In order to understand additional differences between biological and socio-economic evolution, a vital similarity must first be emphasized, namely that 'all evolution is concerned with the growth of knowledge.'[9] In order to avoid confusion, we can distinguish between information which exists independent of receiver/transmitter and information which has been translated into knowledge so that humans understand it. By so doing, we can rephrase the above quote so that 'all evolution is concerned with the growth of information.' Evolution is concerned with

[7] Gould (1987: 18).

[8] In fact, these potential problems are important enough to cause some to reject the evolutionary metaphor for economics. Like Gould, Chris DeBresson (1987) points out similar limitations of evolutionary theory for technical change, but then concludes that evolutionary metaphors should be abandoned in economics. In contrast to DeBresson, Gould argues that given his reservations, an evolutionary metaphor is still interesting for discussing technological change.   [9] Langlois and Everett (1994: 11).

information about the survival rates of different strategies or combinations in a changing environment.

Information must be somehow retained and transmitted within the population in order to be useful. It is so important that it should be seen as an explicit evolutionary principle, along with novelty and selection. Some information has a historical flavour in that it deals with past successes, failures, and survival rates. The information shows which combinations have been selected for in the past, and hence which have been successful in that environment. The environment also changes, however, indicating the need for novelty, which generates new information about which combinations and strategies are currently proving successful and might be so in the future. The generation of information involves adaptive and anticipatory changes in relation to changes in the environment. This is an important reason why an evolutionary approach can be used to analyse how and why technical and economic change occurs.

An important difference between biological and socio-economic evolution is the type and form of information that is collected and transmitted in the population. Whereas biological evolution relies on genes to transmit information in a species between generations, socio-economic evolution relies on the transmission of knowledge, skills, and behaviour in the population. The first mode of evolution is called Darwinian and the second Lamarckian (Saviotti and Metcalfe (eds.) 1991; Hodgson 1993).

In the modern synthesis of Darwinian evolution and Mendelian genetics in biology, genes pass on information which codes for the physical characteristics of organisms. Note, however, that organisms develop as the result of complex interactions between genes and the environment. Any given organism has a specific set of genes, but exactly how the genes will be expressed depends on the environment. The larger population consists of individuals with a variety of similar but not identical genes. Populations thus generally exhibit variety, not uniformity, which is necessary to maintain diversity. In the population, novelty is randomly introduced in offspring through recombinations of parents' genes and through mutations.

In contrast, socio-economic evolution depends on developments in human knowledge. In this Lamarckian mode of evolution, knowledge, techniques, and behaviour are transmitted in the population and also form the basis for the creation of novelty. In both types of evolution, what is important is the ongoing collection and transmission of information among individuals and the population.

In biology, different levels of aggregation are considered in order to specify how evolution occurs. There are three levels, namely: unit of variation, unit of selection, and unit of evolution. In biology, the unit of variation is what contains information and mutates, namely genes. The unit of selection is the expression of those genes and what survives or dies, namely organisms. They are selected in the environment. Finally, there is the unit of evolution, or what changes over time as the gene pool changes, namely populations. These three levels of aggregation express the differences between what is changing (genes), what is being selected (organisms), and what changes over time in an evolutionary process (gene pool; population).[10] In technological innovation, these three correspond to knowledge and techniques; products and firms; and the cumulative bodies of knowledge and firms constituting industries or national economies.

Socio-Economic Evolution

The move from biological to socio-economic evolution and from a Darwinian to a Lamarckian mode of exchange of information leads to additional implications for our understanding of technological innovation processes. The following implications which arise from these differences are particularly important.

First, in biological evolution, each organism can only try out one combination of genes at a time, whereas the population has a diversity of similar genes. In contrast, in socio-economic evolution, one and the same agent can generate a range of alternatives, and can continue introducing changes. Each agent can try out a larger range of alternatives which can then be more quickly subjected to selection. The same firm can produce different models of very similar products; they can also imitate successful strategies of competitors. One reason why cultural evolution moves more quickly than biological is that information is not tied to physical hardware. Agents can instead change information quite rapidly, by developing new information or by imitating others.

Second, there is the question of intentionality related to generation of novelty. Darwinian evolution assumes that a great range of diversity is generated and that this diversity is randomly distributed among feasible combinations. Organisms cannot direct the generation of novelty. In nature, the generation of novelty and diversity is not directed to satisfy environmental conditions. Organisms cannot directly control mutations or new combinations of parents' genes. Instead, natural selection is the force which chooses among random diversity and continues to select those most favourable. Natural selection thus can be said to direct successive change along certain paths definable by characteristics favourable for survival in an environment.

[10] Luria *et al.* (1981: 625).

Socio-economic evolution depends, however, on the purposive beha-viour of human beings.[11] In that humans usually have goals for their decisions and behaviour, humans generate novelty and diversity which is intended to satisfy environmental conditions. The firm, for example, does market surveys to try to determine which of a range of slightly different products are most likely to sell. People use their existing knowledge and skills in order to make new combinations and new discoveries. They direct their knowledge-seeking activities to develop-ing novelty which corresponds to their perceptions of local environmen-tal conditions. This implies that humans internalize some selection mechanisms in order to try to generate novelty which they hope will be successful. Firms use, for example, testing methods to see whether their technology will work in practice as well as they think it will in theory. Testing is very important because through it, firms try to create conditions that the technology is likely to face. By trying to fit innova-tions to environmental conditions, firms hope that it will be more successful than would be the case if it were randomly generated.

Third, because human behaviour is purposive and hence humans generate novelty to meet perceived environmental conditions, neither the search for innovations nor the resulting technical changes are dis-tributed randomly in time or randomly in all possible directions. A firm in the electronics business will not start doing research on genetic engineering unless they can identify benefits. They instead do R & D in areas obviously close to what they already do and to the problems they face.

Although the new knowledge generated is not random, it is generated in blind directions, in the sense developed by the philosopher of know-ledge Donald Campbell (1987). Blind generation means that although agents generate alternatives to fit their interpretations of environmental conditions, they cannot know in advance which alternative(s) will turn out to be well adapted. Agents will generate novelty 'in the dark', so to speak. They cannot see very well in the dark, meaning that they only have an approximate understanding of the environment surrounding them, and of selection criteria. They do the best they can under the circumstances.

Instead of acting randomly, agents search for new knowledge which is relevant for innovations within a limited range of all potentially

[11] Here, purposive behaviour is discussed in relation to the evolution of human artefacts and knowledge, not for evolution of the human race *per se*. The fact that no purposive behaviour is allowed in biological evolution but can be assumed in socio-economic evolution has sometimes been considered important enough to reject an evolutionary approach to economics. In debates in the 1950s over evolutionary economics, Penrose (1952) in particular rejected evolutionary theory in economics on the basis of purposive behaviour.

possible alternatives. Where and how they will search largely depends on what they have known and have done previously, because of the importance of knowledge, capabilities, and institutions. Scientists in, for example, molecular biology are taught a core set of techniques and knowledge, which the scientific community holds in common. Nevertheless, each individual differs, and the types of experiments and problems they are likely to work on will be distributed around the core areas, or paradigms.

Where agents search for novelty is here called search space. Agents have developed maps of these search spaces, and the maps can be thought of in topographical terms, where technical and economic opportunities form the contours of the structural landscape.[12] The map should provide information about what did not work before (dead ends) as well as potentially interesting alternatives. The corporate R & D department has to find some way to organize information about approaches and solutions which did or did not work in the past. The map also contains interesting features which could be further explored. In addition, these maps should also give information about the changing ratios of other species, as this also influences survival.

At any given time, agents will prioritize looking into search spaces deemed most likely to generate novelty fitting environmental conditions. Firms engage in R & D which they can perceive to be important for their economic activities. One implication is that not all search spaces for technical change have an equal chance of being explored, and many areas will be unexplored 'wilderness'. Many technical changes which are possible in theory have not been explored in practice because they are deemed less attractive. One example is the development of solar-powered cars, where the technology has not been developed because it has seemed impossible and because gasoline motors have been more attractive. Government financial support earmarked for this technical development induced some firms to see that technology as more attractive, leading to some investment into that search space. This direction of search has not, however, been successful. Knowledge-seeking activities tend to generate technical change in certain directions, or along certain trajectories.

However, because agents cannot know in advance what knowledge they will develop (otherwise it would not be new), the results of agents' search activities are inherently uncertain. The results will sometimes be quite different from those intended. Anyone who has worked with or managed specific technological change knows how difficult it is to plan in advance. Unexpected things happen, leading, for example, to escalating costs due to unexpected problems or to new ideas which were not

---

[12] This argument is made in McKelvey (forthcoming).

apparent before the R & D was started. This means the results of knowledge-seeking activities should be more randomly distributed than the direction of search activities. Moreover, agents cannot know which alternatives will ultimately be selected in the future, because selection processes are partially outside their power.

Fourth, selection in socio-economic processes cannot be strictly separated from generation of novelty, nor is selection completely external to agents. We have already argued that agents generate novelty to fit their perceptions of environmental conditions. They use tests, for example, to imitate conditions of use and market surveys to try to determine what will sell. For this reason, innovating agents have already winnowed down the range of alternatives available for selection and thereby select alternatives along a developmental path deemed to be potentially feasible. Agents do influence selection criteria and help create environmental conditions.

Moreover, selection processes are fundamentally social processes. They involve decisions made by innovative agents and by others. In fact, because these processes are social, selection of alternatives is complex and cannot be specified in simple variables. Selection involves many different aspects; the most important here are scientific, technological, economic, and political. Market forces are very important, but the decisions and actions of firms in relation to technology are also influenced by the firms' experience and competence, by the state of relevant scientific knowledge, and by government decisions and sometimes public debate. Together, this means that selection is a process of social interactions.

Because selection is social, the selection criteria cannot be fully specified in advance. The firm cannot accurately predict what buyers want or what competitors will do, nor whether their R & D activities will lead to something interesting. This is one reason why the evolutionary metaphor is relevant, because it includes the idea that change is not deterministic.[13] Some social science researchers simply argue that selection means 'that the best survive' without analysing the mechanisms of selection leading to survival. Without analysis, this idea of selection is a tautology and thereby explains nothing. In order to help explain evolutionary processes, the selection mechanisms must be understood, or must be at least understandable, as Nelson (1987) has argued. In the current book, selection mechanisms for technical change are discussed by specifying environmental conditions and their influence on agents'

---

[13] This is the opposite of Milton Friedman's famous argument that selection means that only those firms which act as if they maximized will survive, thereby allowing economists to assume maximization even if not found in the behaviour of individual firms. In Friedman (1953), it is assumed that the selection is set beforehand.

knowledge-seeking activities. It is argued that these complex social selection mechanisms are understandable, i.e. possible to understand.

Finally, an aggregate, evolutionary pattern of technical change is consistent with diversity at the levels of individual agents and of technological innovation processes. In fact, evolutionary theory differs from many theories in that micro-diversity, and creative selection among that diversity to adapt to local environmental conditions, are key elements of the aggregate pattern. We cannot assume global rationality or global conditions. Although lacking a notion of determinacy of outcome, the evolutionary perspective developed here does not deny that many different decisions and actions will result in the aggregate evolutionary pattern. This is why the study of evolutionary innovation in general is compatible with an empirical emphasis on why specific, sometimes co-operating and sometimes competing, innovative activities were pursued.

Technological Innovation as Evolutionary

When biological evolution is translated into terms applicable for innovation processes, it can be used at different levels to specify the relations between agents, environments, and innovative activities. This section will examine evolution as a metaphor of technical change involving the following pattern[14]: (1) generation of novelty leading to diversity; (2) transmission and retention of characteristics in the population over time; (3) selection among diversity; and (4) the assumption that evolution does not necessarily lead to progress or optimal outcomes. This last is correlated to the concept of adaptation to local environments. Improvements are locally good rather than globally optimal.[15]

Using a theory developed in one scientific discipline as a metaphor in a different discipline can, in the worst case, result in misleading analogies, but in the best case, it can be a source of creativity. Geoffrey Hodgson (1993) has argued that the evolutionary metaphor is useful for understanding economic processes.[16] There has been an ongoing discussion in heterodox economics about the value of an evolutionary and institutional approach to understanding economic change. Here, we are not looking at the larger questions of evolution of industries or the economy *per se*, but at evolutionary innovation. This latter focus on

---

[14] The principles articulated in Nelson (1987) provide the starting-point for my interpretation of the evolutionary pattern. There are, of course, many ongoing debates but Nelson's work is the most relevant here.

[15] This assumption has implications for analysing agents' behaviour. Instead of assuming they choose the most optimal solution based on global rationality (the same everywhere) it is assumed that they will choose betweeen alternatives based on local environmental conditions, which may also lead to local rationality, differing from abstract, globally rational choices.   [16] Hodgson (1993: 21).

technical change involves coevolution of knowledge, institutions, and agents.

The value of applying the metaphor of evolution to analysing the characteristics of technological innovation processes is that the metaphor can help identify new events, characteristics, and phenomena. To illustrate, the history of the discovery of penicillin will first be told as if a scientific discovery or technical invention were easily and directly translated into an innovation. The first account only mentions the common distinction between 'invention' and 'innovation', where invention means the initial idea and prototype and innovation means the commercial introduction and sale of a new technical product on the market. If the intervening technological innovation process is not examined, everything which happens between invention and innovation can be thought of as going on inside a black box. Rosenberg (1982) stresses the importance of 'opening up the black box' in order specifically to examine technical change and innovation processes.[17] Following that perspective, the story of penicillin is then told as a continuous, complex history.

An abbreviated history of penicillin which only mentions invention and innovation emphasizes the following points. A medical researcher, Alexander Fleming, discovered penicillin by pure chance in 1928. A biological experiment for another purpose did not work as planned because it became contaminated with a mould. Fleming had the ability as a trained and good scientist to recognize the potential of this mould, i.e. of the contaminant, that he had accidentally obtained.[18] That contaminant was penicillin. This was the invention and perception of a valuable discovery. Penicillin has since been commercially sold as a pharmaceutical and has proved enormously valuable in medicine. Firms have had incentives to produce it because they can reap profits, and penicillin represents a successful innovation.

This strict distinction between invention and innovation can lead to particular policy conclusions. In this case, the conclusion seems to be that science push led to the discovery; that market forces were sufficient to turn that invention into an innovation; and hence that governments should only finance basic research. Implicit in this interpretation of the history of penicillin is that invention and innovation are easily identifiable, discrete events and that the step from one to the other in terms of technical development is fairly straightforward.

In contrast, making the black box of innovation processes more transparent requires an understanding of continuous technical change,

---

[17] See Nathan Rosenberg's seminal book (1982).

[18] Hobby (1985: 8). Both descriptions of the development of a penicillin production process are based on Hobby (1985: chs. 5–9).

as well as an understanding of how the producing firms interacted with other agents and environmental conditions to shape the rate and direction of technical developments. Fleming's 1928 discovery of the mould was indeed partly due to chance, even though the discovery was based on his ability to perceive the importance of a basic scientific experiment which had failed relative to his original purpose. Moving from his discovery to commercially produced medicine took close to twenty years.

In fact, producing penicillin industrially required many technical developments and entailed the involvement of particularly the British and American governments as well as research and development by many pharmaceutical and chemical companies. Firms had to carry out knowledge-seeking activities for many additional improvements in both product and production process in order to produce penicillin. Doing so was difficult, expensive, and resource demanding. For example, Fleming's discovery could not be used directly by firms. The specific species of mould that Fleming discovered produced only minute amounts of penicillin, and researchers spent much time trying to find new moulds or to mutate existing moulds in order to find more productive species, making what turned out to be different versions of penicillin.

Moreover, scientific research results were not enough. Firms had to make many improvements in biological and engineering knowledge and equipment in order to make industrial production possible. For example, in order to make penicillin, firms first had to grow the mould. Initially, the firms thought that the mould would only grow in shallow layers, which represented a severe limitation on large-scale production because shallow dishes take up a very large volume of factory space relative to output. After experiments and specific government support for innovative activities on this problem, an American firm managed to develop a way to grow the mould within deep fermentation tanks. The tanks meant that much larger volumes of micro-organisms could be grown per cubic metre of factory space.

Firms were not just acting in response to market forces. Governments played an interesting role encouraging firms to engage in these uncertain and expensive search activities. For example, the American and British governments supported the commercial production of penicillin during wartime, which, as a consequence, reduced the financial and technical risks that development of industrial scale production meant for firms. Governments also specifically encouraged firms to share technical information about how to produce penicillin, information which firms would have preferred to keep secret. Turning the invention into an innovation thus involved both market forces and government action as well as scientific and technological knowledge-seeking activities.

This brief history of penicillin illustrates some interesting theoretical points made in the literature on innovations. First, producing penicillin on a commercial scale required many complementary engineering inventions. Continuing, small, and very specific technical changes had to be made to enable commercial production of penicillin. The importance of these incremental technical improvements has been consistently ignored by traditional economists.

Second, government support played an important role in encouraging firms and in financing these technical engineering developments. The market did not give firms sufficient incentives to innovate relative to the large technical and economic risks and uncertainty. The theoretical division between scientific activities supported by government and technological activities supported by firms does not hold, due to uncertainty and difficulties.

Third, firms initially thought some technical alternatives were impossible, such as deep-tank fermentation of the moulds. However, investment in concentrated search activities changed their perceptions. New perceptions enabled them to search in new directions, or spaces, where they could develop solutions to challenges initially labelled as impossible.

The differences between the two versions of the penicillin story indicate that explicitly examining the history of technological innovation processes raises new research questions. Here, new aspects of the relationships between markets and governments, and between scientific and technological activities, are highlighted. In the first version of the penicillin history, one easily assumes that market forces sufficed to stimulate technology, whereas the second version indicates the importance of government support of technological activities in order for firms to succeed with commercial scale production. The complex nature of these interactions indicates the need to look more closely at the pattern of innovations over time. Like penicillin, a complex pattern of continuing technical change which is generated and selected in commercially relevant directions can be found in the current book.

If we sum up a large body of research on technological innovation processes carried out over the past thirty years, it portrays a common pattern of several competing inventions and/or technical designs which are developed by different agents.[19] There is often an initial period of competing technical alternatives and uncertainty about the outcome, followed by the selection of one which becomes dominant in the market and in the way engineers and scientists think about the technology. Some approaches allow, however, for continuous small improvements which are cumulatively very important. The different phases can then be concurrent instead of alternating.

[19] A similar argument made in Walsh (1993: 139–40).

A similar pattern of technical change has been identified in the following diverse concepts and research traditions. These approaches are by no means identical, but if reinterpreted in evolutionary principles, they do indicate a common pattern of technical change.

In management literature and in evolutionary economics, the concepts proposed include 'product life cycle' (Utterback and Abernathy 1975), 'technological regimes and natural trajectories' (Nelson and Winter 1982), 'technological guideposts' (Sahal 1981), and 'technological trajectories' (Dosi 1988). In general, these terms deal with the notion that new technologies involve major uncertainty and competition. Existing technologies can be traced as accumulations of small changes to past choices along a path. The creation of a new technology includes first a period of uncertainty, high risks, trial and error, and alternatives which differ in technical and market characteristics. This period of diversity is followed by a period of relative certainty about which technical design is most acceptable, and hence has become dominant.[20]

Selection here means selection of one design or of a few very similar alternatives within the same technical parameters. These are sometimes seen as technical alternatives and sometimes related to how engineers think about the design of a technology. For example, Dosi (1984: 14–16) explicitly builds on the idea of scientific paradigms found in Kuhn (1970) and in research in the sociology of knowledge. Dosi argues that engineers' understanding of technology can be thought of as paradigms of thought. These paradigms include knowledge, relevant questions, and how to think about designing technologies. They form engineers' knowledge and ways of thinking about common, accepted types of problems and solutions. The communality of paradigms shared by engineers working on the same technology can therefore be used to explain why technologies tend to develop along a trajectory or path.

When a dominant technical design is relatively stable, then firms face a situation which can be characterized as follows: (1) more certainty about which technical alternatives are likely to be acceptable and hence pose less risk, and (2) increasing importance of price rather than quality or technical specifications in determining choices between similar products. Ultimately, there is a selection process allowing us to identify which alternatives succeeded and which failed in the market. A major

---

[20] Relative to each other, the two early and late phases can be defined as having distinct characteristics of technical stability. Technology is more fluid in the earlier phase and is more solid in the sense of one dominant design in the second. However, even after stabilization, the dominant technological design may be challenged and improved, but challenges in the later phase are usually less radical than those in the initial phase. The difference between challenges in the early and late phases can be thought of as the difference between, respectively, radical and incremental changes. However, this book argues that even a radically new technology requires many incremental changes and improvements, making this distinction difficult to keep.

question, however, remains about whether these should really be seen as separate phases or whether novelty and selection are continuous processes working at the same time.

In the history of technology and sociology of knowledge, similar concepts include 'technological paradigms' (Constant 1980, 1984) and 'evolutionary technology', introduced by both Basalla (1988) and Vincenti (1990). Constant distinguishes between science and engineering as separate but interacting bodies of knowledge, drawing on Layton (1976). Science and technology are practised by communities of practitioners. They can basically be divided into, respectively, scientists and engineers. These communities develop separate bodies of knowledge which, nevertheless, influence each other in that knowledge and techniques are shared. Vincenti further develops this line of thought by developing categories to distinguish what is specific about engineering knowledge. He also proposes a specifically evolutionary account of engineering knowledge, where the trial and error involved in the empirical testing of theories is initially the most important way to gain information during the first period of uncertainty, after which engineering knowledge becomes more systematized with the growth of knowledge.

In contrast, Basalla's book, *The Evolution of Technology* (1988), makes a strong argument about evolutionary technical change by looking at the competing and changing designs of artefacts. Basalla examines the history of technology and finds multiple designs of technologies (artefacts) intended for similar purposes. On this empirical basis, he establishes the credibility of an evolutionary pattern of technical change. In essence, he argues that we can extrapolate from material artefacts in the same way that biologists extrapolate from genes, fossils, etc. Basalla also has an extensive discussion of the relationship between different social selection principles and the design of artefacts.

In more recent sociology of technology and science, the dominant terms have been 'social shaping' (MacKenzie and Wajcman eds. 1985) and 'the social construction of technology' (Bijker *et al.* eds. 1987).[21] These schools set out to challenge the common idea that existing technologies must be the best or the only possible designs because of the fact of their existence. They show how multiple designs and attempts to innovate are ultimately channelled into one successful design not necessarily because of the intrinsic nature of technology or the superiority of one design but because of social interplay and power politics.

In quite different ways, the research traditions mentioned above thus postulate how and why this common evolutionary pattern of technical

---

[21] The sociologist Stuart Blume makes an interesting attempt to unite sociological and economic factors influencing the development and design of medical equipment (Blume 1992: ch. 2).

change depends upon social, technical, political, and economic factors which set the constraints for what agents perceive to be possible with technologies.[22] Although the pattern of technical change is similar, the explanations differ.

In general, the above-mentioned traditions agree that during the initial phase there are many technical and market alternatives. The institutional setting (environmental conditions)—and the place of the innovating agent in that setting—then play a vital role in influencing which alternative technology or design will be chosen and how it will be further developed. In addition to technical characteristics, the process leading to selection of a dominant design involves the mobilization of interests and resources, e.g. political power, persuasion, knowledge, experience, educational investment, and so forth. Interests are mobilized to establish a dominant alternative, and this lives on when the invested socio-economic interests are relatively stable. This helps explain why a new technology will (initially) have difficulties challenging an existing dominant design. This is so even if the new one is a technically superior solution but based on different principles. The development or design of a technology can thus become 'locked in' to one alternative path. David (1986) illustrates the phenomenon of lock-in in the history of the qwerty typing keyboard, where the standard keyboard configuration is shown not to be optimal for typing but to have become the standard through a combination of technical and social investments in, for example, training.

This recurrent pattern of competition and selection of dominant design or paradigm can easily be restated as an evolutionary process of trial and error, of creation of many alternatives before one is chosen in a selection environment. Nelson describes evolutionary technological change as specific to modern market economies and relates it to the question of allocation of resources to search for novelty. Technological change is

inherently wasteful, at least with the vision of hindsight. . . . Looking backward one can see a litter of failed or duplicative endeavors that probably would never have been undertaken had there been effective overall planning and coordination. . . .

What is it about technical change that makes effective central planning so difficult, or perhaps impossible? The basic matter . . . is the uncertainty . . . Where should R & D resources be allocated? . . . There generally are a wide

---

[22] We can focus on perceptions for a moment. Ultimately, the innovative activities of individuals and organizations are based on perceptions of what the technology should or should not be able to do. In the context of this book, the most important perceptions have to do with scientific, technological, economic, and political factors. These perceptions include expectations about scientific and technical specifications and knowledge, markets, and political aspects. These perceptions include convincing authorities and users to, respectively, allow sales and buy the technology. These factors exist before a specified innovation process begins but usually change during the process.

variety of ways in which existing technology could be improved and several alternative paths toward achieving any of these.[23]

An evolutionary, trial-and-error process can thus appear wasteful in the number of failed alternatives of technologies, but diversity enables selection of a smaller number in a market. Diversity is valuable because there exists uncertainty about which alternatives will work and about which will be selected in the future. No omniscient central planner has to try to choose the best alternative. If one central agency were to allocate all the R & D resources in a population, then this might seem rational because the central agency can weigh the risks and benefits. However, the choice made could be quite wrong because the risks and benefits which will result from knowledge-seeking activities cannot be calculated in advance. What initially appears to be the best choice could, for example, turn out to be a truly suboptimal technology in the sense that it does not work technically or commercially. Diversity of technical alternatives followed by selection is, therefore, an advantage rather than a waste of resources.

Four conditions are proposed below for identifying an evolutionary pattern of technical change. They are proposed based on the above discussion of evolutionary and socio-economic evolution, but represent the current author's own interpretation in regard to knowledge-seeking activities for technical change. Particularly important changes to the generally accepted set of principles in evolutionary thinking include the following. First, the principle of variety has been replaced by a discussion of active attempts to create novelty, which leads to diversity. Secondly, heredity, or accumulation of information, is seen to be so important that it is explicitly discussed as a principle of change. It is defined as the transmission and retention of knowledge, techniques, and behaviour among agents. Thirdly, selection processes are explicitly defined as social, in relation to socially created environments. Finally, the assumption of non-optimization is included in order to address the idea that selection processes take place in relation to an environment rather than in relation to some universally valid conditions.

1. There are multiple attempts to generate novelty, leading to a diversity of alternatives.

To fulfil this condition, several similar but not identical alternatives should be visible in the empirical material. However, in contrast to Vincenti and the life-cycle models discussed above, it is proposed that this creation of diversity and novelty is not one phase, followed by a second phase of selection. Instead, diversity of technical alternatives continues to be introduced over time. According to biological theory,

---

[23] Nelson (1988: 313).

evolution as an aggregate pattern continues to require both novelty and selection in order to function. We admit, however, that the novelty introduced will be more or less radical and the range of diversity larger or smaller, at different times.

So far, nothing has been said about which or how many agents will be introducing the novelty. It should be pointed out that not everyone can innovate. Thus, this proposition does not deny that some agents, whether individuals or organizations, may become locked in to only one or a few alternatives. They may not have the capacity to perceive and act upon new alternatives, such as the many pharmaceutical firms which did not initially see the advantages of genetic engineering. If some agents are locked in to an existing technology, then diversity will be introduced by other agents, either a subset of the initial population or new ones. When novelty is introduced, it in turn changes environmental and survival conditions for those using the older alternatives. This may force those using existing alternative technologies to introduce novelty as well, often leading to improvements in the old technology. The same agent may also, however, continue looking for novelty. Here, what is stressed is the necessity of continuing to generate novelty rather than whether the same agent or new agents do so.

2. The transmission and retention of knowledge, techniques, and behaviour among agents are useful for generating and selecting among technical alternatives.

This condition indicates that individuals and organizations which search for new knowledge draw upon knowledge, skills, techniques, and behaviour which they previously acquired through experience, training, education, and so forth. The concepts 'skills' and 'techniques' are differentiated here in relation to technical change. 'Skills' refers to a property of individual(s) whereas techniques are more general or generalizable skills and ways of doing things. For that reason, 'skills' refers to competences and characteristics of specific individuals whereas 'techniques' indicates general ways of doing things which are available in a population of trained individuals.

Agents have different capabilities and competences. These differences should be reflected in their different propensities to innovate and in their search for new knowledge in different directions. For some activities like basic science, individual characteristics are particularly important. For other activities, like corporate R & D, individuals are still important but so is how the various specialists together solve a larger, systematic problem. In that case, differences among firms' employees, competences, experience, and strategies are crucial. For example, if an established and a new firm which are both developing similar technologies are compared, then we should expect that their differing profiles and competences will lead them to search in different directions, often for different reasons.

3. Selection among alternatives is a social process.

As technology is an outcome of human knowledge-seeking activities, selection also results from social processes. Political, economic, scientific, and technological factors have been argued to be the crucial factors influencing the selection of technology. These four must therefore be included in an analysis of how and why technological innovation processes generate and select among novelty.

For socio-economic processes, selection has also been argued to be closely related to generation of novelty. Agents direct their innovative activities to fit their perception of environmental conditions. They even try to internalize aspects of the selection environment through, for example, testing, so that the alternatives they launch are more likely to be successful than would be the case if novelty was randomly generated.

4. The assumption of non-optimization, where selection occurs in relation to local environments.

The technical alternative which is ultimately selected is better than alternatives in relation to the local environment but does not necessarily correspond to any ideal, universally best alternative. This implies that 'progress' is not general but can only be discussed in relation to specific and local conditions.

Analysing this assumption requires a historical approach. At any given time, it will be impossible to judge which technical alternatives will be selected in the future in an environment, because selection is social, because the environment will change, and because novelty will be introduced. By looking back historically, however, the various alternatives developed over time can be compared. It should be possible to identify technical alternatives which were rejected but which were better than some technical alternatives actually chosen and developed due to local conditions.

One implication of this argument is that what is considered 'successful' in one social environment can be perceived as less successful in another. For example, when economic development and energy production were seen as major goals of society immediately following World War II, nuclear power reactors were hailed. Then, with the rise of environmental accidents, their popularity decreased due to risks of radiation, to rise again later in environmental terms as an alternative to coal-burning power plants, which release substances causing the greenhouse effect. The perceived social value of the same technology, namely nuclear power plants, has thus changed over time. In that this is so, the same technology has been better and worse adapted to local environmental conditions over time.

If all four conditions are fulfilled, the general metaphor of evolutionary technical change is philosophically plausible. In that case, there should be multiple technological innovation processes (generation of diversity and novelty) involving knowledge, techniques, and behaviour (retention and transmission of characteristics), selection among technical alternatives, and non-optimal outcomes. These conditions are discussed in relation to the specific case studies in Chapter 9.

Evolutionary Economics

At a metaphorical level, evolutionary theory cannot be used to directly explain economic and technical change, but it can help structure specialized, social science theories on technology into a unified analysis. The idea of evolutionary innovation as developed here has been argued to draw upon theoretical traditions from several academic disciplines, including evolutionary and institutional economics, history, sociology, and management of technology.

The idea of evolutionary technical change comes largely, however, from evolutionary economics and from historical and sociological research traditions emphasizing communities of engineers developing technologies through shared knowledge and practice. The economists often assume that technical change is evolutionary without exploring the issue. Instead, there is shared agreement that technical change involves multiple attempts to generate novelty, mistakes, competition, and selection, but then these researchers focus on economics-oriented questions such as the dynamics of industrial competition and firms' strategies when technologies change rapidly. This book focuses more on technical than economic change in a wider sense, although the two are closely related. Innovations have, in fact, been defined as technical novelties of economic value, which can be developed as products, production processes, and/or organizational changes.

In that evolutionary economists generally draw upon a neo-Schumpeterian perspective, they emphasize the importance of innovations as the motor of economic growth. More specific to this book, evolutionary economists emphasize the importance of innovations as a means of introducing novelty leading to diversity in the economy. They argue that technical and organizational innovations are fundamental driving forces of economic change.[24] It should be clear that evolutionary innovation has much of its meaning in relation to evolutionary economics.

In that innovations are here defined as novelties adding economic value, it stands to follow that this book particularly focuses on activities

---

[24] See, for example, Nelson (1990), which argues this point.

where economics and technology intersect. As Kline and Rosenberg (1986) stress, innovations have elements of both technical and economic novelty, where the two are intertwined.

It is worthwhile to spend a few pages specifying the perspective of evolutionary economics, partly because the concept 'institutional economics' encompasses very different theoretical traditions and epistemological assumptions.[25] Here, only the subcategory of evolutionary economics is addressed.[26]

This heterodox evolutionary and institutional tradition generally has epistemological underpinnings which bring it closer to the epistemology of other social sciences and further away from that of traditional neo-classical economics. This is due to a reappraisal of how to understand individuals and context, rationality, historical processes, and social institutions.

A unifying characteristic of evolutionary economics has been its criticism of neo-classical economic theory.[27] One of its most fundamental challenges to neo-classical economics has been directed towards the notions of allocation of scarce resources and of economic equilibrium (clearing of markets, etc.) which underlie the neo-classical paradigm.

In contrast, evolutionary economists postulate that economic activities involve continuous disequilibrium and dynamic processes of change involving creation of new resources. The overall outcome of technological, firm, or industrial evolution cannot be predicted in advance. In this perspective, the strategy and structure of firms become quite important. Firms invest in costly search activities in order to create new resources and to find out about environmental conditions. Firms have different competences and strategies and hence act/react differently to environmental changes. Whereas the neo-classical perspective has tended to emphasize that economic change is a rational choice situation involving allocation of scarce resources, evolutionary economics emphasizes uncertainties and contingencies. Firms will make different choices, leading to diversity.

In dialectic with neo-classical assumptions and theories, evolutionary economists have been working to construct an alternative theoretical foundation with which to analyse economies and economic change.[28]

---

[25] Hodgson (1989) gives a useful categorization of differences among institutional economists. According to Hodgson, an important dichotomy in institutional economics is between those who emphasize the primacy of the rational individual and those who see the individual as a social animal. Evolutionary economists tend to fall into the second category. Institutional economics is thus a much larger category than evolutionary economists.

[26] Anthologies providing relevant overviews of this perspective in relation to technology include Dosi *et al.* (eds. 1988), Rosenberg *et al.* (eds. 1992), Foray and Freeman (eds. 1993), Nelson and Winter (1982), and Hodgson (1993).

[27] See comparisons of neo-classical and evolutionary economics in Nelson and Winter (1974, 1982: chs. 1 and 2), Coombs *et al.* (1987: ch. 2), and Hodgson (1988: chs. 2–5).

[28] For evolutionary theories for economics, see particularly Nelson (1987, 1988), Saviotti and Metcalfe (eds. 1991), Witt (1991), Hodgson (1993), and Andersen (1994).

The evolutionary economist Esben Sloth Andersen gives a nice summary of the epistemological assumptions of the field. He identifies six typical assumptions and characteristics:

1. The agents (individuals and organisations) can never be 'perfectly informed', and they have (at best) to optimise locally rather than globally.

2. The decision-making of agents is normally bound to rules, norms and institutions.

3. Agents are to some extent able to imitate the rules of other agents, to learn for themselves and to create novelty.

4. The processes of imitation and innovation are characterised by significant degrees of cumulativeness and path-dependency but they may be interrupted by occasional discontinuities.

5. The interactions between the agents are typically made in disequilibrium situations, and the result is successes and failures of commodity variants and method variants as well as of agents.

6. The processes of change occurring in a context described by the above assumptions and characteristics are non-deterministic, open-ended and irreversible.[29]

The theoretical alternative represented by these six characteristics and assumptions is intended to explain why economic change is a historical, dynamic process involving the use as well as the creation of resources.

The first two assumptions describe the way in which agents, whether individuals or organizations, make decisions. First, agents can never know all information, and therefore when they do try to optimize the outcome of their decisions, the results can only be locally rather than globally superior. Globally superior would be absolutely best.

Second, rules, norms, and institutions affect agents'decision making at least as much as calculations of rationality. Agents use rules, norms, and informal institutions (patterns of behaviour) when making decisions because humans have limited computational abilities and because the future is truly unpredictable. Rules provide guidelines for broad categories of decisions, and thereby help agents cope with more information and decisions than they could otherwise handle. In a broader social perspective, institutions imply stability, because an individual can form an opinion about how others are likely to act/react. Stability of social behaviour helps reduce uncertainty. Although informal institutions may be stable, they also change and new ones are created. Thus, in addition to knowledge, institutions are one way in which humans store and transmit information.

---

[29] Andersen (1994: 15).

The first assumption is in particular based on the cognitive and organizational theory proposed by Simon and elaborated by Cyert and March.[30] They argue, in contrast to neo-classical economics, that we cannot assume that agents make rational decisions based on the calculation of costs and benefits of all possible options. Instead, because humans have limited computational abilities, humans can only exercise rationality within a small subspace of all possible options. This is called 'bounded rationality'. The second assumption about institutions draws upon a large body of literature in sociology and in European institutional economics. The predictive value of these two assumptions is that agents will make future decisions similar to current and past decisions, routines, and competences.

The third assumption in Andersen's list indicates that although agents tend to make decisions close to their current decisions and current informal institutions, they can also act creatively. More specifically, agents are not only confronted with existing environmental conditions to which they must adapt. Agents also learn, imitate, and innovate based on what others do. For socio-economic processes, humans' abilities to innovate are closely tied to human intentionality and to the transfer of learned knowledge, as discussed in the previous section.

The fourth assumption is that both decision making and technical change tend to follow certain paths or trajectories over time. Change tends to be cumulative, even incremental, in a certain direction. Occasionally, there are quite dramatic changes leading to discontinuities (jumps) from the previous path to a new one. The concept of trajectories has been applied particularly to technologies, firms, and industries.

The fifth assumption indicates that no equilibrium is established in the system over time. Instead, competition and selection exist at many different levels in the economy. Andersen mentions competition among variations of goods, routines, and agents. Of the alternatives generated within each category, some are selected and can therefore be defined as successes whereas others fail.

Finally, the above five assumptions and characteristics describe a process which is 'non-deterministic, open-ended, and irreversible'. This means that the outcome of an evolutionary economic system depends on the initial situation, on environmental conditions, and on decisions taken by agents during the process. The outcome cannot be fully predicted in advance using given conditions and an assumption of rationality. The process is instead dynamic and involves qualitative changes.

---

[30] Simon (1957) and Cyert and March (1963). Evolutionary economists thus build on others' theories of rules and institutions in order to explain why agents' behaviour has some elements of continuity.

Together, these six assumptions and characteristics indicate the type of explanations about economic and technical change given within evolutionary economics. Different economists within the tradition will, naturally, stress certain aspects more than others, and some, such as Nelson and Winter (1982), have provided more theoretical discussions of why technical and economic change follows an evolutionary pattern. Nevertheless, this introduction in terms of common assumptions and characteristics gives an overview of the epistemological assumptions of this research tradition. In that evolutionary economics emphasizes the importance of social and historical explanations, it opens up real possibilities for integrating Schumpeterian economics with perspectives from other disciplines in order to study technical change.

Issues about Technical and Economic Change

The relationships between technical and economic change within neo-Schumpeterian economics will be explicated in this section in order to identify some important factors for analysing evolutionary innovation.[31] The general relationships will be supplemented by a discussion of three special issues of relevance to the current book: (1) firms' competences and perceptions; (2) lock-in and trajectories; and (3) radical versus incremental change. These are issues of particular importance for understanding the intertwining economic and technical dimensions of innovations.

Schumpeterian economists argue that innovation, whether in knowledge, organization, or technology, is a recurrent feature which drives capitalist competition. Neo-classical economists agree with that proposition, but it is only in more recent years that technical change has been specifically brought into their analyses. Traditional neo-classical economics tended to view technological change as inventions produced outside the economic system. In this analysis, the economic system is closed, and the actions of buyers and sellers move the system towards equilibrium through prices which clear markets. Technological change can come in from the outside and cause disruptions, after which price signals move the system back towards equilibrium. The emphasis in neo-classical economics has thus been on allocation of scarce resources through price signals. In this scenario, technology flows easily within the economy, either through sales of technology or through firms buying and using 'blueprint information'. Firms do not have to invest specially in technical competences in order to identify, buy, and use new technologies. They instead make decisions based on price information.

[31] Many of these issues are discussed in the contributions to Dosi *et al.* (eds. 1988).

In contrast, Schumpeterian economists argue that market economies involve dynamic, qualitative change. Innovations cause such changes. Specifically technical change is generated both inside and outside the economic system. Outside the economic system, there are agents as well as institutions like universities which store and develop much new knowledge. This is in accordance with the neo-classical idea of changes in knowledge coming from outside the economic system. However, technical change also clearly occurs within the economic system in that firms actively search for innovations. This creates new resources, and hence this perspective demands a different theory of the firm, which emphasizes firm strategy, structure, and competences. Firms are assumed to use their specific strategy, structure, and competences to engage in innovative activities. They have incentive to do so because in the best case, innovations will give them temporary monopoly profits for a product or reduction of production costs. Firms can thus create their own competitive advantages. Corresponding to this view of the firm, technology is argued to be 'sticky' in the sense that some aspects cannot easily be transferred. Technology involves complex knowledge which is partially context-bound.

These differences in understanding technology as blueprint information in neo-classical economics and as complex knowledge in Schumpeterian economics have implications for economic analysis. For example, when technology is seen to be easily transferable, a firm's decision to invest in the building up of new technological competences can seem like an expensive and inefficient distribution of resources. If imitation is very easy, it may not be necessary to absorb external knowledge, particularly when it gives comparatively low short-term returns in the market. When technology is easy to develop and transfer, price signals can steer decisions. Firms make decisions based on the rationale of the market. However, when technology is difficult and partly context dependent as in evolutionary economics, then the development of innovations often requires new combinations of knowledge and experience. The firm needs to understand the logic of knowledge-seeking activities, whether explicitly organized, like R & D, or as part of the general running of the company, like the continuous learning firm. Although investing in the building up of competences can have short-run costs without obvious returns, it can give the firm competitive advantage in the longer term. Because of the importance of innovations for long-term competition, firms must sacrifice some short-term returns in exchange for flexibility and for the possibility of longer-term returns. The perspectives on technology in the two economic traditions can thus result in different choices about firm strategy to be made in the same situation.

Firms' Competences and Perceptions

In a neo-Schumpeterian perspective, firms play a particularly important role in developing technology, and the economic system gives them incentives to develop novelties, which in turn introduce disequilibrium into the economy. Schumpeter argued that major technical changes provide potentials for productivity growth. When entrepreneurs take advantage of these potentials and develop innovations, this creates qualitative change which introduces disequilibrium. Initially, Schumpeter saw entrepreneurs as heroic individuals who broke out of the chains of existing routines. Through their actions and profits, entrepreneurs show the greater productive potential of radical innovations, leading others to imitate because they would also like to profit. The innovation is then put into use both by entrepreneurs and imitators, thereby developing the potential returns of the innovations, and leading to an upward swing in the business cycle. In later work, Schumpeter argued that much of the innovative process was automated in large firms, so that individual effort was replaced by collective effort. Modern economic research inspired by Schumpeter still contains these two strands, one emphasizing individual entrepreneurs and one emphasizing firms. Evolutionary economics recognizes the firm as the most important actor for innovations.

In this strand of the modern neo-Schumpeterian tradition, firms are seen as the most important organizers of technology, knowledge, and competences. Using their competences and perceptions, they organize search processes for new technologies. Pavitt (1991a: 42) argues that there are four key properties of innovations which tend to concentrate technical development in large firms.

1. Technology is largely firm specific and cumulative. This means that even though technology seems independent of context, its development is closely intertwined with firms. To elaborate, firms translate general knowledge into specific practice and conditions of use. Some of the knowledge will be more public and available to others whereas other will be more private, either restricted in distribution by its tacit nature or by ownership.
2. Technology is highly differentiated in different fields and industries. Some technologies offer more opportunities for innovation than others. They have more productive potential and offer more opportunities for improvement.
3. Technology involves intense collaboration among specialized groups. Specialized groups must communicate and co-operate to develop complex technology. In extension, the way in which firms organize the development of new technology is quite vital.

4. Finally, the outcome of search for new technologies in economic terms is highly uncertain. It is not evident that the money spent on R & D will lead to anything usable to the firm.

According to Pavitt, a large percentage of the total knowledge-searching activities in modern market economies is organized inside the R & D of large firms. He argues that large firms can spread risks of search activities and can afford multiple technological specializations. The innovative activities of firms, particularly large firms, are for these reasons of prime importance for explaining technological change in the economy.

The importance of firms for developing technology is, however, not limited to large firms. Small firms are also innovative, and the debate about which size of firm is most innovative for what types of technology will continue. However, whatever their size, firms need to invest resources in gathering and developing information about alternatives in order to innovate. This involves uncertain search processes.[32]

In a neo-Schumpeterian perspective, firms play a particularly important role in translating technical and economic information into decisions about whether and in what directions to pursue technical change. For example, before a new product or an existing product based on a new production technology is sold in the market, there are no existing market signals. Firms must make decisions to create both the novelty and the market. Not only do firms react to their interpretations of market signals, but they also can and do act to influence future and actual sales of the product, and thereby influence the creation of a market.[33]

This implies that just like scientific and technological activities, economic influences are not a priori given but are instead created in social interaction. Because environmental selection processes are social, firms do not just react to an existing environment when deciding whether and how to generate and select technical alternatives. Instead, firms react to environmental conditions, to their perceptions of the environment, and to visions of how to change those conditions in the future. This implies that firms' perceptions of the environment are important in explaining how firms react to and influence the environment.

In addition to having different perceptions, firms also differ in their characteristics, experiences, and resources. What firms know and how they do things affect their decisions and actions. Schumpeterian economics thus resembles that branch of management literature which empha-

---

[32] See discussions in Rosenberg (1990) and Pavitt (1991b) about the relationships between search processes in basic science and firms' search processes for incremental technical changes.

[33] This argument about the construction of a market is developed in Green (1992) for biotech products and is also used in Walsh (1993).

sizes differences among firms. The common conceptualization is that firms differ and that firms actively shape their environments.[34] Their strategies, ways to structure the organization, and competences affect their abilities to make decisions and to develop technologies. An important implication is that no one firm strategy can be optimal because which strategy will be most successful depends on differences among firms and on environmental conditions. This is consistent with the evolutionary principles discussed above.

Thus, in Schumpeterian economics, technology and innovations do not just 'flow' to all firms: instead, it is particular firms which can and do develop them.[35] A very important characteristic of firms is, therefore, their ability to organize learning and searching processes for technical change, such as is visible as organized research and development. Differences among firms, including their perceptions, their current competences, and their routines to search for novelty and knowledge, are assumed to influence how firms develop and use technologies.

It may seem paradoxical that both competences and perceptions are important. Competences include knowledge, experience, and capability, whereas perceptions emphasize vision, imparting that vision to others inside and outside the firm, and so forth. Both are necessary but they will be important to different degrees. For a radically new technology, it is proposed that perception can overcome limited competences. A definite vision can enable the agent to overcome limitations by establishing contacts with external agents. For other firms facing the same radical technology, however, current competences may restrict the organization's field of vision, hence limit their ability to perceive the potential.[36]

Lock-in and Trajectories

The concepts of lock-in and trajectories have already been introduced in relation to technical design and engineers' paradigms. Trajectories result from the incremental process of accumulating competences, experience, and paradigms in communities of practitioners. The community identi-

[34] See Nelson (1994) for a comprehensive treatment, in relation to business literature, of the diversity of firms in evolutionary economics.

[35] Firms' behavioural routines, as well as knowledge and experience with technology and industrial sectors, thus influence the probability that a given firm or population of firms will develop and/or use a technology. This argument is developed by Dosi, Pavitt, and Soete (1990).

[36] This can be related to a discussion of Tushman and Anderson's (1986) work on 'technological discontinuities'. McKelvey (1995a) argues that whether a radical technological change will be 'competence destroying' or 'competence enhancing' depends on the diverse actions of firms, particularly on attempts to build up in-house absorptive capacity versus using external relations in systems of innovation.

fies small changes that can be made to improve the generally accepted dominant design.

Instead of conceptualizing technological trajectories in general, we will here explicitly relate it to firms and to groups of firms in a sector or country. They develop a technology within a narrow range of alternatives, where development can be seen to be the result of many small improvements. An example of a firm-level trajectory is when a firm has chosen one specific set of genetic engineering techniques to make a product and then only makes incremental improvements and does not use new techniques. It is a firm trajectory if that firm follows a path of technical development which is narrower than the alternatives available to and used by the population as a whole. Their particular path is built up over time as an accumulation of experience and competences. Sectoral technical trajectories are specified by collections of technologies in use in an industry, as where pharmaceutical firms share a set of techniques and knowledge for chemical and biological production. This is a sectoral trajectory when the collection of knowledge, techniques, and equipment used are narrower, or are different from, those developed and used by scientists and/or by firms in other sectors.

The concepts of lock-in and trajectory have some predictive power in that certain types of firms are more likely to develop certain types of technology than others. The reason is that firms cannot freely choose from all possible technologies. They can only choose close to what they already know and do. They will often make small changes to existing technologies and to existing firm competences, leading to a firm-level trajectory.

In a population as a whole, some individuals may jump to a new trajectory whereas others continue development along the old. In the car motor industry at the beginning of this century, for example, some continued making steam engines while others were experimenting with gasoline engines. These are quite different technologies but are competing trajectories for similar functions. Moving to the often very different set of knowledge, techniques, and skills involved in a radically new technology involves risks. The outcome and the economic returns of the new technology are uncertain and involve difficult challenges. The firms' old core competences may become obsolete. Tushman and Anderson (1986) argue that when a radical technology 'destroys' the competences of existing firms, new firms are likely to redefine the industry and replace existing firms by introducing the new technology. In the above example, gasoline and diesel motors have completely replaced steam engines to propel cars, and these newer technologies were usually developed by new or different firms. Radical technical change can therefore disrupt existing technological trajectories by introducing a discontinuity with past practice and knowledge. This is based on Schumpeter's idea of 'creative destruction'.

One implication of this perspective is therefore that existing firms are most likely to continue using their old knowledge, techniques, and skills. They will make the many small improvements deemed necessary to compete. New firms are likely to come in for radically new technologies. Technology and innovations will more likely be developed by firms with specific sorts of technical and economic experience and competence. Firms do not have a free choice between all available technologies; they are likely to see (monitor, absorb) only technologies similar to what they already know or which they can identify to be of central importance.

In certain cases, especially of major opportunities or major threats, however, it was argued above that firms' perceptions can compensate for their lack of competence. With a strong perception or vision, often driven by entrepreneurial individuals with authority to get the process going, the firm may develop new competences and thereby move into new technologies. This implies that only existing firms with related competences or those with strong incentives/disincentives are likely to move quickly into a new technology.

Such technological specializations also matter at the aggregate level of national economies. A national economy can be broken down into a number of firms producing in different industrial and service sectors. The firms in a given region, nation, industry, or other population either do or do not have competence and experience with specific types of technologies. Some countries are specialized in mechanical engineering, others in automobiles, pharmaceuticals, and/or financial services. This specialization is reflected not only in the structure of production but also in the pattern of search activities (R & D). The existing structure of production will influence the likelihood that a radically new technological trajectory will be developed within that population. The closer it is to current specialization, the more likely it is. Because, however, existing firms can adopt a radically new technology and new firms can be started to develop that technology, it is also possible that major discontinuities can be introduced into the population of firms in a national economy. The conditions under which this occurs require more research.

The implication of this argument is that the existing industrial structure of a country helps explain which types of technological innovations are likely to occur in the future. It matters, for example, that Sweden has traditionally been heavily specialized in both industrial production and innovative activities like patenting in paper and pulp and in mechanical engineering.[37] It is therefore more likely that Swedish firms will continue innovating within technologies close to their current experience, as indicated by the national industrial structure, rather than jumping to

[37] Archibugi and Pianta (1992: 57). For the implications of this argument for longer-term productivity growth related to R & D-intensive products in Sweden, see Edquist and McKelvey (forthcoming).

new technological fields. There is a relevant body of research which addresses research questions about the relations between existing industrial structure, capabilities to do R & D, and innovation. This is done by developing concepts useful to analyse systems of innovation.[38]

What is interesting about genetic engineering is how and why firms could develop and use a radically new technology which appeared to be so different from existing firm competences and experiences. The strategies of two types of firms—established pharmaceutical and new biotech—are examined in relation to these questions in following chapters.

Radical versus Incremental Change

The question of whether changes are radical or incremental can be linked to the question of whether technical changes are made by agents internal or external to the economic sphere. One reason why the knowledge-seeking activities of firms are placed in relation to other such activities in this book is to explore the internal–external dimension. It is quite clear that firms carry out significant amounts of R & D and that the direction of their search activities is along a different trajectory from that of basic scientists. Firms' activities are placed in relation to other agents which also develop and transmit knowledge and techniques within the population as a whole.

Radical changes which develop completely new technologies or which redefine the core technologies of a sector are often assumed to be developed outside the economic sphere. They are often sparked off by more long-term developments of knowledge such as basic research or government support of military technologies. These are instances where the scientific or technological logic of the epistemological communities takes precedence over more immediate social and economic demands. Incremental changes are often seen to be developed within the economic sphere. This view fits with the notion of technology as 'applied science', where small changes are necessary to translate knowledge into artefacts. However, science is also full of incremental changes, and some of the challenges facing firms may be quite radical.

Instead of dividing it up this way a priori, different ways of analysing the extent to which changes are radical or incremental can be used. First, the discussion of firm competences and lock-in leads us to the idea that radical and incremental changes should be related to agents' competences and experience. Changes are more radical the further they are

---

[38] See, for example, Carlsson (ed. 1995), Lundvall (ed. 1992), and Nelson (ed. 1993). The last two develop the notion of 'National Systems of Innovation' (NSI). McKelvey (1991 and 1994a) provides analytical comparisons of different approaches to NSI, and McKelvey (1993a) analyses Japanese institutions supporting innovation.

from existing experience and practice. One way is to analyse the distance between an established firm's knowledge and the new technology. For all firms, we can think of the distance between knowledge and the artefacts and practice in which it is to be translated. The knowledge may be available long before it is apparent how it could be embodied in an object. Scientists knew DNA should be transferable between species long before they had techniques to do so in practice.

Another perspective is to determine in which dimensions a change is radical or incremental. Bengt-Åke Lundvall has proposed that radical and incremental changes can be discussed in the technical and economic dimensions.[39] A discovery may be technically very advanced but have no economic effect because it is never used for products or in production of marketable goods and services. In contrast, a technically simple change may have enormous economic effects by dramatically reducing production costs or by making a previously specialized product accessible to many, thereby greatly increasing demand. In addition to the technical and economic dimensions, two additional dimensions are introduced here. They are the political and scientific. This thus gives us four categories of dimensions of change which can be used to determine whether early commercial uses of genetic engineering were radical or incremental.

Summary and Conclusions

As indicated by the focal point of the above discussions, this book has shifted the focus of Schumpeterian economics from economic change in general to specifically technical change and technological innovation processes. One reason for doing so is that evolutionary technical change is a core assumption of the evolutionary economics tradition, but an assumption which has not been adequately confronted with empirical material. This has to be done in light of other social science research, and the analysis here therefore explicitly builds upon the broader research on technical change and innovations.

Evolution as defined here draws from an explicit comparison of evolutionary theories for biology and socio-economic phenomena. Important differences include the issues of intentionality; purposive behaviour; non-random generation of novelty due to initial narrowing of alternatives by agents before selection; and the social nature of selection. It has been argued that research on technical and economic change from a number of different disciplines supports the idea of multiple competing technologies, of reduction of alternatives through

[39] Lundvall (1992: 12).

selection. Despite different explanations of why this occurs, a common pattern of evolutionary technical change can be identified.

In order to address whether or not technical change follows an evolutionary pattern, four principles of change have been identified:

1. There are multiple attempts to generate novelty leading to a diversity of alternatives.
2. The transmission and retention of knowledge, techniques, and behaviour among agents are useful for generating and selecting among technical alternatives.
3. Selection among alternatives is a social process.
4. The assumption of non-optimization, where selection occurs in relation to local environments.

These principles should be kept in mind when reading the historical case studies.

The perspective of evolutionary innovation has close ties to evolutionary economics but also to other social sciences. It has been argued that the epistemological foundation of evolutionary and institutional economics includes a reappraisal of concepts of institutions and individuals, rationality and context, which bring it closer to explanations in sociology, history, and some management. This perspective emphasizes the importance of historical, qualitative change to explain both what has happened and to give some indications of future paths of development. Firms face context-dependency in translating knowledge into practice and economic value. In relation to that, three special issues were addressed: (1) firms' competences and perceptions, (2) lock-in and trajectories, and (3) radical versus incremental change. These issues are analysed in relation to the historical material in Chapter 9.

Throughout the following empirical chapters, the historical material is structured to allow a discussion about the evolutionary pattern of technical change. Propositions like bounded rationality, the importance of informal institutions and competences, and incentive structures in environments will be used to help explain why different agents are likely to decide and to act to generate novelty in different directions in response to environmental conditions. It is thereby specified how and why different agents and organizations in market-based economies contributed to and/or hindered technological innovation processes.

3

Science and Technology Interacting

Introduction

Given the perspective developed in the previous chapter on evolutionary innovation and on the relationships between economic and technical change, this chapter analyses similarities and differences between science and technology. In popular discussions, these are often seen as two separate bodies of human knowledge, where science corresponds to basic science and technology to machines and such. The perspective developed in this chapter is somewhat different in that it starts from the proposition that the development of both science and technology relies upon agents' abilities to generate and select among new knowledge and techniques. This is the starting point from which to compare science and technology and to analyse how they interact.

Technological innovation processes can thus be seen as the result of interactions between different agents' knowledge-seeking activities, particularly scientific and technological activities carried out in different environments. Environments include socio-economic and cognitive contexts which influence how and why agents search for novelty. It is here argued that agents direct their knowledge-seeking activities in response to incentives and informal institutions in different environments. Firms, for example, are assumed to have incentives to carry out R & D to compete in the economic sphere. R & D helps transform knowledge into practice and other economic value in innovations. This demands that firms' and other agents' activities are carried out with an understanding and modification of environmental conditions. They need some idea of how novelty will help them compete.

More generally, an underlying assumption here is that although economic incentives are very important for stimulating firms to develop continuously and adapt technology to their specific situations, neither economic incentives nor firms' activities alone can explain technical change. Innovations depend on existing knowledge in society and on a variety of search activities which are carried out both internal and external to the economy. That is why it is important to include other agents, such as universities, which are involved in the development of new knowledge. Novelty also arises from technological as well as scientific activities.

This chapter discusses four environments which promote activities to search for new knowledge, and these are defined by institutional source of influence and by purpose of activity. The institutional source of influence is defined as either market or government. The purpose of activities is defined as either technological—in relation to controlling nature to construct a world—or scientific—in relation to understanding natural and artificial worlds. The four environments are interesting here in relation to the activities of searching for new knowledge. This chapter first analyses technological and scientific activities in relation to markets and governments. These two dimensions result in the description of four environments for knowledge-seeking activities, namely the basic scientific, the techno-economic, scientific-economic, and the techno-government. The next section discusses the public context, which is more general than the environments. The last two sections compare the four environments in more detail and then give specific definitions for each environment.

Science and Technology; Markets and Government

The similarities and differences between science and technology can be initially summarized as follows: science is knowledge and technology is translating knowledge into artefacts. 'Science is about *understanding* nature through the production of *knowledge*' and 'technology is about *controlling* nature through the production of *artefacts*.'[1] Although not always articulated, this distinction is fairly widely accepted. Science is about systematizing our understanding of the world, whereas technology is about making the world of artefacts and machines work. This common distinction will be called into question in this section, leading to a different interpretation of the relationships between science and technology.

This distinction is difficult to make sharply once we look closer at historical processes of technical change. It quickly becomes clear that although technology often takes the form of artefacts like machines, the development of technical novelty also requires knowledge, understanding of processes, and techniques or ways of doing things. Science similarly depends upon techniques and technical artefacts such as instruments, without which the knowledge cannot be generated. Both science and technology thus draw upon knowledge, techniques, and artefacts, so the above distinction cannot be shortened into knowledge versus artefacts. The initial distinction needs refinement.

Instead of thinking of science as knowledge and technology as arte-

[1] Faulkner (1994: 431), emphasis in original. This article gives a good overview of the discussion about science and technology and proposes a complex reconceptualization of them.

facts, we can agree that developing both science and technology involves knowledge but that they draw upon different bodies of knowledge. The purpose of activities also differs: science is about understanding and technology is about using knowledge for practical purposes. This has been most strongly argued in the sociology of knowledge and history of technology, particularly by Edwin Layton, Rachael Laudan, Edward Constant, and Walter Vincenti.[2] Science and technology are two separate but partially overlapping bodies of knowledge. Science has to do with knowledge about the natural world and technology with knowledge about the constructed world. Technological or engineering knowledge, for example, includes generalizable principles and knowledge as well as experimental data and hunches from engineers' experiences with similar cases. Although science and technology overlap, Constant and Vincenti argue that the distinction between science as knowledge about understanding and technology as knowledge about practical utility should be kept.[3]

In that this book deals with technological innovation processes, we are interested in knowledge-seeking activities enabling technical novelty of economic value. Thus, we can expand the distinction proposed by Constant and Vincenti. Scientific activities are concerned with the discovery of new knowledge about the world (understanding the natural world) whereas technological activities are concerned with the designing and fixing of new and existing things (creating an artificial world). The two types of activities may be quite similar but should be distinguishable if we can assume that the purpose (direction of search) influences the outcome.

Scientific activities are concerned with the discovery of new knowledge about the world (understanding the natural world). Thus, in the case of scientific activities, knowledge seems independent of the observer because s/he collects knowledge about an already existing world. This scientific knowledge can be systematized and generalized independently of its use. Like technological activities, scientific activities may make controlled changes to the world. The difference is that in science, the purpose of those changes is to create new knowledge, not to gain access to the controlled changes themselves.

Technological activities are concerned with the designing and fixing of new and existing things (creating an artificial world). In contrast to scientific knowledge, technological knowledge is context-dependent and created by its use.[4] Technological knowledge is valuable in relation

[2] Layton (1976), Laudan (ed. 1984), Constant (1980, 1984), Vincenti (1990). Staudenmaier (1985: ch. 3) provides an overview and analysis of the main questions about science and technology taken up within the community of historians of technology.

[3] Constant (1984), Vincenti (1990).

[4] This is similar to the idea of knowledge proposed in Gibbons *et al.* (1994). They, however, argue that all knowledge production is decentralized and dependent on context. This is argued to be a new mode of knowledge production which is applicable to science. The argument here is that this applies to technology and its commercial uses but is much less relevant to science.

to use, either for direct use, as manifest in artefacts, or for indirect use, such as information about where to search (or not to search) for a specific solution. General categories of technological problems and solutions thus exist but have to be translated into specific uses in contexts. This type of knowledge is very dependent on scientific and other knowledge about the natural world, but the purpose of technological activities is to create controlled changes.

In either the case of science or technology, novelty may be quite radical or quite incremental, depending on how far away, or close, respectively, the novelty is from current knowledge and current practice. This means that for engineers, changes in technology and related knowledge can seem as radical as changes in science. This perspective is incompatible with the sometimes common distinction between science as radically new research and technology as incremental changes. As the economic historian Nathan Rosenberg consistently emphasizes, technical develop-ment as practised by firms depends upon the solving of multiple challenges, some of which are relatively simple and some of which are quite complex.[5] Technological activities in firms thus involve both challenging as well as routine problems. This distinction between radi-cal as far away and incremental as close to current knowledge and practice should be distinguished from distinctions based on impacts or consequences. The change itself may be quite incremental but have large consequences in the technical, economic, scientific, and political dimen-sions as introduced in Chapter 2.

Despite this definition of knowledge-seeking activities through pur-pose (scientific or technological), neither the outcome nor its eventual consequences can be predicted in advance. Agents search 'in the dark', and so novelty is generated blindly. We can, however, propose that science often has more far reaching impacts in the knowledge sphere and technology in the economic sphere.

The respective influence of markets and of governments has been mentioned in Chapter 1 as important for understanding science and technology. Markets and government represent two fundamentally different ways of allocating resources to knowledge-seeking activities. In the market, allocation is based on expected returns to the market activities of selling and buying. This leads agents to emphasize activities that have a chance of making a return, either immediately in the market or indirectly through enhancing agents' competences. Even so, firm management may decide to invest in some basic scientific activities which they think are of direct relevance. The future returns are usually quite vague and difficult if not impossible to determine in advance.

[5] Rosenberg (1976: ch. 4).

Although the uncertainty is similar, allocation based on government distribution is often based on different criteria because governments try to use criteria such as public good, long-term benefits, or equality. When financing basic science, governments usually allow scientists to determine the criteria. Governments often have other rationales, even though economists argue that governments should only intervene when markets do not work properly.

In relation to these broader questions about the relationships between science and technology, this study of specific early commercial uses of genetic engineering identifies complex relations between science and technology, between market forces and government decision making, between firms, universities, and government agencies. This book thus deals with a more fundamental question in analysing innovation: How do market forces and government decision making interact in influencing agents' decisions to develop innovation, drawing upon both science and technology?

This question identifies four key words—markets, government, scientific activities, and technological activities. Figure 3.1 illustrates relationships between these four words on two axes. Neither of the two pairs represents a strict dichotomy. Thus, instead of being four exclusive categories, each pair should be thought of as a continuum such that search activities can be more or less scientific, more or less related to market forces, and so forth. The axes thus represent scales rather than boxes.

Figure 3.1 is an analytical tool for classifying knowledge-seeking activities in relation to markets and government, technology and science, and gives us general categories which are also applicable to other research questions. We are interested in them here only in relation to innovation processes. A few words about what the figure does not do. It does not specify causal relationships between different search activities, in the sense that it does not argue that radical technological innovation processes must show a movement over time from one specific quadrant to another. In fact, it does the opposite by opening up the possibility of identifying various search activities which intersect.

This figure gives us four types of activities involving the search for new knowledge, defined both by the institutional source of influence due to allocation and by the purpose of activities. These four are scientific activities-government (S-G), technological activities-government (T-G), scientific activities-market (S-M), and technological activities-market (T-M). Within each quadrant, multiple, parallel activities to solve similar problems or to take advantage of similar opportunities should also be identifiable, as part of the evolutionary pattern. The history of technology is replete with examples of multiple inventors and innovators competing.

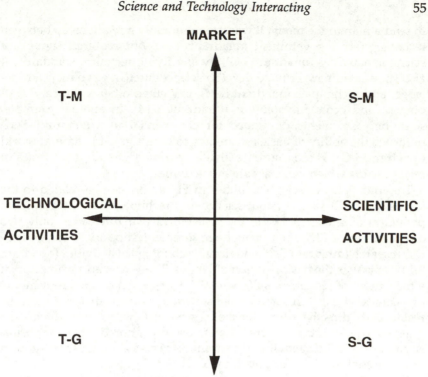

FIG 3.1. Relating market and government to scientific and technological activities

These four environments should be seen as ideal types, or analytical categories. The ideal types correspond best to the outside corner of each quadrant in Figure 3.1. These four ideal types cannot necessarily be found in a pure form in empirical material, but they do help identify crucial features and characteristics of technological innovation processes in market economies. This figure is useful for identifying different types of knowledge-seeking activities ongoing at the same time or identifying relationships between different activities over time. Figure 3.1 illustrates four types of knowledge-seeking activities which may be carried out independently of each other. Independent activities in the different quadrants may also address similar questions but in different ways.

In a specific innovation process, the activities may be related causally and sequentially across quadrants. There are different paths leading to innovations in the sense that different combinations of knowledge-seeking activities contribute to making an innovation possible. An example of a sequential relationship can be found in the American effort to send a man to the moon. It was predominantly a relationship between technology and government (quadrant T-G), but required significant scientific activities (quadrant S-G). By specifying technical standards, it also stimulated new firms to develop science-intensive products, knowledge, and techniques (quadrant S-M) as well as other technical development and economic spin-offs (quadrant T-M). In another example, scientific instruments developed for commercial use (quadrant T-M) influence the ability of basic researchers to investigate the natural world (quadrant S-G). These examples give a flavour of the different types of relationships which can exist among activities.

The four fields of search activities in Figure 3.1 can be related to the discussion in Chapter 1 about science and technology. In the dominant paradigm of science policy in the post-World War II decades, only two categories were identified, namely government support of basic scientific research (quadrant S-G) and firms' technological activities (quadrant T-M). This was the basic division of labour. There was an assumption of a movement of research results from S-G to T-M, called the linear model of technical change. In some versions, it was assumed that one scientific result leads directly to one technology marketable as a product.[6] The other two quadrants in Figure 3.1 were usually ignored. These are firms' support of scientific activities (quadrant S-M) and governments' support of technological activities (quadrant T-G).

The neglect of these latter two types of activities has been mitigated, however, by the realization of a changing role for firms and government. Examples will illustrate this. Quadrant scientific activities-market (S-M) includes activities like contract research by scientific researchers, and such activities have received much attention, not least in relation to biotechnology. Quadrant technological activities-government (T-G) includes activities like civilian industrial policy, development of military technology, and the early stages of scientific projects specifically designed to develop equipment necessary for later scientific research. An example of the third is the first phase of the international Human Genome Project, which explicitly aimed to develop equipment to analyse DNA. These two types of knowledge-seeking activities—scientific-market and technological-government—have thus begun to enter into recent debates over the proper division of labour between firms and governments. Still, many are stuck with the old way of thinking of science as basic science supported by government and technology as R & D supported by firms. The current discussion should widen that perspective.

The four types of knowledge-seeking activities have so far been

---

[6] The linear model is not a model proposed in innovation studies but is an often implicit, unconscious model guiding policy-makers. An implicit assumption is that if governments finance basic research, then market forces will take care of technical developments. It is a hierarchical model from basic science to technology. See overview in Steinmueller (1994).

discussed as quadrants in relation to Figure 3.1. However, we need a more dynamic way of conceptualizing them in relation to theory about innovations and in relation to the historical case studies. Knowledge, techniques, and equipment are assumed to be generally available to trained practitioners in all environments, but each environment can give different incentives for search. It is proposed here that each 'quadrant' defines an environment. The environments are created and implemented in relation to social action, so that the decisions and actions of individuals in relation to the community define selection criteria. An initial flavour of the characteristics of each environment is given immediately below, and later sections explicate them in detail.

Within each environment, the search for new knowledge takes place in relation to existing knowledge and existing social structures. Basic scientists in molecular biology, for example, build upon the knowledge and techniques developed by other scientists in their own and related fields. They then present their results to the same community, who have standards for judging results. So even when one individual is the knowledge-seeking agent, his/her actions are judged and rewarded in relation to the more general social and knowledge context. This is why the environments are defined in terms of direction and purpose of search activities, informal institutions, criteria for success, and incentive structures.

Each environment is composed of two dimensions—the institutional source of influence and the purpose of activities. The institutional source is some degree of either market or government influence. These two different allocation principles give agents different incentives to search for knowledge, and different criteria and priorities for judging results. In relation to knowledge-seeking activities, these institutional influences are generally translated through organizations like firms, universities, and research institutes, such that the first translates novelty into economic value and the latter two translate knowledge to fit into existing bodies of knowledge. An organization, or individual in an organization, may however choose to have parallel search activities within different environments.

The purpose of knowledge-seeking is either technological, in relation to controlling nature to construct a world, or it is scientific, in relation to understanding natural and artificial worlds. Different directions of search are rewarded in the different environments, so that basic scientific activities cannot be directly used to compete in the techno-economic environment and vice versa. If agents in a different environment perceive that novelty to be important, of value, then they must translate and adapt it to fit into their environment. Its use-value does not exist; it must be created.

As mentioned, two of the environments are immediately recognizable from the linear model. The first one corresponds to quadrant scientific activities-government (S-G), here called the basic scientific environment.

These search activities are designed to increase generalizable knowledge about the world, e.g. the internal world of basic research. Governments support these activities through science policy but delegate much of the allocatory decisions and control to scientists themselves. The government gives money to research councils, constituted by scientists, who in turn decide which research projects to fund. Because of the relative independence of scientists, the name of this environment reflects basic research rather than the role of governments.

The second environment is the techno-economic environment and corresponds to quadrant technological activities-market (T-M). It is economic in the sense of new technologies being developed and incorporated into production processes, products, and organization in response to, and anticipation of, market rewards. Because control over nature and constructed worlds must, in the end, incorporate technical and economic aspects in innovations, market forces influence the direction and shape of search activities. These two environments are recognizable from the traditional division of labour between government and firm in relation to, respectively, science and technology.

There are two other environments made visible through Figure 3.1. They are the scientific-economic environment, which corresponds to quadrant scientific activities-market (S-M), and the techno-government environment, corresponding to quadrant technological activities-government (T-G). Each of these environments is a hybrid of the two more obviously recognizable environments. They stimulate knowledge-seeking activities for other purposes and in other directions than the traditional division between science and technology. These will be further discussed below. All four environments are thus specifically defined in relation to activities of seeking for knowledge.

Beyond these environments, which explicitly involve knowledge-seeking activities, there is a larger social context. It will not be considered as an environment here because it does not give specific incentives for scientific and technological activities. For the current analysis, this larger social context is interesting to the extent it sets parameters for what types of knowledge-seeking activities and what types of results (artefacts; knowledge) are generally considered acceptable within the environments. This is called the public context.[7] In relation to new technologies, the public context takes its most obvious form in public debate, informal norms, and formal regulation. Because this book deals with parallel innovation processes in different countries, the extent to which this context is exclusively national or, to which it is national but sensitive to international trends, will be examined.

---

[7] Note that when a government or government agencies act specifically in relation to scientific and technological activities, this will be part of the basic scientific or the techno-government environment rather than the public context.

In Figure 3.1, all four quadrants represent activities of searching for new knowledge, thereby implying agents which are active. These agents can be examined at different levels of aggregation, particularly at the individual or at the organizational level. We can talk about individuals inside or outside organizations, and about organizations as making decisions and acting and therefore being agents of change. By definition, these agents actively seek for novelty.

The case studies in this book specifically explore the conflicts and opportunities which arise when knowledge-seeking activities in separate environments influence each other and when similar activities are simultaneously pursued by agents in different environments. Such opportunities, such conflicts, their resolution, and the subsequent development of new knowledge, techniques, and equipment emerge from related and yet different search activities. In this book, the diverse activities are tied together by their common contributions to parallel technological innovation processes. Over historical time, there is a mutual shaping of ends and means among agents, innovative activities, and environmental conditions.

In biology, coevolution refers to the coadaptation of species, where species adapt and mutually depend on each other, creating niches in an environment.[8] Two species coevolve when they live in symbiosis and influence each other's survival. Coevolutionary innovation takes this analogy of coadaptation and mutual dependency into the realm of technical change. Knowledge, institutions, and agents coevolve during innovation processes. They mutually influence each other within an environment during knowledge-seeking processes. Moreover, agents responding to different environments can mutually influence each other, so that knowledge and techniques developed for one purpose may be applicable for use in other contexts.

Public Context

The relevant aspects of the public context which affect agents' decisions and behaviour in relation to knowledge-seeking activities are defined here as public debate, informal norms, and formal regulation. Only those aspects which specifically influence technological innovation processes are deemed relevant for evolutionary innovation and for coevolution. Public debate related to search activities for a technology or about a technology itself can take quite different expressions—

---

[8] See Durham (1991: ch. 8) for arguments about a different type of coevolution, namely that between genetic and cultural change in human societies. This is much broader and corresponds to changes in the human race as a whole. Here, we only discuss coevolution within cultural or socio-economic change, specifically that dealing with knowledge.

sometimes positive, sometimes leading to the establishment of informal norms, and sometimes pressuring for formal regulation. Formal regulation is implemented either by governments and/or by organizations of practitioners.

These three aspects of the public context—public debate, informal norms, and formal regulation—can be illustrated by the development of practical and relatively easy genetic engineering techniques in the 1970s. Scientific activities led first to debate and internal regulation within the scientific community. These informal restrictions resulted from the scientific debate and set criteria with which an experiment had to comply in order to be considered acceptable. This internal scientific debate subsequently led to public debate and more formal, but still scientific, regulation in the United States and to debate and scientific, then government, regulation in Sweden. In the absence of influence from the public context, agents could have experimented with a wider set of alternative genetic engineering techniques. A public context can thus set parameters in the sense that those activities and artefacts considered unacceptable are stopped or must be reoriented. If no such boundaries initially exist when a radically new technology is being developed, then it is argued here that a public context must be developed.

Public debate, informal norms, and formal regulation can specify the conditions of development and use of either a technology or a group of final products. Restrictions on the use of knowledge, techniques, and equipment used in genetic engineering are a relevant example of parameters for the technology. For final products, there is government approval of pharmaceuticals. Formal organizations generally enforce formal regulation about the uses of technologies and products.

Sometimes, some aspects of the formal regulation of technology are irreversibly related to the regulation of the product as well. For example, commercial use of genetic engineering prompted government agencies regulating pharmaceuticals to engage in discussions with, particularly, doctors and producer firms about the implications of this new production method for existing methods of approving pharmaceuticals. This discussion and the resulting legislation and praxis then specified conditions that had to be fulfilled for firms to gain approval of later pharmaceuticals produced by genetic engineering. Regulation of these pharmaceuticals was thus tied to regulation of the use of genetic engineering to produce them.

Because debate, informal norms, and formal regulation are often national, the public context in different countries often sets different conditions for knowledge-seeking activities. However, national public contexts are not isolated; instead, they are influenced by, and often imitate, those of other countries. Imitation will, of course, make the public context in different countries more similar.[9] The extent to which the national contexts in the cases analysed here were specifically American or Swedish or that they were influenced by international trends, will be analysed.

In relation to technological innovation processes, public contexts:

1. Affect agents' incentives to carry out innovations. When public debate sets a hostile tone against the use of certain kinds of technology, this can discourage agents from exploring that technology. When debate is positive, it may encourage more agents to develop it than would otherwise invest in it.

2. Affect the directions in which agents search for new knowledge. Informal norms and formal regulation often forbid certain types of activities and specify the conditions under which activities are acceptable.

3. Provide both *ex ante* and *ex post* selection criteria about which technical alternatives and innovative activities are considered acceptable. The public context provides *ex ante* selection conditions when it affects the incentives for, and directions of, agents' search activities. When criteria exist while agents engage in knowledge-seeking activities, they are *ex ante* selection conditions if agents try to comply with them as they generate novelty.[10] *Ex post* selection criteria include debate, norms, and regulation which influence selection by helping select among technical alternatives which have already been generated.

The public context is thus assumed to be a national context which influences agents and innovations but which does not give specific incentives to engage in knowledge-seeking activities. For this reason, it has been called a context, which is a more general framework, albeit more geographically bound, than the environments. If the existing public context does not have norms and regulations to deal with a radically new technology, then such a context must be developed through negotiations.

Comparing the Environments

Four environments have been defined, and each has two dimensions—institutional influence and purpose of activities. The environments differ in incentive structures and in informal institutions (routines and patterns of thought and behaviour). These influence the directions of agents'

---

[9] See McKelvey (1993b) for a comparison of the importance of Swedish and American national contexts (national systems of innovation) for genetic engineering to make human growth hormone.

[10] As argued in Ch. 2, intentionality of human actions means that socio-economic evolution involves directed, instead of random, generation of diversity.

search activities, defined either as scientific or as technological activities. Because the underlying bodies of knowledge and techniques are held in common for the different communities, interactions among agents responding to different environments are possible. As a first approximation, we can discuss similarities and differences among the two most familiar environments, the basic scientific and the techno-economic, then elaborate to discuss the other two environments.

The four are argued here to be separate environments. One might, in fact, initially imagine that separate species, or populations, inhabit each environment—universities and scientific researchers in the basic scientific; established firms and their employees in the techno-economic; R & D firms in the scientific-market; and government research labs in the techno-government. Indeed, the specification of the environments initially and partially relies on the notion of population groups of scientific researchers and corporate researchers to help distinguish between science and technology. They are different communities of practitioners. However, in order to analyse the relationships in evolutionary innovation, agents must be distinguishable from environments. This distinction is necessary in cases, for example, where agents or whole populations move from one environment to another, and where agents act to change environmental conditions in a different environment.

It is therefore assumed here that agents and communities of practitioners can be distinguished from the environments. It is further assumed that an agent only responds to one environment at a time with a given knowledge-seeking activity. However, as the boundaries of one environment approach the other environments (quadrants), the ideal types become vaguer. It may therefore be possible that an agent tries to satisfy more than one environment with two sets of knowledge-seeking activities or that agents responding to different environments can compete at some level. There can be overlap, leading to a grey area incorporating features of more than one environment. Agents can also move between environments, and it is clear that knowledge-seeking activities performed in response to one environment influence activities in other environments.

The environments are first defined here in terms of populations, or communities of practitioners. The reason for discussing populations before environments is that these environments are social; both generation of novelty and selection are social processes. Because of this, environmental conditions are formed by social interactions and institutions in the respective communities of practitioners. The knowledge-seeking activities of these communities are in turn influenced by the source of allocation of resources, namely government and market.

Thus, as a first approximation, we can say that the populations inhabiting the basic scientific and the techno-economic environments are, respectively, basic scientists and corporate researchers. It will be assumed for the moment that researchers are doing basic science in independent research institutes and universities, whereas those doing techno-economic activities are employed by firms. Although this distinction does not always hold, it holds enough to help us define the main characteristics of the respective environments. Further along, when the environments are defined, this association between a community and a specific environment and type of organization will be removed.

The population in the techno-economic environment has been called here 'corporate researchers' rather than 'engineers'. One reason is that the term 'engineers' is often defined in relation to hard mechanical worlds, such as Constant and Vincenti's research about aeroplanes. 'Corporate researchers' is a broader term which includes the idea that persons may or may not work with hard machinery. Biological scientists in particular also work with techniques, with biological processes, and with knowledge not directly related to machines. In fact, corporate researchers using genetic engineering often prefer to call themselves scientists rather than engineers. Many identify more with university scientists in related scientific fields rather than with engineers in other disciplines which are based on physical properties. These corporate researchers identify more with scientific knowledge and techniques than with tinkering with machines. Symbiosis does occur, particularly between fields related to genetic engineering and the more established field of chemical engineering. In this situation, it is difficult to talk about engineers representing a separate community and developing a separate body of knowledge. Instead, the corporate researchers using genetic engineering are some combination of scientists and engineers. Therefore, we need different concepts from 'scientists' and 'engineers' in order to specify characteristics of the populations. The terms used here instead are 'basic scientists' and 'corporate researchers'.

These two populations, basic scientists and corporate researchers, can be distinguished according to how and with whom individual members communicate research results. In an earlier contribution to the debate about science and technology, the sociologist Michael Mulkay argued that the distinction lies between 'pure science' and 'applied research'. This is approximately the same division as the one between basic scientists and corporate researchers. The knowledge each develops occurs in specific social situations, including criteria to judge the value of results:

The major characteristics of the social context of pure research are as follows: participants are expected, indeed, they are constrained, to pursue research topics on the basis of their scientific significance. The audience for results consists of other researchers who are working upon the same or related problems and who judge the adequacy of results by means of scientific criteria. Control is informal, in the form of 'scientific criteria' . . .

The context of 'applied research' is significantly different in that participants are expected to produce results which have useful practical consequences. Furthermore, the main audience for these results is composed of non-researchers and this audience determines the activities of researchers by the exercise of formal, bureaucratic authority and direct control over rewards such as salary and promotion.[11]

According to Mulkay, the differences between 'pure research' done by basic scientists and 'applied research' done by corporate researchers are thus in terms of intended audience, in terms of criteria for success, and in terms of who control rewards. Scientists' incentives are internal to science and put priority on publishing novel research results, whereas corporate researchers' incentives are related to practical, technical, and economic benefits for the firm.

Researchers in the 'pure research' world communicate with other scientists, and there are informal controls on, and judgement of, know-ledge, whereas the 'applied research' world requires communication to non-researchers like management as well as more formal control. Basic science has long been analysed as a separate knowledge community, although work by Latour, among others, has strongly challenged this view of independent scientists.[12]

These differences in the two social contexts of the generation of knowledge are argued to affect the type of novelty that agents are likely to generate. Basic scientific activities tend to generate knowledge which generalizes about the world, whereas technological activities tend to generate information and techniques to control nature as well as to generate artefacts by transferring and translating knowledge into the world of applications.[13] The types of knowledge generated can similarly be analysed in terms of use-value for different purposes.

The economists Partha Dasgupta and Paul David have applied economic analysis to the question of scientific research versus technological development. They suggest the following distinction about the purpose and type of novelty generated:

Roughly speaking, the scientific community appears concerned with the *stock* of knowledge and is devoted to furthering its growth, whereas the technological

---

[11] Mulkay (1977: 95).

[12] A long research tradition in sociology following Robert Merton uses the notion of socialization to separate the activities of pure science (scientific research) from applied science (approximately, technical development). Rather idealistically, Merton (1942) argued that the social organization of science is based on scientists' conforming to four pure values in their work—universalism, communality, disinterestedness, and organized scepticism. These values of science assume that scientists follow different ethical codes from the rest of society. More recent sociologists of science such as Latour (1983) argue, in stark contrast, that scientists are very much interested in using their results for personal gain, prestige, and so forth.　　　　　　　　　　　　　　　　　[13] Price (1963).

community is concerned with the private economic *rents* that can be earned from that stock. . . . As would be expected, each community seeks to inculcate in its members, through training and incentives, those attitudes and mores concerning research procedures and findings that tend to further its particular goals.[14]

Dasgupta and David thus define the two bodies of knowledge in terms of use. Scientific activities produce results usable as input into further research, whereas technological activities produce artefacts and knowledge directly usable for economic gain.

Put in a different way which is relevant for the current discussion, these two populations respond to different incentive structures and institutions. Within the scientific community, researchers are rewarded for publishing knowledge, whereas the technological community is rewarded for developing knowledge and techniques which are of economic value. This may sometimes include scientific activities. The informal institutions are created through the actions of the communities and thereby become environmental conditions. These institutions influence the direction of search activities as well as the probable results obtained.

However, this basic distinction between 'pure' and 'applied' research has been increasingly called into doubt in recent years, particularly due to numerous instances where pure researchers have developed results of applied interest and vice versa.[15] This criticism indicates reasons to loosen up the distinction between the two and to agree instead that pure researchers may be motivated by profit instincts and that applied researchers can develop knowledge relevant for basic scientists. This is why, even though environmental conditions are socially constructed, they are discussed as environments in analytical separation from the populations. An individual in one environment may, for example, decide to move his/her knowledge-seeking activities to another environment, as when molecular biologists start biotech firms.

Before defining just the environments, however, there are a few additional points which need to be made about the influence of markets and governments on agents. The previous discussion indicates important points about how the social context, respectively, of independent scientists financed by government and of communities dependent upon market financing gives different communication patterns and different forms of control. Basic science relies on more informal control and much communication goes directly between scientists, whereas corporate research involves more direct bureaucratic control, and in addition to occasionally communicating with external scientists, these researchers are expected to communicate with others, such as managers and lawyers.

[14] Dasgupta and David (1987: 522), emphasis in original.
[15] Rosenberg (1990).

Technical and scientific information must then be translated into a form understandable to others.

These differences in control and communication seem to be based on the communities' relative reliance on funding from markets or from government. In fact, the scientific community can only be a relatively closed group which makes decisions based on scientific criteria when its members are not totally dependent on market financing. When financing is given for basic research and allocated by other scientists, then internal scientific criteria and judgements can be used. In other words, the autonomy of basic science comes from its longer-term support from governments, research foundations, etc. This enables scientific communities to function relatively independently of shorter-term markets and demands for practical consequences. In this situation, scientific research can be carried out in a more isolated cognitive and social context, meaning that practitioners refer to others in their scientific community more extensively than to non-scientists.[16] They do not have to bother with popular versions of science or with whether the results are useful or used by others in society. In fact, in recent years, the independent and vague long-term benefits of basic science have been increasingly called into doubt by political actors interested in more immediate returns. Independent basic science with its own intellectual criteria is under various sorts of fire when governments no longer feel it is their responsibility. They want to see tangible results.

A similar isolated context also exists for certain technological activities, specifically in the techno-government environment. The cognitive context is isolated when it is the technology itself which is important rather than technology in relation to markets. These are often technological systems which are protected from markets and where internal 'scientific' and 'technological' goals legitimate and justify established practice. This would be cases like the Concorde aeroplane, which is technically sophisticated but a failure commercially, mainly because political and social interests other than the market legitimated its development. The government is usually involved one way or the other, either through giving support to the development of technologies which are public goods, like military technologies, or through exercising natural or state-granted monopolies like railways and telecommunication. An isolated social and cognitive context is therefore also a characteristic of the techno-government environment.

In addition to these two situations where government funding allows the development of independent epistemological communities, there are also situations where market forces determine the allocation of resources

---

[16] Argument based on Clark (1987). See also the arguments about the nature of engineering knowledge put forth by Vincenti (1990).

to scientific activities. New knowledge which apparently mostly deals with the stock of knowledge may still be of economic value. For example, much research within biotechnology has been quickly put into practice. In the scientific-economic environment, the criteria to judge the results of scientific activities are made in light of actual and expected market conditions and returns. The practical and economic consequences of scientific activities thereby become more important than adding to the stock of knowledge. The firms may, however, have very long-term time horizons and so by no means expect immediate pay-offs. For firms' management, it is a decision about trade-offs between more immediate day-to-day operations and expenses and longer-term strategic questions.

Because the practical and economic consequences of an investment in knowledge may be neither tangible nor immediate, we can continue to talk about scientific activities even when influenced by market allocation. Rosenberg (1990) and Pavitt (1991b) have argued that in certain cases, firms use their own money to do basic research because otherwise those firms could not understand the importance and relevance of scientific knowledge developed elsewhere. Firms may be willing to develop these intangible skills and competence areas in order to avoid being surprised by more major and long-term threats or, alternatively, in order to open up possibilities for productivity increases. This argument also holds for fields of engineering and technology. Cohen and Levinthal (1989) argue that firms must do R & D in a technological field in order to be able to identify and absorb technical developments made elsewhere. Despite the intangible and long-term nature of these situations, in all cases the organizations responding to market forces are assumed to expect some return on their investment. They are not altruistically building up general and public knowledge, which the government has generally seen as its role. It quickly becomes apparent that markets can influence the direction of scientific activities just as much as technological ones. An important question is, however, how much demand for more immediate returns which can be foreseen can be placed on scientific activities without losing quality.

Defining the Environments

Based on the above discussions, we can now define the four environments in terms of informal institutions, norms, and criteria for success of knowledge-seeking activities.

1. In the basic scientific environment, agents generally engage in scientific activities to increase the stock of generalizable knowledge

for understanding the world. The population of basic scientists collectively create these conditions but they individually respond to them. They tend to carry out scientific research which builds on the knowledge and techniques developed by other scientists and which can be communicated to them. Due to longer-term funding by government and due to independence justified as cognitive guardians of knowledge, the social and cognitive context of basic science is relatively independent from other contexts in society. Scientists can work in an ivory tower because this distance is often necessary to build up long-term bodies of knowledge. Many points of contact outside the scientific world do exist, however, and should not be underestimated.

Because of its relative independence, internal scientific criteria such as contribution to the stock of knowledge, degree of novelty, and theoretical knowledge are used to select among the diversity created. Results are judged by whether they are relevant to building up knowledge to understand and explain the world. Scientists tend to compete within specialized niches where they expect to have some advantage, or at least some possibility of survival, and they can move between related niches. Although basic scientists develop and use significant amounts of techniques and equipment, the incentive structure and hence internalized code of conduct emphasize the importance of knowledge.

In this basic scientific environment, the incentive structure to search for new general, systematized knowledge is thus backed up by selection principles which determine which groups or individual scientists will successfully compete over time and thereby expand (survive). Selection principles within the population of basic researchers include competition for funding of new research, priority through publication, and scientific prestige. Time is an important factor of selection in this environment because date of publication establishes priority, and hence prestige. Competition may be very rapid, even in weeks or days.[17]

2. Within the techno-economic environment, technological activities are done with the expectation of economic returns. These activities are generally organized by, or carried out within, firms and may correspond to formal R & D or to less formal search activities like quality circles. The results are judged not only by others engaging in R & D based on scientific and technical criteria but also by corporate management based on economic criteria. The technical alternatives generated, tested, and selected within this environment are thus expected to fulfil both technical and economic criteria. These two criteria can be summarized as, respectively, 'it functions' and 'it sells'. This does not mean that all

---

[17] See Hull (1988) for an evolutionary analysis of biological evolutionary theory in terms of competing population groups.

alternatives generated in the environment fulfil both criteria, but it does mean that alternatives selected are expected to fulfil both.

Firms have a more direct, formal control over individuals and over the organization of search and innovative activities. As argued in the section on evolutionary economics, firms' most important characteristic in relation to innovation is their ability to organize different search activities to reach common goals. This, of course, has to be carried out with economic considerations in mind.

Moreover, the technical developments desired are often very specific to the firm:

For technological change in its economic aspect involves dealing with innumerable small increments to the stock of knowledge which are, from a strictly scientific point of view, totally uninteresting. . . . It is the essence of technological knowledge that it deals not with the general or the universal, but with the specific and the particular.[18]

This implies that the novelty generated, and the technical alternatives selected, conform to criteria which emphasize improving local, particular technologies useful either in production processes, products, and/or organizational change. Each firm will differ. The techno-economic environment thus gives firms incentives to search for particular kinds of technical change which can be useful when the firm responds to market signals.

In the techno-economic environment, this incentive structure to search for specific, local technological artefacts and knowledge is similarly enforced by selection criteria. These act at the level of technologies, corporate researchers, and firms and determine which will successfully compete over time and thereby expand (survive). Selection criteria expressed through the market are obvious both at the level of firms, particularly their relative survival as firms, and at the level of products, or their success in selling products. Within the firms, selection also takes place in connection with generation of novelty. Selection at this level includes testing procedures imitating expected environmental conditions as well as searches directed by the expectations of researchers. Compared to the basic scientific environment, selection processes can be quite long-term and the degree of novelty less important than the ability to combine technical and economic aspects of innovation.

3. The techno-government environment is a partially isolated social and cognitive context, like the basic scientific environment. These researchers can work in research institutes, universities, firms, or whatever, but the government has often demanded that these groups work separately from others in the organization in order to increase accountability. This is clear, for example, for American firms producing military

---

[18] Rosenberg (1976: 78).

weapons. The government wants to see that it gets something for its money. This community easily becomes self-referential, in that technological improvements are often the main or only criteria for development. This often leads to technically very sophisticated results which are also, however, very expensive.

This environment is less independent than the basic scientific environment. Governments have not been willing to give these engineers and scientists a free hand in developing whatever technologies they wish, as they have been partially willing to do for basic scientists. Instead, governments try to steer technological development according to the principle of providing public good, and thereby try to obtain a satisfactory public good for the money. They often encourage new technology for military protection, for energy provision, etc. Steering development to embody the desired public good quality at a reasonable price is difficult without the market force. Multiple examples show military technologies which embody high technical sophistication but at extremely high prices. Without market criteria to balance choices between trade-offs between cost and performance, technical and scientific criteria seem often to take precedence over government-desired criteria.

In this techno-government environment, the incentive structure sometimes emphasizes search for specific, local technological artefacts and knowledge and sometimes for larger technological systems. Like the basic science environment, the selection mechanisms act through the success or failure of obtaining government funding. The community is partially isolated in activities but has extensive contacts with other researchers, with government agencies, and often with other parts of firms. They attempt to direct technological activities to satisfy the technical specifications of government decisions, but often allow technical and scientific criteria to take precedence. One reason may be that governments have more difficulties enforcing their contracts, or in other words, that the less harsh selection mechanisms allow a wider range of behaviour.

4. The scientific-economic environment encourages scientific activities which have potential returns, although these consequences may be quite intangible and long-term. Like the basic scientific environment, the scientific activities generate new knowledge which can be used to further understand the world. In that it is also judged according to economic criteria, however, this knowledge must also contribute through, for example, enabling more practical techniques, developing agents' competences, or identifying potential opportunities and threats to current ways of doing things. Bell Laboratories, for example, has had a long tradition of supporting a small percentage of basic research which is tangential to their core economic activities. The criteria to judge among alternatives must be some combination of economic and internal scien-

tific criteria, because bad-quality scientific activities do not give the same economic returns as good-quality science. To some extent then, this population must move back and forth between the scientific-economic and basic scientific environments.

Summary and Conclusions

By defining the four environments separately and arguing that agents can only respond to one environment at a time with a knowledge-seeking activity, we give ourselves tools and concepts to identify and analyse whether and how agents direct knowledge-seeking activities in response to environmental conditions. Technological innovation processes involve many different knowledge-seeking activities over a period of time. This implies that agents in more than one environment can clearly contribute, which is evident for science-based technologies.

The two axes of market–government and of scientific activities–technological activities were combined in Figure 3.1, giving us four environments. The combination of scientific activities and government gives us the basic scientific environment. This is the internal world of basic research, where governments support research but scientists retain control over allocation and definition of 'good' research. The combination of technological activities and market gives us the techno-economic environment, in the sense that technical improvements are judged by their practical and economic significance. These two environments are easily recognized, underlying as they do the linear model of innovation, but the figure indicates two other environments as well. These two are the scientific-economic and the techno-government environments. The combination of scientific activities and market gives us an environment which encourages research to create knowledge but where decisions based on market forces are used to judge among alternatives. Examples of market influence include selling of knowledge through R & D contracts and using front-line knowledge to keep an edge on a technology in order to compete in the future. The combination of technological activities and government defines an environment where government influences technology. This often involves the development of expensive, large-scale technologies like nuclear weapons systems.

The environments and their respective selection processes are social, involving the development of human knowledge. The specification of each environment therefore includes: environmental conditions giving agents incentives to engage in innovative activities; informal institutions—i.e. patterns of thought and behaviour—which reinforce these incentives; *ex ante* and *ex post* selection mechanisms for generating and selecting among technical alternatives; and finally, how incentives and institutions interact to direct agents' search activities along specifiable paths. In the case of early commercial uses of genetic engineering, some of these environments already existed in the 1970s and some were created while technology was being developed. The scientific-economic environment in particular was created when these scientific activities were perceived to have economic value.

In addition to these four environments, the public context has been defined. This context is not an environment giving incentives and disincentives to agents to search for knowledge. It is instead a background context, which is more general than the environments. The political context is nevertheless important to the extent it sets parameters for what types of knowledge-seeking activities and artefacts are considered acceptable in the four environments. This influence takes its most obvious form in public debate, informal norms, and public regulation.

In order for environments to influence the direction of agents' activities and hence their relative rates of survival, there must be regulation and feedback between environments and agents. We should therefore expect that agents will be rewarded and punished according to whether the majority of their knowledge-seeking activities are judged successful according to the selection criteria of their environment. It is assumed here that agents only respond to one environment at a time with each activity, although different activities can be directed towards different environments. Agents can, moreover, move to another environment, either by physically moving or by changing the orientation of their activities.

This question of selection criteria at work can be further illustrated. Assume that a basic scientist active at a university or other research institute with a strong basic scientific orientation continually breaks the accepted norms of that community. Maybe s/he always puts commercial interests over scientific ones and even stops producing generalizable research results. In that situation, we should expect that other scientists should give her/him less recognition for the work, reduced research grants, and so forth. That individual then faces a choice between changing orientation of activities to fit the basic scientific environment; finding a research community which emphasizes the importance of commercial outcomes; and of physically moving and/or orienting activities even more towards one of the economic environments and moving out of the basic scientific one. As for a university as a whole, one which blindly concentrates on turning a buck by selling research results and which neglects to participate in developing generalizable public scientific knowledge will lose scientific prestige. Whether or not it will lose government funding depends on whether government policy is oriented towards basic research or towards more immediate returns.

Assume, on the other hand, that a corporate researcher loses sight of the final commercial and practical goals of the knowledge-seeking activities and concentrates purely on technical and scientific criteria. In that case, if the firm buying that research is more oriented towards combining technical and economic criteria, then it should react by firing him/her or forcing that person to work on a different project. Punishment should be expressed if the researcher is supposed to be oriented towards more immediate and specific problems. Different activities within a single firm may, however, be oriented both towards the scientific-economic and the techno-economic environment. It is, for example, rather common practice in biotech firms for researchers to have a small percentage of their time to spend on independent scientific activities. The firm itself may strongly emphasize technical and scientific criteria but if it thereby loses sight of market criteria, it will end up in financial trouble. Even firms oriented towards selling science, like biotech firms, must make it relevant for commercial uses. We should thus expect that environmental conditions are backed up by sanctions which influence the direction of agents' activities and/or which encourage agents to change environments.

Chapter 2 proposed that in technological innovation processes, agents develop a limited number of alternatives based on their competences and their perceptions of environmental conditions. Information about these conditions will often come from other agents so that getting that information requires interactions or communication. Success in the sense of turning an invention into a product which sells is often fundamentally dependent on interactions between innovative agents and other agents like users[19] or universities. These other agents can have specialized knowledge about environmental conditions and/or power to change environmental conditions. They thus provide important technical and economic information to the innovating firm. By influencing the preferences of these other agents which are constraining the limits of the possible, innovating agents may also change environmental conditions. For example, genetic engineering (biotechnology) often requires making whole new markets seem possible, thereby changing buyers' perceptions of what they want. Using radical technology often means acting to change existing environmental conditions to allow the novelty. Because generation of novelty and selection are social processes, agents constitute and change environmental conditions over time, and by placing the specific and particular technical activities of firms in relation to other agents and environments, it is possible to examine the special

---

[19] Lundvall (1988), von Hippel (1988).

characteristics of economic innovative activities and the extent to which technical change is endogenous to the economic sphere.

Knowledge-seeking activities in different environments can influence each other. There are a number of reasons for this, having to do with the public nature of information as well as the level of education and training necessary to monitor changes. One reason is that there is a stock of scientific and engineering knowledge which is public and has accumulated over time. Some basic principles are accepted and taught to students. Individuals then understand and can use this knowledge and these techniques, whatever type of organization they work in.

Just because this stock of knowledge is available somewhere in the world, however, does not mean that everyone has access to it. Knowledge has to be learned. This stock is thus transmitted particularly through teaching and training. When individuals who have learned some of that stock then begin work or move between organizations, they take knowledge and techniques with them. Even without changing organizations, individuals with a certain level of competence will be able to identify and understand new developments taking place elsewhere so that learning continues to take place in the best case. They will also learn from interaction and feedback within the organization. This implies that communication between agents responding to different environments is not just possible but even quite likely and stimulating. Communication can occur without direct personal contact as, for example, when information is moved as written papers.

The accessibility to different parts of this stock of knowledge differs, however. Knowledge and techniques will have different degrees of specialization and so are correspondingly more or less accessible. The more specialized they are, the fewer there are who understand them. In order to understand the more special part of the stock, including recent results, individuals must already have a high level of learning and competence, whereas other parts of the stock are less specialized and require a lower threshold of learning. Knowledge can run on a continuum between very specific, local, and tacit to general. One implication is that some knowledge is more easily accessible and transferred and more easily applied to general categories of problems than other knowledge.

A related reason is that even if scientific activities often deal with knowledge and technological activities often deal with artefacts and control, both types of activities rely on both knowledge and techniques. In scientific environments, localized knowledge such as technical know-how, techniques, and skills are often undervalued in discussions of basic scientific results. These are assumed to be necessary tools for developing knowledge, not goals in and of themselves. Be this as it may, it is exactly scientists' abilities to combine very specific experimental skills with an understanding of general theoretical principles which leads to results in those fields involving genetic engineering. In the same way, corporate researchers often need to draw upon systematized knowledge and general principles in order to solve very local and specific questions and in order to develop techniques. These abilities to use general knowledge to solve particular problems and vice versa also facilitate interactions among agents doing scientific and technological activities.

So, even though only some agents have access to the stock of scientific and engineering knowledge, agents working on both scientific and technological activities can have access to the same knowledge and techniques. For example, some scientific discoveries are only of relevance within a specialized field and some technical improvements only of importance for a firm or industry, but other scientific discoveries and technical improvements have much wider ramifications. They often go hand in hand, so that improvements in scientific knowledge are dependent on improvements in techniques and instruments. Specific improvements in technology can also depend on better understanding general principles. The two do not always interact, but they often do.

The complex processes of technological innovation rely on the development of new knowledge, techniques, and skills and on the constitution of social institutions and selection criteria. These are defined here in terms of agents carrying out knowledge-seeking activities in response to different environments. Agents can also act to change environmental conditions. The institutions and selection criteria have been argued to be specific to the four different environments, giving incentives to engage in knowledge-seeking activities as well as rewards and penalties which direct activities toward specific types of knowledge. Within each of the four environments, there is coevolution between knowledge, institutions, and agents. When one of the three changes, this affects how, why, how much, and in what direction it interacts with the other two. This leads to coevolution across environments.

4

Understanding Genetic Engineering

[Natural scientists] have forgotten how alien the concepts of genes
and cells and molecules are to the layman ... Yet it is vitally
important that the potential and also the limitations of genetic
engineering be made accessible to a wide public.[1]

Introduction to Genetic Engineering for Pharmaceuticals

The words 'biotechnology', 'genetic engineering', 'genome', 'gene
manipulation', 'amino acids', 'steroid hormones' are foreign, exotic,
and unfamiliar to most of us. The layperson's description of the basics
of biotechnology and genetic engineering found in this chapter is
intended to make the remainder of this book more comprehensible.
This chapter gives an overview of some key concepts and principles so
that the scientific and technical essence of these specific case studies does
not completely disappear into the socio-economic context and theoretical
arguments about innovation processes.

The case studies in this book focus on the use of genetic engineering to
make pharmaceuticals intended for human medical use, in particular
human growth hormone (hGH) and to a lesser extent insulin. hGH is a
hormone, which is a specific type of protein with regulatory function in
the body. Proteins are essential for life; all chemical functions in life are
taken care of by proteins.

Human growth hormone is produced in the pituitary glands of all
'normal' humans, after which the hormone is released in appropriate
quantities and at appropriate times to give messages to the body. Its
most important message seems to be to tell the body to grow, although it
is also involved in a number of other bodily functions. Too little hormone, or a correct level of hormone but problems in interpreting the
message, leads to dwarfism; too much hormone can lead to gigantism.
The idea of giving quantities of this hormone to pituitary dwarfs had
been tested, and in many countries, like Sweden and the United States,
became accepted pharmaceutical practice after the 1950s. Treatment with
hGH for this disease begins in childhood and runs for seven to fifteen
years, generally with daily or weekly injections.

[1] Nossal (1985: 3).

Before genetic engineering, the supply of hGH was dependent on its purification from the pituitary glands of human cadavers. This extraction process was performed by different types of organizations. It was done by state owned but for-profit pharmaceutical firms like KabiVitrum (Kabi) in Sweden; by private pharmaceutical firms like Arès-Serono in Switzerland; by institutes supported by the parents of these children, such as the Growth Fund in the Netherlands; and by government-supported organizations like the National Pituitary and Hormone Program in the United States and the Medical Research Council in the United Kingdom.

Some other proteins useful as pharmaceuticals can be extracted from the tissue of pigs and cows. This scenario works if the animal protein is still biologically active on humans, that is, affects human metabolism. Insulin is an example, as it has traditionally been extracted from slaughterhouse remains. However, only human growth hormone is effective in humans. That leaves human cadavers as the only possible source previous to genetic engineering. A third source, chemical synthesis, was impossible for practical reasons. Chemical synthesis could be used to make shorter proteins, but hGH was too long and complex a protein. Therefore, the firms and institutes making hGH before the 1980s were forced to rely on a supply of human pituitary glands from morgues, and thereafter extract and purify the protein. For example, Kabi had an enormous organization for handling hGH; the last year before they switched to genetic engineering, Kabi collected about 200,000 pituitary glands from around the world and sold the resulting product internationally.[2]

If one wanted to push an analogy to the extreme, one could say that firms and institutes previously used other humans as factories to produce hGH and other rare substances made in the pituitary gland, but could not reap their 'production' before those persons had deceased. The same thing is true for blood supplies and other medical products like organs, which were not available from other sources before artificial hearts and the like were developed. This analogy fails, of course, because the organizations did not have control or intention of control over the persons or their respective biological processes. Moreover, donors' actions were generally based on altruism (or benefit to survivors) and free will. However, this analogy does make a point. When genetic engineering made it possible to produce complex proteins outside of human bodies, firms did gain control over nature and over production processes.

Success in manipulating genetic engineering for pharmaceuticals depends on controlling and using the internal chemical processes of

---

[2] Holmström (1992).

cells to make proteins. This book considers two such end-products, hGH and insulin, proteins which work the same way as the natural ones. They do not affect the DNA in the patients' cells. hGH is injected and helps regulate metabolism in the same way as the hormone normally produced in the body or that extracted from human cadavers.

In the late 1970s, basic scientific advances in molecular biology and related fields made it possible for some basic scientific researchers to insert DNA, which was extracted from a cell or built up chemically, into a different cell. Genes are stretches of DNA. It was even possible to transfer DNA between species. Initially, researchers primarily used bacteria cells in experiments and commercial processes, but they have since moved to yeast cells, mammalian cells, and, to some extent, larger organisms.

To make hGH or insulin in bacteria using genetic engineering, the research group needs to do at least the four steps below, represented in Figure 4.1. They first have to find the correct human gene, which gives cells instructions to build it. Having found the gene, the researchers have to find a way to put that gene into the DNA sequence of a different, preferably simple cell, and make the cell 'read' exactly that part of the DNA sequence. As a consequence, the cell should express (i.e. make) the desired protein. In other words, to succeed with this use of genetic engineering, scientists need to find ways to do the following four things:

1. Finding a coding sequence for the protein.
2. Getting the coding sequence into a manipulable piece of DNA.
3. Getting the gene into a bacteria.
4. Turning on the expression of the coding sequence.

These four steps are schematically represented in Figure 4.1.

Having modified cells to produce the desired proteins, firms need to grow the cells, ideally in large batches. Commercial-size batches of cell production are large, for example 10,000 or 100,000 litres of cells and fermentation broth, whereas laboratory scale generally runs 1 to 10 to 100 litres. Initially in a batch, there are only a few cells, but as these cells grow and reproduce, each daughter cell should contain the DNA sequence which tells it to produce the desired protein. Scientists and firms thus want the cells to ignore the other genes in the cells and mainly produce the desired one.

Doing this successfully on a large industrial scale for pharmaceuticals requires a host of complementary skills and technologies. These include growing the cells *en masse*, purification, separation from contaminants, formulating the protein into a pharmaceutical product, developing tests to evaluate the results, and so forth. These commercial technical developments are vital to understanding firms' use of genetic engineering and neither their difficulty nor cost should be underestimated. The old adage

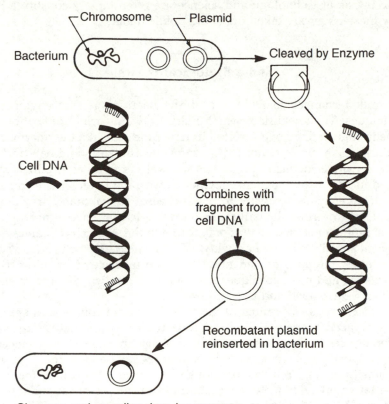

Cleavage and resealing done by enzymes

FIG **4.1.** Schematic representation of recombinant DNA techniques
Source: Nossal (1985: 30), and reprinted with the permission of the authors of the
second edition (Nossal and Coppel, 1989) and Melbourne University Press.

'for every $1 spent on R & D, $10 goes to industrial development and
$100 to marketing' still demands some reflection on the importance of
firms' technical development.

The above description should give enough information to follow the
case studies, as further scientific and engineering explanations are
provided in ensuing chapters, particularly regarding genetic engineering techniques and the development of complementary technologies like
analytical methods. The rest of this chapter gives a more in-depth
discussion of biotechnology and genetic engineering in scientific terms
and in the public debate. The reason that both the scientific basics and
public debate are included here is that, particularly for non-experts, our

conceptions of technology and science are often largely constituted by how these issues are taken up in the public debate.

Some Biological Basics

Controlled changes to DNA are at the heart of genetic engineering techniques. The scientific research fields and industrial applications of genetic engineering have resulted in new products, like the pharmaceutical tissue plasma activator (tPA) against heart attacks and new and/or more sensitive medical diagnostics, as well as familiar products produced in new ways, such as enzymes in washing detergents to remove fats or an enzyme necessary to make cheese. To elaborate, previous to genetic engineering, the natural enzyme needed for cheese-making and called rennin or chymosin was only found in the stomachs of calves or in a fungal substitute of lower quality. With the help of genetic engineering techniques, the enzyme can now be made in bacteria or yeast. New knowledge and new techniques for making controlled changes to genes are being developed and put into use.

Medical uses so far represent the most important commercial applications of genetic engineering, and it is useful to distinguish between different uses in the pharmaceutical industry. In terms of pharmaceutical products, genetic engineering techniques can be used to (1) replace or substitute for products previously obtained from other methods. Alternative methods include extraction of proteins from tissue (animal or human) and chemical synthesis. Substitution may be combined with (2) obtaining products not previously available in bulk. This includes insulin, hGH, and petroleum-eating bacteria. Genetic engineering techniques allow more direct control over the raw materials, and hence the possibility of radically increasing the volume of production. Genetic engineering can also (3) produce completely new products. The last use has gained much media attention, particularly when pharmaceutical and biotech firms launch new products. A common denominator among all three categories is the basis of a production process for pharmaceutical products.

Another currently important trend in the pharmaceutical and other industries is to use genetic engineering techniques as analytical and research tools.[3] For the pharmaceutical industry, these diagnostic tools and research analytical tools enable researchers to analyse the medical effects of drugs at a much more detailed level than was previously possible. Previously, medical researchers in firms and in universities could only see general, clinical effects of drugs on a large number of

[3] Faulkner and Senker (1994: ch. 5).

patients, whereas today, they have the potential to see how things work at the molecular level. One implication is that genetic engineering techniques allow the pharmaceutical industry to be much more precise in designing new drugs. Instead of mass-screening thousands of potentially useful chemical substances, they are trying to develop 'rational drug design'.

Thus, genetic engineering has led and will continue to lead to major changes in both the pharmaceutical industry's products and in basic medical research. These trends indicate significant scientific and commercial use of the techniques by basic researchers, established firms, and specialized biotech firms.

In addition to medical uses, genetic engineering and its applications as biotechnologies are likely to influence many areas of life relating to natural substances such as seed production, use of agricultural materials as the basis of production of industrial goods, waste management, animal husbandry, human health care, new materials, and so forth. These are all examples of how genetic engineering has and will come into our daily lives in sometimes small, perhaps unnoticed, ways.

In fact, biotechnology has long been used to make products we continually come in contact with in daily life such as bread, beer and wine, yoghurt, and penicillin. These are all based on using and controlling micro-organisms to reach the desired ends—and without these biological and chemical processes, none of these or similar products could be made.

Biotechnology can thus be defined more broadly than genetic engineering. The European Federation of Biotechnology offers this definition: 'Biotechnology is the integrated use of biochemistry, microbiology, and chemical engineering in order to achieve the technological (industrial) application of the capacities of microbes and cultured tissue cells and parts thereof.'[4] The American Office of Technology Assessment has a similar definition, as does the OECD, which defines it as 'the application of scientific and engineering principles to the processing of materials by biological agents to provide goods and services'.[5] Biotechnology is thus defined as applications of the biological sciences to purposes which are important in economic, industrial, or technological terms. These official definitions of biotechnology thus clearly refer to a constructed technology, designed to control nature for a purpose.

Such definitions of biotechnology are very broad, and many examples given involve traditional human activities. As the word 'biotechnology' is usually used by many scientists and in the mass media, however, biotechnology is defined only as biological activities dependent on controlled changes to genes, and thereby intimately coupled to scientific

[4] Quoted in FAST (1982: 5).
[5] OTA (1984: 503). OECD definition taken from Yoxen (1987: 9).

fields such as molecular biology and biochemistry and to techniques like genetic engineering and gene therapy. Distinguishing between this broad term 'biotechnology' and a narrower definition of biotechnology is useful partly because it demystifies genetic engineering as something absolutely new and radical, and partly because it makes it easier to relate genetic engineering to other biological and chemical processes. The remainder of this book discusses only such new biotechnology based on genetic engineering techniques.

Understanding biotechnology based on genetic engineering requires a brief review of the biological functioning of cells as given visually in Figure 4.2. Figure 4.2 shows the cell as a whole, including both DNA and other elements which perform the instructions given in genes. All biological processes are fundamentally chemical processes. Thus one can simplify and say that a DNA molecule is a chemical molecule which directs cells to produce other basically chemical substances, such as a protein for a cell wall or a protein which regulates specific bodily functions. The cell consists of different elements like DNA which act as 'brains' and others which act as the 'brawn'.

DNA contains messages which direct the functioning of cells. It functions whether we speak of single-cell organisms or the differentiated cells in a complex organism like a human. The DNA contains messages to the cell and can be thought of as an instruction book for the other parts of the cell. Figure 4.2 shows some of these other elements which act as a factory to execute the instructions found in DNA. These elements are in the cytoplasm. The specific sequence directs elements in the so-called cytoplasm of the cell, and they produce one of twenty different amino acids. These amino acids are then put together into a chain in a specific order and in a specific three-dimensional shape to make proteins.

DNA also contains instructions to start and stop a given process. The start signals are called promoters. These types of signals are important in order to gain control through genetic engineering. When a cell uses a gene to produce an intended protein, the technical term is that it 'expresses' the protein. Those who wish to go further into how the DNA molecule actually works or how DNA is related to, and dependent on, cell biology are referred to the various texts accessible to the non-expert, such as Nossal and Coppel (1989).[6]

---

[6] Many of the words used in biology such as 'genome', 'chromosome pairs', and 'genes' are classifications of segments of DNA. Because this instruction code of DNA lies sequentially, it is important to be able to differentiate between different sections of the DNA molecule. A gene is a section of a DNA molecule. A classification of longer stretches of DNA is a chromosome pair; humans have 23 chromosome pairs. Chromosomes are pairs in that they contain one set of genes from each parent. The term used to refer to all the DNA in an organism/species is 'genome'. To indicate the complexity of controlling DNA, we can ponder the fact that humans have 10^9 base pairs, that is 1 billion base pairs, and 10^5 genes.

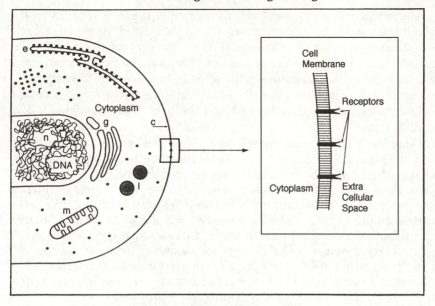

FIG **4.2.** Diagram of a cell
Source: Diagram reprinted from Nossal (1985: 7) with the permission of the
authors of the second edition (Nossal and Coppel, 1989) and Melbourne
University Press.

Continuity or Discontinuity?

The above definitions of biotechnology and genetic engineering contain
two seeds of thought which seem contradictory and can be expressed by
the question: Is genetic engineering revolutionary, or is it just the same
old thing? Proponents for both views abound, but the question runs
deeper than just a mild disagreement. In fact, the answer to this question
relates to the implicit view of historical developments in science and in
technology: Are new discoveries, knowledge, and technologies radical
breakthroughs or are they simply new combinations of existing and
well-formulated theories, thoughts, hunches, and empirical work?

The history of scientific and commercial developments in genetic
engineering can support both interpretations, but the cumulative, sometimes fumbling, nature of scientific discovery is just as clear as the
flashes of genius.[7] Even such flashes of genius and revolutionary upheavals as when the scientists Francis Crick and James Watson determined
the structure of the DNA molecule in 1953 were based on competitiveness and co-operation between different research groups, who in turn
built on previous research.[8]

[7] Root-Bernstein (1989: 354–82).
[8] See these two researchers' accounts of events in Watson (1968) and Crick (1974: 766), or
that of a historian of science in Judson (1979).

The familiar side of genetic engineering, which places it firmly in the traditional practices of biotechnology, is that applications of genetic engineering rely on the biological and chemical processes of cells, micro-organisms, and larger organisms. Additionally, humans can interact and intervene in nature with genetic engineering techniques in similar ways as they traditionally have with other techniques. A couple of examples indicate how the old and the new biotechnologies follow similar logics.

Genetically engineered animals and plants can be compared to selective breeding of the same by humans. Selective breeding is a way to change the DNA pool of the offspring by choosing parents with desired characteristics, and thereby selectively modifying the natural evolutionary process of selection and reproduction. Selective breeding involves a certain amount of trial and error because control is quite loose. Although the selection of appropriate parents narrows the gene pool, much uncertainty remains as to the genotype and phenotype of the offspring, because the DNA will be a fairly random mix of parents' DNA plus sometimes random mutations. Genetic engineering tries to control this mix of DNA more directly. Doing so requires extensive and more detailed knowledge of how genes work in the organism, the sequence of the desired genes, and most difficult, how and which genes are related to which characteristics in the organisms as they develop in an environment. Both genetic engineering and selective breeding thus follow a similar logic to improve nature. The difference is that selective breeding can only do so at the level of the whole plant or animal, whereas genetic engineering opens up the possibility of doing so at the level of genes.

Another example of how genetic engineering techniques can be used in similar ways as previous techniques is the use of micro-organisms to produce substances such as penicillin, antibodies, and vitamins. Since World War II, a number of pharmaceuticals like penicillin have been commercially produced as the by-products of yeasts, bacteria, and the like. These are substances which certain strains of cells produce using the naturally occurring DNA. The basic idea of producing them commercially has been to grow the yeast or bacteria by giving them nutrition, and controlling the conditions so that the micro-organism can reproduce. Afterwards, the desired substance must be separated and purified. The same basic steps lie behind the use of micro-organisms which have a small bit of added DNA which tells the cell to produce other proteins.

For human growth hormone, the human gene which tells a cell in the human pituitary gland to make hGH can be inserted into the DNA of a strain of common intestinal bacteria called *E. coli*. Once a viable strain of bacteria has been devised, the techniques, equipment, and production process flow are quite similar to those used to manufacture other substances produced in micro-organisms, with certain modifications.

Thus, a major difference between the old and new biotechnology production systems is the percentage of the gene for the desired protein which already existed in the wild form of cells relative to the percentage which must be pasted in.

One way of classifying this is to decide whether:

1. All of the genome existed in the original cell,
2. Information for some of the biological steps were already contained in the genome, or
3. None of the information used to make the desired protein was initially there. All the new gene has to be moved in.[9]

Genetic engineering opens up the possibility of the third.

One of the main differences between traditional biological processes and genetically engineered ones is thus how much of the original instructions to make the desired substance can already be found in the genome (the DNA as a whole). With genetic engineering techniques, it is possible to go about pharmaceutical production in a relatively planned and rational manner, i.e. pick a desired protein, discover the relevant (human) gene, and so forth. Previously, discovering which specific micro-organism could make which desired medical substance was more of a hit-or-miss affair. For example, discovering a new antibiotic required that researchers and firms collected various strains of fungi or bacteria and tested them for the desired substance. Even in this example, humans select among bacteria found in nature, often by trying to breed mutants and by modifying the growing conditions in order to reach desired ends. Likewise, medical substances made through chemical synthesis have traditionally required the screening of thousands of chemicals. Today, genetic engineering techniques can be used as a research tool to limit the amount of such testing.

These two examples indicate how commercial uses of genetic engineering follow traditional human practices of modifying nature in order to reach desired results. One important thing to remember is that the resulting molecule is very similar, if not identical, whether the protein is obtained through chemical synthesis, through expression in genetically engineered organisms, or through extraction from tissue. Chemical reactions are the basis of life. This point is important to keep in mind because it is often missing in popular debates and in ongoing discussions and definitions of what is natural and what is unnatural.

At the same time, if genetic engineering is solely a continuation of previous human practices, techniques, and attitudes towards nature, then no discussion of genetic engineering would be necessary here, in the mass media, or anywhere else. What is new about genetic engineering is the increasing understanding of life processes and the ability to control these biological processes. The aspect which is most focused upon in

---

[9] Aharonowitz and Cohen (1981: 106).

popular debates and among practitioners is the working of DNA itself, i.e. how, and perhaps why, scientists can make controlled changes to DNA and the outcomes. Herein lies what is most radically new about genetic engineering.

In the article 'From Understanding to Manipulating DNA', Watson (1986) presents a fascinating and highly readable account of how a community of scientists have, over time, combined scientific knowledge in various fields into an ever more coherent understanding of how DNA works and how to manipulate it. Watson's historical account brings up many vital points about how science develops, but what is most interesting here is how scientists' understanding of DNA and its role in the cell has been so closely related to their ability to manipulate DNA. Knowledge and techniques have gone hand in hand.

For example, the discovery and use of restriction enzymes were important because they allow scientists to cut DNA strands at very specific points.[10] Cutting DNA into fragments enabled researchers to map the sequence of sections of DNA, a technique developed by Gilbert and Maxam at Harvard and by Sanger of Cambridge, England.[11] In addition to cutting, scientists wanted to paste together DNA, and vital research by Paul Berg of Stanford Medical School in 1972 showed that it was possible to paste DNA together using enzymes called DNA ligase. These can paste the DNA strands together at specific points. Cutting and pasting together enabled genetic engineering techniques:

1973 marked the date when the first universally effective method for making recombinant DNA was announced. Then Boyer and Cohen, working nearby to the Berg lab, inserted DNA fragments into tiny bacterial chromosomes (plasmids). . . . Such recombinant DNA plasmids could be made by virtually any trained scientist, and it soon became clear that with time, virtually any gene could be so cloned in bacteria.[12]

In other words, scientists needed to know not only that it was possible to make controlled changes to DNA but also that the techniques could be easily and practically used. Controlled changes were based on understanding genes and cell biology as well as on techniques and tools to cut and paste DNA and to make synthetic DNA.[13]

---

[10] The first effective enzyme became available in 1970 after basic research. Now, multitudes of restriction enzymes are known, and firms supplying them also supply standardized charts of which enzyme is effective at what part of the DNA strand. Restriction enzymes have gone from front-line research to standardized techniques.

[11] Watson (1986: 220).   [12] Ibid. 221.

[13] Scientists can also make synthetic DNA because the DNA molecule is, in the end, a simple chemical molecule. Two of the first scientists hired in the late 1970s by the start up biotech company Genentech artificially constructed DNA, an experiment which at that time was excruciatingly time-consuming and done only by highly specialized persons. Today, innocuous black boxes sit on laboratory benches which can quickly and easily make such synthetic DNA sequences, or else company scientists send a little request form through internal company mail, just as if they were requesting office furniture.

So what is so important anyway about being able to understand and manipulate DNA through genetic engineering techniques? Three main points are the universality, simplicity, and vital function for life of DNA.

1. *Universality.* DNA is universal in that all living organisms have DNA, and in that it functions in cells and organisms in essentially the same way. Based on exterior characteristics, one might imagine that wheat plants had one kind of DNA, bacteria another, and humans yet another, but the basic DNA molecule, its component parts, and many of its ways of functioning are universal for all living things.

2. *Simplicity.* DNA is also simple: the structure of the DNA molecule is relatively simple and easily reproduced in cells. The bases which direct production of amino acids work in an understandable and predictable manner. It becomes somewhat more complex when we are dealing with DNA in humans, but most of the same basic principles apply.

3. *Vital functions for life.* DNA molecules can be seen as repositories for messages which direct the functioning of life.

With genetic engineering techniques, it is possible to take advantage of these universal and simple characteristics of DNA in order to combine genes from different species. An example close to hand is to put human genes into bacteria, and through tricks of the trade, convince the bacteria cells to make the protein for which that human gene codes. This is the use of genetic engineering which is analysed in this book; it was one of the first uses of genetic engineering for commercial purposes and is now common in the pharmaceutical industry. This initial development now belongs to history to some extent, and it is other applications which are challenging.

Public Debate

In addition to giving background material about genetic engineering for pharmaceuticals, a broader aim of this chapter is to stimulate readers to reconsider the current and potential roles of genetic engineering in society and the economy, because such questions come to the surface in social science research which deals with radically new technologies. The main reason for including some discussion about the public debate over genetic engineering is, however, that readers' comprehension of what biotechnology and genetic engineering mean is closely coupled to their understanding of potential applications as reflected in the public debate. Moreover, public debate is analysed in subsequent chapters as an aspect of the public context.

Some individuals know much about genetic engineering, but for most, genetic engineering enters their vocabulary through half-remembered biology from school and from articles, books, and TV coverage of scientists and their fantastic breakthroughs, of successful biotech businesses and busts. This means that many people have a fragmented view of the field. Understanding that DNA is the basis of life can, for example, provoke a perception that all applications of genetic engineering are frightening and of large magnitude. 'Does genetically engineered hGH change the DNA of the person taking it?', one might well ask. The question indicates an understanding of the importance of DNA—hence the fear—but also a misunderstanding of how genetic engineering can be used as a production technique. Although this section by no means claims to cover all the issues, the idea behind it is that laying out a simple discussion of other medical uses of genetic engineering will enable comparison with the specific uses described in this book.

Despite recurrent images of Frankenstein-inspired monsters, of creating or manipulating new life through DNA sequences, scientists argue that genetic engineering is generally not a goal in itself, even if much scientific knowledge is ultimately found by asking the question, Is this possible at all? Experiments such as putting rat growth hormone into mice to get a supermouse have a whiff of manipulating the world and challenging nature, but scientists argue that such laboratory experiments must ultimately relate to some current cognitive logic of a scientific discipline, and must be related to questions about knowledge such as: Why is this experiment possible? How does it relate to known theory? What key questions does it answer?

Moreover, initial research and commercial interest in genetic engineering have been concentrated on human health care, leading to medical questions such as: How does this work in the body? Why? Is it useful and effective? Thus, specific and relevant bodies of scientific paradigms provide a framework within which a particular use of genetic engineering is argued to fit.

Genetic engineering has made a certain measure of mastery over nature possible. Even with our currently relatively rudimentary knowledge of the role of DNA in cell biology—to say nothing of our ignorance of the influence of the environment on the expressions of genes—genetic engineering has still opened up possibilities which were invisible or seemed like science fiction. Even the most optimistic proponents of industrial uses of genetic engineering in the mid 1970s expected viable applications of genetic engineering techniques in future decades, not mere years.

Modern biotech offers promises and fears about its effects on many areas relating to natural substances, although sometimes it will be difficult to separate promises and fears. Promises include new pharmaceuticals, gene therapy, gene surgery on foetuses, cleaning up the environment through petroleum eating bacteria, better seeds and animals, and making materials or substances which are currently rare or impossible to make. Fears include, for example, release of dangerous, genetically engineered organisms which would thereby reduce our possibility of surviving in the natural environment. In addition to fears about catastrophes in the environment, other fear scenarios are based on abuse of information about DNA in order to reach dubious organizational, social, or individual goals. Such fears include making super-humans, reducing the level of genetic diversity in the world, concentration of control in wealthy organizations, abuse of DNA finger-printing in court cases, and so forth.

One of the most discussed scenarios is discrimination based on information in DNA sequences. If we can identify normal genes for various diseases, then those persons with abnormal genes may be identified as potential carriers of the disease, even if we do not know under what environmental circumstances the disease does or does not occur. This information could in turn be used, for example, by insurance companies to differentiate premiums or by employers to choose which worker is most suitable for the job in the long run. As with selective breeding and micro-organism production, there are also historical examples of companies discriminating against workers through drug and psychological tests, etc.[14] In these cases, the potential abuse lies in the use of the information.

Another, more futuristic use of genetic engineering would be to repair or change a gene inside humans or animals to prevent a disease. Modification of DNA in the so-called germ cell (i.e. egg and sperm cells) is a change which can be passed on to offspring; this, however, is not practically possible at the moment. Ideally, in human medical use, the doctors and scientists should be able to change the incorrect sequence in the egg or sperm before fertilization so that the correct sequence is passed on to all the relevant cells in growth. This scenario is most feasible for easy-to-identify, genetic diseases. Of all the millions of bases in a human DNA strand, one base out of place can cause a few genetic diseases, such as sickle-cell anaemia. However, essentially all diseases are much more complex than one out-of-place base.

Even genetically 'simple' diseases can be very heterogeneous in their origin. Sequencing studies of the gene that codes for a critical protein in blood-clotting has shown that haemophiliacs differ from people whose blood clots normally by any one of 208 different DNA variations, all in the same gene.[15]

This complexity of genetically transmitted diseases, plus the fact that all human individuals have somewhat different DNA sequences, indicate the immense difficulties of analysing cause and effect.

---

[14] Another would-be use of genetic engineering is to develop and produce poisons or gases for military purposes (Piller and Yamamoto 1988).   [15] Lewontin (1992: 36).

A related technique is called gene therapy. Like manipulation of germ cells, it relies on the ability to distinguish between normal and abnormal genes for an inherited disease—or possibly an inherited propensity for a disease. Gene therapy means placing a modified gene in a mature organ, for example, putting the correct gene for hGH back in the pituitary gland. The idea is to induce the individual's cells to produce proteins based on this modified, correct DNA instead of the mutated one. The principle is the same as that described above to make pharmaceuticals in factories, only now the mini-factory cells are inside the person's body rather than in a fermenter vat. Gene therapy has already been used to treat children with a rare immune disease.[16] The main difference between gene therapy and the sort of gene surgery discussed in the previous paragraph is that gene therapy does not affect the DNA in the egg and sperm cells and consequently cannot be passed on to offspring.

In order to debate questions about scientific research and its applications, laypersons have a responsibility to understand at least some of the basic principles of genetic engineering, and its potential benefits for and risks to our lives. Sweeping generalizations of the type 'we should reject genetic engineering because it is contrary to nature' can be confronted, for example, with the difficult discussion of what is natural, what is artificial, and what is artificial nature. On the one hand, we need to think about the individual and social choices that new knowledge and practices pose for us, in order to deal with conflicts of morality and ethics. On the other hand, we need to have some insight into the science and engineering side to evaluate for ourselves which claims may be reasonable or unreasonable, what may be possible or not possible.

As argued at the beginning of this chapter, genetic engineering will increasingly come into our daily lives in small, unnoticed ways and probably in dramatic ways as well. The remainder of this book focuses on one such way—namely, using genetically modified bacteria as the basis of industrial production of pharmaceuticals.

------

[16] Lewontin (1992: 36)

5

Generating Research: the Early to Mid-1970s

With a more complete understanding of the functioning and regulation of gene activity in development and differentiation, these processes may be more efficiently controlled and regulated, not only to avoid structural and metabolic errors in the developing organism but also to produce better organisms.[1]

Introduction

This chapter presents historical material from the early to mid-1970s detailing the early history of genetic engineering techniques as the basis of production for human proteins. This history starts with the development of these techniques through scientific research in universities and goes on in subsequent chapters to examine other types of knowledge-seeking activities necessary for early commercial uses. The historical period covered in this and the next chapter—the 1970s—was a decade with major scientific breakthroughs and with the initial recognition by individuals, firms, and other organizations that genetic engineering might be profitable for making certain pharmaceuticals on a large commercial scale.

The scientific results enabling genetic engineering techniques built upon more than twenty years of basic research in molecular biology, microbiology, and related fields on DNA, genes, and on cells. The genetic engineering techniques developed in the 1970s enabled controlled changes to DNA and followed, to a large extent, the logic and possibilities that molecular biologists had understood even when they had theoretical knowledge but no practical techniques. That is the meaning of the chapter epigraph, which is from 1958 and foreshadows these developments. During the first years of the 1970s, experiments began to show that relatively simple techniques could be devised for genetic engineering—relatively simple, that is, for the skilled scientist. Control and regulation of the function of genes and thereby of organisms became

[1] From Edward Tatum's 1958 Nobel Prize lecture (Tatum 1959: 1714). An analysis of the early developments of genetic engineering can be found in Wright (1986: 306–7).

practically possible. Direct medical applications of the new technology also appeared to be within the reach of science, although still in the future. Much of these developments occurred in the basic scientific environment.

Alongside basic research unlocking the secrets of life and of molecules like DNA, another type of use of genetic engineering was beginning to develop in the 1970s, namely commercial uses of genetic engineering to produce pharmaceuticals. The 1976 founding of the Californian biotech firm Genentech is often seen as the start of this new biotech industry, where basic scientists and venture capitalists joined together. These small biotech firms generally sold R & D contracts to established companies. These contracts were to develop new scientific knowledge and techniques in order to be able to adapt what had initially been scientific activities to commercial purposes.

The American pharmaceutical firm Eli Lilly (Lilly) was quickly interested in this technology for insulin, as was the Swedish pharmaceutical firm KabiVitrum (Kabi) for human growth hormone. Their interest led to two of the first R & D contracts recognizing the economic and technical potential of genetic engineering techniques. Genentech carried out the respective R & D contracts on genetic engineering for Lilly and Kabi.

Thus, although scientific research was vital for the generation and development of genetic engineering techniques in the 1970s, it was also an important period of developing and shaping genetic engineering techniques for commercial purposes. This changed the directions and search spaces of agents' knowledge-seeking activities, and thereby changed the probable results obtained. In the early 1970s, the scientific-economic environment was just beginning to be constructed for this type of activities involving genetic engineering. The same knowledge and techniques could also be applied to advantage in different environmental conditions.

The dual uses of genetic engineering knowledge, i.e. to further the scientific endeavour and to further the profit motive, seem to fit the two categories of 'basic science' versus 'applied science'. One might even assume that during the 1970s, governments were funding scientific activities and firms were funding technological activities. They were, and this is a basic trend. In addition, however, firms were funding some scientific activities in molecular biology, and some basic science funded by governments was used to develop new technology relevant for commercial profitability.

Thus, the history of events exemplified by insulin and human growth hormone does not fit with the implicit assumption that scientific research necessarily has to reach a point where useful techniques or ideas can be handed off to industry before firms will become interested in science. Instead, as Kline and Rosenberg have argued, firms will directly fund basic science when no other sources of information are available.[2] Lilly, Kabi, and Genentech did so for insulin, hGH, and similar products in the 1970s because they could see the technical and economic potential of genetic engineering techniques. The firms funded scientific activities in an economically relevant direction and wanted knowledge, techniques, and biological material necessary for this new context of use.

The Recombinant DNA Controversy and Scientific Activities

In the early 1970s and based on much previous research, basic scientists developed experimental techniques which allowed them to combine bits of DNA; these were the basic genetic engineering techniques and gave scientists some control over nature. Moving specific genes had previously been a theoretical possibility, but scientists had lacked practical, functioning techniques. Genetic engineering techniques were thus generated within the basic scientific environment, which had accumulated knowledge and techniques over several decades. These scientific fields were strongly oriented towards basic science and usually had few contacts with other environments.

When genetic engineering techniques appeared practically possible, basic scientists had many questions about how well the techniques would work in practice, about the consequences of experiments, and about whether formal regulation should be devised to determine which experiments were safe in the sense of being acceptable. Their version of regulation was to be internal to the basic scientific environment, regulated by scientists based on scientific research and criteria. Unusually perhaps for basic scientists, but with the nuclear physicists and their earlier appeals to stop atomic weapons development in mind, these scientists were active early on in trying to encourage debate and formal regulation thereby shaping and creating a predictable public context for the technology.

On 26 July 1974, a handful of American scientists published a letter which would subsequently influence formal regulation of genetic engineering, also called recombinant DNA (rDNA), in many countries. This started what has been dubbed the recombinant DNA controversy. Following appeals voiced at the 1973 Gordon Research Conference on nucleic acids, the American National Research Council formed a committee of eleven leading researchers to investigate the potential dangers of genetic engineering experiments. The committee was headed by the renowned biochemist Paul Berg, who had performed early experiments indicating the feasibility of these techniques. This committee developed

[2] Kline and Rosenberg (1986: 290).

some recommendations to regulate experiments, including the forbidding of some, and subsequently published a letter in the influential magazine *Science*.

This was the letter that would influence much of the subsequent course of events. In it, the Berg committee proposed a voluntary, international moratorium on certain genetic engineering experiments which 'could prove biologically hazardous'.[3] A main reason for concern was that experiments in laboratories had indicated that researchers could link sequences of DNA from different species, leading to truly new and unknown combinations.[4] This moratorium was internal to science, partly because only a handful of élite basic researchers had then actually mastered the genetic engineering techniques necessary to succeed with experiments. Moreover, the appeal and subsequent debate were mostly published in scientific journals like *Science*, and the regulatory guidelines which most debaters had in mind would be designed, watched over, and evaluated by scientists.

Even those scientists who felt the proposed moratorium was overly cautious felt compelled to act—especially to delay experiments—once the letter became public. The moratorium was voluntary, but in the informal institutions of the basic scientific environment, norms are often internalized. Individuals felt compelled to follow the rules and norms which were to be agreed upon collectively, even when control was informal. In the words of Professor Lennart Philipson from Sweden, who planned an early recombinant DNA experiment with Pierre Tiollais of the Pasteur Institute, France:

Once the information was out in the open, we had to wait for the reaction, and for some sort of guidelines. Our feeling was that we had to hold back until there was an agreement on how to perform the experiment. . . .

I felt very early on, in fact, that maybe this letter, and the whole uproar that followed, was an effect of biochemists being concerned with problems not previously encountered. Medical microbiologists have been exposed to similar dangers for a long time and sort of learned to live with them. Guidelines and rules were available.[5]

Despite early arguments among scientists about whether the Berg committee had overstated the risks, the Berg letter and subsequent debate had the desired effect of stopping certain types of experiments until the envisioned risks could be evaluated. During a period, basic scientists defined a new public context and closed off certain technological trajectories of development.

[3] Berg *et al.* (1974: 303). The initial public appeal for regulation by scientists was Singer and Soll (1973). See also Krimsky (1982) for a historical account of this controversy in the USA.   [4] Wright (1986: 314).
[5] Philipson (1977b: 1st para. from p. 43, 2nd from p. 33).

On the voluntary, informal level, the moratorium on some scientific experiments lasted until May 1975, when scientists met at the Asilomar Conference. They agreed on classification of experiments into risk groups, with corresponding requirements about physical containment. *Science* again acted as the forum to diffuse information, as a summary of the executive report was published on 6 June.[6] The report included guidelines for classification of experiments, and it would ultimately steer scientists' experiments for a year, until the American National Institutes of Health (NIH) established their safety guidelines in June 1976.[7] The NIH is the major medical research council in the USA as well as the home of major medical research institutes. Their guidelines were also followed internationally in this research community, until national guidelines were developed in other countries.

Following the Asilomar recommendations, the NIH classified experiments into four risk types, called P1 to P4. The numbers run from the least to the most restrictive category, and each has specific physical and biological containment requirements for experiments. The NIH guidelines were to be followed in all publicly funded research in the United States, but did not legally apply to American industry, only morally. These guidelines were made by scientists for scientists, with little or no public insight, probably because scientists felt they could best evaluate the risks.[8] Basic scientists did not directly attempt to regulate experiments for other environments, partly because genetic engineering techniques were then considered only of interest within the basic scientific environment.

Although the 1973 Gordon and 1975 Asilomar meetings took place in the United States, scientific research is an international activity. Those scientists asking similar research questions in Europe and elsewhere were aware of the American discussions through a range of interactions, from visits by American researchers, Europeans spending a post-doc year in the USA, international conferences, and direct participation in discussions.[9] For example, Philipson and others from the European Molecular Biological Labs participated in the Asilomar conference, and like American scientists, followed the Berg letter guidelines. They restricted experiments until the norms of safety in the international, basic scientific environment could be agreed upon. Moreover, scientists in many countries tried to communicate the importance of

---

[6] Berg *et al.* (1975). The five scientists listed as authors were the members of the Organizing Committee for the whole meeting.   [7] NIH (1976b).

[8] See Wright (1978: 468) and *Science* (1978).

[9] A post-doc is a position of limited duration—usually one or two years—where a scientist who has recently got his/her Ph.D. degree works at another university. The advantages of a post-doc position are that it gives the individual a chance to learn new skills and knowledge, or to improve existing ones. The disadvantages are that this position confers very little power on the individual and is temporary.

genetic engineering and its risks and benefits to society and to develop national regulation.

Despite the international character of science, scientists located in the USA made many of the relevant breakthroughs, even if their work was based on an international community of researchers. Philipson argued that 'it was clear that most of the technology, the restriction enzymes and the recombinant technique, emanated from the United States.'[10] At the same time, much of the foundation of knowledge necessary for genetic engineering had previously been developed in Europe, and many younger European scientists worked in the United States and contributed to those scientific developments. This cumulative nature of science must not be forgotten when evaluating the relative role of different national research systems and when discussing how knowledge is accumulated. Here, however, it is not possible to give credit to the many researchers who contributed through experiments and theoretical work. Instead, this section will take up a few of the major scientific developments relevant to the history of the commercialization of these techniques for hGH and insulin.

In addition to Berg's own research, one experiment which started the recombinant DNA controversy involved at least one basic scientist who would soon thereafter act to realize the commercial potential of genetic engineering. In 1973, two active research groups in relevant scientific fields were centred around Professors Stanley Cohen of Stanford University and Herbert Boyer of the University of California, San Francisco (UCSF). Cohen and Boyer put together a series of techniques to manipulate DNA, the so-called recombinant technique. The recombinant technique is really a series of techniques, including cutting segments of DNA with restriction enzymes, pasting together two fragments with ligases, and getting the genes into a bacteria cell through a circular fragment called a plasmid.[11] Not only could researchers cut and paste genes, they could do so at specific points, thereby having more precise control. Their technique was initially quite rudimentary, but it worked. In that Cohen

---

[10] Philipson (1977b: 49).

[11] See Cohen's own account of events about the discovery and their subsequent patent application in Cohen (1982). Their discovery would lead to an important patent. In 1992, the Cohen-Boyer patent pulled in $14.6 million in revenues for Stanford and UCSF. Stanford, the second most successful US academic licenser in 1992, pulled in a total of $25 million, indicating that its success with technology transfer is highly dependent on this one patent (Lehrman 1993a: 574). Interestingly enough, Cohen and Boyer's research came to the attention of Stanford University through the mass media rather than through internal university information channels. Mr Niels Reimers of the Office of Technology Licensing at Stanford read about their work and the practical implications in a front page article in the *New York Times*, and then encouraged Cohen and Boyer to apply for a patent (Cohen 1982: 215). This was possible in the USA because patents are given based on the principle 'first to discover', and there is a one-year 'grace period' after the discovery's becoming public information during which the inventor can apply.

and Boyer developed this technique in 1973, useful and relatively simple techniques were only just being developed when the international, internal scientific moratorium was called in 1974.

With the establishment of, first, the informal guidelines in 1975, and then the formal ones by the NIH in 1976 (copied by a number of countries), these basic scientists could get back to research which used or developed genetic engineering techniques. In the mid-1970s, they had a handful of techniques and a handful of powerful theories about DNA, its universal character, and its importance in instructing cells to make proteins. The simplest type of genetic engineering is inserting a bit of DNA into a single-cell bacterium like *E. coli*. This had only recently become possible and was only relatively 'simple' in the sense of being able to do without huge mobilizations of labour and resources.[12] Scientists still had to be trained to utilize these techniques.

What these basic scientists did not have in the mid-1970s was the certainty that the mixing of techniques, biological materials, and theories would lead in practice to the results to which scientists thought they ought to lead. Theories had not been confirmed. It might not work. Despite relative agreement over theories, scientists experimented with different approaches to practical techniques, partly because no one was sure which path would prove most fruitful. We can say that uncertainty about which experimental approaches would work in practice encouraged competing scientific research groups to generate diversity. Moreover, because conditions in the basic scientific environment include incentive structures which reward those scientists who publish first and accurately, competing groups had incentives to spend resources to try out quickly alternatives which seemed most promising. Speed and high quality in relation to internal scientific criteria were encouraged.

Scientists developing these techniques also faced a series of unanswered questions about the viability of genetic engineering for actually expressing human proteins. In particular, in the early to mid-1970s, no one had yet proved the next step after cutting and pasting DNA segments, namely whether or not bacteria cells could actually 'read' a gene as an instruction to make a specific human protein. Even before the moratorium, various scientists were considering experiments to explore this possibility. Until shown in practice, scientists remained uncertain about whether or not this would be possible.

Theories predicted it should be possible, but questions remained in a

---

[12] It bears repeating that one of the reasons that the first commercial applications of genetic engineering were for producing proteins (used as pharmaceutical products and enzymes) was that this was comparatively simple. Scientists only needed to know and be able to handle genes and specific simple cells, which then act like mini-factories. It is scientifically and technically much more difficult to succeed when dealing with higher organisms, e.g. when genetically modifying plants and animals.

number of dimensions. Could a bacteria build proteins normally only found in humans? Would the DNA sequence stay inside the bacteria or would the bacteria reject it and revert to what is known as a 'wild type'? How could scientists build their own DNA sequences in the lab? By using the fundamental chemical components, they would no longer have to rely on DNA already existing in cells. Even if the bacteria succeeded in producing the desired protein, would the protein keep its chemical and physical structure over time? Would it be folded correctly? Would other parts of the bacteria (immediately) attack and destroy the protein in the cell?[13] Expression should work if DNA was as universal as theory predicted, but it was difficult to prove and required the development of experiments and techniques. These unanswered questions will also be used later to help explain why experiments with human growth hormone in 1979 were considered scientifically—as well as commercially—interesting.

As mentioned above, pioneering work on the rDNA technique was developed in the early 1970s at the élite, private Stanford University and at the California state-funded UCSF, which had research of special renown in medical fields. These two universities, as well as the California state-funded University of California, Berkeley (Berkeley), all did significant research leading to genetic engineering techniques. They all lie in or nearby San Francisco, California, in the so-called Bay Area, within an eighty-kilometre (fifty-mile) radius.

Even though science is international, this local university climate should be kept in mind as the focus of this and the next chapter narrows more and more to specific individual researchers, university departments, biotech firms, and pharmaceuticals firms which contributed to the use of genetic engineering techniques for insulin and human growth hormone. For, if we jump from 1976 to 1979, we see that not one but two research groups in the Bay Area published scientific papers in respected journals about how to use bacteria to produce hGH.[14]

Moreover, one group was situated at a university, UCSF, and the other group at the biotech firm, Genentech. Both organizations had active basic researchers; both generated basic scientific results; and both car-

---

[13] These questions are based on discussions with researchers active at the time.
[14] The two most significant papers on rDNA hGH at the time were the UCSF paper (Martial et al. 1979) and the Genentech paper (Goeddel et al. 1979), based on impressions given by active scientists and on a database search through the Science Citation Index. Researchers at the Pasteur Institute in France apparently developed a similar bacteria expression system around the same time for Sanofi (Roskam 1987), but they were not perceived as being part of the same race by the Genentech scientists (Yansura 1993a). The database search showed that the Goeddel et al. paper was cited 331 times and the Martial et al. paper was cited 269 times. As a comparison, an article in *The Economist* (1992a: 93) examines the most cited scientific articles which were based on experiments as of 1992. The number one paper had been cited 4,608 times; the tenth most cited only had 1,505 citations. This indicates that over 300 citations is a relatively high number.

ried out research financed by established pharmaceutical firms. Concentration of researchers in one geographical area, in this case, did not entail pooling of resources to perform one joint project but instead entailed competing groups. In fact, there were conflicts as well as co-operation between these groups, as further explored in the next chapter.

The explicit ties between UCSF and Genentech are closer than first meets the eye. To uncover the tangled relationships, the remainder of this and the next chapter moves chronologically from 1976 to 1979, starting in a university department and drawing in other individuals, firms, and organizations as their activities touch upon the technological innovation process for hGH. In this way, the factors and mechanisms underlying the pattern of coevolutionary innovation are highlighted from the perspective of both basic scientists and corporate researchers. The implications should therefore be of interest to government policy-makers, universities, and firms alike.

Inside University of California, San Francisco and Genentech

Inside UCSF, scientists in several departments worked on research questions that either directly or tangentially enabled further development of genetic engineering techniques. Dr William Rutter, head of the Department of Biochemistry and Biophysics since 1969, was building up the department's strength in basic research by attracting researchers who had ideas and the ability to pull in research grants and who could develop labs with fancy and mundane equipment.[15]

One of the three senior researchers in Rutter's department who would eventually be co-author on a scientific paper applying genetic engineering to human growth hormone was Howard M. Goodman. A second was John D. Baxter, a medical doctor with his major appointment in medicine, but who sometimes worked closely with Goodman. These were the last two (out of four) authors on the UCSF paper on hGH published in 1979. A third UCSF faculty member, Herbert Boyer, also had an appointment in this department but had his major appointment in microbiology. Boyer is particularly interesting because he started the biotech firm Genentech, which also published an article on human growth hormone in 1979. Thus, one department at one university

---

[15] In 1975, Rutter himself had two NIH grants, one for research on gene expression, a well-established field which is a necessary component of genetic engineering. This was R01GM21830-01 on 'Gene Expression and Replication in Eukaryotic Organisms'. His other project, P01GM19527-04 0006, was on 'Human Genetics—Growth & Differentiation of Exocrine and Endocrine Pancreas (Mice, Rat, Dog)' (NIH 1975). Although Baxter and Boyer had their primary appointments in other departments, they were closely affiliated with the Department of Biochemistry and Biophysics, and each had a joint appointment there.

sufficed to generate two different attempts to answer almost the same research question. It is therefore interesting to know more about how the informal institutions of basic science worked to stimulate this diversity. Moreover, we can ask whether these individuals were responding to the same environments or whether both the basic scientific and the scientific-economic environments were important.

An understanding of how Goodman, Baxter, and Boyer came to be doing hGH research in the late 1970s should be based on their previous research projects. In 1975, Baxter was working on medical questions about hypertension whereas Goodman was clearly working in a field related to genetic engineering, in his third year of NIH support for the project 'Structure and function of tumour virus DNA SV40'.[16] Moreover, Goodman had previously worked intimately with Boyer on a number of experiments. Boyer had developed restriction enzymes and sequenced the nucleotides left after the enzyme Eco RI cut DNA at specific points.[17] The scientific research of the last two thus involved both knowledge and techniques enabling genetic engineering to work.

Because these three senior researchers co-operated in different constellations over time, it is interesting to ask why Goodman and Baxter competed with Boyer over hGH in 1979. This raises the larger question of how a scientific field which is just beginning to be perceived as commercially interesting experiences tensions beneficial, or destructive, to the creation of diversity. In this case, the tensions relate to activities which are potentially relevant for more than one environment.

One reason for tensions has to do with perceptions about the proper relationships between knowledge developed in a university and in a firm. To different extents in different fields and different times, university researchers have had contacts with firms. Individual scientists have been active in both scientific and commercial development of a number of technologies. However, when a research community has not traditionally had relationships with firms and has instead been a more isolated epistemological community, then new problems and discussions arise when their scientific activities begin to be perceived as being of economic interest.[18]

Such tensions are relevant here because within this very same department, another trend affecting knowledge generation was simultaneously

---

[16] (NIH 1975). Because viruses are essentially non-living bits of DNA that can invade cells and make the cells reproduce the said virus, they provided scientists with a way of getting genes into a cell. SV40 was a much-studied virus for this purpose in mammalian cells.

[17] When this restriction enzyme is used to cut two strands of DNA, the strands are cut at different points, leaving tails known as 'sticky ends', which have a great affinity to their corresponding nucleotide sequences. Sticky ends made it easier to combine two DNA strands later.

[18] As documented and analysed for biotech by, among others, Kenney (1986), Orsenigo (1989), Krimsky *et al.* (1991: 280–5), Sharp (1991: 221–5), and Laage-Hellman (1986).

getting under way, namely commercialization of genetic engineering. In late 1975, the venture capitalist Robert Swanson discussed commercialization possibilities with the basic scientist Boyer, and this led to their forming a partnership in January 1976 and incorporating a company in April. That company is the first dedicated biotech firm, named 'Genentech'. At the time, Boyer was a tenured faculty member at UCSF and remained so for many years, but he simultaneously consulted for Genentech and helped steer its early research.

In the literally hundreds of articles written about Genentech, it is often not the scientific side—and hence the role of Boyer and other scientists—which is emphasized. Instead Swanson, the venture capitalist founder, gets the credit for perceiving the commercial potential of genetic engineering, signalling the start of a whole new industry. Swanson was no outsider to the business. He had both scientific training in chemistry, with a Bachelor of Science from Massachusetts Institute of Technology (MIT), and knowledge of the commercial world, with a Masters of Business Administration from MIT. Swanson also had experience from working first at Citibank 'specialising in setting up small companies with venture capital' and then in 1974 at Kleiner and Perkins in California, a small venture capital company.[19] Swanson personally had the potential to understand both the scientific-technical and economic potential of genetic engineering, as did Boyer, but their competences were largely complementary in that Swanson was specialized on the economic and financing side and Boyer on the scientific side. Swanson might recognize the potential of the science but could not carry it out.

Swanson also had a strong vision for the new biotech firm, which helped form some of their early decisions: in the long run, Genentech would not only do contract R & D but also move into manufacturing.

For Genentech, the strategy from the very beginning was to be able to make and sell our own products. Therefore, we need not only to generate the products but to manufacture them and build the marketing force to sell them.[20]

This vision guided many of their early strategic decisions about R & D.

In order to finance a longer-term diversification from R & D contracts into manufacturing, Genentech had to have both short- and long-term goals and enough short-term financing to reach the longer-term goals. In Genentech's case, this initially translated into attracting money from commercial R & D contracts as well as capital from private investors, including Swanson's old employer Kleiner and Perkins. This money would give them a foundation to build up competences in house and to move into commercial production of a product. In the short run,

[19] Quote from Lewin (1978: 925). [20] Swanson (1986a: 58).

however, Genentech had to prove its basic scientific prowess before it could sell research in the scientific-economic environment. This was necessary because genetic engineering was largely basic science at the time, and high-quality science would presumably sell better (and function better) than science of low quality.

The founding of Genentech led to mixed reactions within the UCSF department about the proper type of relationships between universities and firms in general. For example, when it became known that Boyer was planning to start a company, a then first-year assistant professor, Keith Yamamoto, recalls that he brought up the topic at a small, informal faculty meeting. He was critical of using publicly funded research to make personal profits and so put forward a proposal to stop the firm in 1976. His criticism was ignored.[21]

No one disputed that Boyer's research had been to a large extent publicly funded, mainly through NIH, although Boyer had other sources of funding like the private foundation Howard Hughes Medical Institute and contracts from pharmaceutical companies.[22] No one disputed that the knowledge and skills that Boyer had personally acquired were largely financed by public money, or that he was likely to use his competences to benefit the firm—and by extension, benefit himself. He could help select scientists for the new firm, use his research abilities to judge and direct projects, transmit some of his competence to the firm's researchers, and so forth.

Basically, though, there were no rules against starting a firm within the university and indeed, the university had an interest in industrial relations if contract money accrued to support further research at the university. Moreover, scientists in this field had very different opinions about the proper form of relationships between university and firms. Many of the senior scientists at UCSF (and elsewhere) later became involved in starting new biotech firms, and others began working for firms, either moving there or remaining at a university but acting as consultants.[23] UCSF as a whole had no objections at the time about Boyer starting Genentech. Tensions nevertheless arose.

[21] Yamamoto (1992).
[22] NIH (1975, 1976a, 1977, 1978, 1979). Boyer's partner Swanson indicates that Boyer's funding was long term, as he mentions that Boyer's research had been partly funded by the government for fifteen years. Swanson emphasizes how government-funded research can give rise to the formation of a new industry: 'Or as [Boyer] likes to put it, "Who would have dreamed that my work on how bacteria have sex could combine with other pieces of basic research to help form a new industry?"' (Swanson 1986b: 430)
[23] Baxter, Goodman, and Rutter had already been involved in contract R. & D. for pharmaceutical firms at UCSF. In addition, all three later developed significant, long-term ties with firms. Baxter formed California Biotechnology, Inc., and was later joined by at least three other researchers from UCSF (Robbins-Roth 1991: 35–6). Instead of opening a new company, Goodman opened a whole new department in 1982 at Massachusetts General Hospital (MGH) with money from Hoechst AG, the giant West German chemical company. Hoescht committed '$70 million over 10 years to completely equip and support a

In the first two years, from 1976 to 1978, Genentech existed as a legal company, but it had no labs or location of its own. Genentech instead signed contracts with researchers in universities and research institutes to perform scientific activities. Of course, Genentech did not ask just anyone in the field. For its first project on somatostatin, the firm signed an R & D contract with a pioneering scientist, who also happened to be a co-founder, Boyer. The very fact that this contract was signed indicates that both partners found the arrangement satisfactory in 1976–7.

As said in a report from a later investigation by the UCSF Academic Senate, Committee on Rules and Jurisdiction:

Boyer founded a company, Genentech, of which he is Secretary, a member of the Board, a major stockholder, and a paid consultant. . . . The company raised money and then let a contract to the university for work to be performed in Professor Boyer's laboratory for initial experiments to incorporate structures of DNA known to code for the desired proteins into plasmids so that the human gene products could be manufactured in bacteria. . . .

The principal representing Genentech in contractual matters . . . was Robert Swanson, Genentech's President. The principal representing the university was Professor Boyer.

An exclusive licence to use any patentable material was given by the university to Genentech. Because Genentech did not have any operable laboratories of its own, initially the experiments were carried out by Professor Boyer and two postdoctoral fellows in laboratories within the department.[24]

The relationship between Genentech and UCSF legalized in this contract thus boiled down to a relationship between Boyer and Swanson. Genentech directly drew upon UCSF researchers and facilities for its scien-

brand new Department of Molecular Biology. Goodman is its director' (Culliton 1982b: 1200). Goodman had originally planned such a new department at UCSF, but was courted away to MGH. Goodman perceived there was too much red tape at the publicly-funded university. Although MGH is affiliated with Harvard Medical School, it is an independent entity with its own decision-making structure. In 1981, Rutter helped create another major biotech firm, namely Chiron Corporation. He founded it along with researchers from Berkeley, which is just across the San Francisco Bay. The third major competitor on the insulin research—Professor Wally Gilbert at Harvard—started Biogen in 1978 with researchers from MIT and the University of Zurich (Robbins-Roth 1991: 35–6, 86).

All five of the top researchers mentioned here—Boyer, Baxter, Goodman, Rutter, and Gilber—thus developed significant ties with industry, many starting their own small biotech firms. Moreover, all five researchers had already succeeded in fulfilling the academic criteria for success before moving into the corporate world. Chirgwin, who was a post-doc at UCSF in the 1970s, reflects on the move of famous basic scientists to the biotech industry. 'What is left when you already have a big lab, a c.v. full of important papers, have been Department Chairman perhaps, are a member of the National Academy? In academics, becoming dean or university president is not a step upwards, it is the admission that you are over the hill intellectually and want to become a paper-pusher. Why not show those Harvard MBAs that you can beat them at their own game?' (Chirgwin 1993: 10)

[24] Wolff (1979: 2).

tific activities which, in the long run, would have technological goals of manufacturing human proteins in bacteria.

This research contract gave Genentech the right to negotiate a licence with UCSF in the future, and inventions and research samples remained the property of the university. A licensing agreement between the two was signed in 1980, resulting in the payment of 'substantial royalties . . . from the sales of human insulin and human growth hormone'.[25] The university thus gained money not only directly for the R & D contract but also in the long run from royalty payments.

Boyer worked on this project, as did two former post-docs from the department. Although Boyer and the two former post-docs, Herbert Heyneker and Francisco Bolivar, were from the UCSF Department of Biochemistry and Biophysics, they worked closely with researchers at a large medical research hospital in southern California named 'The City of Hope National Medical Center'.[26] City of Hope researchers were crucial to the project because they had special competences, particularly in relation to synthetic DNA. Carrying out this initial project required co-operation between researchers with different skills, in this case located at different places in California.

Boyer, however, was not the only scientist at UCSF who was interested in putting together genes, plasmids, and bacteria. Other scientists there were interested in developing scientific knowledge and, as a by-product, expressing human proteins. Co-operating, and rival, labs and research groups were never far away. For example, by 1977, Goodman was dealing more generally with this same class of problems, and Baxter had four NIH grants, all of which dealt with medical questions relating to hormones, but two of which were tangential to genetic engineering techniques.[27]

As another indication, Baxter and Goodman are listed as co-authors on a series of important scientific papers about genetic engineering published in 1977. Labs and experiments rely on the expertise and efforts of many individuals, and the first name on a paper generally means most work done. Therefore, it must be noted that the first authors on these papers were neither Baxter nor Goodman, but post-doc

[25] Kleid (1994).

[26] Bolivar and Heyneker had been European post-docs at UCSF but are listed in the research paper, namely Itakura *et al.* (1977), as being from their home European institute. According to a UCSF investigation in 1979, 'those postdoctoral fellows who worked on the project were subsequently hired by Genentech at salaries considerably higher than those available to other postdoctoral fellows in the department' (Wolff 1979: 3). The validity of this statement has not been substantiated.

[27] NIH (1977). Baxter's four grants were: R01AM-18878-02 (END) 'Mechanisms of Thyroid Hormone Action (Rats, Cattle)', R01AM-19997-01 (END) 'Growth Hormone Gene—Purification and Regulation (Rats)', R01EY-01785-02 (VISA) 'Mechanisms of Hormone Hyperresponsiveness in Glaucoma (Humans)', and R01HL-16918-04 (CUB) 'Role of Steroids in Hypertension (Humans)'.

researchers, including Peter Seeburg, Axel Ullrich, and John Shine.[28] It is praxis for senior researchers to be listed on the research of post-docs in these fields because the lab directors provide learning opportunities, ideas, advice, and the facilities for experiments.

Like the Boyer *et al.* group at UCSF and City of Hope, the constellation of researchers around Baxter and Goodman at UCSF were trying to answer some basic research questions by using genetic engineering techniques. They were testing the limits of the possible by putting a rat insulin gene and a rat growth hormone gene into bacteria, but the value in the basic scientific environment was not in making the protein but in finding the correct mammalian genes.[29]

In May 1977, the UCSF group reported success in isolating the rat insulin gene and in inserting the gene into bacteria, but the bacteria was not then able to use that DNA fragment to make mammalian insulin. Although the scientists gained knowledge about the correct DNA sequence due to this experiment, it still left the practical question, Was it possible to express a human protein in a bacteria? Their work was picked up by the press, and added to the public debate over genetic engineering.[30] In general, Baxter's and Goodman's research groups at UCSF were quite active in developing new procedures and experiments. This constellation of scientists was clearly of the quality to compete in the international basic scientific community.

Later in 1977, the Boyer *et al.* group, on contract money from Genentech, showed that the techniques also worked in practice. Bacteria could assemble human proteins! The Boyer group published a paper in *Science* on 9 December 1977, about making a short, fourteen-amino-acid-long, human protein called somatostatin in *E. coli* bacteria. The list of authors included, first, four from the City of Hope hospital, and then the three from UCSF.[31]

The City of Hope researchers played a key role in this experiment. Their contribution to this and later projects helped Genentech succeed with developing techniques to make synthetic DNA. In particular, according to John Chirgwin, then a post-doc at UCSF, the City of Hope researcher Itakura

developed the practical synthesis of small DNAs in vitro. Khorana at MIT, with whom Itakura trained, worked out the basics and synthesized a complete tRNA gene. Like the Chinese insulin, this [Khorana's method] was a tour de force but utterly impractical.

Genentech had the foresight to embrace practical synthetic DNA [as developed

---

[28] Ullrich *et al.* (1977), Seeburg *et al.* (1977), Shine *et al.* (1977), and Seeburg *et al.* (1978).
[29] Chirgwin (1993).
[30] See, for example, *Science News* (1977).   [31] Itakura *et al.* (1977).

by Itakura] before almost anyone in academia did. It served them well at the time, gave them tools that most universities could not provide.[32]

Synthetic DNA has thus been important for commercial uses. Genentech's scientific activities were relevant not only for the basic scientific environment but were also relevant for the techno-economic environment, because they developed techniques to control nature. Practical techniques are often necessary in scientific experiments but are crucial for commercial uses. It is also a clear example of how basic scientists help develop knowledge and skills in their students, thus transmitting specialized knowledge and techniques among the population. The Genentech scientist Goeddel has pointed out, however, that this quote is incorrect, in that Itakura actually trained with Narang, who had in turn trained with Khorana.[33]

By developing practical techniques to make synthetic DNA, the Genentech scientists could construct their own DNA, rather than pulling it out of a cell. Thus, if they knew in advance which sequence they required, they could make a copy chemically. They gained control over nature, the main purpose of technological activities.

As to the experiment as a whole, on the one hand, the outcome of this experiment—namely somatostatin—can be seen as a hormone without medical value or known market value. Somatostatin was much shorter than the human proteins known to have medical value, indicating that larger proteins might present more problems in expression. Moreover, the experimental test results which indicated that somatostatin was expressed in bacteria did not give much information, only a band on a gel. The practical value of this experiment could thus be called into question. On the other hand, the experiments did show that some output of human protein was produced in bacteria, thereby showing that genetic engineering techniques were feasible. In this way, somatostatin was a test case, making it easier to perceive that genetic engineering might also work for longer proteins like insulin and growth hormone. Boyer *et al.*'s experiment did indicate the feasibility of this technique and also opened up important relationships for Genentech with agents in other environments than that of the basic scientific.

Although the 1977 experiment developed what was in many ways a very rudimentary technique, and only partially allayed scientists' uncertainty, it did indicate important potential trajectories for future develop-

---

[32] Chirgwin (1993: 6). 'Chinese insulin' refers to research by a group of mainland Chinese to chemically synthesize insulin. 'It was a technical tour de force, but of no practical value whatsoever. One dose would cost a million dollars' (Chirgwin 1993: 1). Chemically synthesizing insulin was technically too complicated and required intensive labour.   [33] Goeddel (1993).

ments within different environments. The results opened up new search spaces both for scientific activities and for technological ones.

Having a positive answer about the feasibility of the technology reduced uncertainty and thereby allowed the scientists to ask new questions and try new combinations of techniques, knowledge, and biological material. It likewise reduced uncertainty for firms about their intended commercial uses, by developing technological activities to control nature. As the 1977 scientific experiment showed the potential feasibility and practicability of genetic engineering techniques for making human proteins, several firms acted on their perceptions of the technical and economic potential of this new technology. The technology offered new potential ways of competing. Established pharmaceutical firms moving in early wanted genetic engineering as an alternative source for making existing products, whereas new biotech firms wanted to sell scientific knowledge and possibly also use it to make pharmaceutical products with niche markets.

American Regulation and News about Research

Although the Genentech-financed somatostatin experiment was seen as important within the basic scientific environment, it also had consequences for firms and for the public context. So far, these had been only potential commercial and medical benefits which did not exist as such; they had been perceptions that the involved agents actively tried to create. In cases of radical technological change like genetic engineering, perceptions are vital to shaping political, economic, scientific, and technological environmental conditions. Somatostatin was clearly used for such a purpose.

Scientific results are usually presented at scientific conferences prior to publication but are usually not announced in the mass media before publication. News about somatostatin followed a different pattern, and its publicity was clearly used to shape the public context in the United States.

News of the experimental success with expressing a human protein in bacteria did not wait until its scientific publication on 9 December 1977. It was hot news! A full month earlier, the somatostatin results were made public at a Senate subcommittee hearing, and influential newspapers like the *Washington Post* and *New York Times* published their accounts. The *San Francisco Chronicle* also ran several stories in November and December 1977. In these, Boyer is sometimes identified as a UCSF researcher and sometimes as co-founder of Genentech, but not both at once.[34] By neglecting Boyer's dual role, this indicates that public

[34] Cohn (1977: A9), *San Francisco Chronicle* (1977), Petit (1977a, 1977b), Hannon (1977), *Business Week* (1977), and *Medical World News* (1977).

debate differentiated more strongly between scientific and technological activities than the agents themselves.

A major reason why the press identified somatostatin as important scientific research was that Philip Handler, who was then president of the National Academy of Sciences, leaked the news to a Senate sub-committee hearing. He called it a scientific triumph of the first order. Paul Berg, the leading Stanford molecular biologist and previously head of the Berg committee, similarly testified by stressing the scientific importance of this experiment. Regardless of the scientific significance of the somatostatin experiment, its publicity was also a useful trump card in the political pack. This Senate hearing was held when the US Congress was debating national regulation of genetic engineering in both firms and universities.[35] Scientists were wary that these political attempts to shape the public context would not allow them to continue with their knowledge-seeking activities. 'Dr. Handler told the subcom-mittee he believed that the gene-splicing risks did not exceed those of everyday, unregulated, routine hospital practice. He urged Congress to hold off passing a DNA-control law until more is known.'[36] The scien-tists were thus very positive about Genentech's results.

During 1976 and 1977, more and more scientists—including those who had previously supported the moratorium and regulation—began to feel the risks were being overstated in the public debate. They were concerned because at the same time that new experiments indicated the safety level was higher than previously assumed, the mass media were increasingly critical of genetic engineering in general. Scientists were worried that if national legislation were passed, their informal morator-ium would turn into a monster, leading to strict regulations.

In particular, Senator Edward Kennedy's proposed bill to the US Congress would have imposed harsh penalties and strictly regulated genetic engineering research, to a level unacceptable to scientists accus-tomed to freedom of enquiry. Therefore, many scientists worked to convince Congress not to legislate, and they were either active indivi-dually or organized in, for example, the American Society for Micro-biology. Amidst this political negotiating, research which showed the

[35] An article from 5 April 1979 says that 'various concerns on Capitol Hill [are being raised] such as whether private industry's voluntary compliance with the [NIH] . . . guidelines provides' adequate safety (Dickson 1979: 494). Another interpretation of events is that 'Senator Adlai Stevenson, Chairman of the Subcommittee on Science, Technology, and Space, presided over hearings aimed at examining the effect that proposed legislation would have on freedom of inquiry' (Pfund and Hofstadter 1981: 141). There was an outcry because a UCSF scientist, Axel Ullrich, had done an experiment which was prohibited, but only because there had been a mistake and a mix-up. The UCSF scientists thought this particular prohibition had already been lifted. When they found out that the experiment was not allowed, they simply redid the experiment using the accepted standards. When discovered, this led to outcries that the UCSF scientists had covered up the incident.   [36] *Medical World News* (1977: 17).

positive medical benefits of genetic engineering and which could cool the legislative zest was welcomed.

Positive publicity about the medical benefits of genetic engineering did help researchers modify the public context. The US Congress did not pass legislation, even though most contemporary observers had thought they would. Instead, the NIH rules continued to be in place, to impose guidelines for certain experiments in universities.

Thus, on one level, the somatostatin results came at a time when American scientists were becoming concerned that the public debate would impose harsher regulations than the scientists thought neces-sary. Basic scientists were therefore interested in changing the attitude of the public debate from negative to positive. The Swedish debate lagged behind the American debate, and somatostatin was not impor-tant in the Swedish debate.

On another level, Genentech itself was interested in getting publicity for somatostatin because this result indicated that genetic engineering could be used practically—and eventually commercially. More impor-tantly for the firm, it indicated that Genentech could deliver such commercially relevant scientific results. On that level, somatostatin was important for Kabi's subsequent actions of contacting Genentech. Knowledge-seeking activities in response to one environment could thus influence knowledge-seeking activities in another environment as well as the public context.

This discussion of somatostatin and of legislation should be related to the ongoing debates over genetic engineering. To the wider public in the United States and in Sweden, the scientists' own fears, research ques-tions, and previous debates over the technology were unclear, and their experiments were often represented as mysterious attempts to manip-ulate nature. Many were uncertain about what genetic engineering techniques would and would not make possible. As one journalist said in retrospect about the United States, 1976 was not a

particularly propitious time for the start-up of a genetic engineering company. The headlines were heralding monsters, not miracles. . . . Public concern about possible epidemics of cloned killer viruses prompted the city of Cambridge, Mass., to delay DNA work at Harvard and M.I.T. for months.[37]

According to a survey on how American newspapers and news maga-zines reported on genetic engineering between 1976 and 1979, the height of the American mass media controversy over recombinant DNA occurred between late 1976 and mid-1977, after which the articles began stressing the benefits of genetic engineering more often and omitting the views of critics.[38] By mid-to late 1977, scientists were beginning to argue

---

[37] Benner (1981: 66).
[38] Pfund and Hofstadter (1981: 142). They charted American articles about industry involvement in recombinant DNA in seven major newspapers, ten magazines, and six science/medical periodicals.

and to show with experiments that it ought to be possible to make useful medical substances like insulin. Positive public opinion about genetic engineering techniques meant that calls in the public debate for stricter formal regulation faded away in the United States.

Swedish Regulation and News about Research

In July 1974, the Berg committee letter was published, and the fears and risks expressed there were taken seriously by Swedish scientists as part of the international community. Important work to implement regulation in Sweden was also taken by Professor Lennart Philipson and by Professor Peter Reichard, who sat on the Swedish Science Research Council.

A core of concerned scientists arranged meetings to spread information about genetic engineering in Sweden and to discuss the potential need to regulate its development. The first meeting was held in December 1974 between scientists, politicians, and some industrial representatives. Professors Lennart Philipson, Peter Reichard, Nils Ringertz, and Tage Eriksson informed Forskningsberedningen, the scientific advisory board to the Swedish government, about recombinant DNA. Along with scientists and politicians, the board included several representatives from industry, including Dr Bertil Åberg, a medical doctor and professor of clinical chemistry who had moved to the pharmaceutical firm Kabi.[39] No regulatory initiatives were taken by the Swedish government at this time. The scientists felt regulation of the technology was up to them for the moment.

On the initiative of Professor Reichard, the Science Research Council formed a Genetic Manipulation Advisory Group Committee (hereafter GMAC) in 1975, which was also approved by the Medical Research Council. Reichard again approached the government, this time the Minister of Education Bertil Zachrisson, and suggested he appoint one or more members, but Zachrisson declined.[40] This committee was similar to the NIH committee which reviewed research grants using genetic engineering techniques.

In contrast to the American NIH committee, which was constituted by scientists, the Swedish committee brought together scientists and a range of interested parties such as trade unionists.[41] This corporatist pattern of participation is common in Swedish politics. The committee had its first

[39] Except where explicitly noted otherwise, the next four paragraphs are largely based on Philipson (1977b). My account of Åberg's participation is based on Åberg (1982: 54).

[40] Reichard (1993: 2). Zachrisson suggested instead that the Researchers and Parliamentarian Organization (RIFO) appoint someone.

[41] The committee members and the organization they represent are listed in DsU (1978: app. 1, 169–70).

official meeting in September 1976, with Professor Reichard the chairman. It had two main functions: diffusing information about rDNA to the public and to represented organizations, and reviewing research grants. The Swedish research councils had agreed only to fund experiments which had undergone review. The committee was thereby given some control over the direction of experimental developments, following accepted international praxis.

In addition to politicians and corporatist partners, the industrial sector most likely to be initially affected by genetic engineering also sat on this GMAC committee, namely pharmaceutical firms. Although none of the Swedish pharmaceutical companies had in-house R & D in molecular biology in the late 1970s, the Swedish scientists working for regulation asked the pharmaceutical association to participate. The Swedish association of pharmaceutical companies, Läkemedelsindustriföreningen (LIF), was thus involved in the first attempts in Sweden to regulate this technology. This indicates that scientists clearly saw that genetic engineering could soon be used by commercial firms.

LIF initially appointed the head of research of Astra, another large pharmaceutical firm, as their representative; later, that person was Åberg from Kabi.[42] In 1976, the representative, 'on behalf of the pharmaceutical companies, agreed to the guidelines that we finally adopted, the procedure we had to review any research being done in this area, whether in a pharmaceutical industry or in a university'.[43] In other words, the pharmaceutical association agreed in 1976 to abide by the GMAC rules, which were informal, without direct government legislation. Their representation on the committee also gave Swedish firms early information about the possibilities of recombinant techniques. GMAC can thus be seen both as a non-government, regulatory body and an organization diffusing information about the potential of the technology.

Just as Swedish scientists participated in and reacted to the calls in 1974 of scientists working in the USA to impose a temporary moratorium, so too the Swedish media reacted to and published articles similar to American articles. *Dagens Nyheter*, one of Sweden's most influential and respected newspapers, published the article 'Lord Knows what Monsters you have in your Test Tubes' on 6 March 1977. The article first sets up the views of a Harvard biochemist against the mayor of Cambridge, Mass., then discredits the biochemist while taking the fears of the mayor seriously:

In the closed world of science, the debate about the new and forward-moving boundaries of genetic research has been going on for about five years. . . .

But the eyes of the public were not opened until Al Vellucci [mayor of Cambridge] sounded the alarm last year. . . .

---

[42] Ibid. app. 1.   [43] Philipson (1977b: 60).

One day when he heard about what went on in the laboratories in his city, he said straight out, 'Damn it, I would just like to know what monsters are going to crawl out of those damn researchers' test tubes.'[44]

According to the tone of this article, genetic engineering was definitely dangerous and in need of political control. One of the final sentences of this article was that 'society must take the final responsibility for the actions of individual members.' This illustrates a recurrent theme among Swedish critics of the technology: not only should the Swedish state take responsibility for the direction of scientific and technological activities, it should also tightly control these dangerous scientists, who would otherwise become real-life Frankensteins. Scientists should not be left to regulate themselves.

As in the United States, authors of Swedish debate articles can be divided into proponents and opponents of genetic engineering, where both often wished to use their arguments to influence national regulation. In mid-June 1977, *Dagens Nyheter*, as the first Swedish paper to do so, ran a series of debate articles on genetic engineering. The first, written by the Social Democrat and active debater Nordal Åkerman, was entitled, 'What Right does Research have to be Free?' Åkerman's implicit answer in the article was 'very little'.[45] The second, written by Lars Wieslander, a medical researcher at the Karolinska Institute, reacted to the implication that there was 'any connection between Harvard's [genetic] research and monsters that people had seen on the streets!' and instead detailed the scientific basics of genetic engineering in his article.[46] The final article in this series, 'This Concerns Survival Itself', again written by Åkerman, restated the need for social control.

The articles by these two authors—a critical, professional public debater and a medical researcher—reflect an on-going dilemma in the debates about genetic engineering. For the medical and natural-sciences researchers, genetic engineering has been something understandable, techniques that can be defined and explained. For many of the debaters and the public, genetic engineering has meant possibilities and dangers, something which will be developed and used in unforeseen ways in the future. Communication becomes difficult because of these differences in basic assumptions.

By mid-November 1977 and running through spring 1978, the Swedish debate intensified, especially the negative side, which meant that Sweden could be perceived as one of the countries hostile to developments in genetic engineering. Åkerman again set the negative tone in 'Stop the High-Risk Laboratory!' in *Dagens Nyheter*, but other news-

---

[44] Hamrin (1977: 23), my translation.
[45] Articles in this series: Åkerman (1977a), Wieslander (1977), Gerholm (1977), Rapp (1977), Lambert (1977), Holmberg (1977), and Åkerman (1977b).
[46] Quote from Wieslander (1992), my translation.

papers also ran articles.[47] The catalyst for debate this time was the plans of the Biomedicinskt centrum Uppsala University to build a P3 high-security lab inside the university city of Uppsala. Due to the intensity of these debates, but especially due to a decision by Uppsala City Department of Health (Uppsala kommun hälsovårdsnämnd), these building plans were shelved at that time. Ulf Pettersson, one of the researchers working with Professor Philipson, then carried out some experiments at the Pasteur Institute, Paris, France.[48] This incident happened at about the same time that American scientists and public debate were praising the benefits of genetic engineering as shown in the somatostatin results.

In other words, just as the American media began emphasizing the benefits of genetic engineering and celebrating somatostatin, the Swedish media—particularly the debate articles—were emphasizing its risks. In the late 1970s, the United States offered a more favourable public context than Sweden for both scientific and technological activities involving genetic engineering. Because genetic engineering was a radically new technology giving rise to much debate and to various proposals for regulation, the public debate played an important role in shaping national public contexts which would ultimately allow—or forbid—certain types of genetic engineering techniques and experiments.

Early Commercial Interest from Kabi in Sweden

One of the first firms in the world to approach Genentech about an R & D contract was the Swedish, government-owned pharmaceutical company Kabi.[49] Kabi moved to investigate the potential of these new

[47] The initial article in this series was Åkerman (1977c). Åkerman summed up his view of these technological developments with: 'We must quite simply learn to say no to the so-called devil's doctrine which demands that all that can be done must be done' (1978: 2, my translation). In response, Professor Philipson wrote, 'Instead of worrying and being afraid of what we do not understand, there are reasons to try to penetrate the questions in detail and to build our own opinion about what basic research is.' He argued that one of the reasons there were so many misunderstandings in the debate about recombinant DNA was that 'journalists and the public have gathered their knowledge from utopian novels like Aldous Huxley's *Brave New World* and George Orwell's *1984!*' (Philipson 1977a, my translation).

[48] Pettersson (1992). Pettersson and Philipson carried out the first experiment with recombinant DNA techniques in Sweden in 1975. It was by no means unusual for researchers to go abroad during periods of intense debate or uncertain and/or restrictive regulations. Ullrich, who did the main work in the Baxter-Goodman group on insulin, did some experiments in France in 1978 (Dickson 1979: 495). Additionally, 'Tiollais from Pasteur worked at SBL in Stockholm at one point when the opinion in Paris was negative to recombinant DNA work!' (Reichard 1993) 'SBL' stands for Statens Biologiska Laboratorium, the government biological lab.

[49] Kabi was itself the result of a merger in 1971 of four state owned pharmaceutical companies—Kabi, Vitrum, Recip, and ACO. The Swedish state had bought 60% of Kabi from Pripps brewery in 1969, and the remaining 40% in 1971. The Swedish pharmacists' association had started and run ACO and Vitrum, but when all pharmacies became state-owned in 1969, the government also took over ownership of these two companies (Norgen 1989: 45).

techniques for producing their main product quite soon after Genentech's somatostatin experiment. Through their involvement in GMAC and through in-house research groups, some of Kabi's researchers and management had heard about genetic engineering much earlier than the Swedish public.

Kabi's decision to access the new knowledge and technology through Genentech rather than in-house will make more sense if we first examine Kabi's historical involvement with pituitary hGH as interactions among corporate and university researchers, with the Swedish government playing a role. Kabi researchers had had contacts with Professors Luft and Hall at the medical research institute, Karolinska Institute.[50] In fact, Kabi's relationships with the nearby universities and medical institute had been important for the company's whole involvement in hGH extracted from pituitary glands. In the late 1960s, Professor Luft had, in association with assistant professor Paul Roos, suggested that Kabi make hGH. Kabi began working on pituitary hGH in 1967, started clinical tests in conjunction with Luft in 1968, and registered the product in 1971.[51] This seems like a clear-cut example of university researchers coming up with an idea for a product which pharmaceutical firms then put into practice after having seen its economic value.

However, Kabi's initial involvement with pituitary hGH was not quite as straightforward as this depiction may seem, mostly because of firm-level decisions being countered by issues related to its government ownership. In 1969–70, Kabi's upper management almost decided not to develop pituitary hGH as a pharmaceutical product because several market surveys indicated that a pharmaceutical designed for six or seven persons per million was uninteresting and unimportant as a product. The contemporary company directors seriously questioned whether Kabi should enter this market.

Management thought the market was quite simply too small to be interesting, but the government stepped in. As Åberg tells the continuation of this story: 'Through the intervention of the then Minister of Industry, Krister Wickman, manufacturing of hGH continued, however, and today [1982] the hGH preparation Crescormon® is Kabi-Vitrum concern's most profitable product.'[52] In 1981, Kabi sold Crescormon for seventy million Swedish crowns per year, or about $10 million. The government owners ended up supporting a product which

[50] Sievertsson (1992).

[51] Professor Luft was at the endocrinological clinic, Karolinska Institute, Stockholm, whereas Dr Roos was about an hour north, at the Department of Biochemistry, Uppsala University (Norgren 1989: 77–8).

[52] Åberg (1982: 57). Åberg continues by saying that Wickman personally wanted to see Kabi produce pharmaceuticals for more uncommon diseases. At this point, Statsföretag—literally, the state's companies, which was a holding company—had not yet been formed and Kabi's stock was handled by the Department of Industry (Åberg 1982: 57).

was much more profitable than the firm's management could initially imagine.

It is clear that Kabi's initial and continued involvement in proteins extracted from pituitary glands directly benefited from contacts with Swedish basic researchers and from government support. This indicates interesting hypotheses, such as that the reasons firms become involved with a technology may be quite local and not necessarily based on market assessment. Moreover, it indicates that if a person has power to finance a risky technological project, then personal, political, or long-term visions can override decisions based on short-term market prognoses. This seems necessary for technological changes involving major technical or economic uncertainty, or both at once.

In addition to the GMAC committee, Kabi kept itself somewhat up to date with scientific activities involving genetic engineering. They were not specialists in molecular biology but heard about Genentech's success with the somatostatin experiment. According to Hans Sievertsson, who was then Kabi's research director, Kabi had a small research group of about five people who studied the complex of proteins released by the pituitary gland and the hypothalamus. They studied interactions between hGH and other proteins, among other things.[53] Sievertsson was a member of this group and had a Ph.D. for research on hormones in the hypothalamus. Like all research groups, these corporate researchers monitored scientific developments in the field. They could monitor these particular experiments and understand their significance, without being able to duplicate the work in-house.

In 1977, this Kabi group thought Genentech's research on somatostatin was 'fantastically exciting'. Sievertsson recollects that it was natural for them to wonder if other proteins could be produced the same way.[54] Based on this perception, Sievertsson called Genentech during a business trip to Chicago in late 1977. He wanted to establish contact with Genentech and to look into the possibility of an R & D contract for hGH. Upon Sievertsson's return to Stockholm and after Sievertsson had talked over matters with his boss, Bengt Karlsson, Kabi invited Swanson and Boyer, as Genentech's representatives, to Sweden.[55]

[53] This complex of proteins is important for understanding the physiological and medical details of hGH because hGH works in tandem with other proteins, including ones that stimulate the release of hGH, ones that inhibit its release, and ones that are in turn stimulated by hGH (somatomedins).

[54] Sievertsson (1992). Secondary sources in Sweden have indicated that Åberg heard about 'synthetic', i.e. recombinant-DNA, insulin at a symposium (Norgren 1989: 78). However, the case of hGH shows that Kabi approached Genentech long before Genentech published anything on rDNA insulin. They published in September 1978, about the time the final contract was signed. As Åberg was a highly public and visible person in Swedish debates, many different interpretations of his actions have been published.

[55] Sievertsson (1992).

Some research managers at Kabi thus perceived the potential of genetic engineering and acted accordingly to see whether and how these scientific activities would be applicable to corporate goals in the long run.

Åberg, as research director for KabiVitrum, was also intimately involved in these discussions. In a debate book from 1982 entitled *Safe Enough? About the Introduction of a New Technology into Sweden, Recombinant DNA*, Åberg reminisces about the course of events:

I remember how Peter Reichard, professor in biochemistry at Karolinska Institute, asked me, in connection with the awarding of the Nobel Prize to Roger Guillemin—the discoverer of somatostatin—what Kabi intended to do about the new technology. The answer was that Kabi's current research director Hans Sievertsson and I, who was research director for the group Kabi-Vitrum-ACO, had already invited Herbert Boyer to come to Stockholm and discuss the possibilities for co-operation in some of the product areas that were important for Kabi. The meeting occurred in the first week of December 1977, and Boyer was accompanied by Robert Swanson, managing director for a newly formed Californian company, Genentech Inc. Kabi was represented by Hans Sievertsson and, from the research side of the group, myself and my closest colleague, Kerstin Sirvell, Master of Science. It was clear after the meeting that it would be possible to clone human growth hormone (somatotropin, hGH) in a *coli* bacteria.[56]

Kabi and Genentech representatives thus met in Stockholm to discuss an R & D contract for genetic engineering very quickly after the somatostatin experiment had gathered attention. About the same time, the scientist Reichard encouraged Kabi to explore commercial uses of the technology, but Kabi did not mention that they had already moved to contact Genentech.

Sievertsson confirms that Boyer and Swanson came to Stockholm on 'Nobeldagen' 1977, that is, 10 December, the day the Nobel Prizes are awarded. Their fee for coming was the price of their plane tickets: Genentech was interested in finding customers to whom they could sell their R & D contracts. Another researcher omitted in Åberg's account was also present at the meeting, namely Linda Fryklund, who was then department head of the Recip Hormone Laboratory.[57]

Note, moreover, that there were overlaps between agents responding to different environments at this time as well as a chasm between an optimism in the knowledge-seeking environments and a pessimism in the public context. First, Kabi was exploring the commercial feasibility of

---

[56] Åberg (1982: 55), my translation. Despite the implication of Åberg's remarks—that Kabi acted even before Swedish academics had considered the industrial prospects— Fryklund argues that Åberg had a very wide network of contacts, and 'although I don't know his thought processes at the time', Åberg undoubtedly contacted many experts who told him genetic engineering was not as far-fetched as it sounded at the time (Fryklund 1992).   [57] Fryklund (1992, 1993).

the technology about the same time that the Swedish media was exploring the risks. Many of the debate articles were trying to shape the public
context by mentioning the dangers. As discussed above, the Swedish
public climate was sceptical about scientific—much less commercial—
uses of genetic engineering at this point, but that did not stop Kabi from
acting on their perceptions.

Second, the basic scientific environment lay very close to the two
economically oriented environments. The first overlap has to do with
the dual nature of Genentech's somatostatin experiment, relevant for
both basic science and commercial use. The second overlap was
between different ways of producing the same proteins, e.g. tissue
extraction versus genetic engineering. As Åberg points out, Drs Guillemin, Schally, and Yalows were concurrently awarded the Nobel Prize in
physiology/medicine for their work on peptide hormones.[58] Guillemin
had discovered the medical significance of somatostatin and had
extracted it from tissue. Scientific recognition for research on hormones
like somatostatin thus occurred parallel in time and within a few kilometres of the commercial recognition of a new technology which could
make similar proteins.

The scientific versus commercial demands on quantity produced with
the two different technologies ultimately differed by several orders of
magnitude. Both Guillemin's group and Genentech's group had made
about five milligrams of somatostatin, a tiny amount, before Nobeldagen
1977. However, whereas Genentech could make it in bacteria, with the
potential of replicating the experiment in thousand-litre tanks, Guillemin
obtained his five milligrams by grinding up almost a million sheep
brains.[59] Genetic engineering promised control over what was an apparently unlimited supply, and large-scale production was a necessary
condition for this type of commercial use.

Kabi was interested in the possibilities that the new technology offered
for producing their most profitable pharmaceutical product, human
growth hormone. Kabi was a so-called pure, ethical pharmaceutical
company which mainly produced pharmaceuticals based on biological
processes.[60] They had no competence in molecular biology, as Genentech
did, but did have complementary assets and complementary technologies. Kabi had technical and engineering experience with, for example,
separation of blood products, with complex proteins, and with controlling microbiological processes such as penicillin and streptokinase. Due

[58] *Uppsala Nya Tidningen* (1977: 10).
[59] Cohn (1977: A9). Of course, unlike Genentech, Guillemin was not trying to develop a
method for mass production.
[60] In its technical sense, 'ethical' means available only with a doctor's prescription. In
1990, Åberg claimed that hGH accounted for two-thirds of the profits of the whole
company (Andersson 1990: 12).

to this competence and experience, Kabi retained and could transmit knowledge, techniques, and equipment developed from other biological production processes and products to new projects using relatively similar new technologies. The question was, How similar would genetic engineering prove to be?

Kabi had an alternative technology for production of hGH, namely extraction from tissue, specifically extraction from human pituitary glands. In the late 1970s, Kabi was the world's largest commercial supplier of hGH extracted from human pituitary glands (pituitary or pit hGH). The nature of the international market and of supplies was an important factor underlying Kabi's decision to move into genetic engineering.

The disease hGH is supposed to treat, hypopituitary or severe dwarfism, was then estimated to afflict six to ten persons per million. This means that in 1979, Sweden, with a population of eight million, should have had about eighty cases and the USA, with a population of 220 million, about 2,200 cases. The estimated costs of one year of treatment per patient was $5,000–$10,000 in 1979, and treatment lasts about ten years, up until puberty. Either the state medical service or other medical insurance paid for the treatment. Human growth hormone extracted from tissue thus had an established, if fairly small, market. Management could easily project that the same product made with an alternative technology like genetic engineering should have at least an equally large market.

For this product, size of market was closely linked to supply of pituitary glands. The pituitary glands were often in short supply. In the late 1970s, Kabi collected about 150,000 to 200,000 glands from around the world. On average, Kabi needed 50 pituitary glands to provide enough hGH for one patient for one year, so Kabi could provide treatment for approximately 3,000 patients per year. They had 70% of the world market, with their main international competitor being Serono, a Swiss company, but there were also non-profit, government-financed agencies like the National Pituitary Agency (NPA) in Baltimore, Maryland. The NPA gathered 6,000 pituitary glands a year, a contrast in size to Kabi. Whereas Kabi was mainly run as an independent firm, the NPA distributed the glands to medical researchers who purified out hGH and other rare brain hormones. The NPA then in turn distributed the doses to about 1,600 children without charge. The American federal government paid for extraction and distribution as part of medical research, as they felt the market would fail to provide incentives to make this pharmaceutical.[61]

In addition to the 1,600 children provided for by NPA, an additional estimated 400 children in the USA bought from firms like Kabi. Assuming Kabi had 70% of the American market, that means about 260

[61] Glasbrenner (1986: 582–3).

American patients plus around 50 in Sweden, if the estimated frequency is correct. This implies that Kabi sold hGH to about 2,660 patients in other countries in the mid-1970s, indicating the truly international nature of their market.[62] Although Kabi provided hGH to countries which had shipped them the pituitary glands, the biggest markets lay in the East, especially Japan and Australia.

Commercial firms and government-financed organizations had different understandings of the potential of expanding the market for hGH. Government-financed organizations like NPA had no incentives for, or ways of, organizing a move into the new technology because of their dependence on individual medical researchers and because of the structure of direct funding. They were given money by the government to extract hormones this way. Salvatore Raiti, director of NPA in 1979, maintained 'that all patients with diagnosed hyposomatotropism are receiving the hormone'.[63] In other words, too little supply was not seen to be a problem, and therefore no new production technologies were needed. Raiti's statement was made in December 1979 at the symposium where Genentech announced their success in making hGH in bacteria. Since the NPA was not moving to develop the new technology, partly due to the organizational and institutional structures, genetic engineering threatened their *raison d'être*.[64]

Kabi had a different understanding of the potential for expanding the market in the 1970s, and this affected their perception of the potential of genetic engineering. Kabi felt it could sell all the hGH it could make because the current supply sufficed for only the most severe cases of dwarfism. Many potential patients of this disease, hence customers, simply could not get hGH. In addition to the known and established market for dwarfism, there were indications that hGH could be used for other medical conditions like burns, Turner's syndrome, and so forth. The market could be much larger than the current one expressed through pit hGH.

Even though Kabi perceived this potential market, greatly expanding the supply of pituitary hGH was not so easy. Kabi already had international contacts to collect pituitary glands (from morgues), but they continually faced a situation where potential demand was greater than supply. Raw material from biological material was not only in limited supply, it was also difficult to deal with. Åberg later claimed that these latent sourcing needs, rather than profit incentives or availability of new knowledge, pushed pharmaceutical companies into genetic engineering.[65] Genetic engineering offered the possibility of unlimited supply

---

[62] Fryklund (1993). The NPA's average use of about forty glands per patient per year compared to Kabi's fifty was due to somewhat different purification and isolation techniques. Kabi felt that the NPA's process resulted in a less pure product.
[63] Gonzalez (1979: 702).   [64] See further in McKelvey (1993b).
[65] Laage-Hellman (1986: 59).

because the protein would be made in bacteria or other simple cells which would rapidly multiply, each daughter cell also making hGH.

In relation to expanding the supply, the possibilities for profits were quite clear. Kabi as a firm faced economic uncertainty about the future. Kabi was having financial difficulties and needed a boost to survive in the industry in the longer term. At the same time that pituitary hGH was Kabi's most successful product and an important generator of income,[66] Kabi teetered at the edge of bankruptcy several times in the late seventies. This implied that if Kabi could use a new technology to increase the supply of a known product thought to have a larger market, this strategy would facilitate the firm's survival in the longer run. It could give Kabi what is today known as dynamic competitiveness. Kabi contacted Genentech about the possibility of an R & D contract due to the technical and economic potential of the technology.

Largely because Genentech was willing to sell R & D contracts which developed genetic engineering techniques for specific applications, Kabi contacted them rather than any Swedish researcher in the field. Although there was some Swedish research in tangential fields—above all nearby in Uppsala—Swedish researchers did not work on the specific application of genetic engineering which had attracted Kabi to exploring the techniques. In this case, a firm in one country could fund scientific activities in another country in order to be able to move into a new technology. Scientific competences relevant for commercial use did not have to be available locally or nationally.

Moreover, it appears that during the first negotiations between Kabi and Genentech, few outsiders to Kabi, even within Sweden, knew about the specific discussions that Åberg and Sievertsson had begun or about Kabi's general intentions to use genetic engineering. As shown above, two of the most active Swedish researchers in the field, also actively involved in regulation, were Professors Reichard and Philipson. The above quote from Åberg indicates that Reichard was unaware of Kabi's intentions in December, and Philipson had a similar opinion in July of 1977:

I don't think any one of them [Astra, Pharmacia, Kabi] is involved in recombinant DNA research at the present time. I don't think there are any plans to use it

---

[66] Their dependence on hGH can be related to some of their other products. One Kabi employee, a technician, thought that some of the other products, such as blood plasma, were not profitable but only broke even. However, they cannot be discontinued because Kabi has agreed to supply these items to the Swedish state in times of war (Florell 1992). There is some truth to this because Kabi was 100% state owned in the 1970s, and according to its mandate, it was supposed to provide medicine on the basis of social need. At the same time, Kabi has mostly functioned as a commercial firm on the basis of profit and losses.

in the foreseeable future. But of course, they would like to have an option and a procedure to follow in case they would be interested.[67]

Of course, Philipson was right that Kabi was not involved in recombinant DNA research, or even in contact with Genentech, in July 1977: their first more formal contact with Genentech was in December of that year. Their plans did, however, come in the foreseeable future. Neither was Kabi involved in the contemporary mass media debates over the technology, which otherwise would have indicated their interest publicly. Reasons for Kabi to keep silent about their intentions could include the hostile tone of the Swedish public debate at the time as well as the competitive advantage of moving into and starting to develop a new technology before their competitors knew what they were up to.

Following the meeting between Genentech and Kabi in December 1977, the heads of the joint Kabi companies, that is, Bengt Andrén, Bertil Åberg, and Hans Sievertsson, made a decision to work out an agreement with Genentech to carry out research on hGH. They signed a 'Letter of Intent' in December 1977, which indicated their agreement to try to come to an agreement, and the lawyers from the respective companies set out to hammer out a legal contract during 1978. Kabi thus thought it likely that Genentech could successfully carry out the research project.

Summary and Conclusions

The 1970s was a crucial decade for genetic engineering techniques; the early to mid-1970s was analysed in this chapter, and the late 1970s in the subsequent chapter. There were knowledge-seeking activities which led to novelty enabling commercial uses of genetic engineering techniques. Initially in the early 1970s, basic scientists developed these techniques and knowledge through scientific activities intended for the basic scientific environment. Research in a number of fields, such as molecular biology and biochemistry, had built up the accumulated knowledge foundation from which recombinant DNA techniques could be developed. This research was mostly funded by medical councils financed by governments or by private foundations, but both distributed funds according to scientific criteria. This was research internal to the basic scientific environment.

This chapter began by discussing the debate about, and actions to implement, regulation inside the basic scientific environment. This occurred when genetic engineering techniques became practically pos-

---

[67] Philipson (1977b: 68).

sible and relatively easy to use in the early 1970s. This first section addressed what basic scientists knew (knowledge) and what they could do (techniques). Scientists' uncertainty also indicates the level of risks involved for firms, which had perceived the potential of adapting genetic engineering techniques for use in other environments.

Because the new genetic engineering techniques were relatively easy and practical to use and because no existing regulation applied to the technology, basic scientists called for an informal moratorium on certain experiments in the early 1970s. Scientists felt they had to create and implement regulation for certain experiments in order to prevent two undesirable situations: (1) Everything goes. In a situation without regulation of a powerful technology, dangerous experiments might be attempted, leading to undesirable accidents and consequences. (2) Nothing goes. Without some boundaries defining acceptable experiments, if an accident should occur, then public debate and formal regulation could become so hostile that all experiments would be banned. Both situations were suboptimal compared to finding acceptable rules and regulation for continuing scientific activities.

Even those scientists who were convinced that the initial guidelines were overly strict felt there were reasons to consider seriously the criticisms launched against unregulated development of the technology. They also felt compelled to follow the voluntary moratorium launched by other scientists. In the mid-1970s, the scientists involved developed guidelines at the Asilomar conference, and these guidelines were later adopted by the major financier of medical research in the United States, namely the National Institutes of Health (NIH). As in the USA, Swedish scientists informed the Swedish government about the technology during the early 1970s, but when the government showed no inclination to regulate it, scientists implemented regulation through the Genetic Manipulation Advisory Group Committee (GMAC). This committee evaluated research grant proposals for the research councils. Whereas American regulation remained heavily represented by scientists, a broader range of interest groups were represented in the Swedish committee. Agents internal to the basic scientific environment thus shaped the public context by developing norms and regulations according to internal scientific criteria such as risk evaluation.

Following the establishment of scientific guidelines, basic scientists developed and used scientific knowledge and genetic engineering techniques in order to try to express human proteins in *E. coli* bacteria. Much discussion centres on the two research groups who later both worked on experiments on human growth hormone and insulin. These groups were more or less within the same university department at the University of California, San Francisco (UCSF). UCSF thus had several research groups of high quality doing this type of research, and they sometimes competed and sometimes co-operated. Some individuals focused on scientific activities for their basic scientific environment, whereas others were more directly interested in commercial applications. Even the latter had to engage in scientific as well as technological activities, as shown by the somatostatin experiment.

Scientific knowledge for the basic scientific environment placed priority on, among other things, understanding how DNA functions in cells. Developing this knowledge required making things work in practice, and this depended on a number of practical techniques, such as identifying and cutting out the relevant gene sequence and expressing the protein. This was the basic approach enabling control over nature, which also made it possible to make pharmaceuticals using genetic engineering.

Up to the mid-1970s, agents mainly carried out knowledge-seeking activities in response to the basic scientific environment. Their actions were regulated by debate, norms, and informal regulations within this scientific community. Some scientists, however, began orienting their knowledge-seeking activities towards other environments.

In the mid-1970s, some agents recognized and acted upon the economic potential of genetic engineering techniques. The new technology could be relevant for other uses and for agents other than basic scientists. The first dedicated biotech firm, Genentech, was started at this time by the basic scientist Boyer and the venture capitalist Swanson. Boyer remained a professor at UCSF. Established firms invested some money in in-house research, university research, or other R & D contracts. There was sometimes commercial as well as scientific rivalry, indicating co-evolutionary trends between activities for different environments.

By 1976–7, only very rudimentary techniques had actually been developed. Not even the question which most interested firms, namely, 'Can genetic engineering techniques force bacteria to produce human proteins?', had been answered. Firms interested in this commercial potential therefore faced conditions of uncertainty. Reducing this uncertainty required relatively radical results, potentially found in a combination of scientific and technological activities.

At the same time that scientists, universities, and firms engaged in knowledge-seeking activities for their respective purposes, the public context for the technology, initially shaped by scientists, was coming under scrutiny. Debate was used to influence public opinion and often called for the creation or modification of technology regulation. On the one hand, in the mid 1970s, the NIH guidelines for genetic engineering were relaxed in the United States and subsequently so in Sweden. The NIH relaxed the severity of its guidelines after scientific experiments indicated that the danger was much lower than the initial, worst case scenarios had postulated. Scientists wanted some regulation in order to continue doing experiments but only as much as deemed necessary.

On the other hand, public debate in both the USA and Sweden increasingly discussed the risks, consequences, and ultimately, the potential of the new technology. When the debate about genetic engineering became more public after 1976 in the USA and after 1977 in Sweden, the range of fears and optimism increased, and there were suggestions to forbid all experiments with genetic engineering within a city and/or within a nation. Scientists were therefore concerned when the US Congress debated federal sanctions and regulations that would have seriously restricted some types of experiments. This change would undoubtedly have affected other countries as well. While the US Congress was debating this legislation in 1977, research results were obtained which indicated *E. coli* bacteria could express the human protein somatostatin. Publicity helped create favourable public opinion for the promised medical benefits of genetic engineering, and thereby helped put off government regulation. In order to shape the public context, scientists used scientific results indicating benefits for the public at large.

The somatostatin experiment used to influence the American public context was carried out in a university lab at UCSF and at the public research hospital City of Hope. The two groups worked together under contract from the new biotech firm Genentech. Boyer, who was one of the senior scientists at UCSF and who had developed the recombinant DNA technique along with Professor Cohen, started Genentech.

The firm Genentech was initially a mixture of venture capital and basic science, with the aim of selling R & D contracts in what has been called here the scientific-economic environment. Genentech's first R & D project, internally funded but carried out externally, was this somatostatin project. It was also important because this project led to scientific research results indicating the feasibility of making other human proteins using the new technology. This experiment led to economically useful research results for Genentech. It helped establish the scientific legitimacy and integrity of this new biotech firm. For example, these research results prompted the established Swedish pharmaceutical firm Kabi to contact Genentech in order to investigate the possibility of an R & D contract for hGH. The American pharmaceutical firm Lilly was similarly in contact with Genentech about insulin.

Kabi's exploration of Genentech's possibility of selling R & D contracts took place during a relatively heated Swedish debate in late 1977 and early 1978. Although this national debate had many negative tones, it did not stop Swedish firms from being interested in the economic and technical potential of genetic engineering. The Swedish public debate did play a role in mobilizing opinion about genetic engineering and its regulation, but cannot be seen as a decisive element affecting technological innovation processes. In this political context, Kabi initially remained silent about their decision to contact Genentech and to explore genetic engineering.

The events in the USA and Sweden up to 1977 concerning somatostatin, public debate, and the selling of the R & D contract have thus indicated a number of things about evolutionary innovation. At this point, the development of genetic engineering techniques significant for hGH was still largely the result of scientific activities carried out within research institutes, and acclaimed by scientists as interesting. Nevertheless, alongside this basic scientific environment, Genentech's research on somatostatin also had technological objectives in that this work helped develop practical techniques, like those for synthesizing DNA. It also served as an advertisement for Genentech's scientific potential and their willingness to sell R & D contracts to firms. Science would be made relevant for managers.

Genentech's strategy was successful in that persons in powerful positions at some established firms perceived the economic and technical potential of the new technology and of Genentech's ability to deliver. Kabi had monitored external scientific research in its internal R & D departments and had participated in associations and committees which helped diffuse information about the new technology. Kabi had economic as well as scientific and technical reasons to search for a new way to produce their most successful product. For them, genetic engineering offered an alternative to tissue extraction.

The research agreements between Genentech and Kabi and between Genentech and Eli Lilly would affect the directions in which genetic engineering techniques would be developed in the future. They are further explored in the next chapter. Clearly, genetic engineering would no longer be an exclusively academic development, nor were firms willing to wait around for research results intended for the basic scientific environment but which were also applicable within the economic environments. Some firms instead acted to support knowledge-seeking activities in order to get access to knowledge which was otherwise not available. A combination of scientific and technological activities were necessary to develop techniques which no one was quite sure would work. Exploring the search space and technical alternatives involved uncertainty. Managers and researchers had to take the risk of trying to develop knowledge and techniques which were uncertain, and at the time, scientific activities were the only way of doing so.

6

Generating Research: the Mid- to Late 1970s

Introduction

This chapter continues the analysis of early scientific and technological activities relevant to commercial uses of genetic engineering, now in the late 1970s. In particular, this chapter examines firms' strategies and interactions between firms and universities, which thereby created tensions and new possibilities.

In late 1977, the somatostatin experiment described in the previous chapter indicated the potential feasibility and applicability of using genetic engineering techniques as a method of producing human proteins. It also indicated that the biotech firm Genentech could do scientific research but directed towards firms' goals. Many questions relevant for firms were left unanswered, however, particularly whether bacteria could make the larger human proteins that were medically interesting.

1978 was a year in which several agents acted on their respective visions about using genetic engineering to make insulin and human growth hormone. Corporate and university managers and researchers could interact and meet in the newly created scientific-economic environment. This chapter first examines the strategies and actions of three firms—Eli Lilly, Genentech, and Kabi—as they worked to develop favourable technical, economic, and political conditions. They were interested in, respectively, insulin and hGH; hGH and genetic engineering in general; and hGH. The strategies and activities of these three firms and of one university department at UCSF are described in relation to insulin and hGH. These early-moving firms had to support research which at the time might be relevant for either the basic scientific or the scientific-economic environment.

The story of competitive basic scientific research is, in this case, complicated by the funding of research by established firms and by the starting up of new biotech firms. The 'competitors' could thus sometimes be found in other firms and sometimes in universities. For example, Genentech worked on the hGH project using Kabi's money and partly based their work on research done by former UCSF researchers.

Genentech worked in competition with a UCSF research group which had money from Lilly.

Interactions among environments was quite intense at this time, due to the negotiation and creation of a new scientific-economic environment. The results generated by what had traditionally been basic scientists were suddenly perceived to be of interest for firms and commercial uses. There were different types of interactions. The distance between knowledge-seeking activities was quite close at this point, and individuals could directly or indirectly influence agents responding to a different environment.

Moreover, in 1978, these firms had to help create and shape national public contexts which would enable them to exploit the productive potential of the new technology. The public debate, informal norms, and formal regulation setting parameters for the technology were under negotiation.

As the firms had to rely heavily on basic research in the late 1970s, either in-house or at universities, this chapter continues to examine rivalry and co-operation within university science. In particular, the relationships and conflicts within UCSF and between UCSF and Genentech are further examined. This gives a better indication of how the creation of a new environment, the scientific-economic environment, impacted on environmental conditions. In fact, many of these early interactions led to conflicts and to discussions about how to change existing informal institutions.

In relation to this discussion, the similarities and differences between research responding to different environments is explored. The discussion focuses more specifically on two scientific papers, one published by UCSF and the other by Genentech. Both papers indicated how genetic engineering techniques could be applied to human growth hormone. Although the scientific activities were carried out at, respectively, a university and a biotech firm, both research projects were funded by pharmaceutical firms. Nevertheless, there were differences in orientation and in outcome.

The final section summarizes the chapter from the perspective of evolutionary innovation and draws some preliminary conclusions. Throughout the chapter, the historical material is structured according to an evolutionary pattern of technical change. We can thereby specify how and why different agents and organizations in market-based economies contributed to and/or hindered technological innovation processes. Propositions from evolutionary economics, like bounded rationality, the importance of informal institutions and competences, and incentive structures in environments will help explain why different agents are likely to decide and to act to generate novelty in different directions, in response to environmental conditions.

Eli Lilly's Active Search for a New Supply of Insulin

Swanson and Boyer of Genentech were not just sitting around, waiting for established firms to understand how genetic engineering could fit existing or new needs. They were actively looking for commercial users of genetic engineering in order to sell R & D contracts. In 1978, Boyer and Swanson therefore approached the American pharmaceutical firm Eli Lilly and Company (Lilly), the dominant world-wide supplier of insulin, and a firm very interested in keeping its market share for this profitable product. Lilly signed an R & D contract with Genentech in September 1978. Lilly were also, however, very actively searching for alternative sources of insulin supply.

Problems with the supply of insulin were similar to those with the supply of hGH, giving firms incentives to explore new types of technologies. The insulin then used by diabetics was extracted from cows and pigs and was not identical to human insulin. Although the existing insulin functioned properly, genetic engineering promised to make insulin identical to human insulin. Moreover, like hGH, insulin was a pharmaceutical product for which the firms projected future shortages of raw materials. Establishing control over source would give more possibilities for maintaining market share. Kabi and Lilly thus had similar reasons for being interested in genetic engineering for human proteins. These pharmaceutical firms were interested in the possibilities that genetic engineering offered for solving the problem of shortages—or potential shortages—of their major products.

In 1982, Lilly had 85% of the American market, worth a total of $155 million in sales. Lilly also had a strong presence in Europe and the rest of the world, worth a total of, respectively, $140 million and $60 million in sales. In contrast, the number two firm in the market was the Danish firm Novo. Novo had 30% of the world-wide market of $350 million and about 15% of the American market.

That pharmaceutical firms in the insulin market were more interested in making human insulin than in the technology of genetic engineering is indicated by their diverse strategies for finding alternative sources. According to Swanson, Genentech also approached Lilly's arch-rival Novo in 1978.[1] Novo were not interested in Genentech's offer of an R & D contract for genetic engineering, not only because genetic engineer-

---

[1] The scientific journalist Stephen Hall has documented a fascinating account of the competition over basic scientific results for insulin. Hall has, however, a different interpretation of these events. He writes, 'Early on, around the beginning of 1978, Swanson held discussions with Lilly's arch-rival, Novo Industri. The Danish manufacturer never expressed great interest, according to Swanson, because "Novo didn't believe it could be done. They didn't believe the technology would work, basically." Lilly's interest remained steady but non-committal' (Hall 1988: 268).

ing techniques were very uncertain and Genentech an unknown new firm, but also because Novo were already exploring a different technological option for producing human insulin. Novo were exploring the use of enzymes to transform animal insulin into insulin chemically identical to human insulin. Novo had much experience with enzymes, and to them, this seemed more likely to pay off. It was also closer to their core competences. Novo long questioned the economic viability of recombinant DNA techniques.[2]

In contrast to Novo, Lilly felt genetic engineering was an interesting alternative technology to tissue extraction. The main question for them was whether Genentech could prove its ability to use genetic engineering to make insulin. Lilly claims that in the mid- to late 1970s, it was a firm actively looking for alternative sources of supply. Whether Lilly had actually started work on an alternative, as Novo had, is less clear.

Irving S. Johnson, vice-president of research at Lilly Research Laboratories in 1983, gave his account of Lilly's strategy to make 'Human Insulin from Recombinant DNA Technology' in *Science*:

Because of the uncertainty of the insulin supply and because of the forecasts of rising insulin requirements, it seemed not only prudent but a responsibility as well for the scientific community and insulin producers to develop alternatives to animal sources for supplying insulin to the world's diabetics. Lilly established several internal committees of scientists to examine various solutions to the problem. They considered augmentation of insulin production from pancreas glands, transplantation of islet of Langerhans cells, chemical synthesis, beta cell culture, directed-cell synthesis, and cell-free biosynthesis, as well as insulin replacements. These discussions touched on the technology called genetic engineering.[3]

Johnson thus mentions that Lilly explored a number of different options which could potentially make synthetic insulin. Lilly's internal corporate researchers, backed up by research managers, were actively evaluating alternatives which were all highly uncertain.

Johnson also stresses that the firm had a moral responsibility to find an alternative source of insulin due to shortages. In fact, insulin derived from pigs and cows was available in sufficient quantities in the 1970s; it was pure and worked well for 95% of diabetics. The 'shortage' Johnson mentions was a prediction about future supplies, and a prediction with which some disagreed.[4]

---

[2] In the 1980s, Novo did develop a production process based on genetic engineering and abandoned the enzyme approach. See further in Chapter 9.   [3] Johnson (1983: 632).

[4] It is therefore difficult to know whether Lilly and other firms believed in future shortage and acted accordingly to find an alternative source, or whether this argument was constructed afterwards to justify publicly the necessity of genetic engineering. The 'raw materials' for hGH were in even shorter supply, but then again, hGH was used by only six to ten persons out of a million during a limited number of years, whereas insulin was used throughout life by a much larger percentage of the population.

Whatever the reasons for genetic engineering, this quote indicates that Lilly kept themselves informed of alternative technologies and scientific activities which might provide new supplies of insulin. Corporate researchers monitored scientific activities in the basic scientific environment. They became aware of developments in genetic engineering as well as other possibilities for making insulin. However, their monitoring of scientific trends does not in itself indicate that Lilly researchers were doing this type of research in-house before they signed an R & D contract with Genentech in 1978.[5] They were clearly interested before contacting Genentech. In March 1977, the same Irving Johnson, as head of Lilly's R & D department, testified to the Subcommittee on Science, Research, and Technology of the US House of Representatives. In his testimony and in submitted written material, Johnson stresses the commercial applications of genetic engineering for pharmaceuticals.[6] Note that Johnson testified before signing the R & D contract with Genentech.

Later on, Johnson described Lilly's history thus:

We contracted with a new California company, Genentech, Inc., for specific work on human insulin. . . . In the Lilly Research Laboratories, we have also used recombinant DNA technology to produce human proinsulin, the insulin precursor. The successful expression of human insulin (recombinant DNA) in *E. coli* was announced in 6 September 1978. This was a first step.[7]

Johnson seems to imply that this proinsulin was the research result announced in September 1978, but in fact, that is not so. The 'successful expression of human insulin' announced then was based on Genentech's research, and the Genentech expression system at this time made the A and B chains of insulin separately. After purification, these two chains were combined to make human insulin. Later, Genentech introduced and gave Lilly a second bacteria expression system to make human proinsulin.[8] The Lilly researchers also apparently worked on the techniques and biological material for proinsulin, although a functioning expression system arrived from Genentech.

Based on the R & D contract with Genentech, Lilly received the initial and then upgraded bacteria expression systems. They also developed their own competences to grow the bacteria, purify it, modify genetic engineering techniques and biological materials, and so forth in their in-house labs. Lilly had the money to expand in-house labs quickly in relevant scientific fields.

Johnson's statement also indicates that Lilly explored and considered a variety of alternative techniques based on scientific research. The

---

[5] In fact, the amount of molecular biology knowledge and genetic engineering techniques that Lilly had previous to the Genentech contract was one of the questions which the legal dispute was trying to sort out.   [6] Bud (1993: 179–80).
[7] Johnson (1983: 633–4).   [8] Yansura (1993b), Kleid (1994).

managers wanted to know about potential options in order to retain control over their large market share. Genetic engineering was only one of a number of approaches for increasing supply, but the most promising to develop further and test. This description of Lilly's actions is in line with arguments that firms search for solutions close to existing problems, knowledge, and product areas. In making these management decisions, which specific technology would be chosen was less interesting than that the technology worked for their purposes. Management and researchers also realized that there could be a transfer of knowledge between projects based on different technologies. Like Kabi, Lilly could use knowledge, techniques, and equipment developed for animal insulin as a partial aid for making genetically engineered insulin.

Johnson's description of the research and search process is also in line with evolutionary innovation. We can see that Lilly researchers identified a variety of solutions. In this case, one agent gathered information about different technologies from many different sources and explored the feasibility of different possibilities. This diversity helped identify different possible trajectories and enabled a certain evaluation of options. Such choices about radically new technologies are made on calculations of success and failure in the environment, but in a situation of true uncertainty. Managers had to place their bets and find ways to implement their decisions.

Genetic engineering was perceived to be the most viable alternative, so much so that Lilly acted to gain control over alternative approaches using it. Lilly did not simply rely on Genentech to access genetic engineering for insulin. Indeed, Lilly supported Genentech only late in the game. Lilly hedged its bets by supporting rival scientific research groups and thereby tried to guarantee that they would have access to, and ownership over, alternative ways of using genetic engineering to make insulin.

A whole year before the Genentech contract was signed, Lilly supported Drs Baxter and Goodman, the two UCSF researchers discussed in the previous chapter. They worked on research involving both hGH and insulin. Lilly gave them research money to do basic science in their labs, in return for which Lilly got the right of first refusal. UCSF would retain ownership of the resulting material, techniques, etc., but would ask Lilly first if they wanted to license the results. The student newspaper at UCSF reported their relationship thus in 1978:

There are the huge drug company contracts, including a five-year, $1.3 million deal between Eli Lilly and UC with Drs Rutter, Goodman and Baxter (growth hormone and insulin work) the principle researchers.[9]

---

[9] Bader (1978: 1). The sum for the contract between Lilly and UCSF was also reported in Dickson (1979: 495) at $250,000 per year.

It is interesting that Lilly contracted UCSF for work on human growth hormone as well as insulin. The two projects on human proteins were sufficiently close due to the similarities of the techniques. It is interesting because Lilly did not make pituitary hGH, so perhaps they were interested because hGH seemed like an easy market to move into or perhaps the UCSF group suggested it because the scientific research was similar. It is not clear whose interests were represented. Perhaps both, as the university and firm perceived the R & D contracts as mutually beneficial. Like the contract between Genentech and UCSF for somatostatin in 1977, the Lilly and UCSF contract supported basic scientific activities.

Lilly's initial strategy was first to support one group at UCSF in early 1978, e.g. Baxter and Goodman. Lilly thereby gained access to those results and could license them. When, however, other research groups successfully demonstrated similar but different solutions to these same questions, Lilly acted to gain control over those competing results as well. As indicated above, Lilly also signed a contract with Genentech in 1978, but they actually only signed that contract after Genentech had obtained results by performing experiments that showed their techniques worked (see next section). The UCSF contract, in contrast, was given to directly support UCSF scientific activities. The UCSF contract thus supported the generation of novelty, whereas the Genentech contract bought very new but, still, already existing novelty.

Moreover, Lilly also approached a third American research lab which was successfully working on insulin. According to the scientific magazine *Nature*,

A major pharmaceutical company is providing backing for two of the leading three teams investigating the possible production of human insulin by bacteria (and has tried—unsuccessfully—to gain a licence to develop the results of the third team).[10]

There were three major research groups in the USA working on genetic engineering to make insulin. These three were the group at UCSF, Genentech, and a group headed by the renowned scientist Professor Walter Gilbert at Harvard University. Although Lilly bid on a licence for Gilbert's insulin technique, that licence went to Gilbert's own biotech firm, Biogen.[11]

Interestingly enough, the UCSF patent application on insulin was only a few weeks before Genentech and Lilly had a joint press conference. The UCSF patent application on insulin was filed on 11 August 1978 and the Genentech press conference was on 25 August. From Lilly's perspective, they had exclusive rights to decide whether to use this UCSF patent, and

[10] Bader (1978: 1).
[11] Just as in the history of technology, interesting research questions could be asked about an examination of university and industry relations that failed to materialize.

a few weeks later, Lilly also had access to and a licence on Genentech's work on insulin.

Thus, although there was a race between UCSF and Genentech researchers over insulin, Lilly was the one who benefited from the competition. They gained access to diverse approaches to the same technology. If a technique or technological approach is uncertain, it is more likely that competing groups using somewhat different approaches will, between them, find at least one functioning technique than if only one group is working on it. Diversity is beneficial but expensive. Managers can reduce immediate costs by only choosing one alternative and hoping they back the winning horse, or they can increase costs but get access to (ownership of) several horses in the same race. There can be a trade-off between short-term costs and long-term benefits, but these ratios often have to be made on guesswork, due to uncertainty.

Lilly's interest in all three research groups working on insulin reflected the importance of the product to the firm as well as Lilly's recognition of the potential commercial importance of genetic engineering. Lilly wanted to guarantee that they would have alternative approaches if one of the techniques failed. They also wanted access, including ownership through patents and licences, to other possible approaches in order to block others from using the technology to enter the market. Blocking competitors' access to a new technology is one often-used corporate strategy to protect inventions/innovations.[12] Not only were Lilly very early into the genetic engineering race, but they were willing and able to spend money to help develop the technology and thereby gain ownership. The techniques which worked best for commercial purposes were initially Genentech's.

Genentech's Activities

During 1978, Genentech expanded rapidly and worked intensely on designing a bacteria which could produce insulin for Lilly. In the journalistic historical account of science in Stephen Hall (1988), Lilly only signed the research contract after Genentech proved they could deliver genetic engineering techniques to make insulin. 'According to Irving Johnson . . . Lilly signed its agreement with Genentech on August 25, 1978—one day after Goeddel completed the confirming experiment, two weeks prior to the press conference.'[13] This press conference included Lilly, Genentech, and City of Hope, where the researchers announced their results on 7 September 1978.[14]

---

[12] Levin *et al.* (1988).   [13] Hall (1988: 271).

[14] Andreopoulos (1980: 744). Moreover, according to the same source, the US Congress and Senate were enthusiastic about this insulin experiment, and members made statements about how government-funded science could lead to such medical breakthroughs. This is another indication that early cases of genetic engineering were used for political purposes.

The Genentech and City of Hope researchers had submitted but had not yet published their insulin results in a scientific journal. Holding a press conference endowed them with scientific legitimacy and with success in commercial applications in the eyes of the public and mass media. Legitimacy within the basic scientific environment comes from publishing in respected journals, however, so such activities created some tensions.

Much of the value of Genentech's work lay in the development of practical techniques to synthesize DNA. By synthesizing it, they could reproduce it and not be limited to existing biological material. The experiment involved both basic scientific and technological activities. Economic goals directed the path of knowledge-seeking activities towards controlling biological processes as well as understanding them.

It is less clear whether Genentech began work immediately and in parallel on human growth hormone after contact with Kabi in December 1977 or if hGH came after insulin. According to Kabi, Genentech worked on hGH parallel with the insulin work during 1978.[15] In contrast, Genentech employees remember insulin as the initial research project dominating this period, but Genentech's legal complaint for their patent dispute with Lilly argues that 'virtually from its inception in 1976, Genentech embarked on a research effort to develop human growth hormone through what is called recombinant DNA technology.'[16] Genentech probably initially worked on insulin but were working on hGH as well as insulin by late 1978, although the latter was less urgent.

In relation to the question of timing, there is an interesting question about whether Genentech signed the hGH or insulin contract first. Although the insulin contract has had the most publicity, according to Åberg, who signed the hGH contract for Kabi,

The [Kabi hGH] contract with Genentech was the world's first industrial contract in the area of genetic engineering. A few weeks later, the second contract was signed—between Eli Lilly & Co and Genentech dealing with manufacturing human insulin using the same technology.[17]

This quote indicates that Genentech signed the Kabi contract before the contract with Lilly.

Note, however, an important difference between the R & D contracts for insulin and for hGH. The Lilly contract was signed after Genentech's scientists proved it could be done, that is after the confirming experiments. The announcement of this R & D contract was made in connection with the announcement of scientific results. In contrast, the Kabi

---

[15] Sievertsson (1992).
[16] Respectively, Yansura (1992) and Genentech (1987: 4). Hall (1988) strongly makes the argument that insulin was the only on-going project at Genentech during this period.
[17] Åberg (1982: 59) my translation.

contract gave Genentech twenty-four to thirty months from August 1978 and forward to fulfil the conditions and express hGH. Thus, by the time Kabi signed their final contract with Genentech for hGH, Genentech had already performed the majority of work on the insulin project in order to woo Lilly. Lilly paid for already executed knowledge-seeking activities, although those results were in no sense final, and further improvements were necessary to fulfil the contract conditions. In contrast, Kabi paid for future knowledge-seeking activities.

Commercial research contracts usually have check-points and deadlines that have to be fulfilled before a letter of intent is transformed into a full and binding contract. A letter of intent thus allows the partners to test something unknown but leaves an exit if the project does not develop as promised. Because Genentech's commercial contracts involved several benchmarks and because Genentech as a firm completed the majority of the insulin work first, in the United States the common story is that Genentech signed the contract with Lilly first of all its contracts.[18]

One of the reasons for the American interpretation of history may be that Genentech gained prestige in the USA by associating their name with huge, well-established firms like Lilly, whereas a small Swedish firm offered few publicity points for Genentech. Prestige could help sell additional R & D contracts. In Sweden, on the other hand, Kabi's early contact with Genentech is known in certain circles and confers prestige on Kabi. Publicity played a role both in publicizing the benefits of genetic engineering, thereby creating positive support for the development of this technology, and in publicizing the foresight of those firms which either performed or ordered R & D contracts.

In April of 1978, Genentech moved into their own buildings. Their new building was a renovated warehouse in South San Francisco, an industrial area, and strategically close to San Francisco, including access to UCSF, Stanford University, the airport, and bridges across the bay to Berkeley. Initially, Genentech only took up a corner of an empty warehouse, with none of the trappings of an R & D-intensive firm. The first employees were the venture capitalist Bob Swanson, a secretary, and a manufacturing expert who soon left the company; the basic scientist Boyer remained at UCSF but consulted for Genentech. Even with the move into the new buildings in April 1978, 'it [was] a very very small place', with only five newly hired technical and scientific staff.[19] Between March and June 1978, the first three scientists to be hired were the fourth, fifth, and sixth Genentech employees. They were, respectively, David Goeddel, Dennis Kleid, and Daniel Yansura.

The backgrounds of these individuals are interesting examples of

---

[18] There are different interpretations even within Genentech (Raines 1993).
[19] Kleid, quoted in an interview with a journalist, namely Lewin (1978: 925).

which types of scientific knowledge Genentech initially prioritized for their scientific and technological activities. It also indicates how individuals transferred knowledge and techniques from universities and other firms to Genentech.

Kleid received a Ph.D. in organic chemistry in 1968, then worked on a post-doc at MIT with the Nobel Prize winner H. G. Khorana, on developing synthetic organic techniques for making DNA. This is the same Khorana mentioned in relation to Itakura at City of Hope. In addition, another person working with Khorana at the time, Marv Caruthers, went on to become a professor at the University of Colorado in this field. Caruthers trained the other two scientists then hired by Genentech, namely Goeddel and Yansura. From working on techniques for synthetic DNA with Khorana, Kleid became interested in DNA sequencing after a time and worked with Mark Ptashne at Harvard BioLabs, who in turn collaborated with the highly renowned scientist Gilbert.[20] Gilbert's group worked on insulin.

In 1974, Kleid got a job at the Stanford Research Institute south of San Francisco and started a lab. He then hired the post-doc Goeddel, who had studied synthetic nucleotides with Caruthers. Goeddel's colleague had been the graduate student Yansura, but he stayed at Colorado for the moment while Goeddel moved to San Francisco. According to Kleid,

At Stanford Research Institute we began to develop our own little programme following the somatostatin work, because we thought that work was such a major breakthrough. What we decided to do was to synthesize some small genes as well.

But then I [Kleid] met with Herb Boyer and Bob Swanson because they invited me to dinner with them to talk about Genentech. They were ready to move out from the university and City of Hope and start their own place and they wanted somebody to come and work on these projects. And since they were exactly what we were interested in anyway, you know we were kind of dragged—not really dragged—but the idea of working on human insulin was something we had avoided because we knew they were working on that one—but to be involved in that project would be really, really fun.

So we left Stanford Research Institute virtually a few weeks after talking with them . . . I think we talked to them in February and Dave joined them in March and I joined in April . . . And from March to June, we were buying glassware and trying to set up with all the things you need to do molecular biology. But in the mean time, the project couldn't wait so we commuted to Los Angeles, to the City of Hope. Where the insulin cloning project was being done.[21]

Boyer and Swanson thus actively recruited Kleid and Goeddel to start at Genentech to work particularly on the insulin project with City of Hope.

The quote from Kleid also indicates that he considered insulin to be a

---

[20] Gilbert and Maxim developed a new DNA sequencing technique which revolutionized the field. Their technique was practical.   [21] Kleid (1993).

hot research project but that his little group at the Stanford Research Institute had avoided it. With Genentech's resources and collaboration with Boyer and City of Hope, Kleid and Goeddel would be part of a group scientifically strong enough to compete on the insulin project. There are thus also mechanisms within the basic scientific environment which work against an infinite number of approaches to the same problem. The prospects of success and failure within niches, and consideration of who else is doing such research, can discourage groups from working on some projects. Scientists avoid areas where they feel they will not make a contribution. This process instead works to generate diversity of projects, so that those scientists who avoid an overcrowded or intensely competitive niche can work on a different project. In this case, competitors were within universities as well as in biotech firms.

Once Kleid and Goeddel decided to work at Genentech, Goeddel called Yansura and told him they had a job waiting in California, and Yansura started in June 1978.[22] The Genentech scientists collaborated with the same researchers from the City of Hope Medical Center as had worked on somatostatin. Itakura again played a vital role with his work on practical synthetic DNA. They succeeded first with insulin then continued with insulin, in parallel with hGH.

Research involving genetic engineering in the following years at Genentech was not confined to these two projects on insulin and hGH. Genentech used its specialized scientific competence in genetic engineering for a multitude of projects. After their success with insulin, Genentech worked in the succeeding years on a number of different products, generally for other firms, including interferon alpha and beta for Hoffman-LaRoche; a vaccine against hoof-and-mouth disease in co-operation with the US Department of Agriculture and funded by the International Minerals and Chemical Company; and a vaccine for hepatitis.[23] As with insulin and hGH, the Genentech scientists competed to some extent with university scientists working on similar projects.

There were, however, some differences in approaches, and Genentech saw their specific ability to generate new products potentially profitable for themselves or for another firm as the main purpose behind these scientific and technological activities. Reaching these goals, nevertheless, often required quite path-breaking scientific activities. The R & D contracts with Lilly and Kabi were thus part of Genentech's larger strategy to sell scientific and technological activities in genetic engineering for various firms.

The legal terms of the R & D contracts give insights into property

---

[22] Yansura (1992, 1993a).
[23] Sources on these various products include Wade (1980: 34), Yansura (1992, 1993a), Lin (1993b), USDA (1981), and Genentech (1981).

rights, including payments of licensing fees as well as the types of knowledge, techniques, and biological materials specified. Under the contract with Lilly, signed 24 August 1978,

Genentech agreed to provide Lilly with recombinant DNA micro-organisms, including plasmids (recombinant DNA-containing material) capable of producing insulin, related patent rights, trade secrets, technology and know-how in return for research fees and continuing royalty payments of 8% of Lilly's insulin sales.[24]

Genentech thus agreed to transfer all the knowledge, techniques, and secrets that Lilly needed to know about the insulin-producing bacteria.

Quite importantly, the R & D contract stipulated that Genentech had to deliver micro-organisms which could produce a commercially viable amount of protein at a certain level of purity. This was one of the most important bench-marks for commercially-viable-scale production, and it took until 1980 before Genentech reached that goal. This indicates that even after scientific research, Genentech had to continue to engage in knowledge-seeking activities to solve such challenges. Solving these challenges often entailed changing some of the genetic engineering techniques and biological materials. In this case, firms' necessity of solving all the practical problems involved in translating knowledge into practice required the expression of proteins at a sufficient quantity, quality, and reliability.

The contract also limited the extent to which Lilly could use the said genetic engineering knowledge for purposes other than insulin. The techniques and knowledge were only for insulin. The contract 'granted Lilly the exclusive right "to use Genentech Recombinant Microorganisms *for the limited purpose of manufacturing, selling and using Recombinant Insulin"'.*[25] Genentech thus did not want to transmit knowledge, techniques, or biological material which would be public and generally valid for this purpose. They wanted to sell them to Lilly solely for insulin. Because Genentech specialized in selling research contracts, their interest lay in getting paid for each new application of genetic engineering and not in the development of general and publicly available techniques and knowledge. This is not to say that Genentech never engaged in the development of public and/or scientific knowledge, but that the context-dependent applications were intended to be sold one by one. A major reason for the Genentech and Lilly conflict in the US courts was Lilly's potential breach of the above clause. Genentech alleged that Lilly

---

[24] Genentech (1987: 6).
[25] Ibid., emphasis in original. On 14 July 1980, the contract was amended to define Recombinant Organisms very specifically, thereby covering many different interpretations and giving Genentech ownership over all possible mutations and changes to their original material, even if Genentech were not involved in these later transformations of the material.

used knowledge and techniques given for insulin in order to develop animal and human growth hormones.

Genentech's insulin and hGH contracts are interesting partly because they were two of the very first R & D contracts based on genetic engineering to be signed. They set the common pattern of specialized biotech firms selling genetic engineering knowledge, know-how, and biological material to established firms. It is still difficult to know all the details about these contracts because secrecy about details is endemic in business contracts to protect firms' investments, even for ones signed so long ago.

Because there has not been a patent dispute, and hence there has been more secrecy, the details of the Kabi and Genentech contract are less clear than the Lilly contract. One of the Kabi signers, Åberg, has written that the hGH bacteria cost a million dollars, or approximately seven million Swedish crowns; another declined to comment about costs fifteen years later.[26] In addition to this one million dollars, e.g. the up-front costs for the knowledge-seeking activities, Kabi also agreed to pay an undisclosed percentage in royalties to Genentech, which would in turn also be divided with City of Hope and UCSF.[27] The 8% that Lilly pays would be a qualified guess for the Kabi contract, although Kabi employees say the percentage has changed over time.[28]

Transfer of knowledge and know-how was seen as important for the fulfilment of the contracts. For example, the hGH contract gave Kabi the opportunity to learn from Genentech through direct co-operation. The contract stated that Kabi was entitled to send one or two individuals to Genentech to learn about the bacteria expression system. Know-how thus involved more than the written word, and it appears to have required transfer directly between individuals—what we can call hands-on experience and experimentation. Kabi and Lilly also had the right to improvements that Genentech later made in the respective bacteria expression system. Genentech ultimately gave Kabi at least three bacteria expression constructions with improved yields. Lilly got both the A and B chain insulin, and the proinsulin, expression systems.

The place of hGH in Genentech's strategy must be related to Swanson's vision that Genentech should develop into an integrated pharmaceutical firm. Genentech could choose from a number of potential products to manufacture based on genetic engineering, as indicated by

---

[26] Figures from, respectively, an article based on interviews with Åberg in Andersson (1990), Åberg (1982), and from Sievertsson (1992). At one point, the internal leader of Kabi's development team for recombinant DNA hGH, Linda Fryklund, pulled out the thick Genentech-Kabi contract. After checking the date of the signatures but not showing the document, she carefully locked the document away again.   [27] Kleid (1994).
[28] Holmström (1992).

the breadth of projects listed above. Originally, Genentech only intended to perform the R & D contract for Kabi, not develop hGH into their own product. According to Kabi employees, Genentech's idea of manufacturing hGH 'developed during 1979–1980 as commercialization appeared realistic'.[29] hGH was only one of several projects that Genentech could have chosen to develop, but there were important differences between markets for different products. Lilly was not willing to share the insulin market or jointly develop insulin production with Genentech. Nor was Genentech overly eager to try to enter a market that was so completely dominated by only a few firms.[30] Insulin was therefore not particularly appealing as a first product for a new firm.

According to Genentech employees, the firm viewed human growth hormone as a sort of test case, a pilot run before making a really profitable product. hGH would teach them how to develop the necessary component technologies to support a production system based on genetic engineering. They would also develop experience and competences about how to get approval for, and market, a pharmaceutical. hGH was thought to be a small product, with a potential market of about $10 million in sales.[31] It would be a decent-sized product for a new firm, and one with only a few competitors.

The market seemed quite open. Kabi was at least willing to divide up the world market for genetically engineered hGH (rDNA hGH). hGH had no dominant commercial supplier in the USA, in that the government-financed NPA supplied the majority of patients. It was likely that the government would stop financing these activities once a market alternative had been established. There was also a clear potential to expand the market beyond that which the existing supply could cover. In the original 1978 contract, the two firms had non-exclusive rights to the American market whereas Kabi had the rights to the rest of the world. Kabi and Genentech had 'semi-exclusive rights' to the American market, meaning both could sell recombinant hGH there; in 1980, however, that was changed to give Genentech exclusive rights.[32]

Because Genentech was interested both in selling R & D contracts and in manufacturing pharmaceuticals, the management/owners perceived a need to accumulate and develop scientific and technical knowledge, skills, and equipment to meet both goals. They had to succeed both in the basic scientific and scientific-economic environments with genetic engineering and in the techno-economic environments with a biological production system for the pharmaceuticals.

---

[29] Fryklund (1993).　　　[30] Clayton (1986: 64).　　　[31] Young (1992), Kleid (1993).
[32] Fryklund (1992). Kabi also gave up the rights to the Canadian market. 'The decision was made not to enter the US market at that point' (Fryklund 1993).

hGH would be a test case for products, just as somatostatin was a test case for genetic engineering techniques for human proteins. In later developing production systems, Genentech researchers experimented, for example, with the hGH bacteria in parallel with other proteins like somatostatin and insulin.

In 1978, however, Genentech concentrated on the basic scientific side of genetic engineering. No existing scientific activities for the basic scientific environment had independently developed the novelty that was needed to apply the technology to commercial goals. Reaching commercial goals required risk-taking; knowledge-seeking activities could be financed but the outcome and consequences were uncertain. Genentech expanded to a total of about twenty employees and four laboratories by the end of 1978.

Kabi—Swedish Politics and Commercialization

Although Lilly, Genentech, and Kabi all perceived the economic and technical potential of genetic engineering for the manufacture of pharmaceuticals, Kabi faced somewhat different tasks to translate perception into innovation in the late 1970s. Genentech had in mind the development of genetic engineering for multiple commercial uses, whereas Eli Lilly monitored different technologies and tried to gain access to different genetic engineering techniques for insulin. The Swedish firm Kabi concentrated on its R & D contract with Genentech for hGH. Unlike the new firm Genentech, which lauded genetic engineering *per se*, Kabi wanted an alternative source of supply for their main pharmaceutical product. Kabi was less focused on the genetic engineering and basic scientific results than Lilly.

Individuals at UCSF, at Genentech, or who eventually moved from one to the other, pursued ideas and experiments dealing specifically with genetic engineering. Kabi, particularly the powerful upper research management Sievertsson, Åberg, and Andrén, faced different types of tasks enabling commercialization. In this initial period, their role mainly involved influencing the public context and in taking care of both the hGH expression system and genetic engineering in general.

Kabi management also recognized that genetic engineering represented a break with their past production system for pituitary hGH extracted from tissue. We can say that Kabi needed to find a way to jump to a new technical trajectory based on genetic engineering. At the same time, they did not intend to give up the technical trajectory, including knowledge, techniques, and material, that the firm had developed around tissue extraction of hGH. They would develop the two technologies in parallel and might be able to use their competences and experiences to jump to the new trajectory. Basic scientific research in molecular biology and related fields was definitely not Kabi's main activity, but Kabi tried to develop quickly the ability to take care of techniques and biological material developed on the basis of such knowledge.

Kabi's management tasks were concentrated on commercializing the technology and the final product. In addition to financing various types of knowledge-seeking activities, this involved shaping environmental conditions and the public context. It included obtaining financing, putting together internal research groups, and so forth. Like Lilly, Kabi was an existing firm, with an existing profile of products and competences, who wanted to develop a new technology. Signing a letter of intent with Genentech in December 1977 was just the beginning of a series of decisions and events enabling Kabi to explore, and push forward, the possibilities for commercialization of genetic engineering.

Initially, this involved keeping an eye on the hGH project that the Genentech scientists were supposed to be doing. The R & D contract was signed in August 1978, but that was preceded by the letter of intent in December 1977. The research managers Sievertsson and/or Åberg travelled to South San Francisco about once a month during late 1977 to early 1979 in order to check up on their project. In an interview, Sievertsson said that there were two main reasons that they followed the hGH project so closely: (1) It was such a major, expensive research project compared to Kabi's budget, and it was therefore natural to see the advances first-hand. (2) Due to the uncertainties. At that time, it was 'incredibly futuristic to think that a stomach bacteria could make human proteins'.[33] In other words, it seemed like a pipe-dream and involved large risks. Kabi was curious about whether or not Genentech would be able to deliver the scientific breakthrough they had promised.

In addition to checking up on Genentech's search activities, Kabi had the months between December 1977 and August 1978 to plan how to take care of both genetic engineering techniques and the specific bacteria for hGH within the firm and within Sweden. Although Kabi had experience with biological processes, neither they nor any other firm in the world had previously worked with genetically engineered bacteria on a commercial scale. In addition to learning about the bacteria, the research managers felt it was also imperative that Kabi develop their own experience in genetic engineering for future products. Thus, although Kabi became interested in the new genetic engineering trajectory for their main product hGH, they also saw the potential that the new technology offered for generating new products and/or improving production of existing ones.

---

[33] Sievertsson (1992).

To develop competences related to genetic engineering, Kabi helped start a biotech company named KabiGen in 1978. This was an alternative to starting up a new department within the firm. It should be emphasized that despite this strategy to develop molecular biology competences for other products, Kabi clearly relied on Genentech for the rDNA hGH project. As to why Kabi started KabiGen, there are many interpretations. The upper research manager Åberg explains the strategy to start KabiGen as follows:

I felt a strong NIH—Not Invented Here—complex against the recombinant DNA adventure in KabiVitrum. Bengt Andrén and I therefore thought that it was better to locate this development project to a special company, especially since one could see the necessity of Kabi acquiring its own competence in the area of recombinant DNA, if the project succeeded. So KabiGen AB was built in 1978.[34]

Bertil Åberg became the first managing director of KabiGen, and even more than Genentech, KabiGen was initially a very, very small place, but did not expand as rapidly as Genentech.[35] As Åberg says in the quote, 'if the [hGH] project succeeded' and thereby showed that genetic engineering could live up to its perceived commercial potential, Kabi wanted close access to, and control over, basic research competences related to biotech. Kabi felt it needed to act quickly to have the possibility of developing its own commercial applications of the technology in the future.

Åberg thus presents one explanation of KabiGen, the Not Invented Here complex, implying that his vision of genetic engineering met stiff resistance within Kabi. In other words, genetic engineering represented a new and uncertain technical trajectory for the firm that threatened Kabi's existing core competence and experience base. In his written account, Åberg (1982) argues that Swedes in general (in public debate) and particularly politicians were hostile to the new technology and made its commercial development difficult.

The other upper R & D manager driving this innovation process at Kabi, Hans Sievertsson, says, 'All innovations meet resistance' and shrugs off Åberg's account.[36] In short, innovative firms and individuals should expect resistance and act to mitigate it as best they can. Sievertsson's interpretation has been seconded by Fryklund, who was later

[34] Åberg (1982: 59), my translation.
[35] There was a serious fall-out between Åberg and Kabi in 1982, at which point Åberg left KabiGen to start his own biotech company, Skandigen. This new company was heavily financed by the venture capitalist Thomas Fischer. It was more a clearing-house for genetic engineering, which made deals between firms and which supported research in general—rather than trying to develop its own products. By 1982, Sievertsson had also left Kabi to move to Bofors; he returned to Kabi (Pharmacia) in the early 1990s.
[36] Sievertsson (1992).

project leader for the rDNA hGH project. Fryklund continues, 'This [NIH explanation] is not true. The reason for KabiGen was to permit Kabi's own development for other products. All the work done on hGH was done by Kabi [not KabiGen] scientists.'[37] The last comment indicates some conflicts between KabiGen and Kabi, where Åberg and KabiGen seem to have received too much credit for the rDNA hGH project.

Another reason that Kabi started KabiGen may have been to protect Kabi from a scandal or backlash against genetic engineering. If something dramatic happened, then it would be KabiGen which would be hurt, not Kabi. As mentioned earlier, a heated and critical public debate about genetic engineering was then under way in Sweden.

Starting KabiGen was also an economically strategic decision by Kabi in relation to the rDNA hGH project. By placing the contract with Genentech in KabiGen, the initial costs for travelling, and the contract itself, could come out of KabiGen's budget rather than Kabi's already strained research budget.[38] KabiGen's first bill was about a million dollars, up front, to pay the Genentech R & D contract. Åberg has written that they knew they could not just take that million dollars out of Kabi's normal R & D budget but instead had to find an alternative source of funding.[39] Such external R & D did not come out of Kabi's ordinary R & D budget.

KabiGen was the first biotech firm in Scandinavia, started in 1978. Kabi jointly started and owned it with Statsföretag, the holding company for Swedish government-owned firms. Why, then, was Per Sköld, head of Statsföretag, interested in joint ownership of KabiGen and in financing the R & D contract with Genentech? Sievertsson says that Sköld was interested because he had studied some chemistry and molecular biology and could see the possibilities. 'It doesn't have to be more remarkable than that.'[40] Åberg was also very well connected with individuals and groups in Swedish public life and very energetic about creating support for genetic engineering. Personal relations build a basis for trust, which can facilitate financing for long-term or risky goals.[41] Important as well in this context, Kabi was 100% owned by the Swedish state, which therefore had a direct interest in its development.

For whatever reason that Kabi succeeded in getting the Swedish government to finance KabiGen, this financing was vital for the hGH project. Without those Swedish crowns and without Statsföretag's support, Kabi could not have moved as quickly into genetic engineering. Sievertsson indicated that without both their financial and moral support, he did not think the rDNA hGH project would have got off the

---

[37] Fryklund (1993).   [38] Åberg (1982), Sievertsson (1992).   [39] Åberg (1982).
[40] Sievertsson (1992).
[41] Swanson similarly relied on personal relations for the initial financing of Genentech from his former employer, the venture capital company Kleiner and Perkins.

ground at all. In the worst-case scenario, resistance within Kabi might have overwhelmed these managers' attempts to introduce genetic engineering into the firm. Kabi scientists have said that there was no resistance among scientists.[42] Obviously, however, a firm is composed of many categories of employees, and the corporate researchers involved with the technology should be more positive than others. One implication is that individuals within a firm who actively try to introduce and develop a new technological trajectory will face resistance but can overcome that by relying on support from powerful outside allies.

In January 1979, Statsföretag sold its 50 per cent share of KabiGen to two firms in the Swedish Cardo business group, namely Sockerbolaget (literally, 'sugar company') and Hilleshög (a plant development company).[43] These two firms were interested in using genetic engineering to improve plants, and thereby saw a different type of technical and economic potential for genetic engineering than the pharmaceutical potential envisioned by Kabi. Thus, another explanation for the formation of KabiGen was to make genetic engineering available to Swedish firms in general. After all, Statsföretag and then two established firms went in and helped finance KabiGen; surely they expected something out of the deal. Over the years, KabiGen's corporate strategy has oscillated between providing genetic engineering research and knowledge only to Kabi and providing it to Swedish industry in general. It has thus played several roles in relation to the introduction and use of this new technology in Sweden.

The Swedish state helped Kabi begin its technological trajectory into the commercial use of genetic engineering in another way as well. In addition to getting money to start KabiGen and to finance the R & D contract, Kabi also immediately applied for a special eleven-and-a-half-million-crown ($1.5 million) loan from the governmental Industrial Fund (Industrifonden). Kabi received the money later but Åberg and Sievertsson applied around 1978. This was a state agency which loaned Swedish companies money for (risky) product development work, initially for large industrial projects like Saab civil aircraft. Such loans reduced risks for the firm, as the firm only had to repay the loan if the product was successful. Swedish technology policy thus included direct support for

[42] Fryklund (1993), Fhölenhag (1992).

[43] Sievertsson (1992), Brunius (1992a). Later, other companies owned parts of KabiGen, but it has since been incorporated into Pharmacia, which was the result of a merger in 1990/91 between KabiVitrum and Pharmacia, a company which was more into diagnostics, research equipment, and medical equipment. After the merger, KabiGen changed its name to 'BioScience Center' and later integrated into the company. Many Swedish companies were initially quite interested in genetic engineering; for example, in October 1982, four Swedish organizations—Alfa Laval AB, the Wallenberg Foundation, AB Fannyudde [Volvo], and D. Carengie and Company—bought $20 million of shares in Genentech, and Harry Faulkner, Vice-President for Alfa-Laval, sat on Genentech's board of directors.

product development, based on the argument that scientific research does not transform itself into a product. Much of the initial seed money for KabiGen and for Kabi's hGH project thus came from Swedish government agencies rather than from market financiers. This is quite different from Genentech, financed through the market, and from Eli Lilly, financed mainly by retained earnings. Swedish political agencies complemented market forces more directly and were thus important factors explaining why Kabi was able to start a new technological trajectory.

Financial factors were not the only ones affecting Kabi's ability to develop products based on genetic engineering. Concurrent with Kabi's manoeuvring in 1978 to build support for a new biotech firm, the Swedish government was pressured to implement official regulation for genetic engineering. The Swedish public context was in a period involving much debate over the technology. Pressure on the government came partly from the scientists in the Genetic Manipulation Advisory Group committee (GMAC) and partly from the political necessity of acting on a hot media topic when there was a parliamentary election the following year.[44] The debate called for the creation of a new public context which would be under government control and which would direct the exploration of scientific and technological activities using these techniques.

Åberg's account of that period stresses the intense tone of the debate and in particular the negative attitudes:

A great controversy among the public creates among decision-making politicians, of course, partly agitation and partly the feeling that something must be done. Certain facts were systematically wrong in the mass media, and it is impossible to judge where this occurred due to dubious intentions—to increase the customer base—or due to their unwillingness to obtain scientific facts.[45]

Åberg was thus cynical about the reasons that debaters had negative opinions about the techniques, including accusing some political parties of attempting 'to increase the customer base' by playing to popular opinion, which was hostile to new technology. As mentioned earlier, a Swedish mass media debate had started in the autumn of 1977 over Uppsala's high-safety lab, and this largely negative debate ran through spring 1978.

Kabi, represented by Åberg and his colleague at KabiGen, Kerstin Sirvell, published their first significant debate article about the technology in *Dagens Nyheter* on 3 February 1978. Like the scientist Professor Philipson in Uppsala, they criticized the unscientific tone of debate,

---

[44] However, the really big Swedish debate at the time was about nuclear power.
[45] Åberg (1982: 62), my translation.

especially in Åkerman's articles, and wanted to give a different picture of the potential of genetic engineering. Just as Åkerman painted the fantastic dangers of the new technology, Kabi wanted to show the fantastic possibilities and the negative consequences of not following them up. More particularly, Åberg and Sirvell argued that prohibiting recombinant DNA experiments would make Swedish universities and industry dependent on foreigners and that Sweden would take the risk of losing jobs in the future. These are arguments that weigh heavily in many debates in Sweden, a small neutral country always struggling for independence and high-paying industrial jobs.

Åberg and Sirvell also had a plan to nip further opposition in the bud by calling for the creation of new official regulations which would make it clear to everyone what trajectories of knowledge-seeking activities were and were not allowable. They wanted to

Replace voluntary reporting to the research councils' committee [GMAC] with obligatory reporting for all researchers in Sweden active in the field! Legally see to it that the recombinant DNA committee gets the right to decide on prohibition or permission for certain research. Place democratic representatives on the committee.[46]

Åberg and Sirvell thus clearly called for official regulation, including features, such as democratic representation, that also met the demands of critics. The view they represented was heard by the government.

Indeed, the centre-right, three-party coalition government decided on 16 February 1978 to empower the Minister of Education Wickström to investigate legislation and to make regulatory proposals. Instead of a government investigation (*statlig utredning*) which involves many people and much time, the Swedish government gave the investigation to the Department of Education, who in turn appointed one man. The investigator, Bertil Wennergren, was ready ten months later, on 1 December 1978, with the report *Recombinant DNA Under Control*.[47] In short, Wennergren proposed legislative changes to place activities using recombinant DNA technique and molecules under the existing environmental, workplace, and public health laws, as well as proposing a special committee to take over the supervisory tasks of the GMAC committee. This new committee was to propose guidelines for activities and would be official rather than organized by scientists. The proposal was similar to American and British regulations, and committees.

Like those Americans making policy, these Swedes felt genetic engineering could be handled within existing laws and therefore rejected the idea of making completely new, special laws for the technology. A

---

[46] Åberg and Sirvell (1978: 2), my translation.
[47] DsU (1978), my translation. See also the description of this investigation in a later official investigation (SOU 1992 ch. 3).

parliamentary decision about these proposals came in late 1979 (see next chapter). The Wennergren report was quite up to date on American debates and risk classification, so it is not without importance for both countries that in December 1977, the same month that Wennergren presented his report, the American NIH revised its guidelines, making them less strict.

Both the Swedish debate and the resulting proposal for Swedish legislation were initially stimulated by events in the United States, but soon gathered their own momentum, where events internal to Sweden, like the Uppsala lab, the election interests of political parties, Kabi's industrial interest in genetic engineering, and the Wennergren report were used to shape the public context to direct knowledge-seeking activities in Sweden.

Rivals at and in UCSF and Genentech

This chapter has so far followed the strategies and actions of the three firms Lilly, Genentech, and Kabi in their attempts to generate and access scientific and technological knowledge and techniques for the economic environments in 1978. The actions and perceptions of these firms and of UCSF influenced each other but also represented parallel knowledge-seeking activities for different environments. These three firms clearly affected the rate and direction of scientific activities for the basic scientific environment by developing closely related activities for other environments. Their knowledge-seeking activities involved scientific research and the development of techniques applicable within both the basic scientific and scientific-economic environments. This section will more closely examine incentives and institutions within the basic scientific environment which led to the creation of novelty leading to diversity relevant for commercial use of genetic engineering.

Backtracking to explore scientific activities at universities relevant for insulin and hGH, we can recall that Genentech was one of three American research groups trying to clone and express insulin; the other two were Baxter and Goodman's group at UCSF and Gilbert's group at Harvard. These competing groups were all high-prestige, élite groups, and the fact that they were working on insulin acted to discourage smaller and less prestigious research groups. For human growth hormone, Genentech and UCSF both co-operated and competed.

The basic scientific environment did not have incentives to generate a maximum diversity of attempts to solve one problem. There was instead limited competition among similarly gifted and resource-strong scientists. These groups often had somewhat different approaches, which in turn allowed them to co-operate as well as compete. Perhaps most interestingly, both the insulin and human growth hormone projects showed that the technological activities of new biotech firms could compete with scientific activities of university scientists in certain cases. Nevertheless, the basic university scientists and the corporate researchers worked in response to different environmental conditions. Each tried to answer somewhat different questions relevant to their current environment, but their activities and results were similar enough also to allow direct co-operation and discussions.

The university lab at UCSF involved in both insulin and hGH is particularly interesting, partly because one of the co-founders of Genentech, Boyer, was a tenured faculty member there and partly because some conflicts arose between Genentech and UCSF and between individuals originally working at UCSF. Some of these conflicts had to do with the assignment of academic credit between the older scientists who had built up the labs and the younger scientists who worked in that lab for a limited period. Other conflicts had to do with the personalities of the individuals or with conflicts of interest between basic scientific and commercial goals.

Just as Kleid and Goeddel moved north the thirty-five kilometres (twenty-three miles) from Stanford Research Institute to Genentech in early 1978, a number of individuals moved south the fifteen kilometres (ten miles) from UCSF to Genentech in late 1978 and 1979. Eventually, Genentech hired at least three former post-docs from this department, including Axel Ullrich, Peter Seeburg, and Herb Heyneker. Genentech also later hired the full tenured professor Dave Martin, who had been a post-doc there as well.[48] The conflicts between Genentech and UCSF had some consequences for the direction of scientific activities related to rDNA hGH.

Although the following two accounts of events should be seen as only one side of the story, they provide indications of tensions between senior scientists and some post-docs within the Department of Biochemistry and Biophysics at UCSF.

In fact, one person clearly contributed to the hGH research of both UCSF and Genentech, namely the UCSF post-doc Peter Seeburg. He worked on this project at UCSF before moving to Genentech. According to an article in the *New York Times Magazine* based on an interview, Seeburg came to UCSF as a post-doc from Germany with the idea of synthesizing a human gene, and subsequently worked with Boyer, Goodman, and Baxter on different projects. He had conflicts with all of them.

---

[48] Robbins-Roth (1991: 36) names all four as former UCSF post-docs. Goeddel (1993), however, points out that Martin was a full professor when he moved to Genentech.

One day, it occurred to Seeburg that human growth hormone might be an ideal prospect. Baxter seized upon the idea. [But there were conflicts between medical doctors like Baxter and the Ph.d.'s] . . . . They [Boyer and Goodman] told me, 'You either do it on your own or you don't do it. We don't want Baxter in it', Seeburg recalls. But that would have been impossible. . . . So during the day I worked on something that Boyer and Goodman wanted and at night I worked on human growth hormone with John Baxter. . . . Later, Goodman began to collaborate with Seeburg and another young recombinant DNA scientist, Joe Martial.[49]

In this account, Seeburg perceives that he came up with an ideal research project on human growth hormone but in order to carry out his idea had to work secretly with Baxter. Goodman and Boyer were then co-operating. Goodman later became interested in the project described here as Seeburg's idea.

This description of the conflict says much about Seeburg's contemporary perception of the conflicts. A very different perception of the conflicts is given by another post-doc working on insulin in the department at the time. According to him, Seeburg as a post-doc 'served at the pleasure of the laboratory director and should not have been doing experiments against the wishes of the laboratory director'.[50] Moreover, in the long run, Seeburg needed both Baxter and Goodman to find and clone mammalian, and eventually human, growth hormone genes. Seeburg could never have carried out the project on his own or in collaboration with only one of them. As a medical doctor and an endocrinologist, Baxter

would have appreciated the importance of hGH. He would also have been able to get the human pituitaries and GH secreted tumors (if these were used) necessary for this project. Baxter at this time could not have provided the resources for Peter to do the cloning, but Goodman could.[51]

Seeburg thus needed Baxter as well as either Goodman or Boyer to complete this hGH project. In this situation, where the post-doc was dependent on the wishes of the lab director, Seeburg felt his contributions were ignored:

As Seeburg recounts it, he and others in the lab achieved key results in a series of experiments that clearly would lead to the hormone, and this occurred during one period when both Baxter and Goodman were traveling. 'When they came back,' Seeburg says, 'we told them what we had done and the next thing we knew they had drafted a patent without even including my name. This clinched it. I felt exploited so much I couldn't work there anymore.'[52]

The expression of anger is apparent in his feeling of being exploited. However, there is some confusion as to what patent is referred to here:

[49] Stockton (1980: 20).   [50] Chirgwin (1993: 8).   [51] Chirgwin (1993: 4).
[52] Stockton (1980: 20).

Seeburg did not do significant work on insulin, and therefore should not have been included. It may refer to a 1977 UCSF patent application for rat insulin cDNA, which was dropped soon after filing.[53] The conflict referred to above, however, was in 1978.

Hall (1988) gives a similar account of tensions between these UCSF post-docs and the senior, tenured researchers, but this time from the perspective of another post-doc, Axel Ullrich, who mainly did work on insulin. In 1978, Ullrich was carrying out experiments in France which could not be done conveniently in the USA at the time:

'I heard about that [the Rutter-Goodman-Baxter patent] while I was in France and got really angry,' says Ullrich. 'Peter [Seeburg] was angry, too. Peter said he had been approached by Swanson again, and Swanson offered him a job and reactivated the offer to me, to all three of us—John Shine, Seeburg and me. So I accepted.'[54]

Both Ullrich and Seeburg felt their contributions had been ignored according to these accounts, although again, it is not clear which patent should have included both Ullrich and Seeburg. Another interpretation for Ullrich and Seeburg's leaving the university is that Genentech offered a more stable research position than a temporary UCSF post-doc position.

The conflicts between UCSF and Genentech and the conflicts between individuals within UCSF involved both scientific prestige and commercial benefits. Individuals working in different types of organizations could carry out parallel scientific activities. Moreover, the very same individuals could respond to different environments with different activities within the same organization and/or s/he could move from an organization mainly representing one environment to another one. Seeburg and Ullrich were quite clearly hired by Genentech because they were scientists who could work with genetic engineering and solve some of the basic challenges confronting Genentech in working on the R & D contracts.

These conflicts helped generate a diversity of approaches to solving similar questions. Just like Genentech, Baxter and Goodman were also interested in commercial applications to some extent, as they accepted

[53] Kleid (1994: 3). In the opinion of Yamamoto, one faculty member not involved in this research but who was worried about the influence of commercialization on science, commercial interest could be seen in many of the post-docs' work. 'In 1977, following the cloning of rat-insulin DNA, a fellow faculty member confided that the ensuing patent application and press coverage seemed to be affecting the motivation of some of his postdoctoral colleagues, and that the potential for financial gain was an apparent consideration in the planning of their experiments' Yamamoto (1982: 197). The post-docs on that particular paper included Ullrich, John Shine, John Chirgwin, but not Seeburg (Ullrich *et al.* 1977: 196). This statement is clearly only Yamamoto's opinion and contested by Chirgwin (1993).   [54] Hall (1988: 279).

research money from Lilly for insulin and hGH, and they took out a patent instead of just publishing a paper. They had agreed to assign exclusive licences, if Lilly wanted them, for any patents arising from the hGH and insulin research projects, and licences require patents. Moreover, patenting has long been common praxis for American universities, who are major beneficiaries of patents taken out in individual researchers' names. A percentage of royalties is funnelled back into the department to support further experiments and further expansion for the university.[55] If research results can be used to compete within both environments (whether that competitive advantage is in the short- or long-term), then both a firm and a university can perceive that there are mutual benefits from interactions and joint projects.

In Hall's account of events, Seeburg and Ullrich made the decision to leave the department soon after the Baxter-Goodman-Rutter patent application in August 1978, but they remained at the department until the final months of 1978. Hall implies that the post-docs continued to work on basic scientific research during this period, probably for their (previous) advisers.[56] Eventually, Seeburg and Ullrich did leave UCSF for Genentech.

However, if the conflict between Seeburg and Ullrich versus Baxter and Goodman was as serious as Hall implies (see previous footnote), then it seems unreasonable that the two sides could have continued professional relations. They might have ignored each other's presence at the department and/or have been forced to 'sit out' a given contract period, but it is also possible that they resolved the conflict and kept collaborating. In the latter case, Hall is overstating his case. In fact, Seeburg continued collaborating with the UCSF professors during

---

[55] In Sweden, the individual researcher holds the patents and receives all royalty payments, and so the university has less institutional interest in whether individuals take out patents and whether firms license those patents. There has been some debate about changing to imitate the American situation, where the university holds the patent and royalties are divided between the university and researcher.

[56] Compare *Medical World News* (1979: 20), which similarly writes, 'One of the Genentech team, Dr. Peter Seeburg, had until late 1978 worked in Dr. Goodman's UCSF laboratory.' Another account follows. 'In November 1978, Seeburg began expressing the human growth hormone gene at UCSF despite the fact that he had already announced that he would soon leave for Genentech. Howard Goodman and Seeburg had a confrontation over this, which ended with Goodman forbidding Seeburg to continue sequencing the hGH gene in his lab. Later that night, Seeburg returned to the lab to help a fellow postdoc and suddenly he noticed that all of his test tubes had disappeared from his freezer. Those test tubes contained the answers to his experiments. Goodman had taken all that and put it in his own freezer. As Seeburg recounts it, "Instead of taking these racks, they [the test tubes] had just been thrown into his freezer. They were all lying upside down. . . . I was totally shattered. I just sat there. I couldn't believe my eyes"' (Hall 1988: 282–3). As to the validity of this story, Hall writes, 'The account of this episode comes from Peter Seeburg and was independently confirmed by two other members of the Goodman laboratory; Howard Goodman declined to be interviewed' (Hall 1988: 282). As mentioned, however, postdocs work at the discretion of the lab director. Rather than the interpretation offered by Hall—an example of how terrible Goodman was—this incident can alternatively be seen as a clash between two strong personalities, where Seeburg bears some of the blame for doing experiments explicitly forbidden by the lab director.

1979, that is after leaving UCSF for Genentech. They collaborated on 'cloning and DNA sequence analysis of hGH *genomic* DNA . . . Such work was of no commercial significance and was jointly published with UCSF.'[57] This indicates co-operation as well as competition among the groups, when the scientific activities were not relevant to the economic environments.

When the UCSF scientists moved to Genentech, they transferred a certain amount of knowledge and skills. To the extent that education and training are individual, it moves to the new organization. There is a range between a general body of knowledge and techniques to skills and perceptions which are individual. In either case, when a trained researcher moves from one organization to another, this adds to the retained knowledge and techniques of the new organization.

Transferring equipment and material between the old employer and the new was, however, more controversial. Because any science which relies on experimentation is more than ideas and theories, these scientists have to have access to the right material. In this case, this includes biological material such as sequence data, vectors, operons, and so forth. Biological material was necessary to carry out additional experiments. When Seeburg then moved from UCSF to Genentech in late 1978, he took some hGH clones to Genentech.

'I had largely started the growth-hormone project and worked on it since 1975. Why shouldn't I take material which I had acquired?' Seeburg asks. 'I didn't take anything exclusively. Whatever I took I left some behind.'[58]

Seeburg's statement here takes the extreme opposite position of Chirgwin, also a post-doc in the department at the time:

If your major professor permits you to take anything of your own creation with you when you leave, you consider yourself fortunate. When I left UCSF, I took no reagents with me and later asked in writing for a couple of cloned insulin probes, nothing more.[59]

Taking material, even your own creation, when you leave a university is a complicated issue in experimental fields. It is a question about how much is the private property of the individual or of the research group at an organization and how much is privately held or public information. Transferring biological materials is a potential problem which goes well beyond the post-docs and their irritations with the senior UCSF researchers.

On the one hand, researchers in the field routinely gave away samples of their biological material to other researchers, so it would not at all have been unusual for UCSF researchers to give hGH clones to Genen-

---

[57] Kleid (1994: 5), emphasis in original.   [58] Stockton (1980: 20).
[59] Chirgwin (1993: 4).

tech or to other researchers working in the same field. After all, exchanging material is necessary to repeat experiments.[60] In later experiments, for example, Genentech got new promoters from university groups. On the other hand, UCSF and Genentech considered each other competitors to some extent in these experiments. Whereas UCSF would have been willing to send material to Genentech after they had published a paper and hence after receiving scientific credit, they might not have wanted to do so beforehand. It was probably not in UCSF's interest to send out biological material enabling Genentech to carry out a similar experiment before UCSF had published. An initially restrictive flow of material hampers direct imitation and may thus be a mechanism inside science which helps generate diversity among competing groups.[61] The incentive to restrict flow is that being first with high quality results is important in the basic scientific institutional context.

That Seeburg moved material from UCSF to Genentech is not under dispute, but one question debated in the extensive patent disputes between Genentech, UCSF, and Lilly has been whether Seeburg had any right to take material considered UCSF property as well as what he actually brought with him. Seeburg moved to Genentech at the end of 1978, but the two scientific papers on hGH were published almost a year later. Many have wondered what advantages Seeburg's material conferred on Genentech. Could Genentech have done the research as quickly without these materials? Patent distrust lead to a situation of dispute and concealment so these questions have a variety of answers.

The most important thing that Seeburg could have taken with him to Genentech was the hGH cDNA clone. Finding the original gene can require searching through the ten thousand to hundred thousands of base pairs in a mammalian gene for those few segments which code for it. This was time- and resource-consuming. Instead of finding the whole gene, researchers can make a copy of the final, much shortened message (mRNA) as sent to the cytoplasm of the cell. This is called a cDNA clone.

---

[60] Genentech was later involved in a similar conflict with UCSF over whether the company could make a commercial product out of a freely-given cell line. In autumn 1980, Hoffman-LaRoche filed suit against UC over damage to reputation about a conflict over interferon. According to an article in the *San Francisco Chronicle*, UC had been considering suing LaRoche and Genentech for 'unauthorized use of interferon-producing cells sent to them for testing'. Genentech had received the cell culture from the National Cancer Institute, which in turn had received samples from two UC researchers. UC claimed that the companies could not market interferon, because it came from a strain of cells discovered at UC. In contrast, Genentech and LaRoche claimed that the cells were given without restrictions. These two firms viewed their own work in modifying them with genetic engineering as the novelty, not the strain of cells *per se* that the medical researchers had provided. Hoffman-LaRoche therefore sued UC for damage to reputation (Benfell 1980).
[61] See *Science* (1990) for an interesting discussion of this topic. The argument there is that researchers are less willing to share samples today.

To get such a copy of the message for hGH, human pituitary glands secreting hGH were a necessary starting point. Seeburg had access to such glands at UCSF through Baxter. In addition, he needed to do many experiments to find the right sequence and Goodman (or Boyer) could provide the lab and equipment necessary for these scientific activities. The university lab had offered Seeburg the possibility of finding and sequencing the cDNA clones for hGH, and he did scientific research on this project there. In their published paper on hGH, the Genentech group acknowledge that the RNA used was prepared by Seeburg while at UCSF.[62]

Like UCSF, Genentech needed these cDNA clones. Or rather, Genentech needed the gene which could allow them to make some synthetic DNA for hGH. There are many interpretations of whether or not there were conflicts. One of the Genentech scientists involved, Yansura, recollects, 'Yeah, I can't remember. I think Peter Seeburg had cloned it over there, in Howard Goodman's lab or something like that. And then Dave [Goeddel], I guess he recloned it here so we could have it separately.' When asked why Genentech would have to reclone the hGH, Yansura replied, 'We didn't want to just ask them to send the clone over. First of all, they probably wouldn't have done it. And secondly, it wouldn't look too good in legal terms if we had used their DNA.'[63] A person then working at UCSF but with no inside knowledge comments, 'I certainly had the impression that Peter isolated the hGH cDNA clone and then used it to barter a position at Genentech.' In his view, 'Seeburg's cDNA had both immediate and mid-range commercial possibilities.'[64] The Genentech scientist thus argued it would have been silly to do anything other than reclone it, whereas the 'outsider' had a more conspiratorial view.

Genentech scientist and now legal consultant Kleid recounts this sequence of events:

Dr. David Goeddel cloned Genentech's cDNA for hGH (encoding amino acids 24–191) *at Genentech*. The procedures were straight forward compared to that used by UCSF. . . . After 1978 the NIH Guidelines were relaxed, so Dr. Goeddel and Genentech didn't have to do that [enrich human cDNA to greater than 99%, or do an experiment done in a P4 lab or out of the country]. Genentech used the standard procedures. The hGH cDNA cloning by UCSF was done in mid-1978 (or late 1977) with a cDNA fragment that was highly purified. The cloning of the full-length hGH cDNA [by] UCSF may have been done in mid-1978 out of the country. All of this work was already published by UCSF, and patents filed. . . .

---

[62] The hGH paper, done at Genentech (Goeddel *et al.* 1979: 548), specifically states that 'RNA used was prepared by P.H.S. while a postdoctoral fellow in the Department of Biochemistry and Biophysics, University of California at San Francisco.' This same article also refers to articles which list Seeburg as co-author along with Martial, Baxter, and Goodman.   [63] Yansura (1993a).   [64] Chirgwin (1993: 4).

The controversy with UCSF (long settled), apparently surrounded one of several samples of pituitary RNA belonging to Dr. Seeburg that Dr. Goeddel may have used in related work. Dr. Seeburg apparently had one RNA sample left over from the previously completed work done by himself and Martial *et al.* . . .

The only hGH sequence information Genentech had were from its own data derived in 1979 or were previously published by UCSF and/or provided to Genentech during various public seminars given by Goodman, Baxter, Martial and Seeburg.[65]

Genentech have thus argued that the information needed was public and/or the firm had skilled scientists in-house to replicate the experiment. This allowed them to use 'standard procedures' to obtain the desired cDNA clone and thereby find the hGH gene. The interpretation of events about the transfer of material versus the use of common and public knowledge has thus been under some dispute.

One reason that this has been a point of contention between Genentech and UCSF is that the importance of an hGH clone derived from naturally occurring mRNA goes beyond its use for hGH. It could be important for related research projects. It 'could be used, by cross-species hybridization, to pull GHs [growth hormones] from other species, such as bovine, etc.'[66] Indeed, later on, Genentech entered an R & D contract with the giant American agricultural chemical company Monsanto to provide genetically modified bacteria which could produce bovine growth hormone. Thus, the knowledge, techniques, and biological material that Genentech built up internally with genetic engineering for hGH could be used to successfully complete other but similar R & D projects.

This discussion of UCSF and Genentech has concentrated to a large extent on conflicts. Earlier, there had been more co-operation between the research groups. In fact, one of the first scientists hired by Genentech, Dennis Kleid, was under the impression that Boyer and the UCSF scientists were collaborating. 'When I joined Genentech [in April 1978], I thought they [Goodman-Baxter-Rutter and Boyer] were friends, but then I found out fairly soon on that they weren't anymore. You know, I was kind of surprised by that!' In Kleid's account, the conflict came from the UCSF scientists: 'We used to work with them in the old days, but then, these guys at UC decided they could get more money by working with Lilly. So they signed a deal with Lilly that allowed Lilly to have all of their technology instead of Genentech.'[67] This indicates that Genentech would have been willing to license UCSF's technology. Moreover, according to Kleid,

The relationships [between Genentech and UCSF] were not 'bad' at that time (late 1978 and early 1979). . . . The relationships became 'bad' later, in mid-1979

---

[65] Kleid (1994: 4 and 5), emphasis in original.   [66] Chirgwin (1993: 4).
[67] Kleid (1993).

after Genentech (with Dr. Seeburg) was successful in actually producing hGH from *E. Coli* and setting the stage for developing a commercially viable process. . . . After the 1980 agreement between UC and Genentech, again the relationships were not 'bad'.[68]

Genentech's successful expression of hGH in bacteria apparently stirred up conflicts. Under the 1980 agreement which mitigated the conflict, Genentech have paid substantial royalties to the University of California system for materials (and licences) made at UCSF.

Science and Commercialization

Scientific activities leading to results (knowledge; techniques) were necessary to enable these commercial uses of genetic engineering. Because the technology was so novel, developing techniques to control nature depended upon increasing knowledge about nature, and vice versa. The two scientific papers using genetic engineering to modify bacteria to make hGH were used in Chapter 5 to identify the researchers and organizations involved in scientific research. The experiments and the scientific papers resulted from knowledge-seeking activities by two groups within the San Francisco area. These were the Genentech group and the Baxter and Goodman group at UCSF, financed respectively by Kabi and Eli Lilly. The groups also overlapped to some extent, as some individuals moved from one group to another.

As seen above, Lilly funded UCSF for research to express insulin and hGH in bacteria and funded Genentech for insulin. Kabi funded scientific activities at Genentech for hGH. One outcome of Lilly's and Kabi's funding of scientific activities was the development of practical techniques and knowledge about how to develop and use genetic engineering. These would be used later to improve the expression system in order to fulfil bench-marks in the R & D contracts about level of expression, purity, and so forth.

There could be some interesting tensions here between firms' attempts to keep their discoveries secret and scientists' desires to publicize their findings. Secrecy about scientific and technological results can be advantageous for firms in certain situations, such as getting a head start over competitors in adapting to a changing techno-economic environment. Scientists responding to the basic scientific environment, on the other hand, had few incentives to keep results secret, once their results have reached a competitive stage and can be published. What is interesting here is that both the firms funding and carrying out scientific activities as well as the scientists at universities had reasons for making some of the

---

[68] Kleid (1994: 4) emphasis in original.

results public. Both found it was important to establish basic scientific success, whether for the basic scientific or for the scientific-economic environment.

The competition over rDNA hGH extended to competition over publicity to establish the success of one group. Press and prestige through publicity of high-quality research results is one way of gaining recognition for a research group. In the basic scientific and scientific-economic environments, publicity is often necessary to succeed. It is important that each researcher or group produce research in specialized fields in order to be considered successful within the community defining the selection criteria. In firms, publicity of scientific results is sometimes necessary to establish scientific legitimacy. At other times, firms must concentrate on technological activities to transform knowledge into practice. Although scientific and technological activities are sometimes quite similar for different environments, the question still remains, To what extent did they compete with or complement each other?

There were two papers published in 1979 dealing with expression of hGH using genetic engineering techniques. In this case, a biotech firm and a university research group published competing papers in scientific journals. The first paper published was by the UCSF group. It was entitled 'Human Growth Hormone: Complementary DNA Cloning and Expression in Bacteria' and was written by four researchers. These are identified as working at the private Howard Hughes Medical Institute and at the Department of Biochemistry and Biophysics, UCSF. The four authors are Martial, Hallewell, Baxter, and Goodman. Their paper was submitted to *Science* on 8 June 1979, and published on 10 August.[69]

The second paper was submitted by Genentech researchers. It was entitled 'Direct Expression in *Escherichia coli* of a DNA Sequence Coding for Human Growth Hormone'. Their paper was submitted to *Nature* on 6 July 1979, accepted on 16 July, and published on 18 October.[70] The Genentech paper brought together a large number of specialists, with ten authors, of whom three were from the City of Hope.

UCSF thus won the race to publish first. However, the research groups were in somewhat different races in that they were directing knowledge-seeking activities and hence expected results to fit two different environments. From that perspective, UCSF lost the race to express hGH. Genentech's bacteria construction expressed hGH whereas UCSF made an uncleavable fusion protein.[71] The articles, and underlying experiments, were similar in some ways but different in orientation. UCSF were more directed towards scientific activities and Genentech more

---

[69] Martial *et al.* (1979). [70] Goeddel *et al.* (1979).
[71] Goeddel (1993), Yansura (1993b).

towards technological activities. Nevertheless, they can be considered close enough to be competing to some extent.

Both articles used similar genetic engineering techniques and biological materials. For example, UCSF cloned cDNA 'in the plasmid pBR322 and *E. coli* $_\chi$1776' and Genentech report using the same plasmid and strain of *E. coli* to find the correct DNA sequence[72] which codes for hGH. This supports the argument made in Chapter 2 that new combinations resulting from knowledge-seeking activities rely on existing knowledge, techniques, and material. These are learned and/or transmitted in the community but can be used for different purposes.

One reason for this similarity was quite simply the NIH regulation which stated that experiments must be performed on weakened strains of *E. coli* bacteria which can only live in very special conditions. These strains reduced the risk of spreading the bacteria and included the strain mentioned above. In other words, regulations in the public context induced similar research approaches.

A second reason for similarity was that both groups drew upon experience and knowledge developed in the same scientific activities previously done at UCSF. Knowledge, skills, and biological material were retained among these individual scientists, some of whom moved from the university to the firm.

A third reason is that researchers often chose to work with well-understood and much-studied biological materials as the basis of new combinations. For genetic engineering techniques, creating novelty relied on many types of biological materials and techniques being put together like puzzle pieces to constitute the experiment as a whole. In that situation, uncertainty is reduced if many of the elements have been studied and are relatively well-known.

These two experiments differed, however, in their relative orientation towards scientific activities to develop knowledge or towards technological activities to develop control over nature. Each experiment was some combination of scientific and technological activities, but they did differ in the main orientation. The heart of an experiment to use genetic engineering for commercial applications was really in getting *E. coli* bacteria to express hGH, whereas the heart of the scientific experiments was to understand how biological processes work, including identifying the gene sequence. Genentech were most specifically interested in realizing their commercial perception, whereas UCSF was most interested in the scientific questions.[73] The two groups clearly differed in emphasis.

[72] See, respectively, Martial *et al.* (1979: 603) and Goeddel *et al.* (1979: 544).

[73] Popular science articles point to significant differences in the approaches of the two groups, especially when the journalist asked the opinion of a scientist involved. In general, the reports indicate that the UCSF team saw both papers as great achievements, whereas Goeddel and Seeburg strongly argued that the Genentech experiments were the ones that were truly novel and that would introduce less clumsy techniques useful for a range of proteins. See González (1979) and *Medical World News* (1979).

These differences in emphasis were reflected in techniques and in choice of biological materials. UCSF used only DNA obtained from mRNA preparations, that is from human pituitary glands. The purpose of their experiment was mainly to find the hGH gene, a scientific purpose.[74] The UCSF group never realized expression of the protein in this experiment. The Genentech group, on the other hand, combined segments obtained with the cDNA techniques used by UCSF with chemically synthesized DNA. This gave more control and was set to realize the commercial purpose of expressing hGH.[75] The alternative purposes in response to different environments thus generated diversity of approaches even though the underlying knowledge-seeking activities were similar.

The knowledge-seeking activities of these two research groups thus led to different results in response to different environments. The environment which Genentech helped create was a hybrid one integrating scientific and economic conditions. A newly started biotech firm selling R & D contracts in the scientific-economic environment needed to build scientific prestige and reputation. Genentech scientists had to deliver results that were both basic science and applicable to commercial goals. At the time, scientific activities were necessary for being able to work with genetic engineering and highly dependent upon basic scientific knowledge and techniques. Scientific recognition in the basic scientific environment was therefore important for proving the quality of Genentech's activities.

Acclaim in the basic scientific environment is won by being first to produce new results of high quality, and both UCSF and Genentech scientists had reasons to want scientific acclaim. Genentech published after UCSF, but they did not lose the race they were running. Even in the basic scientific environment, their results were valuable because Genentech did something new: they coupled together synthetic DNA with an existing copy of a gene. In the scientific-economic environment, being able to make and use practical synthetic DNA proved necessary for controlling nature for commercial applications.

Like somatostatin and insulin before it, the scientists' hGH experiments were reported in the mass media. As in the somatostatin case, the experiments were discussed in the mass media before scientific articles were published. In the case of hGH, both research groups gave out press releases, resulting in mass media stories based on unpublished papers.

[74] To see whether hGH gene sequences can be expressed in bacteria, [the UCSF group] 'used the plasmid p*trp* ED5-1, which contains the regulatory region [(po)La], the first gene (*trp* E), and 15 percent of the second gene (*trp* D) of the *E. coli trp* operon' (Martial *et al.* 1979: 605).

[75] They then joined together the two separately cloned hGH DNA fragments, and used 'a plasmid (pGH6) having two *lac* promotors' to express hGH in *E. coli* (Goeddel *et al.*, 1979: 545).

Spyros Andreopoulos of the News Bureau of Stanford University Medical Center examined this phenomenon for 1978 to 1980 and compared the promises with the scientific results in the published paper.[76] In an article in *The New England Journal of Medicine*, Andreopoulos discusses three cases of so-called 'press-release science' about pharmaceutical products, all promulgated by new biotech companies:

1. Genentech and City of Hope's press release in September 1978 that they had produced 'human insulin' using recombinant DNA techniques.
2. Genentech's and UCSF's competing press announcements in July 1979 on human growth hormone.
3. Biogen's announcement of 'clones of interferon-producing bacteria' in January 1980.[77]

Two of the three cases analysed thus involved Genentech and the third one involved the biotech firm Biogen, started by Gilbert. Andreopoulos argued that these press releases contained information which had not yet been substantiated by other scientists but which was used to gain publicity for the firms.

Publicity highlights successes, not the trial and error and failures of a process of evolutionary innovation. All three of Genentech's initial and successful R & D projects for pharmaceuticals thus came into the limelight, whether by design or by luck.[78] Research work done by Genentech on agricultural applications similarly made the news. For example, the US Secretary of Agriculture, John R. Block, announced that Genentech had succeeded in making a vaccine for hoof-and-mouth

[76] See also *The New England Journal of Medicine* (1980) and Culliton (1981). In the article discussed in the text, Andreopoulos is specifically concerned with reporters' acceptance of unpublished data as true, with problems associated with establishing scientific priority. In other words, 'Is the press conference the proper avenue for publishing scientific results? And should science reporters give them unqualified coverage?' (Andreopoulos 1980: 743) Twelve years later, Andreopoulos (1992) specifically relates his concern about press coverage to other discussions in the university about conflicts of interest between universities and commercialization of genetic engineering. In particular, he mentioned the Pajaro Dunes conference, organized by Don Kennedy, President of Stanford, to discuss potential conflicts of interest. (See also the discussion of Pajaro Dunes in Culliton 1982a.)

[77] Andreopolous (1980: 744–5). Biogen was a biotech company based in Switzerland but largely based on American academics, particularly from Harvard. Biogen's claims about interferon were based on a paper written by 'Dr. Walter Gilbert, a Harvard professor and chairman of the scientific board of Biogen, and Dr. Charles Weissman, a professor of molecular biology at the University of Zurich' (Ibid. 744). Biogen was also financed by the same venture capital company that financed Genentech.

[78] Genentech's earlier results done at City of Hope on somatostatin had already gained a lot of publicity. In the case of somatostatin, circumstances were fortuitous and its role in political negotiating a contributing factor. For Genentech, Hall's book indicates that the press conference on insulin was pushed as a business strategy, but also brought various conflicts up to the surface. Kleid (1994) argues that it was City of Hope which pushed for and arranged the press conferences, and not Genentech.

disease in 1981.[79] Of course, those research projects which did not work or which were abandoned never made the news. The multitude of projects worked upon should not be forgotten, mainly because failures are also an important part of doing knowledge-seeking activities.

In the case of hGH, Genentech and UCSF released press statements on 9 July 1979. This is three days after Genentech submitted its article but about one month before it was actually accepted.[80] *Medical World News* reported:

By a margin of only a few hours, Genentech was the first to go public with news of the bacterially synthesized hormone. It issued a press release that, a day later, was followed by a formal presentation of the firm's results by Dr. David V. Goeddel at a polypeptide symposium in Baltimore.

Alerted to the Genentech disclosure by local newspaper reporters, the UCSF team—whose work was still in press for publication in *Science* this month—quickly issued a report of its own achievement.[81]

Although university press offices continually produce press releases, a number of typos and grammatical mistakes in UCSF's original press release do indicate that they may have been alerted at the last minute about Genentech's pending announcement:

Several steps are still necessary *before* the hormones can be available for therapy. . . . and the *precurser* of the protein hormone need to be removed from it. . . . Nevertheless, these steps do not involve any new conceptual hurdles and the scientists *believe are* not major obstacles.[82]

The UCSF press release emphasized the medical uses of hGH, including problems in actually reaching the medical goal, rather than advances in genetic engineering. However, the typos and the *Medical World News* report that the local papers alerted UCSF do not prove that this sequence of events actually occurred. In fact, Genentech representatives argue that the firm had filed for

its hGH semi-synthetic gene patent on July 5, 1979. Dr. Baxter heard about the project from either or all of Drs. Seeburg, Shine, and Ullrich before the 9th . . . UCSF, Genentech, City of Hope, and Kabi organized news releases to coincide with Miles Symposium seminars to be given by Dr. Goeddel (on hGH expression in *E. coli)* and Dr. Seeburg (on the human hGH gene) the next day.[83]

Genentech had thus already filed a patent and organized the press release to coincide with the scientific announcement. Like UCSF, they

[79] USDA (1981), Genentech (1981), and Yansura (1993b).

[80] González (1979: 701) reported that 'Goeddel and Seeburg announced the synthesis of HGH' at the 'International Miles Seminar on Polypeptide Hormones, held in Baltimore'. Goeddel (1993) indicates that Seeburg was not involved in the announcement. González may have mentioned Seeburg anyway because she emphasizes the conflicts between Seeburg and UCSF in this article, giving her incentives to play up Seeburg's role.

[81] *Medical World News* (1979: 20).   [82] Reichman (1979), my italics.

[83] Kleid (1994: 5–6).

wanted to emphasize the medical uses of hGH, but also wanted publicity for their skill with genetic engineering techniques *per se*.

Unlike UCSF, Genentech had indeed succeeded with the genetic engineering techniques, thereby getting expression of hGH. It was, however, not certain then whether the hGH described in the press conference and in the scientific paper was biologically active or not. The submitted Genentech paper indicated that the structure was the same as natural hGH, indicating it should also be recognizable by the human body. Although medical doctors were concerned about biological activity, a quote from the head of the Genentech group, Dr Goeddel, indicates how differently researchers in molecular biology could view the same problem: 'But if you believe in the genetic code, this material is going to be all right.'[84] Science would triumph.

However, expression of a protein in bacteria does not assure its biological activity, as Genentech were well aware. In order to investigate biological activity, Genentech hired Ken Olson at this time, who had been doing DNA enzymology and protein purification at Hoffman-LaRoche, to purify hGH.[85] As soon as he could purify sufficient quantities of hGH, they used the hGH bio-assay to assess biological activity (see Chapters 7 and 8).

Conflicts of Commercialization within UCSF

In the American university world, the spawning of the biotech industry, starting with the creation of Genentech out of UCSF, focused a number of persons' attention on the actual and potential conflicts between universities and firms. The commercialization of scientific activities meant using and redirecting basic science and it meant basic scientists pursuing a perception of commercial potential. This question of commercialization was by no means unique to these scientific fields and time, but the problems seemed immediate and acute.

The University of California, San Francisco is particularly interesting because it was the source of several new biotech firms like Genentech. There were also the subsequent relationships and competition between individuals at UCSF and Genentech. There were a number of conflicts between UCSF and Genentech, between the strong-minded individuals involved, and everyone was relieved when Genentech built its own laboratories in South San Francisco in 1978.

There were tensions and discussions within universities about the

---

[84] *Medical World News* (1979: 24). This quote was given at the Miles Symposium, the next day, when Goeddel gave a formal presentation of their research results.
[85] Olson (1993a, 1993b).

proper roles of universities and firms in carrying out research. Both scientists and universities had to cope with a changing environment, where the scientific-economic environment was being created. It was relevant to scientists who had previously been restricted to the basic scientific environment.

The tensions which arose had to be dealt with. The UCSF Academic Senate appointed a committee to look into Genentech's relations with the campus on 11 January 1979. This was an internal Committee on Rules and Jurisdiction, consisting of university researchers. In September 1979, the committee reported to the Academic Senate about its investigation into the relationships between Genentech and UCSF,[86] and on 2 October, this report was sent to the Director of News Services and Publications Office. Incidentally, this is the same person who wrote their 1979 press release on hGH. The report was confidential and was to remain confidential until the Academic Senate discussed matters with the Chancellor of the University.

The report mentioned that one important issue was the disruption of communication and jealousy. 'A recurrent theme was that people were loathe [sic] to ask questions or give suggestions in seminars, or across the bench.'[87] This implies that individuals were not sharing information freely, presumably because the researcher was afraid that someone else would take the ideas and become a millionaire. However, the description given in the committee's report must be interpreted with caution as a reflection of general trends in the university. It was based on testimony by only five researchers, including one of the most vocal critics. Other researchers who were in the department at this time disagree with this interpretation of the stifling of the flow of information.[88]

The committee argued that any stifling of academic communication was closely tied to jealousies and philosophical perceptions:

It seems to many of these people that is within the academic spirit to give freely of ideas and suggestions, if they are used to advance our knowledge (and even eventually to benefit mankind). It is not all right to do the same if another person is to make money out of it, even if by so doing he also helps mankind.
. . . . Not all of the faculty is that idealistic, however, and the committee believes that the situation was exacerbated by simple jealousy.[89]

One reason for the jealousy alluded to in the report was that Boyer was on his way to becoming a millionaire, as well as maybe some of the post-docs, whereas other scientists who had done similar research were for

---

[86] Glass (1979a, 1979b).   [87] Wolff (1979: 2).

[88] Those giving testimony included: Professors Bruce Alberts and Brian McCarthy, acting co-chairmen; Professor Boyer; Professor Goodman; and assistant professor Keith Yamamoto—who had until recently been a post-doc. Another post-doc in the department at the time, Chirgwin (1993), strongly disagrees with their conclusions.

[89] Wolff (1979: 3).

the moment stuck with research grants and university salaries. In contrast to that interpretation of jealousy, we should keep in mind that no one enters university science, particularly not post-doc positions, to become millionaires.[90] The motivations and goals of researchers responding to the basic scientific environment are usually based on scientific criteria. When, however, two researchers do similar research, and one only gets scientific acclaim and the other much money, jealousy cannot be ruled out.

It is noteworthy that by the time of this committee's report in 1979, the worst of the conflicts between individuals at UCSF and Genentech had already subsided. The most apparent conflicts over the scientific versus commercial value of knowledge-seeking activities had physically moved out. After all, many of the scientists hired by Genentech had already left UCSF, and Boyer was no longer conducting contract research for Genentech in his UCSF labs. Moreover, it is noteworthy that the fact that Goodman and Baxter had been doing contract research for Lilly raised no immediate conflicts. Other scientists in the department would soon follow Boyer in starting a biotech firm or in working for one.

This committee decided not to satisfy itself with only examining the contract between Swanson and Boyer to carry out research in the UCSF labs. It instead saw that contract as one example of many potential conflicts of interest within the university. The university wanted to know a much broader question about the pattern of interaction, namely What was the proper form for relationships between firms and the university? In the perspective developed here, the question was, How to develop informal rules, or institutions, which could regulate how scientists at universities respond to both the basic scientific and scientific-economic environments? The committee used the Genentech example as a forum to give more general suggestions about how the university (UCSF) should handle industry relations in the future.[91] What was important was developing rules to regulate a large number of interactions, not each individual case. They wanted to create informal institutions, or patterns of behaviour, which defined what would be acceptable.

This section has illustrated how both individuals and organizations found ways of dealing with conflicts of interest. There were different strategies, such as moving between organizations, changing the orientation of research, developing informal institutions, and so forth. This type of conflict was important enough to lead to a discussion of the proper

[90] Chirgwin (1993).
[91] This led the committee to suggest that the university 'refrain from making contracts in which work will be done by a university faculty member who also has a *major* financial interest in a concern, as this amounts to a contract between the person and himself, with the university's role only being incidental' (Wolff 1979: 4), emphasis in original.

interactions between universities and firms. The presidents of five leading American research universities—namely Harvard, Stanford, California Institute of Technology, Massachusetts Institute of Technology, and
the University of California—met with representatives of eleven cor-
porations in late March 1982 to discuss perceived problems in biotechnology, particularly in relation to contract disclosures, patents, licences,
and conflict of interests.[92] This is known as Pajaro Dunes, named after
the place in California where the meeting took place. Firms had an
interest in solving such conflicts because they were fundamentally
dependent on university science and scientists in these fields and continued to need basic research. The universities were interested because
they were eager for money with which to expand but also wanted to
maintain their scientific reputations. The purpose of these institutions
and guidelines was not to forbid or unduly restrict interactions among
university scientists and firms. The purpose was, on the contrary, to find
ways to co-ordinate acceptable patterns of interaction among the different communities responding to different environmental conditions. This
new pattern was intended to facilitate communication and stimulus not
only of knowledge and techniques but also of individuals.

Summary and Conclusions

Usable, practical genetic engineering techniques did not just appear,
ready-made, as a side effect of university research. This and the preceding chapter have instead shown that university and corporate researchers developed different, but overlapping, areas of expertise. The mid- to
late 1970s was a period with more involvement of firms in scientific and
technological activities. Both knowledge and techniques had to be
developed. Agents responding mainly to the basic scientific environment and those responding mainly to the techno-economic environment
interacted in knowledge-seeking activities in the scientific-economic
environment. Overlapping scientific and technological activities in
response to different environments has been argued to direct the generation of knowledge in commercially relevant directions.

This chapter has concentrated on scientific and technological activities
for using genetic engineering to express insulin and human growth
hormone in bacteria. Several research groups at universities or at biotech firms competed to achieve similar research results. Not only the
scientific knowledge but also the techniques, biological material, and
equipment used were quite similar when these researchers competed
contemporaneously. This is visible in, for example, choice of promoters,

---

[92] Culliton (1982a).

strains of bacteria, and DNA sequences. They drew on a common body of knowledge, skills, and behaviour but for two different purposes.

Multiple groups competed, each developing an alternative knowledge-seeking strategy, and each solving the challenges in somewhat different ways. Despite different approaches and purposes, the researchers mentioned here were all successful within the basic scientific environment, judging by scientific publications. Each group published scientific results which contained some element of novelty. There were three major groups successfully competing for insulin—Gilbert's at Harvard; Baxter's and Goodman's at UCSF; and Boyer's at Genentech and City of Hope. There were two major groups for human growth hormone—Baxter's and Goodman's at UCSF, and Boyer's at Genentech and City of Hope. UCSF and Genentech were in turn financed by established pharmaceutical firms—respectively, Eli Lilly and Kabi. Lilly also tried to obtain patent licensing for Gilbert's work on insulin. However, UCSF researchers were more interested in understanding and developing knowledge for the basic scientific environment, whereas Genentech was more interested in developing practical techniques, but this also required new scientific knowledge.

There were thus two types of firms involved in scientific activities—biotech firms and established pharmaceutical firms. The first carried out activities, and the second financed them. One important difference between the firms was that biotech firms like Genentech needed to continue generating publicity and scientific legitimacy through scientific research results to attract financiers and further R & D contracts. Established pharmaceutical firms like Kabi and Eli Lilly, in contrast, needed the new technology to develop an alternative supply for their main products. They wanted it for specific contexts of use.

An interesting difference in the direction of knowledge-seeking activities has been identified. In the case of university researchers funded by a pharmaceutical firm (UCSF financed by Eli Lilly), the researchers were still mainly oriented towards the basic scientific environment. The design of the research experiment and results were strongly directed towards addressing internal scientific questions about DNA sequences and how cells function. Lilly seems to have seen their role as funding basic science, rather than more immediately directing it towards commercial goals. In the case of research performed at a biotech firm and funded by a pharmaceutical firm (Genentech financed by Kabi), the orientation was more towards the scientific-economic environment. The design and results were strongly oriented towards making the techniques work in practice and allowing control over nature in order to make specific changes (synthetic DNA; expression achieved).

The results thus differed in the degree to which they were directed towards the basic scientific or scientific-economic environments. The knowledge-seeking activities and results were nevertheless similar, and so we can say that several research groups worked on competing research projects and generated diverse knowledge and techniques. Scientific activities were required to orient knowledge-seeking activities towards practical techniques and control and vice versa.

The dual purposes of knowledge-seeking also had ramifications for universities. This chapter has indicated a number of tensions and problems which arose within the basic scientific environment. These conflicts had to do with either the orientation of research or the physical moving of individuals between environments. These conflicts had different dimensions, including the assignment of scientific credit, jealousy, disruption of communication, and the possibility of transferring biological material. Much unclarity remains about the extent to which the conflicts between individuals had to do with individual personalities, or whether these conflicts were inflamed by the new situation of commercial benefits from scientific activities. The greatest tensions centred around patent applications and around the moving of techniques and biological material. At the same time, however, the experiments described did not require unusual or unavailable material, indicating that the transfer of knowledge and techniques through the skills of individual researchers could have sufficed to allow Genentech to repeat the same experiments. The economic potential of activities previously only relevant within the basic scientific environment led to a situation where the community of researchers needed to find new ways to regulate interactions.

This type of conflict led to the development of informal institutions and more explicit guidelines to specify which types of contacts between industry and universities were acceptable (UCSF Academic Senate; Pajaro Dunes). Communication ought to be possible without destroying the unique characteristics of research for either environment and without substituting one for the other. The two different types of knowledge-seeking activities would instead live in symbiosis.

In the mid- to late 1970s, genetic engineering was coupled to much risk and uncertainty. It was not at all clear whether or how well the knowledge could be translated into techniques and technology. Nor was it clear how well the technology would function technically and economically in practice. It was even less certain it would work on a commercial scale of production. Many potential users of the new technology, such as other pharmaceutical firms, had good reasons to do as they did and wait and see what happened with the technology. The slower-moving firms wanted to know whether, and how, genetic engineering would be developed before changing the orientation of their production towards the new technology. They were more cautious.

Some established pharmaceutical or chemical firms, and obviously the new biotech firms, acted early to exploit the technical and economic potential of genetic engineering. They directed knowledge-seeking activities towards such ends, either in-house or through financing others. The firms' motivations to take quick action to develop the technology included ownership of information, first-mover advantages into a product, and the potential for profits. Firms willing to take the risk of moving into genetic engineering often had strong incentives to do so, such as leading market share and shortage of supply of substitute products, and/or were started up to specialize in genetic engineering. These firms recognized the potential of profits from selling R & D contracts or genetically engineered products in the market.

Funding knowledge-seeking activities, however, does not automatically lead to expected results. By definition, a radical technology initially involves much uncertainty about whether or not the knowledge-seeking activities will lead to results and whether or not the idea will be realized in practice. This uncertainty of results holds for both firms and university researchers. Even when firms are willing to fund scientific activities, it is possible that firms' perceptions cannot be realized in an absolute sense (they are impossible) or cannot be contemporaneously developed due to deficiencies in the existing (retained) knowledge, techniques, and equipment. In these cases, scientific activities would fail to provide the desired results. Funding scientific and technological activities by no means always leads to solutions of the challenges, but was an important way of generating new alternatives and evaluating existing ones. In cases of radical change, it is often the only way of generating a number of alternatives, which can then be tested according to expected environmental conditions.

This chapter has shown that perceptions were based on ideas which could not be immediately realized because the necessary knowledge and/or techniques were not available. The uncertainty of the results of knowledge-seeking activities was one reason why knowledge and techniques go hand in hand for radical changes. Both were necessary; both were complementary; and so cross-stimulus between scientific and technological activities was facilitated.

In performing scientific and technological activities for university peers, for firms, or for both at different times, scientists in these fields had to get their experiments to work. Only if the techniques functioned in practice could scientists address whether or not the empirical experiments confirmed, denied, or developed a larger body of theoretical knowledge about the world. In this chapter, discussions about the difficulties scientists had in finding and further developing functioning genetic engineering techniques indicate that the actions of scientists doing experiments resembled the actions of engineers developing technology in the sense discussed by Constant and Vincenti.[93] Like their

---

[93] Constant (1984), Vincenti (1990).

engineers, the scientists had to make technology and experiments function in practice and not just theoretically.

The difference, however, was that scientists responding mainly to the basic scientific environment demanded that experiments, technology, and techniques function within different parameters than of scientists responding to the scientific-economic environment. For basic scientists, technological activities were generally not an end in themselves but a means of developing a body of knowledge about the world. In contrast, researchers working in the scientific-economic and techno-economic environments faced different constraints. Techniques and equipment used by firms had to function within strict economic and technical parameters. They had to work reliably at a reasonable cost, and so forth. Firms demanded continuing small improvements to solve their local and particular questions, whereas university scientists had the freedom to work on new generalizable questions.

Genetic engineering in general and particularly for commercial uses was not 'discovered' in the sense of passive observation, nor did it passively trickle down from universities to firms. It was instead actively developed by individuals and organizations with specific scientific and economic interests in genetic engineering. Agents engaged in knowledge-seeking activities in response to different environments. They perceived economic and technical potential, and they developed knowledge and techniques based on accumulated bodies of knowledge but did so for their specific trajectory.

7

Specific Firm Challenges, 1979–83

Introduction

This chapter examines the technical and economic challenges and opportunities which firms acted upon to integrate genetic engineering techniques into functioning production systems. These challenges differ from those involving genetic engineering *per se* which were encountered in the two preceding chapters. Here, the challenges are specific and local to firms' use of genetic engineering to manufacture pharmaceuticals, but sometimes also represented general categories of problems. This chapter thus analyses firms' knowledge-seeking activities in the context of interactions with external agents and environmental conditions.

The preceding chapters illustrate how both scientific and technological activities were necessary for developing knowledge and techniques for genetic engineering. The challenges in those chapters were told mainly from the perspective of researchers working with genetic engineering, in relation to different types of organizations and environmental incentives.

The challenges described in the current chapter focus more specifically on the integration of genetic engineering into production systems in firms. Using genetic engineering as the basis of production required different types of scientific and technological activities, involving all the downstream processing. This system involved many other component technologies, such as fermentation, purification, and analytical methods. Integrating them led to additional investment in R & D. We can call this a commercial trajectory of large-scale production of human proteins, but there were also individual firm-level trajectories.

Instead of investigating these scientific and technological activities within firms, one could dismiss corporate R & D as applied science, as problem-solving which is less creative and inherently less interesting than basic science. This assumption would be correct according to the linear model, where basic science is assumed to generate technology. What is most interesting are the developments in basic science. Here, however, it has been argued that scientific and technological activities draw upon similar knowledge and techniques, but for different purposes. Both types of activities can be creative and can imply radical changes. Their contributions to technological innovation processes should therefore be analysed. In contrast to a linear model over time, the argument here is that parallel, sometimes co-operating and sometimes competing knowledge-seeking activities are complementary and inter-active. Feedback among them is vital.

To dismiss the firms' contributions would be to miss the heart of innovation processes in the economy, a major question addressed in this book. Scientific research involving genetic engineering techniques and in designing a modified bacteria did not provide the once-and-for-all answer. Instead, new questions arose as scientific knowledge was translated into practice in the form of bacteria, which were in turn integrated into production systems. A number of different technolo-gies, based on somewhat different bodies of knowledge, had to function together as a whole in order actually to produce the protein used as a pharmaceutical. This part of the innovation process was mainly organ-ized in firms, with the design of new combinations based on knowledge, techniques, and equipment. Sometimes these corporate researchers inter-acted with the broader community of researchers, sometimes not. The continuing innovativeness and improvements that are required to trans-late new knowledge into practice in firms has long been neglected.

To engage in these innovation processes, firms relied on the compe-tences and experiences of employees and of the firm as a whole, but also interacted with external agents to access relevant knowledge and tech-niques. The extent to which corporate researchers and managers made improvements in-house, based on general knowledge and skills, relative to the extent to which they communicated with others, differed for different parts of the technology and during different periods.

Making the production systems work consistently, at high yields, and with a high quality of final product, was crucial for corporate success in the techno-economic environment. The techno-economic challenges required many incremental changes and improvements within a nar-rower range of parameters than basic science. On the one hand, these were often general problem areas and general solutions for categories of challenges. On the other hand, these general aspects were modified, changed, and applied to specific, local, technical developments within individual firms. These corporate developments of technology thus involved both general and specific dimensions of problems.

Firms had more direct control over the development of trajectories when the design of production systems and marketing were more important than basic scientific results. In particular, firms used testing to internalize perceived selection criteria. Testing approximates (imi-tates) those conditions deemed likely to be encountered. Testing also helped develop model systems, useful for giving the general parameters for a class of similar products or of problems. If firms could develop standard or generalizable techniques, then those components could be used for other activities, thereby reducing additional costs. Despite firms' attempts to internalize environmental conditions through testing, uncertainty remained. This included uncertainty about the outcome of search activities; about whether the results would function in practice; and about future environmental conditions.

Because pharmaceuticals have very stringent demands on quality control and on documentation of all phases, including production, the firms had to decide at some point that they had a relatively efficient set of genetic engineering techniques for hGH. They could then concentrate on developing the fermentation and purification techniques, identifying the resulting product, and getting approval from government agencies. Having made this choice, the firms ignored much of the diversity of genetic engineering improvements generated by science or by in-house R & D. Nevertheless, the efficiency of the production system could depend on the specific set of genetic engineering techniques chosen. The firms would therefore take notice of major improvements in the genetic engineering techniques if the returns were high enough to compensate for investment and time that would be lost by changing to a new alternative.

This chapter covers Kabi's and Genentech's decisions and actions from 1979 through the early 1980s. The next section outlines the component technologies of a production system, in relation to genetically modified bacteria. The subsequent section covers Kabi's interactions with other Swedish agents to create a favourable public context for their early experiments with genetically modified organisms. These early experiments and technical developments were in close co-operation with Genentech. The third section then concentrates on the broader challenges of integrating genetic engineering into a functioning production system, as encountered by Genentech and Kabi. This chapter thus analyses the active role of firms in responding to, and changing, environmental conditions as well as firms' technical challenges. Kabi had to spend more energy in forming environmental conditions during this period than Genentech.

Much of this story about the technological innovation processes thus focuses on the actions of firms, especially those R. & D. activities which contributed to functioning production systems.

Directing Integration Towards Commercial Use

Many of the researchers involved in the rDNA hGH projects at both Kabi and Genentech talk about the unexpected challenges which had to be solved to make a functioning production system. Novelty had to do with the integration of old and new knowledge, techniques, and technologies.

They make statements about how things did not turn out quite as expected:

In 1979, it was really, [we] really didn't know what we were doing. We were incredibly naïve! When I think back, when I reflect back on what we were trying to do![1]

These corporate researchers initially believed that they could quite quickly solve the potential technical and economic bottle-necks of integrating genetic engineering techniques into production. Looking back, they realized that the challenges had been much greater than initially expected.

The evolutionary perspective of technological innovation processes developed in Chapter 2 leads us to expect that researchers will face a number of challenges and propose alternative technical solutions. The alternatives will be generated and selected continually along the way, but particular problems or challenges will focus the agents' attention and innovative energy on the bottle-necks.[2] According to the analytical framework of this book, these bottle-necks may be induced by scientific, technological, economic, or government factors. Testing also plays an important role in knowledge-seeking activities as the firms try to internalize perceived selection criteria (environmental conditions). The firm internally generates knowledge about the advantages and disadvantages of alternatives in order to make bets by choosing among them. The firm thereby develops a map for its search spaces.

This theoretical perspective leads to additional questions about how firms and other agents identify diverse opportunities and problems concerning the development and adaptation of knowledge into practice. This section will identify the major interdependencies in this type of biological production system, involving both technical and economic aspects. This overview gives a structure for the later discussion of specific technical challenges faced by these firms when they engaged in integrating genetic engineering into their production systems.

Figure 7.1 illustrates the typical steps of a biological production system, from fermentation on the upper left to patients on the upper right. Fermentation means that cells are grown, cells which in turn divide into daughter cells. Through this division, more and more cells are grown, resulting in a certain cell mass. The resulting solution must be purified so that the desired protein is separated from other substances. After a number of intermediary steps, the purified protein must be made into a pharmaceutical which is stable and long-lasting, a step called

---

[1] Kleid (1993). Similar sentiments can be found in Florell (1992) and Fhölenhag (1992).
[2] See Rosenberg (1982, ch. 3).

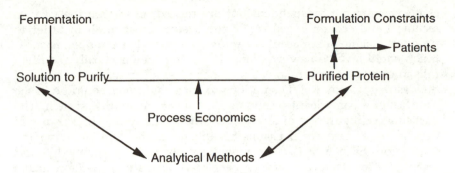

FIG 7.1. Relationships in a biological production scheme[3]

formulation. Each step is dependent on the others in technical as well as economic considerations, as shown in Figure 7.1.

Figure 7.1 thus indicates how a biological production process is composed of a number of steps, each involving a body of knowledge and techniques. The trick is integrating the steps into a functioning system.

More specifically, Figure 7.1 indicates that a fermentation process results in a liquid solution (solution to purify). This solution is composed of a number of elements, such as the desired protein, the nutrients upon which the cells fed in order to grow, other proteins, and a number of contaminants. The goal is to purify out the protein (purified protein) and formulate it as a pharmaceutical (formulation constraints; patients). Doing so requires the use of analytical methods to test alternatives and considerations of costs (process economics).

According to Figure 7.1, firms' decisions about which techniques and equipment to use are based on:

1. Process economics. It is particularly important to relate cost to the level of purity. Higher purity often means higher costs but is necessary for selling pharmaceuticals.
2. Analytical methods to determine the purity of the protein as well as what has to be removed.
3. Formulation constraints on the protein. Formulation constraints for pharmaceuticals include parameters like stability, activity, impurity, delivery rate, and so forth. Pharmaceuticals have to meet high standards to be used for human beings. The protein needs to be analysed in terms of these constraints and also produced at a price acceptable in the market(s).

Each of the steps shown in Figure 7.1 could involve new challenges, and many of them did so, as described in subsequent sections. The

---

[3] Diagram and next paragraph adapted from Ho (1990: 15–18).

challenges are not independent but are related, in that all the various technical and economic aspects of the system must mesh in order to produce a viable pharmaceutical at a viable price. For example, fermentation could involve new problems in getting the genetically modified cells to grow up to a certain cell mass, or when there was a low yield of the desired protein. R & D solutions to such challenges could lie in the specifics of a component technology or in the integrative system. The particular configuration of any given production system in a firm will depend on a series of decisions taken within the firm pursuing the innovation. Each firm decides how to apply general knowledge and techniques for its specific use in each step. Firms will therefore make different choices about steps, and each step may have consequences for the next step, or for the system as a whole.

Purification, for example, could involve new challenges. Difficulties arose from the many trace contaminants, including

pyrogens, viruses, and transforming DNA, inaccurately translated or glycosylated forms of the protein, degradation and oxidation products, aggregates and conformational isomers which are similar to the desired product.[4]

In other words, contaminants included substances which could induce fever or illness (pyrogens and viruses) as well as a number of molecules which are very, very similar to the desired one and yet different in key aspects. These must be removed to get the purified protein. The ultimate goal of purification is thus to reach as homogeneous a product as possible, but process economics relative to formulation constraints also had to be taken into account. Corporate researchers could identify different trade-offs, but management had to decide which choice would be most appropriate for the environmental conditions.

Genentech and Kabi knew that selling genetically engineered hGH as a pharmaceutical required ultra-purity and a stable formulation. These were constraints on the outcome of the system. In that sense, problems identified after analysis of the protein could in turn be used to identify strengths and weaknesses of alternative designs of the system. Due to the nature of both technical and economic trade-offs, different designs would give somewhat different yields, price, etc. These constraints were imposed on the firms by existing conditions in the pharmaceutical market and by formal government regulation.

At the same time that both regulatory and commercial agents were aware of general constraints on pharmaceutical products, the firms were using a radically new technology as the basis of production. The outcome might have differed from products made with other technologies. This led to questions in firms and in government agencies about how genetic engineering techniques differed from alternative production

---

[4] Landisch *et al.* (eds. 1990: 3)

technologies and hence about the consequences for safety and risks. Negotiations therefore had to occur between firms and other agents in their environment, and innovation involved collective creation of selection criteria.

These negotiations centred around the product, specifically on whether and how the new technology, and hence firms' specific production systems, affected the pharmaceutical. The outcome was a protein, but questions remained. What exact proteins did these bacteria modified by genetic engineering techniques produce? Was the protein identical to the known substance the firms wanted to produce? Were the proteins folded correctly? What contaminants did the *E. coli* bacteria introduce which had not previously been present? These questions could only be addressed through further knowledge-seeking activities, including analytical methods and tests.

Because both the genetic engineering technology itself and its specific use to make pharmaceuticals was novel in the early 1980s, the public and regulatory framework of how to analyse and interpret the pharmaceutical was under negotiation. New rules of behaviour and new criteria for judging among alternatives had to be created and agreed upon. There was a need to modify some aspects of the formal regulation in order to take the peculiarities of this technology into account. The initial, genetically engineered pharmaceuticals approved were insulin and hGH, and they provided a model, or pattern, for government approval.

The starting point for this negotiation was obviously the existing national procedures for approving pharmaceuticals. For example, regulatory agencies required that rDNA hGH be put through pharmacology/toxicology tests on animals before clinical tests. In contrast, naturally occurring human substances like hGH extracted from pituitary glands had never had to go through such tests, because they were human products. The initial rDNA hGH with the extra methionine differed from natural hGH by one amino acid, and this meant that it could have other effects on humans. Moreover, there could be, for example, contaminants introduced by the bacteria.

A sketch of the general government procedures for approving pharmaceuticals is shown in Figure 7.2. The pharmaceutical regulatory agencies required that these firms take rDNA hGH through these approval stages.

Figure 7.2 gives information about the different phases of the approval process, including whether the tests are on animals or humans, and the general size of the clinical studies. These boxes represent the typical steps for getting a new pharmaceutical approved.

Because no one knew the special implications of genetic engineering, the firms and regulatory agencies had to find novel ways to analyse and interpret the resulting proteins. The existing knowledge, techniques, and

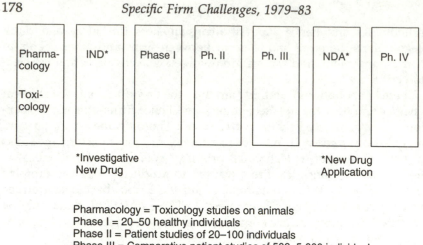

*Investigative
New Drug

*New Drug
Application

Pharmacology = Toxicology studies on animals
Phase I = 20–50 healthy individuals
Phase II = Patient studies of 20–100 individuals
Phase III = Comparative patient studies of 500–5,000 individuals
Phase IV = Continuation of Phase III or post-marketing survey

FIG 7.2. Overview of clinical testing for pharmaceuticals

methods about how to analyse other pharmaceuticals were useful and necessary starting-points. When they did not suffice, however, new ways of doing things were developed instead. Testing procedures and analytical methods were very important, but sometimes represented a bottleneck. By 1980, when these two firms' respective employees had got rudimentary production systems for rDNA hGH running, some of the challenges came from the peculiarities of genetic engineering, or from not fully recognizing the challenges of integrating genetic engineering with biological engineering.

Thus, before commercial firms used genetic engineering to produce and sell truly new proteins for medical purposes, it was helpful to have a test run to produce known proteins with the new technology. This would facilitate negotiations over regulatory standards. Making a known product in a new way could give both firms and regulatory agencies some criteria by which they could argue that genetic engineering techniques had succeeded. The aspects which were more general could later be applied to truly new products which could only be made with genetic engineering. By comparing the products resulting from the new and the old technological production processes, they could identify problems stemming from the genetic engineering techniques and production system *per se* rather than from the protein itself.

It was therefore useful to have knowledge and techniques for analysing a known and naturally occurring protein to compare with the rDNA version. This was a major reason why Kabi's experience with pituitary hGH was initially considered valuable by both Genentech and Kabi.

Having identified some challenges with the new technology (rather than the protein), the firms could try to develop knowledge in directions which enabled them to analyse and solve these new challenges. Although this dependence on previous competences seemed logical, agents soon discovered that genetic engineering had modified some of the playing rules.

The directions in which the corporate researchers developed the systems thus depended on their perceptions and on the formation of a selection process for the final pharmaceuticals. Discussions, negotiations, and interactions among firms, government regulatory agencies, and market conditions helped define the directions in which corporate R & D decided to search for solutions to the challenges. The environmental conditions were not wholly determined in advance, but could instead be changed. This is shown not least by firms' attempts to change those conditions and by the fact that firms generated novelty to fit their expectations of environmental conditions. In that those conditions were changed through action and not all selection criteria were obvious in advance, other alternatives were selected *ex post*, through, for example, the market or negotiations with agencies.

Integrating Genetic Engineering into Kabi in Sweden

Kabi's actions to develop a production system for rDNA hGH during this period included funding Genentech to generate the new scientific techniques; the transmission of knowledge and biological material from Genentech to Kabi; some collaborative generation of novelty; and interactions with Swedish and other national government agencies to meet existing regulatory standards and to define new ones. Initially in 1979 and 1980, many of the management actions were directed at influencing the Swedish public context and developing the firm's competences and R & D activities. Kabi researchers initially co-operated with Genentech in developing relevant new knowledge and techniques.

The commercial trajectory of integrating genetic engineering into a production system can be clearly seen by the firms' emphasis on technological activities to make the system function. For example, even when Kabi funded Genentech for scientific activities, Kabi were interested in the generation of useful genetic engineering techniques applicable to its main product. In short, Kabi funded Genentech not for general scientific knowledge, in the way that governments often fund basic research, but in return for a bacteria strain which could produce hGH. Contrary to the linear view, this does not deny that Genentech had to carry out scientific activities to fulfil Kabi's specific goals. Scientific and technological activities stimulated each other.

The R & D contract between Genentech and Kabi stipulated that Genentech had twenty-four to thirty months from August 1978 to develop a bacteria which could produce hGH. Instead of taking so many months, Genentech came up with an initial bacteria expression system only seven months after the contract was signed. Bertil Åberg, the head of research at KabiVitrum, and then at KabiGen, writes, 'In April 1979, I got the message that the bacteria was ready and that it made hGH.'[5] The Genentech scientist named first on the subsequent hGH paper, David Goeddel, says, however, that their first clear experimental results came in late May.[6] In either case, the message came several months before either Genentech or UCSF submitted their scientific papers to the respective journals.

In that the message came earlier, the bacteria developed was not 'ready' in any final or usable sense even for the basic scientific environment. It was even less ready to meet the criteria of reliability, functionality, and so forth which were demanded by firms. These initial results were followed up by a whole process of improvements. Nevertheless, such communication gave Kabi early access to information that the technology was feasible for this use. It also indicated to the Kabi management that additional action would be necessary. It indicated that Sievertsson's and Åberg's previous preparations for taking care of the bacteria and for genetic engineering within the firm and the country were not in vain. Those preparations would be worthwhile when the knowledge-seeking activities led to functioning techniques. It did give the visionaries in each firm confidence that they would eventually integrate and use the technology. They could start organizing additional search activities which would generate further information relevant for the new contexts of uses.

Still, showing that bacteria could make human proteins did not solve corporate questions about the efficiency of the bacteria construction. These included questions about the level of expression. These could be related to genetic engineering questions, such as how well the signals to start and stop translation worked. Answers to these types of questions would require additional R & D activities. Nor did the making of human proteins in bacteria address the commercial question of whether rDNA hGH could be produced at an economically viable quantity and price. Generating the information that genetic engineering techniques could express human proteins was the beginning of a process.

Based on such assurances, Kabi began in a modest way to bring together its own research engineering group to handle the commercial production side of the project. In the spring of 1979, Sievertsson asked

---

[5] Åberg (1982: 59), my translation.   [6] Goeddel (1993).

Björn Holmström, a microbiologist with extensive fermentation experience at Kabi, to start the rDNA hGH project.[7]

Just like the United States in late 1979, Sweden did not have national legislation to regulate genetic engineering; it only had the informal regulation of the scientists' Genetic Manipulation Advisory Group Committee (GMAC). As Åberg of Kabi sat on the GMAC, Kabi were well aware of which experiments and labs could be considered acceptable. KabiGen applied for a permit from the committee, and on 27 April 1979, it got a permit to grow *E. coli* bacteria modified with an hGH gene on a ten-litre scale. Because, however, neither Kabi nor KabiGen had laboratories which met the required physical specifications, they could not utilize the permit.[8] At the time, researchers from Kabi and Genentech were instead using Genentech's facilities to ferment (grow) the bacteria in California.

Kabi's particular actions were not carried out in isolation in Sweden. Their plans to build an appropriate lab to utilize the GMAC permit created controversy, including objections from critics who argued that Kabi should be forbidden from all such activities because the technology Kabi wished to develop was too risky. Some critics in the public debate thus tried to stop technical development well before any innovation had been introduced into a market.

On 15 August 1979, Kabi's plans to build 'Sweden's first risk laboratory for gene research' made front page news in the influential newspaper *Dagens Nyheter*. Kabi planned to renovate an existing, unused virus lab up to the so-called P3 standards of safety then demanded by the Swedish GMAC (and American NIH) guidelines. This lab was located next to Kabi's headquarters in Kungsholmen, central Stockholm.

The front page *Dagens Nyheter* article, 'Criticism in Stockholm against Kabi's Plans: Risky Research in the Middle of the City' had a critical tone, but the criticism was even more pronounced in the daily debate article.[9] The debate article was written by Guy Ehrling of the Centre Party (Centrepartiet), which traditionally represented agricultural interests but had increasingly emphasized a 'preserve nature' angle. There was an underlying assumption in Ehrling's argument that genetic engineering was artificial, contrary to nature. More specifically, Ehrling argued that research involving genetic engineering was dangerous, that a 'risk lab' should not be built downtown, and that the government must take a decision to implement laws for recombinant DNA based on Wennergren's proposals from December 1978. Erhling thus wanted

[7] Holmström (1992) and Lin (1993a). It is important to point out again that this R & D work on commercial production based on genetic engineering occurred within the established pharmaceutical company Kabi, not in the specialized biotech company KabiGen. As to the genetic engineering side, Genentech did the work but the R & D contract and initial expenses were under KabiGen's budget.

[8] The permit was granted in KNM (1980a: 2). Sievertsson (1993) gives this explanation about why Kabi did not use the lab.   [9] *Dagens Nyheter* (1979: 1, 11), Ehrling (1979a: 2).

cautious regulation and development of the technology, and he used public debate to try to brake Kabi's move into genetic engineering. In fact, this turned out to be a very short debate, running only in August 1979.[10] Kabi was silent for the moment.

These were clearly influences from the public context attempting to direct and limit the rate of knowledge-seeking activities. One reason that Ehrling's protest was heard was that his attack on genetic engineering, coming as it did from the Centre Party, came at a particularly sensitive moment politically. It was August 1979; Sweden had parliamentary elections coming up in September; and a three-party, centre–right coalition between the Conservatives (Moderaterna), Centre Party, and People's Party (Folkpartiet) wanted to win a majority of votes to form the national government. From 1932, the Social Democrats had been leading the government in Sweden, now and then in co-operation with one other party. Then in the 1976 elections, Thorbjörn Fälldin had managed to unite these three more-to-right political parties into a coalition government, but in the autumn of 1978, the government resigned, and the People's Party built a minority government. The coalition wanted to regain power and its legitimacy in the new elections.

This political situation would temporarily restrict Kabi's range of choices about developing genetic engineering. With the parliamentary elections only a month away, these three parties could ill afford debate over questions which might split the future coalition and which would thereby reduce their legitimacy as an alternative to the Social Democrats. It was no time to start a major debate over genetic engineering which might split the parties. This was particularly important since during the period 1978–9, Sweden was already in a heated and consequential debate over the future of nuclear energy.[11] In these Swedish debates, technology was no longer seen as unequivocally positive; instead, there were mainly arguments to increase social control.

In this sensitive political situation, the Swedish government, led by the People's Party, chose an alternative to a new debate on genetic engineering. They chose a temporary, voluntary moratorium for industrial experiments. At the time, KabiGen was the only firm considering genetic engineering experiments in Sweden, so this moratorium was directly aimed at them. It is thought-provoking that the moratorium

[10] There were only two articles by Ehrling and one by Hans Boman, Professor of Microbiology at Stockholm University, respectively, Ehrling (1979a and 1979b), and Boman (1979: 2). Boman, with the approval of the University, had written a contract with KabiGen to enable university microbiologists to use the planned P3 lab.
[11] This debate culminated in a referendum in March 1980 about whether or not to close down all of Sweden's nuclear power plants. Simply put, the choices were yes, no, and maybe, with the voters choosing 'maybe' and the Parliament later deciding to close all plants by the beginning of the twenty-first century. (As the deadline approaches, this decision has been called more and more into question.)

came quickly after the beginnings of a debate, launched by Erhling, about whether or not KabiGen should build a lab inside Stockholm. This three-party coalition won the September 1979 elections, allowing them to form the new government.

After this, Åberg and Sirvell explained their position in the press when the debate resumed:

Just before the election, the government requested that Swedish industry should voluntarily refrain from doing recombinant DNA experiments until the government had organized a regulatory body and had passed a law to control such activities. KabiGen will of course follow this request, which was conveyed through the daily press . . .

We at KabiGen consider it is our duty to follow [international technical developments] and despite unclear political conditions on this question here in Sweden, we 'will save what can be saved' for the future of Swedish industry. . . . We are following the government's request, conveyed through the mass media, to do nothing in Sweden.[12]

Åberg and Sirvell clearly saw the voluntary moratorium on industrial experiments as a political move by the government, particularly since the request was conveyed in the public debate. That this temporary moratorium was due to political negotiations within the coalition is substantiated by the fact that the Centre Party's national convention had voted in 1978 to try to implement a moratorium on rDNA research and on the building of new labs until a broad debate had been held and legislation implemented.[13] The Centre Party wanted strong control in the public context in order to be able to direct future technological developments.

In contrast to the Centre Party, the firms saw the temporary moratorium, as well as calls for additional moratoriums to stop all genetic engineering, as very negative factors. From KabiGen's perspective, even a temporary moratorium could have the very unfortunate consequence of slowing down their knowledge-seeking activities compared to international trends. The Kabi firms were not behind their competitors then, as they were one of the first to explore commercial uses of the technology, but they argued they would soon be left behind. Whereas the Centre Party might have argued that if that is true, then slowing down technical development is a good thing for society, Kabi argued it was very bad for industry.

At the same time that Åberg and Sirvell perceived genetic engineering as a future money-maker for the Kabi firms, the above quote also indicates that they had a broader vision of genetic engineering. They used the argument that it would become a necessary technology for

[12] Åberg and Sirvell (1979: 3), my translation.   [13] Ehrling and Ekengard (1980: 68–9)

many products in Sweden's industrial future, and they would there-fore 'save what can be saved'. Åberg later argued that hostility in the public debate was the real reason Swedish firms moved so slowly into genetic engineering.[14]

Åberg overstates his case, however. The moratorium only lasted three months, and comprehensive legislation came into effect as of 1 January 1980.[15] Moreover, this moratorium was of no practical importance for Kabi because they were then working jointly on rDNA hGH with Genentech in California. It only potentially affected KabiGen's plans to use genetic engineering to develop other products. This means that the particular Swedish public context did not slow down Kabi's work on rDNA hGH.

Nevertheless, the Swedish public context was not giving clear signals about the extent to which genetic engineering was acceptable or not as a trajectory. There were even differences among Swedish government agencies. On the one hand, the Swedish government called this volun-tary, temporary moratorium on industrial applications in autumn 1979. This represented an informal but politically loaded selection criterion against genetic engineering. In the longer term, it appears that the Swedish government in fact wished to legislate national regulations which would clearly define what was acceptable or not. This would calm the debate, and researchers in all environments could get back to work. Even the most critical political party worked towards defining formal regulations, where the outer limits of the trajectory would be defined politically.

On the other hand, the commercial possibilities of genetic engineering had also been seen by some persons at the Swedish Board of Technical Development (Styrelsen för Teknisk Utveckling, STU). STU was an official agency, formed in 1968, and its raison d'être was to facilitate and develop closer contacts between universities and firms in order to promote industrially relevant technology. In contrast to the govern-ment's brief moratorium, STU encouraged diverse industrial applica-tions from 1979. In particular, Gerhard Miksche of STU pushed for government support of genetic engineering. STU was divided into 'needs areas' or research divisions, one of which supported research

[14] LO/TCO (1982: 53).

[15] Wennergren's original proposal was criticized when the respective government authorities and other parties received it for comments. Based on the account given in SOU (1992: ch. 3), the following events occurred. After some revisions, the Ministry of Labour developed propositions for the Swedish Parliament. The parliamentary working committee for these questions (socialutskottet) suggested the Parliament pass the proposi-tion, but added that ethical, humanitarian, and social questions about recombinant DNA in a longer-term perspective should be investigated by a parliamentary committee. This eventually led to the official discussion presented in SOU (1984) *Genetisk integritet* (Genetic Integrity). The Swedish Parliament took the decision on 13 September 1979, and on 20 December the government gave four decrees to implement it.

on food technology, including biotechnology, and was headed by Charlotte af Malmborg. Miksche was head of pharmaceutical technology.

Miksche and af Malmborg thought that genetic engineering, or biotechnology, could be a way to dynamize research in these sectors. In
1979, they therefore generated support for and launched a framework
research program called Gene Technology. The program was to run for
several years. 'The purpose of this project [Gene Technology] is to build
competence about recombinant DNA technology which is directed
towards the needs of Swedish industry.'[16] Although STU never supported work within Kabi or KabiGen on hGH,[17] STU recognized the
need to develop commercial scale processes as well as enabling technologies. This included, for example, process technology, process control,
and separation technology as well as more basic research.[18] STU, a
government agency supporting technical development, thus quickly
joined Kabi's enthusiasm and were willing to invest large sums of
money, several million crowns, in scientific research at universities or
institutes of technology. The research was intended to have commercial
applications. STU specifically wanted to encourage novelty and some
diversity along a commercially useful trajectory.

The year 1979 was by and large a period of uncertainty for Kabi and
KabiGen. The Swedish public context gave both positive and negative
signals, although stability increased near the end of the year. There was
also financial uncertainty within the firm, leading to uncertainty about
how to finance the expanding R & D project. KabiVitrum had gone from
a profit of 27.2 million Swedish crowns ($3.9 million) in 1978 to a loss of
22.3 million Swedish crowns ($3.2 million) in 1979.[19] This was one
reason that government support was so important. Kabi and KabiGen
also faced opposition to their building plans for a P3 lab and some
opposition to genetic engineering experiments in general, as well as
uncertainty about when the government would pass regulatory laws
and how restrictive those laws would be. By mid-to late 1979, however, it was clear that the Swedish government and Parliament would
soon act, leading to a stabilization of the public context. The state played

[16] STU (1982: 6). Because the food division wanted to distribute a large sum of money,
the decision had to go up to the STU board. In addition to approving the distribution of
funds, the board also requested that the moral issues of genetic engineering be discussed,
eventually leading to the book *Etik och Genteknik* (Ethics and Genetic Engineering) (STU
1982). Similar questions were being raised by the Swedish government in SOU (1984) as
discussed in the previous footnote.

[17] Much later, Åberg thanked af Malborg for STU's early support in a public seminar
on biotechnology (Rosén 1991). STU gave no support directly to Kabi or KabiGen, and af
Malmborg (1992) said in an interview that she did not know why Åberg had said that
STU supported them.

[18] Sources include af Malmborg (1992, 1993) and STU (1979: sect. 5D). Although a
number of diverse projects were supported, by far the largest grant went to Lennart
Philipson, Microbiology, Biomedicinskt Centrum in Uppsala. These projects were
handled by af Malmborg.   [19] Ehrling and Ekengard (1980: 63).

an important role in complementing the market, both through direct financing and through developing a framework for action through regulation.

Knowing that the situation would stabilize, Kabi could concentrate on integrating genetic engineering into the production system. Doing so required experimentation and hands-on experience because challenges arose as a consequence of practical applications. Experimentation would help generate alternatives likely to be adapted to conditions of use. This experimentation was initially done in collaboration between Kabi and Genentech.

Before growing the bacteria in Sweden, Kabi's fermentation expert Holmström needed to learn more about the specific characteristics of the *E. coli* bacteria strain producing hGH. This was best done in collaboration with Genentech, which both had relevant knowledge and were situated in a favourable public context. Testing alternatives was also necessary to develop the genetic engineering techniques and biological material because they had to function according to corporate parameters of use. This knowledge, techniques, and biological material was part of the R & D contract and transfer from the United States to Sweden which was specified as part of Kabi's licence.

For these reasons, in September 1979 Holmström went to Genentech to work for five weeks with Genentech's fermentation expert Norm Lin.[20] Genentech had the specialized genetic engineering techniques and had developed the bacteria, but they had not yet grown it on a large scale. Nobody had. Just like Holmström, Lin needed to learn more about the peculiarities of this bacteria strain, particularly the conditions for optimizing cell growth, how to turn the promoter on, how to maximize hormone production, and so forth. In order to learn more about the alternatives, the researchers experimented, tested alternatives, and strove to develop a model fermentation process which functioned.

At this stage, these corporate researchers clearly saw the fermentation process as a continuation of the large scale, commercial fermentation of other products like antibiotics. They had standardized equipment and techniques to use in addressing engineering questions, which were similar to questions from other commercial uses of biological materials. They acted as engineers to develop technology in directions relevant for the techno-economic environment, not as basic scientists responding to the basic scientific environment. This was so despite the strong science base of the technology and despite the necessity of integrating scientific and technological knowledge and techniques.

Using existing knowledge, techniques, and equipment, Lin and Holmström set to work growing the genetically modified bacteria in South San

---

[20] Holmström (1992).

Francisco. The American restrictions were the NIH guidelines, which allowed ten-litre fermentation but which also required that the micro-organisms be killed before removal from the fermenter. Indeed, NIH guidelines were formally only for university research, but firms followed them, partly to prevent negative public opinion. Holmström and Lin's initial problem was just getting the bacteria to grow.

As a strategy which was a compromise between the regulatory environments in the United States and Sweden and between the respective competences of the firms, Holmström and Lin grew the hGH cultures in San Francisco, and broke apart the cells, called cell lysate, at Genentech. Thereafter, as Lin puts it:

we would put it in bottles, freeze it, and send it to Kabi for product recovery. Because at the time, we [Genentech] had just started doing recovery ourselves but I think Kabi knew much better how to purify this protein than us, so they were ahead of us.[21]

Åberg and Sirvell said the same thing publicly in Sweden at the end of October 1979:

We [Kabi] can not bring home this [hGH-producing] bacteria in the current situation. The bacteria is cultivated abroad, after which the bacteria are killed. The bacteria free solution is then sent here to Sweden and attempts have been started to develop an industrial technology to purify the growth hormone.[22]

Kabi's contribution was analytical as well as helping develop the production system. Bacteria producing human growth hormone thus had a commercial-scale reality as well as its scientific reality described in the scientific papers from summer/autumn 1979. The bacteria could be simultaneously used for diverse purposes for diverse environments.

At this very early stage, Genentech and Kabi had a division of labour, each doing a complementary step of the production process. Genentech fermented, and Kabi purified. Åberg and Sirvell indicate that the reason for the division of labour was the respective legislation (or lack thereof) in the two countries, whereas the researcher Lin emphasized division of labour based on the specialized competences of the two firms. Other scientists second Lin's interpretation.[23] Initially in this co-operation, both firms perceived that Kabi's experience with pituitary hGH would give them a competitive advantage over competing firms like Lilly. Knowledge, techniques, and equipment about the existing tissue extraction technology would help guide their attempts to develop new combinations. Biotech and pharmaceutical firms would need each others' competences and experiences.

Because the firms were trying to make a product identical to an

---

[21] Lin (1993a).   [22] Åberg and Sirvell (1979: 3), my translation.
[23] Fryklund (1993).

existing product but based on quite different technology and knowledge, another initial major concern was that the hGH produced in bacteria had one extra amino acid, a methionine (met). It had 192 amino acids instead of the 191 in hGH produced in the body. The first can be called met hGH, and the second met-less or natural hGH. The methionine gives a start signal for the translation of the gene, and Genentech had no way of cutting it off after it had fulfilled this function. Originally, the bacteria produced a mixture of met and met-less hGH, but when the fermentation method was under better control, the recombinant organisms only produced the met hGH.[24] To prove that the met hGH worked as well as the natural one, the firms needed to have something with which to compare it. In other words, they needed to know the physical characteristics of pituitary hGH and techniques for purifying and testing it. This is why Kabi's previous experience came in handy for the new project.

Thus, although the relationship between Genentech and Kabi involved transfer of genetic engineering techniques for a specific application from the USA to Sweden, this initial division of labour between fermentation (Genentech) and purification (Kabi) also indicates elements of mutual complementarity. Each wanted to move into the other's core competences. Managers and researchers felt that this mutual complementarity was important for their joint collaboration, since many initial challenges arose due to the integration of the old and the new.

Due to the interlocking nature of the production systems, more than cell fermentation was required. Kabi and Genentech also had to develop and refine all the complementary techniques and equipment, such as purification and analysis. They also had to make the component technologies function together at a cost-effective level.

The project was placed into a Kabi R & D group studying peptide hormones from the pituitary gland. Although some in the group had been involved in Kabi's initial contact with Genentech after somatostatin, their real involvement came in 1979 with the appointment of Linda Fryklund as project leader.

Despite Kabi's openness in the mass media about developing the purification process in Sweden for the 'bacteria-free solution' in October 1979, Åberg has said that in December 1979 he secretly brought the hGH-producing bacteria into Sweden. As much later reported in a widely read, weekly newspaper for engineers, *Ny Teknik*:

Smuggling professor made genetic engineering profitable. It began with a bacteria, smuggled in the research director's waistcoat pocket . . . For six months, it lay in amidst the food in the professor's own refrigerator, and eventually ended up at Kabi.[25]

[24] Fryklund (1993).
[25] Andersson (1990: 12). Åberg also threatened to move activities abroad in November 1979 if legislation was not passed soon (*Scrip* 1979: 3).

He probably did bring in a bacteria strain, but there is a question about the relative importance of this event. In this account, Åberg presents his smuggling trip as one of the key steps in the innovation process.

Although Åberg was a driving force for Kabi's move into genetic engineering and deserves much credit,[26] this physical act of importing a strain of the bacteria was just one of countless steps along the road to commercialization. Åberg's role has been emphasized in popular Swedish accounts to the exclusion of all the subsequent R & D at Kabi. In the case of bringing the bacteria to Sweden, for example, other variations of the genetically engineered bacteria were later brought into Sweden by Holmström or just shipped through the mail.

Moreover, according to Fryklund, whether or not Åberg 'smuggled' the bacteria to Sweden was irrelevant to Kabi's R & D work. In 1979 Kabi and Genentech were running fermentation in California. Holmström and Lin were 'trying to persuade the bacteria to make the right hGH. Before then it was not necessary to bring the bacteria to Sweden at all!'[27] On this view, Kabi had little reason to challenge the norms in the contemporary public context. They were still having technical problems in California.

Moreover, changes to the Swedish public context at this time paved the way for Kabi to ferment the bacteria. On 1 January 1980, Sweden got comprehensive national legislation regulating the use of genetic engineering, based on Wennergren's earlier recommendations. These included legislative changes to place rDNA experiments under existing laws as well as to replace the research councils' GMAC with an official Delegation for Recombinant DNA Questions (Delegationen för DNA-frågor).[28] In particular, firms wishing to use genetic engineering now had a specific legal procedure and structure through which to negotiate. This replaced voluntary compliance with the research council's committee and reduced uncertainty. Largely as a result of this legislative decision, the Swedish public debate trying to stop the development of genetic engineering pretty much died out. By setting clear formal regulations, the Swedish state facilitated firms' knowledge-seeking activities.

The firms' desires to develop genetic engineering were tangential to

---

[26] Reichard (1993).   [27] Fryklund (1993).

[28] The decision was taken on 20 December 1979. Like the GMAC, the Delegation had a subcommittee for risk classification of experiments and held hearings to advise government decisions. After 1 January 1980 all work in Sweden with recombinant DNA techniques—whether in industry or universities—had to get permission from two government authorities, the Board on Working Environment (Arbetarskyddstyrelsen) and Public Health (Koncessionsnämnden för miljöskydd). In fact, organizationally, the Delegation was placed under Arbetarskyddstyrelsen, which is a ministerial body for making and enforcing laws on working life. Gunnar Danielsson, the first chairman of the Delegation, was also director-general for Arbetarskyddstyrelsen. Koncessionsnämnden set the conditions for industrial activities by making and enforcing laws on environmental protection.

the interests of the new Delegation and the committees under existing bodies of legislation. They were positive. Gunnar Danielsson was the first chairman of the Delegation and director general for the Board on Working Environment. As he put it, we 'also wanted rules, not to prevent activities but to help them . . . [We wanted to create] a model to regulate activities that people could accept.'[29] Stable, politically agreed upon regulation proved necessary to legitimize industrial use of genetic engineering in Sweden.[30]

Although the political framework was in place as of January 1980, getting permission to do experiments was not immediately forthcoming. Kabi moved as fast as it could to obtain a permit. On 3 January 1980, KabiGen applied for permission to the Public Health Committee to (1) do research generally with recombinant DNA techniques and (2) grow *E. coli* bacteria which could express hGH in a volume of up to ten litres. KabiGen intended to carry out these two activities in the now renovated Kabi virus lab. The strain of *E. coli* mentioned in the application was, of course, the one developed by Genentech, namely an *E. coli* K12 strain 1776 with RV308 using the plasmid pBR 322.[31] Interestingly enough, KabiGen's application specifically states that 'the company wishes to grow this bacteria in volumes of max 10 litres in order to develop purification technology necessary to produce pharmaceuticals.'[32] Technological activities in relation to production had clear precedence over scientific activities by this point.

Following Swedish praxis, the Public Health Committee in turn sent out the request to interested authorities for comments and finally had a meeting on 12 June 1980.[33] The Public Health Committee decision came on 4 July (the paper is dated), but KabiGen did not get the broad permits they were seeking. Instead, KabiGen only got permission to grow *E. coli* to produce three specific proteins in scales of up to ten litres volume.[34]

---

[29] Danielsson (1992), my translation.

[30] Countries which did not pass comprehensive legislation and/or where the public debate continued to be largely negative have in recent years been more hostile public environments to developing genetic engineering. Germany, for example, got comprehensive laws in 1990, and it is quite restrictive and time-consuming to fulfil the rules (Kahn 1992: 524). For example, Hessen, a region in Germany, delayed a Hoffman-LaRoche factory for producing insulin with genetic engineering for several years (Abbott 1992: 402).

[31] This bacteria strain was the one later used to produce Kabi's first hGH, with the brand name of Somatonorm (Holmström 1994).   [32] KMN (1980a: 2).

[33] The application was sent to a number of potentially interested parties, such as research councils, government ministries, and local Stockholm government bodies. The majority supported KabiGen's application, but stipulated that the application should be for specific projects, not general research using recombinant DNA (KMN 1980a: 1, 5–7).

[34] KMN (1980a: 10). The board decided that the application for general research using recombinant DNA techniques was too general and therefore did not take a decision. They instead allowed KabiGen to come in with a modified application before 31 December 1980. On 9 December , both KabiGen and KabiVitrum applied. KabiVitrum applied for permission to carry out development work with rDNA material and KabiGen to expand their permit to carry out research with rDNA technology (KMN 1980a, 1980b, 1980c).

While the biotech KabiGen were waiting for this decision in 1980, the pharmaceutical firm Kabi continued their collaboration with Genentech, expressing the bacteria in the United States and purifying it in Sweden. Kabi's R & D fermentation expert Holmström returned to Genentech several times for some weeks at a stretch to work with Lin. There was communication between Holmström and Lin, of course, and transfer of knowledge, but the two quickly developed individualized processes in collaboration with their respective downstream processing groups.

After KabiGen were granted their permits in June 1980, Holmström used KabiGen's labs to grow the hGH bacteria in Sweden. Then in November 1980 another Kabi employee, Cirl Florell, joined Holmström in fermentation. Unlike Genentech, which initially had to hire new people for each new task, Kabi drew on current employees for the hGH project. In this case, both men had extensive experience in fermenting Kabi's other products, like streptokinase and penicillin. Their knowledge, skills, and experience thus built upon retained knowledge organized within the firm and transferred to a new R & D task. This phase of the innovation process required much trial and error based on empirical work to identify potential problems and solutions.

Moreover, time was of the essence due to competitive pressures in the international markets. Initially, Holmström and Florell utilized the ten litre limit to the maximum by running one cultivation a day. As it took about seven hours to grow up the bacteria to the desired cell mass, they took turns at coming to work at 6 a.m. Kabi were in a hurry! During this initial R & D in Sweden, sufficient money was available through the money borrowed from the governmental industrial fund.

The corporate research managers also had to decide which types of activities should be given priority at each stage. In other words, they continually had to make decisions about the directions in which to develop the complementary and component technologies. For example, in 1980 the rDNA hGH group at Kabi got information that their 192 amino acid hGH was biologically active. This vital information showed that it could be used as a pharmaceutical. Knowing this made Genentech's research to get rid of the extra amino acid less of an urgent task than it had been. Instead, R & D related to the production system, and particularly to purification, was given top priority.

During the two years 1979 and 1980, Kabi thus began to engage in in-house R & D to integrate genetic engineering into a production system. Nevertheless, they had been faced with uncertainty and strict limits on genetic engineering activities in general in the Swedish public context.[35] Even at the end of 1980, things still seemed unsettled, implying risks and

---

[35] It was also during this period that Genentech decided to make hGH when commercialization seemed possible.

uncertainty for the firm. It could not be certain that they would be allowed to continue experimenting with the technology, and therefore, it was uncertain whether they would eventually be able to reap benefits from this R & D investment. In mid-1980, Kabi and KabiGen had got permits to work on a ten litre scale, but Kabi could not be sure whether they would be given a permit to grow the bacteria on a large scale in Sweden. Although permission would probably be forthcoming, new debates or protests might derail it.

Moreover, the contacts with Genentech had functioned well, but both firms needed all the hGH they could get for their preclinical and future clinical tests. The two developed marginally different production processes, but such differences were relevant for the official testing procedure. They stopped collaborating. For such reasons, Kabi needed an alternative source of production which could produce hGH according to Kabi's specifications. This is why Hans Sievertsson and his boss Bengt Karlsson looked for alternative possibilities for growing the bacteria at the end of 1980. They found a willing partner in the British Department of Health, which owned the Centre for Applied Microbiological Research at Porton Down. Most importantly from Kabi's side, Porton Down had the localities to grow cultures and to do experiments classified as high risk in large volumes. Reasons for British interest included the fact that the Department of Health had been actively encouraging Porton Down to be involved with commercial applications, and moreover, that Kabi agreed to help the British authorities with their extraction of hGH from pituitary glands.[36] An agreement was signed in December 1980 that Porton Down would ferment the bacteria for hGH during a short period. Kabi thus reacted against what it perceived as a limitation in the Swedish public context by finding a specialized lab in England to carry out experiments.

As with the earlier fermentation work done with Genentech, the cell paste was flown from Porton Down to Stockholm for purification, product recovery, and analysis. Cell paste is the concentrated remains of the fermentation process. Only fermentation of the genetically modified bacteria was moved abroad, and Kabi's special competences in the succeeding stages were again used.

The actions of the Swedish regulatory agencies were in fact clearly pro-commercial in this case. They accepted that ten litres of cell paste brought in from abroad was equivalent to the ten litres of fermentation broth for which KabiGen had a permit. Ten litres of fermentation broth means ten litres of nutrients, liquid, and variant cells with only a small portion of hGH. For that reason, ten litres of cell paste actually corresponded to the approximately 400 litres of fermentation broth that

[36] Walgate (1980: 528), *Svensk Farmaceutisk Tidskrift* (1980: 623).

Porton Down produced. The Swedish authorities' acceptance of this difference between permit and reality came from an expressed desire to encourage commercial use of genetic engineering within Sweden.[37] Moreover, the authorities seem also to have expected that the Swedish regulations would soon be revised to allow larger volumes and less stringent conditions, as Swedish legislation was expected to imitate such American revisions. For example, when fermentation was later initiated in Sweden, Kabi's first production tank was already 1,500 litres in size.[38] So, although Kabi sometimes perceived the Swedish public context as restrictive, government agencies could flexibly interpret Swedish regulations to promote commercial uses.

Despite such points of positive support, in general during the late 1970s and the year 1980, Sweden initially lacked but then started developing a stable public context, including official regulations. The supporters of recombinant DNA at the two Kabi companies, especially Åberg and Sievertsson, actively and publicly worked to create legislation and positive public opinion about the medical and commercial benefits of genetic engineering by engaging in public debate, testifying to the government, and so forth.

Thus, in developing their commercial uses of genetic engineering, Kabi had to start by developing the public context in terms of debate, informal norms, and formal regulation. By so doing, they reduced uncertainty about their own future by creating conditions which allowed them to pursue a commercial technological trajectory but with a firm specific path based on their specific competences and experiences. Without legislative rules, unexpected and uncontrollable public or political opinion might again have endangered their plans to realize the economic and technical potential. With legislative rules, the firm could identify which specific activities were allowable. They could thereby assure that their knowledge-seeking activities fell within the boundaries of the acceptable.

This consolidation of the political context took some time but was not excessively slow. For Kabi to work on a ten-litre scale with genetically modified bacteria, it took fifteen months from application to the granting of the initial GMAC permit (when Kabi did not have labs) and seven months for the permit under the new official regulations. Because a functioning production system based on genetically engineered bacteria required physically bringing together and trying out the various steps, not being able to carry out the work inside the firm in Sweden was a handicap for Kabi. Initially, however, collaboration with Genentech was primary, where fermentation was done in South San Francisco and product recovery and analysis in Stockholm.

[37] Holmström (1992), Brunius (1992b).   [38] Holmström (1994).

However, because both Kabi's and Genentech's R & D projects were in essence shaped by market forces rather than the knowledge forces internal to science, time was a vital factor, and Kabi needed their own source of the protein.

Commercializing Genetic Engineering from Genentech's Perspective

Across the Atlantic, Genentech did not have to go about creating a stable public context as Kabi was doing, because such a context existed in the USA, especially through the NIH guidelines. Negotiation over regulation mainly consisted of relaxing the guidelines, and by the end of 1980, Genentech could use 750-litre fermenter tanks.

In contrast to Kabi's position as a government owned firm selling established pharmaceutical products, though, Genentech's existence was much more dependent on the market. Genentech continued to need positive publicity to attract financiers, R & D contracts, and eventually, buyers of their stock. Genentech as a business proposition made the American news increasingly often during this period, culminating in an enormously successful share offering in October 1980.[39] In light of this dependence on the market in relation to its scientific reputation, Genentech concentrated on research on various rDNA proteins up through the end of 1980. Their knowledge-seeking activities challenged existing scientific and technological knowledge in order to expand their economic constraints. However, they also needed to develop competences similar to Kabi's in order to produce and sell a pharmaceutical.

As Genentech was a new firm, it had no retained knowledge, techniques, or equipment which could be transferred from an old project to the new ones. Genentech instead had to hire and organize a new combination of employees. In 1979 and 1980, Genentech hired a wide range of persons for its nascent departments and research groups, including molecular biologists, protein chemists, and specialists in fermentation and other engineering R & D work. Among the basic scientists, Genen-

---

[39] Based mainly on the research results for somatostatin, insulin, and human growth hormone as well as much publicity, Genentech gave out a public offering of shares in October 1980. It managed to raise $36 million. The shares were initially offered at $35 per share, rocketed to $89 within 20 minutes, but soon moved back to the low $40s (Benner 1981: 62). 'Not one penny of Genentech's meagre profits has yet come from the sale of a product. . . . Even so, investors' white-hot reception for the company turned the $500 that Messrs. Swanson and Boyer each had kicked in to their original partnership into fortunes worth more than $65 million each' (Christensen 1980: 1). The idea of scientific breakthroughs can generate much optimism! Publicity is important because science is worth whatever people are willing to pay for it.

tech went for post-docs, full of ideas but without steady university positions.[40] In addition to scientists specializing in genetic engineering techniques and related knowledge, they hired a number of persons with industrial experience in areas necessary for large-scale growth of bacteria, such as fermentation, analytical chemistry, protein chemistry, and purification.

Genentech management recognized the need for interdisciplinary interaction, particularly between genetic engineering and biochemical engineering, as shown by the background of many of the people they hired. Maybe they learned from an early mistake. The third Genentech employee, who was the first person hired as head of Genentech's process development, is said to have had the attitude, 'Just give me the bugs and I'll grow them.' The bugs (bacteria) proved to be finicky and required special handling. This person did not stay long at the firm, probably because he did not consider feedback between process R & D engineering and the genetically engineered bacteria.[41]

In fact, growing the bacteria on a large scale proved difficult, as the co-founder Swanson put it:

Scientifically, we [Genentech] began at 'square one' by taking microorganisms out of the small laboratory scale and putting them into much larger stainless steel tanks. You know, learning how those organisms work in that new environment wasn't easy. The first time we did it, they all dropped dead—they didn't like it.[42]

As the R & D staff confronted these modified micro-organisms with new conditions, such difficulties led the firms to develop new fermentation conditions more amenable to the modified bacteria. In the above quote, the technical constraints included the new physical conditions of large-scale stainless steel tanks. The novelty generated during Genentech and Kabi's co-operation was directed towards challenging the existing constraints. They wanted to do new things.

Genentech hired persons who could understand the relationships between the knowledge bases of genetic engineering and biochemical engineering and who could build up this integration of knowledge in the firm. This can be exemplified by two early employees, Norm Lin, who worked on fermentation, and Ken Olson, who worked on protein purification. Lin had an undergraduate degree from Taiwan in agricultural chemistry, after which he had worked four years in glutamic acid fermentation, which ran in very large scale (100,000-litre) batches. He then came to the USA for a Ph.D. and then a post-doc position, working on aspects of gene regulation and restriction enzymes, before moving to Worthington Biochemical, where he did enzyme fermentation.[43]

---

[40] Clayton (1986: 67).   [41] Kleid (1993).   [42] Swanson (1986b: 58).
[43] Lin (1993a).

Olson similarly both had industrial experience and had done graduate work relating to the techniques of genetic engineering. He had an MA in biochemistry, then worked for Hoffman-LaRoche doing enzymology and protein purification. In particular, Olson worked at Hoffman-LaRoche's Institute of Molecular Biology, where in the early 1970s, they made a synthetic gene, put that together into a double stranded DNA using annealing techniques and DNA ligase, and put it into a Lamda phage virus. 'This was one of the very first examples of recombinant DNA!', Olson states.[44] Note that this was in a corporate lab. Thus even before the biotech firms were started, some corporate researchers were involved in both scientific and technological activities. The point here is that as individuals Lin and Olson integrated knowledge about genetic engineering techniques with commercial aspects of production.

Lin and Olson joined Genentech in August 1979 when Genentech had about forty employees. Instead of just 'taking the bugs and growing them', the new research management emphasized that growing cells and improving yields would require interdisciplinary approaches between different scientific and engineering fields. This new commercial trajectory would require new combinations of novelty which differed significantly from basic scientific activities.

In 1980, the third Genentech employee who just 'wanted to grow the bugs' left the firm, and Genentech hired a person away from Eli Lilly, namely William Young. Young had some experience with large scale, genetically engineered bacteria from Lilly's work on insulin, and while at Lilly, Young had worked with Genentech. By this time Genentech had about three people in manufacturing development and maybe five to ten researchers who had moved to manufacturing R & D. Young's job was to form a process development group. In other words, his job was to organize the different kinds of knowledge and experience needed within Genentech to carry out the goal of production.[45]

Genentech's new combinations of biochemical engineering and genetic engineering were applied to develop production systems for a variety of potential products. This variety contrasts with Kabi's emphasis on hGH. In Genentech, there were a number of process development projects going on simultaneously over the early 1980s, including hGH, insulin, somatostatin, bovine and porcine growth hormones, human serum albumin, and alpha and beta interferon. These were the same projects for which Genentech had sold R & D contracts for the proteins. That Genentech also worked on process development indicates that Genentech management had identified the challenges both of genetic engineering *per se* and of integrating it with process technologies.

---

[44] Olson (1993a). The scientific paper describing this experiment is Harvey *et al.* (1975).
[45] Young (1992).

One reason why Genentech worked on multiple products was that they wanted to develop a general model system for genetically engineered proteins. On the one hand, such a model would be generalizable, including indicating the broad parameters for mass production. On the other hand, the model would be useful for a number of specific R & D projects carried out by the firm. Both the general and the more specific knowledge would give knowledge directly applicable for the firm. Thus, although both firms had to solve specific and local technical problems, they also strove after more generalizable techniques, knowledge, and models.

Although Genentech's model system was intended to be generalizable for similar proteins, it should be pointed out that the knowledge and technologies so generated were not necessarily meant to be general in the sense of public knowledge. Some specifications would be privately kept knowledge, industrial secrets. They would hopefully give Genentech an advantage in competition with others. Other aspects would be published or patented, and both strategies would lead to the diffusion of knowledge, although publishing generates public knowledge available to all who can partake of it, whereas patenting diffuses information but also assigns private ownership.

In that Genentech was trying to develop a general model, we can say that R & D at Genentech worked to reduce the diversity of technical choices. The problem with diversity was that it was expensive to generate and to maintain. An alternative to diversity is to generate models which limit the range of choices. In the best case, the models would concentrate the alternatives, weeding out diversity which is not immediately relevant.

Thus instead of diversity, Genentech's development and process science researchers hoped that the model system would allow standardization. Lin says this about the fermentation:

At first we thought it would be the same. What you're going to do is insert a gene in *E. coli* and tell the *E. coli* to express it so it'll be the same. But it turns out that every protein is different as far as how to grow the *E. coli*, how to do the fermentation control, you know, so on and so forth. So every new product is a challenge for me.[46]

There is, of course, a continuum between standardization and diversity, that is, between standard models and new challenges for each project. Lin indicates that there have been more challenges than expected. For researchers, the challenges involved meant that each new protein was more interesting to work on. Each would involve a search for new and very specific knowledge and techniques relevant to exactly that problem.

[46] Lin (1993a).

New challenges also, however, made developing each additional protein more expensive relative to using a standardized model applicable to all.

One reason it has been challenging is that the products the cells are making are foreign to the bacteria and can make the cell 'sick'.

You have to individually optimize each fermentation process. Because actually each protein produced in *E. coli* has a different impact on the *E. coli*. OK? So some are very toxic to the *E. coli* and you really have to do some trick to make it grow.
The most common trick is you repress the expression to allow [the cells] . . . to grow to a certain cell mass. Just imagine each cell is a factory; if you don't have enough cell mass, you don't have enough product.[47]

Instead of 'just taking the bugs and growing them', the foreign genes lead to special problems and necessitate 'tricks' to make the cells ignore the toxins. Growing 'healthy' cells requires fermentation techniques specialized to each strain of bacteria. This knowledge is often specific to individual firms.

Not only do different proteins have different effects on the bacteria, but also the same protein can be expressed using different genetic engineering techniques and biological material. The differences often lie in what can be seen as small modifications, although deciding what those modifications should be may take much effort.

As to the specific strain of bacteria used to produce hGH, in 1980 both Genentech and Kabi were growing the *E. coli* bacteria expression construction detailed in Goeddel *et al.* (1989), a bacteria which had a lac promoter. Although this construction did instruct the bacteria cells to make hGH, there were problems, not least because of the low yields. Only about 5 per cent of proteins produced were hGH.[48] One problem causing the low yield was the number of variants, which are proteins similar but not exactly identical to the one desired. Another was that the bacteria made so many other proteins. Genentech had similar yield problems with their other products, like insulin. There was thus a general problem in that the technology functioned but was not efficient enough to meet the firms' demands.

Low yields implied high cost, and reasonable cost represented a very serious constraint on a new pharmaceutical. Reasonable cost of the final product was necessary to compete, and in fact, low yields and high costs have been general problems for commercial use of genetic engineering as a means of production.

Yield was also vital for the specific R & D contracts. 'One of the most important bench-marks' of the contract between Lilly and Genentech was that the bacteria make ten milligrams of insulin per litre of fermenta-

---

[47] Lin (1993a).   [48] Kleid (1993).

tion broth at a specified level of purity, lot size, and cost. The other contracts also contained very specific demands. If Genentech could not increase yield satisfactorily, they could not fulfil their R & D contracts and would thereby forgo that money and prestige and endanger their whole existence as a firm.

Genentech therefore needed to generate new techniques, or imitate existing external ones in order to increase yield. This problem was then significant scientifically as well as technologically, even if scientists responding to the basic scientific environment were not interested in exactly this question. Corporate researchers would be rewarded for working on very specific contexts of use involving purity, lot size, cost, and so forth, but not basic scientists. According to a later Genentech lawsuit document, the stipulated 'production levels would represent a dramatic technological breakthrough without which the profitable commercialization of such a recombinant DNA product would not be possible.'[49] To realize this 'breakthrough' which made a commercial trajectory possible, Genentech management could choose between a variety of strategies, including carrying out in-house research, contracting out specific projects, monitoring knowledge and techniques developed elsewhere, and/or adapting general principles for their specific goals. Each could in turn potentially influence scientific activities.

To increase yield of proteins, it was not enough to improve the purification process. The bacteria also needed to express a greater proportion of the correct protein. Some of the Genentech researchers therefore continued searching for ways to improve the genetic engineering techniques and biological material by, for example, improving the DNA sequence giving the signal to start expressing proteins. A more efficient signal would have the effect of increasing expression. For hGH, the researchers also wanted to get rid of the extra amino acid (methionine) since that differentiated their product from the 'natural' protein.

As with their hopes to develop a standardized fermentation process, Genentech were interested in improving the yield of not only hGH but also other proteins. For this reason, they felt it would be advantageous to standardize the genetic engineering techniques used. They could then introduce the same improvement across the board for all products rather than devoting time and resources to design unique improvements for each. The firm again had incentives to decrease diversity in order to decrease costs. Such attempts to make genetic engineering techniques more reliable and standard clearly differentiated the commercial technological trajectory from the scientific trajectory.

To standardize genetic engineering techniques and biological material, the corporate researchers wanted to be able to use the same signals and

---

[49] Genentech (1987: 7).

just 'plug in' genes coding for different proteins. This at least was Genentech's strategy, so they could experiment with different promoters to find the one which encouraged the bacteria to produce the best yield. That promoter could then be used for all the proteins.

At this point, the firm's researchers were asking questions about nature that reflected not the laws of nature in which basic scientists were supposed to be interested but instead questions about how to control nature. In this work, the corporate researchers used basic scientific knowledge and techniques but were not looking to answer basic research questions. They instead wanted to develop techniques in specific directions which would enable cost-efficient commercial mass production. Their knowledge-seeking activities were specifically generated to fit their perception of market conditions, but doing so relied on feedback and interactions among scientific and technological activities.

The types of questions that both researchers and managers were asking included the following: Can we increase the yield and reduce production costs enough to make the product competitive in a market? (The market included not only identical proteins made with genetic engineering but also proteins from other sources.) Can we improve the quality and increase the percentage of the desired protein with fewer variations? Can we reduce the number, the time involved, and hence the cost for all the intermediary steps in the production system?

Sometime about a year after Genentech's original 1979 scientific experiment proving *E. coli* could make hGH with the lac promoter, they tried a number of different promoters, including one called tryptophan or trp. The trp promoter had been studied in Charles Yanofsky's lab at nearby Stanford University, and perhaps Giuseppe Miozzari, who came to Genentech from Yanofsky's lab, was the one who suggested they try trp.[50] The corporate researchers did not know in advance if the trp promoter would work better than the lac promoter, but thought it might.

One day, the Genentech scientist Daniel Yansura was hooking up trp to one of Genentech's other products, maybe hepatitis surface antigen, when his supervisor Dennis Kleid asked if he could throw in hGH and hook it up, make the plasmid, get it into the cells, and all that. Yansura did not have time to do the induction (grow the cells) so Kleid grew up the cells, then starved them of trp, thereby giving a signal to start producing hGH. Kleid recalls, 'We saw just tons of hGH!' and 'It looked like half the cell might be our protein!'[51] Yansura recollects, 'Instead of making 5 per cent, it made a third of the cell protein! Making a third of

[50] Yansura (1992, 1993a).
[51] Kleid (1993, 1994). The specific amount and/or general range of cell protein made as given by sources varies between 10% to 50% in Kleid (1993, 1994), Yansura (1993a, 1993b), Fryklund (1993), and Olson (1993b).

the cell protein was an enormous increase in yield over the 5 per cent previously produced.'[52]

As with the lac promotor before it, the academic lab studying the trp promotor sent it to Genentech free of charge. Transmitting biological materials was a normal part of the flow and reproduction of scientific experiments. Moreover, the academic labs working on promoters had publicized quite a bit of information about how they functioned. This understanding facilitated use for the specific commercial goal of increasing yields. The firm could thus adapt and apply general knowledge developed in the basic scientific environment, but the firm had to invest resources to make adaptations relevant for their differing, commercial goals.

Increasing the yield, here achieved by changing the genetic engineering techniques and biological material, was one of the most crucial steps towards commercialization.[53] Genentech had to solve this particular bottle-neck of yield both for their own goal of commercializing a pharmaceutical and also for fulfilling R & D contracts. By getting this result, they changed the existing limitations of scientific and technical knowledge and techniques.

In connection with this, Genentech was again looking for a more standardized model for other proteins. Genentech scientists concurrently used the trp promoter on a number of projects such as thymosin alpha 1, somatostatin, insulin A and B chains, and pro-insulin.[54] Accomplishing this by just 'plugging in the genes' was not quite as standardized as it sounds, at least not in 1980, because Genentech had to worry about finding the right place to cut the DNA to insert the new genes and so forth. They had only a handful of restriction enzymes to cut at specific sites. In addition, they had to take into account the distance to the ribosome binding site. These similar and yet different experiments thus demanded that a number of parameters be taken into account for each case.

Despite these challenges, trying out new promoters on the bacteria expression systems did not have the same novelty as their first cloning jobs such as insulin. In the initial cloning job, everything had to be correct, double-checked, and there was no functioning system against which to check that it worked. Changing the promoter could be tricky, but they had something with which to compare it. By having done some experiments, the firm had thus built up specific as well as general knowledge and techniques which could be usefully applied to other products. These generalized and standardized aspects, or models,

[52] Yansura (1993b).   [53] Genentech (1987).
[54] Kleid (1994). The rest of this paragraph is based on Yansura (1993a) and Kleid (1993).

reduced the degree of novelty required for similar but subsequent experiments. Firms could thus learn.

Of all the trials and errors and only half-successful attempts to modify genetic engineering techniques and biological material in their search to improve the economic and technical potential of genetic engineering, these Genentech researchers only sent the improvements on down the pipeline to the R & D process researchers if there was a big change, like the enormous increase in yield with the trp promoter. The decision had to be based on a combination of technological and economic criteria. The change had to be significant enough to recuperate the cost in time and money of dropping the development and regulatory work already invested in the previous strain. Corporate R & D thus generated diversity by testing different solutions, but the firm had internal selection routines which directed it to choose only technical improvements giving relatively large economic advantages. What those advantages would turn out to be could not be calculated a priori but had to be guessed at, believed in.

The interactions between corporate researchers working on the genetic engineering techniques more for the basic scientific environment and corporate researchers working on the production system are, however, more complicated than simply transferring improvements from 'scientists' to process production people. This linear perspective is negated by the intensive feedback between various types of knowledge-seeking activities. For example, the reason Genentech researchers were examining different promoters in the first place was that low yield had been identified as a serious problem. Changing promoters was identified as one way to solve it. The existing knowledge, techniques, and biological material in the firm did not suffice to solve it. They needed to look elsewhere.

That those corporate researchers might be the ones who could solve this problem was evident through feedback with other corporate R & D groups involved in, for example, fermentation or purification. Lin explains this interaction thus:

Yes, we have to constantly feedback actually. If one hook-up for expression turns out to be difficult and the yield poor, then we always go back to the people doing the cloning and we talk with them and analyse the problem. And then we do another hook-up, changing promoters, changing whatever we thought might be beneficial and then come back and try fermentation again. So, it is a constant sort of feedback system.[55]

Interactions among specialist researchers corresponding to specific parts of the system helped identify challenges as well as the direction of

---

[55] Lin (1993a).

knowledge-seeking activities. There were a number of specialist groups inside the firm who were organized to work together on the system, but each group was also in turn a member of a larger community of specialists in other firms and in universities. They could then draw on established knowledge available in the community.

Inside the firm, different groups could discuss what was problematic and what was possible from their different perspectives, based on their respective competences and experiences. In other words, they could help each other identify opportunities, challenges, and bottle-necks. One advantage of a firm as compared to a university is that a firm's more formalized control structure for regulating search activities may facilitate the development of communicative, interactive patterns which facilitate interactions among specialists. They must discuss common problems and joint knowledge-seeking activities to reach common goals. In the best case, incentive structures in firms reward individuals for doing so.

Other Challenges of Complementary Technologies

As argued above, the firms initially used existing knowledge, techniques, and analytical methods for pit hGH and other proteins to compare the output of the new production systems with the protein extracted from human pituitary glands. Of course, convincing themselves did not suffice, because the firms also had to convince government regulatory agencies for pharmaceuticals that bacteria could produce human proteins. Such negotiations over technologies, testing methods, and characteristics of the output helped define the conditions which the new proteins needed to fulfil in order to compete.

In this dialogue between firms, doctors, and government agencies, the national regulatory agencies had to decide which criteria could be used to evaluate the safety and efficiency of rDNA pharmaceuticals. Regulatory agencies in Europe and the United States discussed matters extensively with firms involved in genetic engineering in the early 1980s.[56] They wanted to set guidelines, patterns of regulation, to establish what types of knowledge and tests were necessary to judge this new category of pharmaceuticals. These guidelines could be based on the initial products like insulin and hGH. The regulatory agencies would use specific knowledge found, for example, in clinical testing to develop general criteria for judging genetically produced pharmaceuticals.

A relevant example is a two-day conference of American government

---

[56] Fryklund (1992), Fhölenhag (1992).

officials and of university and corporate researchers called by the Food and Drug Administration (FDA) in May 1981.[57] This conference resulted in a book. In the words of the organizer, the FDA

convened this state-of-the-art conference on *Insulins and Growth Hormone* as a forum for the discussion of various aspects of the preparation and use of hormones obtained by recombinant DNA techniques. . . . The FDA staff reviewed criteria and tentative technical and administrative procedures by which the hormones from recombinant organisms will be evaluated for clinical use and marketing.[58]

In this and similar discussions, university scientists, firms, and governments were jointly creating criteria and conditions for evaluating rDNA pharmaceuticals. They needed to have a basis for comparing alternative analytical methods, testing, production methods, and so forth so that they could modify the existing pharmaceutical approval process in order to evaluate the new products.

The discussion over approval criteria was underway before any firm had submitted such a New Drug Application (NDA). For example, Eli Lilly would submit an NDA for rDNA insulin within a matter of months after this FDA meeting on insulin and hGH.[59] It is quite interesting that the FDA, this regulatory agency giving government approval for pharmaceuticals, was trying to create informal institutions which established criteria and routines to allow commercial exploitation before firms had specifically applied. Based on other passages in the book quoted above, it is apparent that there was pressure on the agency to avoid being accused of slowing down the innovation process. Pressure to move fast apparently gave them incentives to act a priori to set standards.

Both Genentech and Kabi participated in this American conference on rDNA insulin and hGH. This was the case even though Genentech and Kabi had divided up the world market, giving the American market exclusively to Genentech in 1980. Fryklund says that Kabi was invited because the FDA considered Kabi an actor. Kabi's pituitary hGH was already on sale there, and they were moving into the new technology.[60] At this conference, participants presented scientific and medical papers oriented towards the technology or the final protein. Genentech participated with two papers about aspects of genetic engineering and about comparing natural and rDNA polypeptides, whereas Kabi's paper compared the biological activity of rDNA and pit hGH using rats as models.[61]

---

[57] This conference was called by the Division of Metabolism and Endocrine Drug Products, Bureau of Drugs, Food and Drug Administration.
[58] Gueriguian *et al.* (eds. 1981: preface).
[59] In 1981, Eli Lilly's work on insulin was far ahead of any company making hGH.
[60] Fryklund (1993).
[61] Papers by Genentech are Miozzari (1981), Ross (1981), Stebbing *et al.* (1981), and by Kabi, Skottner *et al.* (1981).

Comparison between the two was essential to prove similarity—in other words, that the output of the different systems were similar.

The preface to this conference book indicates some tensions between seeing genetic engineering as a radically new technology and seeing it as something traditional:

A scientific consensus appears to have emerged at the conference. It became clear that recombinant DNA technology is not esoteric, mystical, or even mysterious; rather, it is the product of the evolution of biochemistry and molecular biology.

However, the possibility exists that very low levels of extraneous bacterial material present in the final products may cause untoward side effects, particularly during continual long-term therapy. It is within these limits that regulatory decisions will be made in the future.[62]

It is a reflection of the mood in the early 1980s that a government regulatory agency felt compelled to write that genetic engineering was 'not esoteric, mystical, or even mysterious'. Indeed, it indicates that public debate over the technology was still along those lines and that the agency wanted to tone down the radically new side of genetic engineering.

The FDA as well as other participants at this conference wanted to anchor genetic engineering firmly within the basic scientific environment, and thus within the ability of natural science to explain and evaluate nature. The argument that recombinant DNA was 'the product of the evolution of biochemistry and molecular biology' reflects an argument that genetic engineering is very close to existing bodies of knowledge and scientific research. If it is close, it is not so radically new after all. On the other hand, it opens up wondrous new possibilities. There is thus a dual argumentation which could help create optimism about future benefits as well as reduce fears about the consequences.

The second paragraph of the quote also indicates that new challenges for analytical methods had arisen but had not yet been solved. This is indicated in the above quote by 'extraneous bacterial material . . . may cause untoward side effects'. This reflects a specific problem with the new technology. More specifically, it reflects an incident which had taken place at Genentech and perhaps elsewhere. Initially there was a disagreement over the causes of this incident, but it was soon decided that Genentech had trouble with pyrogens. Firms and government agencies knew that proteins extracted from animal or human tissue could be contaminated with many things, from viruses to other mammalian proteins to variants of hGH itself. These were all things made or existing within human bodies. Now, when genetically modified bacteria

---

[62] Gueriguian *et al.* (eds. 1981: preface). See also Chapter 4 for a discussion about the extent to which genetic engineering is radically new or traditional.

make human proteins, the bacteria also make many other bacteria proteins than the one intended. This happens partly because the commonly used *E. coli* bacteria has about 3,000 genes, and some of these genes code for proteins toxic to humans, so called pyrogens. Pyrogens can be found in any organic material which may have been infected by bacteria, and so it was a known problem.

In the purification process, the desired protein has to be separated out from a fermentation solution. The problem of pyrogen contamination may be related to the specific configuration and components of the production system. Solutions to this problem could be either made worse or facilitated by different sets of genetic engineering techniques and biological materials. Firms' specific choices in production were dependent on the specific set of genetic engineering techniques. This mutual dependency thus imposed technical constraints on the directions in which a firm could search for solutions.

For example, separation was more challenging for Genentech's two first hGH expression systems using the lac and trp promoters, because these bacteria made hGH inside the cytoplasm of the cell. To get at the hGH, the firms had to break apart the cell (to make the cell lysate). As a result, the other contaminants spilled out into the fermentation broth, requiring extensive purification, which was expensive.

There were also general constraints on the direction of search activities. For example, all pharmaceuticals need to achieve ultra-purity, that is, get a very homogeneous product. Ultra-purity was specific for commercial use as compared to basic scientific research involving the same techniques and proteins. University researchers doing contemporary experiments with genetic engineering techniques similarly purified their proteins of bacteria contaminants, but the requirements for purity differed greatly. For a university lab experiment, the protein did not have to be very pure, maybe only 50 per cent or even 5 per cent pure, because the most important thing in developing scientific knowledge then was whether and how the expression system worked. How much it produced was less interesting. When Swanson and Boyer came to Stockholm back in 1977, they were invited because experiments had shown that bacteria could make the protein somatostatin, but the results were still highly uncertain because of the low purity level. The corporate need for ultra-purity was not met by early basic scientific research, which focused on whether the techniques and approach were feasible.

When the purpose of an experiment was to develop pharmaceuticals, a vital condition for use of the technology and hence of the outcome was purity. For pharmaceuticals, the protein must be close to 100 per cent pure. Reaching this required very specific, extensive, and expensive purification steps. This demand for ultra-purity of pharmaceuticals and consequent criteria in designing component technologies could clash with the commercial demand for speed in the innovation processes. This clash between purity and speed at Genentech seems to be at the essence of one of the incidents which prompted the FDA to write that 'very low levels of extraneous bacterial material present in the final products may cause untoward side effects, particularly during continual long-term therapy.'

Having developed a reasonable fermentation and purification process for rDNA hGH, Genentech moved full steam ahead to start toxicology tests. These tests were run by Genentech employees at the private Stanford Research Institute, affiliated with Stanford University, but working on more commercial terms. 'Bob Swanson had already decided that growth hormone was going to be approved by 1981 or 1982'[63] so Genentech did preclinical tests, known as toxicology tests, on monkeys at Stanford University in 1980. At least one person at the Stanford Research Institute was concerned that the Genentech people monitoring the tests were just out of university and had never monitored such a thing before, and that the monkeys were unhealthy. These were serious comments in that the tacit knowledge built up through experience was important for properly running and monitoring such tests. These concerns were voiced to some Genentech employees in private. In contrast to these worries, 'There was this guy who was doing the animal studies, who was under a lot of pressure to make sure everything was going smoothly.' There could thus be conflicts between corporate goals of pushing towards commercialization and evaluation of scientific tests.

In contrast, Kabi was not then moving as quickly into preclinical trials. A journalist at the time argued that this delay was partly due to a cautious attitude about quality and partly due to lack of protein material.[64] Looking back, Fryklund says that Kabi was working according to plan and did not want to take the risks of having trouble with pyrogens by rushing into Phase I tests. 'A set back could have ruined the whole project'.[65] Their attitude was more cautious, due in part to their previous experience with pyrogens involving other products.

Based on Genentech's toxicology tests at Stanford University which were interpreted as OK, the firm decided to do a Phase I clinical test on a handful of Genentech employees in early 1981.[66] Twelve Genentech employees showed up at a special room set up by Genentech. These employees ranged from a biochemist, a protein chemist, a pharmacologist, and a lawyer to the director of business development. Six got Genentech's preparation and six got the pit hGH. Soon thereafter, six people reacted, getting a touch feverish and red in the arm near the

---

[63] Kleid (1993).   [64] Walgate (1980: 528).   [65] Fryklund (1993).

[66] This paragraph is based on Kleid (1993, 1994), Olson (1993a, 1993b) and a journalist's account in *Genetic Engineering News* (1981: 1, 7). Olson participated in the Phase I clinical trials.

injection. 'Everybody was convinced that the commercial stuff was no good', reflecting the genetic engineers' conviction that they were remaking the world. 'But it turned out our stuff was no good!'.[67] One of the participants in the Phase I study argued that saying it was no good was an exaggeration. The reactions were mild and simply indicated that some improvements were necessary.

What went wrong? It was not carelessness. Although the Phase I clinical test had been pushed forward to get a commercial edge in registering their pharmaceutical preparation before their competitors, Genentech had tested their protein according to the standards of the day. According to those analytical methods, the product was clean, and the hGH in the preparation was identical to the one wanted (not a variant). Still, these mild reactions in the six test persons indicated that something was wrong. What could it be?

There were various hypotheses, reflecting contemporary uncertainty and lack of knowledge. Some postulated that it was impossible for *E. coli* bacteria to assemble a human protein correctly and that this would be an insurmountable problem for industrial production. This argument was particularly convenient for producers of pit hGH who were not moving into the new genetic engineering. Some argued that the one extra amino acid on Genentech's product, the methionine, was the root of the problem. There had been some small uncertainty about this, even within Kabi and Genentech. This methionine, after all, was the most obvious feature which distinguished the rDNA version from the natural version. Even Genentech's management took this into account, and when time and resources allowed, they later pushed for development of a met-less hGH.[68] Genentech employees were, however, already working on this question of whether or not the rDNA hGH was biologically active and whether the extra methionine might have adverse effects.[69]

There were thus two hypotheses about the cause of the problem which seemed specific to genetic engineering. These were: (1) it is impossible to make human proteins in bacteria, and (2) the problem was caused by the extra methionine. There was also one hypothesis specific to bacteria rather than the technology, namely that the problem stemmed from pyrogens, or known contaminants from bacteria. This was eventually shown to be the correct hypothesis.

When Genentech tested for purity before the Phase I preclinical trial, the standard tests of the day were what is known as SDS gels. These separate molecules according to molecular weight, and when dyed, they

[67] Quote from Kleid (1993).   [68] Lin (1993a), Olson (1993b).
[69] Olson (1993b) and the scientific paper Olson *et al.* (1981). The implications of this work were also reported in *New Scientist* (1981: 238). In February 1981, the protein purification group led by Olson submitted a paper to *Nature* which showed it was biologically active and probably clinically active.

show protein content as a band. Each band corresponds to a protein so that one band indicates one protein. This gel can be used to test the initial fermentation solution as well as the outcome after protein purification (see Figure 7.1). The results of Genentech's tests in 1981 indicated purity, i.e. that the hGH was homogeneous because the SDS gel gave a single band. This test in fact indicated that it was even purer than the pituitary version, leading to optimism within the firm.[70] Not only was their hGH good, analytical tests indicated it was better than the pituitary version.

The physical reactions of the employees tested indicated, however, that the SDS gel only captured part of reality, a reality that was sufficiently true for the hGH extracted from tissue but that was not sufficient for the rDNA version for some reason. Something which was not visible in the SDS gel was in the pharmaceutical solution. That something focused Genentech's attention on the necessity of developing more sensitive analytical methods and a new purification scheme.

To observers at Kabi, however, the explanation was soon thought to lie not in contaminants invisible to the standard tests but instead in Genentech's inexperience with this type of problem. 'They probably didn't do the pyrogen test properly. They also did not appreciate the environmental requirements (i.e. pyrogen-free water and a 'clean' environment) for producing human proteins.'[71] According to this interpretation, the challenges lay in better using existing methods for existing problems.

Initially, all such ideas were conjectures, in that no one really knew which of the hypotheses correctly identified the cause of the physical reactions. The corporate researchers needed more information, often requiring new techniques, in order to decide which was most likely correct. The physical reactions indicated that the current knowledge and techniques would probably not suffice to decide which explanation was correct.

This was one of the very first times that anyone had demanded that human proteins made in genetically modified bacteria be ultra-pure. From the firms' perspectives, this novelty plus the reactions presented a discontinuity from previous experience and understanding. Standard biochemistry procedures used in the production process did not appear to remove the contaminants. So solving this problem would require new knowledge-seeking activities.

About the time Genentech identified this challenge, the firm divided up its process department into a protein biochemistry department under Mike Ross and a process development department under Bill Young. Ross was a molecular biophysicist, who hired quite a few persons with biophysical backgrounds, 'who understand proteins, their structure,

[70] Olson (1993b).   [71] Fryklund (1993).

how you can treat them, and the physical basis of the analytical separation methods'.[72] Young similarly hired persons who understood proteins. Young says that he hired a number of individuals trained as scientists rather than engineers to run the process development work because engineers did not understand the parameters of what could and could not be done with proteins. Because of the traditional orientation of engineering education towards physics and mechanical processes, the engineers lacked sensitivity to biological processes.[73] Unlike such traditional engineers, those trained as scientists understood biology.

These specialized R & D groups worked together, as generally represented in the areas shown in Figure 7.1, such as fermentation, protein purification, analytical methods, and so forth. To solve challenges and identify new opportunities, the Genentech R & D groups specializing in different fields not only gave feedback information to influence the direction of each other's search activities but also co-operated more directly. The protein biochemistry group under Ross thus worked, among others, with the protein purification group. Together they wanted to eliminate the unseen contaminants indicated by the Phase I clinical tests.

The mutual dependency of different bodies of knowledge and techniques meant that each group in the firm could pursue a diversity of designs for each component technology, but that changes in one often entailed changes in others. In that way, bottle-necks in one aspect of the system would concentrate efforts on solving that challenge and often led in turn to changes in other parts of the system. The interactions of design within the system thus caused dynamic development.

Ross's biochemistry group hired a protein chemist at this time, Andy Jones, who was one of those given the task of solving these new challenges. Because Genentech had done standard tests which showed that there were no pyrogens in the hGH, the mission given to Jones was to remove the pyrogenic protein thought to be in the solution. Jones recounts:

Since it wasn't the conventional pyrogens, based on the fact that it had passed those tests, it must be something specific to *E. coli* and probably a protein.[74]

Later developments in analytical methods discredited this hypothesis:

We now know that that wasn't the case—that it was probably just regular pyrogen—a large chunk of the dry weight of an *E. coli* is endotoxin, which is a pyrogen . . . And it was the tests that were misleading![75]

This final interpretation of events is the same one that the Kabi employee gave. However, when this incident occurred in the early 1980s, Genen-

[72] Jones (1993).   [73] Young (1992).   [74] Jones (1993).   [75] Ibid.

tech had to find ways to generate new knowledge to decide which hypothesis it thought was correct as well as to suggest means of solving the problem.

Genentech managers and researchers needed better analytical methods. They felt that the existing standard gels and stains could not tell what substance was causing the problem. The contaminant was therefore invisible, in that the tests had indicated the hGH was pure whereas the clinical test had indicated a problem. If the contaminant could not be seen, then when Olson or others in the protein purification group tried to improve their part of the system, they would not be able to tell whether that outcome was better, worse, or the same as the previous outcome. In short, if the output could not be analysed, then changes to the system would also be invisible.

In order to improve purity, Genentech's chemists had to find a more sensitive way of distinguishing between batches of hGH produced differently. Clues about how to identify contaminants causing this problem had been published in the basic scientific literature around 1979, namely how to use silver staining to improve the sensitivity of SDS gels. This gave a first clue. Genentech had not used silver staining for the hGH. The reason was that this analytical technique used lots of silver, was expensive, and it was difficult to get to work reliably! Some researchers at Genentech had previously tried the silver staining technique to test other proteins but found that it had too many bugs and troublesome steps, like cleaning the glassware with nitric acid to remove all proteins. This analytical technique had therefore not seemed relevant to firms' contexts of uses. Making it relevant by improving silver staining to be reliable, less troublesome, and less expensive would require R & D time and resources. Before this incident, this technique had not seemed relevant enough for commercial use to develop it according to such parameters.

The Phase I clinical trials of rDNA hGH indicated, however, a great need for more sensitive analytical methods. University scientists had already published an improved silver staining method in the journal *Analytical Biochemisty* in early 1981, and it was this improved method that Jones took and further modified and improved for use within Genentech. In working with silver staining of SDS gels, Genentech's main effort went into making the technique reliable, standardized, and easier to use.[76] This type of criterion was thus similar to those imposed on the integration of genetic engineering with fermentation and purification techniques as discussed earlier. It took Genentech about six months to develop this improved analytical method, identify the contaminant, devise a new protein purification procedure, and retest the hormone.[77]

---

[76] Jones (1993).   [77] Lerner (1981: 18).

For commercial manufacturing, the point of such analytical methods was to measure very low levels of *E. coli* protein contaminants in very large quantities of product and solution. Silver staining SDS gels was only one of many analytical techniques used to test the hGH resulting from various configurations of Genentech's and Kabi's production systems. They were looking for knowledge and techniques relevant for their contexts of use.

The FDA also demanded that Genentech develop another analytical method to prove purity, namely an immuno-assay. This demand arose from the FDA's previous discussions with Eli Lilly over genetically engineered insulin, which, as the first genetically engineered pharmaceutical, had set some standards for later products.

In an immuno-assay, antibodies are used to test for the presence or absence of particular proteins, and this configuration results in a more sensitive analytical method than those previously available. Genentech researchers thought at first that making such an immuno-assay would be too difficult, or impossible, but they tried out different possibilities and then came up with a configuration of antibodies in an assay that worked.[78] Having solved that task, they and others saw that each assay only worked for one specific system, that is, for one specific means of purification, for specific cells, and so forth. An immuno-assay was thus a general category of test but had to be specifically designed for each use.

Although based on scientific knowledge and methodology, analytical methods also had very specific dimensions related to specific uses. An immuno-assay like the one for hGH became by its very nature and specificity corporate property. It was also an individual firm asset, in that the specifics of its configuration had little value outside the firm precisely because it could not be used effectively elsewhere. At the same time, however, corporate R & D groups tried to identify some general features about how to design immuno-assays. Genentech published some of their results in order to try—arrogantly or not—to set some sort of industry standard on immuno-assays, whereas many other firms did not make this information public. There is thus a very interesting research question here about the extent to which commercial translation and use of knowledge would benefit from a wider discussion of challenges and solutions encountered in the population of firms relative to incentives for secrecy.

The fact that analytical methods built on knowledge and techniques that were partly general meant that sometimes, developing one method for one product could be useful for other products. At least in analytical chemistry fields which ultimately led to many of the new analytical methods, hGH turned out to be a test case. Jones states that:

---

[78] The next few paragraphs based on Jones (1993).

Many of the issues we faced in hGH, discussing them with the FDA, were, looking back on it, somewhat trail-blazing. The issues were being raised for the first time and the pros and cons of this potential risk or the benefits of this method versus that one.[79]

The trail-blazing nature of analytical methods for insulin and hGH thus stemmed from the way they could set the issues as well as distinguish deadends from viable search strategies. By identifying general categories of problems and the pros and cons of specific approaches, later searches to explore ways to test other proteins could be carried out within narrower boundaries in the search space.

High Pressure Liquid Chromotography (HPLC) was also developed in the early 1980s. Although HPLC—like silver staining—was initially developed by university scientists, firms worked to get out the bugs and make the technique more reliable and standardized. Without corporate innovative activities, these techniques would have been of low value to the firms.

HPLC was both faster and gave more information than gels, as Lin explains:

[With HPLC] you can analyse a protein so fast. You can take a sample of *E. coli* in a fermenter. You crack it open and then you don't even have to do more manipulation. Just inject it into the HPLC. It tells you right away, in thirty minutes, how much protein is there. If the protein is intact or degraded. It can even tell you if it is in an active form or inactive form and much information. So you know how to improve and optimize your fermentation to make the right product . . .

We used to only run a gel, an SDS gel. [It takes] about two hours to run a gel, but gels don't give you as much information as HPLC.

Because, for example, on a gel, if it's an additional amino acid, it cannot tell the difference . . . Also, if there's a clipping—very often, the molecule is still held by disulfide bond if not reduced but it is already clipped . . . So you think you are making a good product but you are making a clipped product.[80]

HPLC was thus a large improvement over previous methods because it was sensitive and faster. Because this new technique could quickly identify minor differences, the variants such as a shorter (clipped) protein could also be identified. They could then be either discarded or else improved, such as refolded to reassemble the desired protein.

The analytical techniques of silver staining of SDS gels and of immuno-assays were just two of the many new analytical techniques developed in the 1980s. These went hand in hand with commercial use of genetic engineering techniques! Although the basic ideas for this diversity of testing and analytical methods were often initially gener-

[79] Ibid.   [80] Lin (1993a).

ated within the basic scientific environment, they had to be refined and standardized for use in the techno-economic environment. This generated new types of knowledge and techniques. The importance of this trend lay in providing quick, reliable information about previously 'invisible' contaminants and variants of the protein.

Without the physical reactions in the early clinical trials, which in turn led to attempts to identify and remedy the problem, these impurities and variations might not have been identified and hence 'seen' by more sensitive tests. Both firms and government agencies demanded these more sensitive analytical methods once their value had been demonstrated. Firms wanted high quality, too, even though more sensitive tests had the negative effect of identifying variants of hGH. Before this, variants were counted as full proteins, so that the methods had the unwanted side-effect of apparently reducing the final yield, which thereby increased costs for the remaining complete proteins.

It should be pointed out here that even the hGH extracted from human pituitary glands contained a number of different variations of 'the' hGH. In fact, the pituitary version was much less pure than the rDNA version, but many of its variants and contaminants simply could not be 'seen' with the traditional analytical methods. Not being visible, they were therefore not removed systematically. This higher purity of the rDNA hGH could constitute an important marketing argument for counterbalancing the appeal of 'natural' (pit) hGH for future sales.

Even though the above discussion has mostly focused on Genentech, multiple agents were involved in these negotiations about where regulatory standards for genetically engineered pharmaceuticals should lie. Like Genentech, Kabi developed new analytical methods in discussions with Swedish and international regulatory agencies, but their attitude and actions were less aggressive than Genentech in the early 1980s. One reason was that Genentech pushed clinical tests early on and therefore ran into difficulties which helped them identify the need for new analytical methods, whereas Kabi stressed that the final product must be of exceedingly high quality before attempting to move into trials involving human beings. Another reason is that Kabi thought that they as a firm already knew so much about hGH, especially about the protein and the appropriate tests and analytical methods, that they were satisfied with the existing ones.

These different attitudes led to somewhat different corporate strategies for R & D, resulting in somewhat different technological choices and direction of search activities. Kabi's belief in the importance of their own experience may even have been an obstacle at some points.[81] It could

---

[81] Fryklund (1992).

have made them blind to the necessity of searching in new directions, in opening up their search map. For example, Kabi had extensive contacts with clinicians experienced with pituitary hGH and used the standard ways of measuring antibody formation rather than trying to develop a new test. (Measuring antibody formation was important because it indicated whether the patients' bodies accepted the drug or not.) Thus, at the same time that Kabi's experience and contacts could be a strength useful for identifying existing best practice and knowledge, it could also lock them into current ways of doing things.

This can be exemplified in contrast with Genentech. Genentech were not satisfied with standard ways of measuring antibodies and instead used a new test developed by an external medical researcher. The test indicated many reactions, which initially caused a stir. There was uncertainty about whether the results were clinically relevant or not, meaning whether the test measured antibody reactions which could or could not be related to growth.[82] Later, it was established that they were not clinically relevant, and so the tests gave information which was not relevant for judging the efficacy of the pharmaceutical.

As another example of the firms' different perceptions, when Genentech were developing and standardizing use of silver staining in the early 1980s, Jones tested Kabi's product and found contaminants that could not otherwise be seen. Jones thought Kabi was initially uninterested, as if they could not believe that contaminants had been found through use of analytical methods.[83] One explanation lies in the fact that Kabi were proud of the purity of their pit hGH compared to other existing suppliers, and that this pride plus their reliance on previous experience stood in their way in accepting contradictory new knowledge. Kabi's emphasis on quality meant, however, that they also quickly adopted the new analytical methods.[84] In other words, genetic engineering had first appeared to be competence-enhancing for Kabi but was in fact competence-destroying for some parts of their knowledge-base about proteins.[85]

When discussing the two firms and their reactions to developments in analytical methods, the firms' perceptions of each other should be kept in mind because the above discussion partly relies on employees' perceptions of the other firm. The differences and sometimes criticisms of each other partially reflect a difference in culture where each prided itself on its respective competences. Genentech valued their molecular biology and genetic engineering knowledge very highly, especially because they viewed themselves as building a completely new firm, even new industry. In turn, this led some Kabi people who were

---

[82] Fryklund (1992).   [83] Jones (1993).   [84] Fryklund (1993), Fhölenhag (1992).
[85] Concepts based on Cohen and Levinthal (1989: 570). Fryklund (1992) argues that Kabi initially thought their experience with pituitary hGH would be helpful, but that knowledge may have stood in the way of developing the genetically engineered version.

interviewed to see Genentech as too self-assured, as too focused on their basic scientific achievements. Genentech seemed to overemphasize the science side of 'getting it right' to the detriment of the commercial goals of 'being first' and capturing the market, although Genentech did move quickly into the clinical tests. This move was not, however, considered positive. 'In fact, Kabi's perception was that Genentech was extremely foolhardy trying to coerce a regulatory authority into approving a product that wasn't quite ready for human testing.'[86]

Kabi, on the other hand, valued their knowledge of proteins and purification, and their experience in the pharmaceutical branch. They felt they knew how to deal with regulatory agencies, including when to start tests involving human beings. Some Genentech people interviewed saw Kabi as slow moving and a bit wary of new developments. This included making unwise trade-offs between waiting for a more efficient set of genetic engineering techniques and choosing a less efficient set in order to work towards getting government approval.

Genetic engineering for pharmaceuticals involves techniques faced with an extreme amount of formal regulation compared to many other technologies. This implies that proponents of the new technology had to interact with regulatory agencies proportionately more, and that they had to specifically shape the technology and analytical methods to fit such demands. Environmental conditions thus shaped the direction of search activities, thereby also influencing outcomes of the production of knowledge. In this case, firms used the knowledge and techniques of the new analytical methods in order to try to convince the regulatory agencies that the production systems and final pharmaceutical were safe. Firms actively shaped environmental conditions set by other agents.

In the special case of pharmaceuticals, users are patients. Their interests are taken into account from the beginning of such innovation processes, but they are only indirectly represented through organized, professionalized doctors and later through standard clinical testing. As medical doctors, firms, and government agencies jointly defined which standards could be considered relevant, efficient, and safe from patients' perspectives, then analytical methods which could specify where those standards lay were also developed.

Negotiation over general standards and tests for early genetically engineered pharmaceuticals helped develop criteria and rules of engagement for later, similar products. Agents were developing informal institutions and scientific knowledge which would provide a pattern for deciding about later products produced this way. Each product

---

[86] Fryklund (1993).

and production process would be specific, but there were also general standards and categories.

Analytical Methods and Protein Purification

This section particularly examines the close connections between analytical methods and protein purification. It gives more concrete examples of how challenges in one component technology often affected other aspects of the systems.

Some challenges for protein purification were immediately recognizable as challenges, whereas others only became apparent as the new analytical methods were put into use. These were particularly obvious during the period when corporate researchers tried to develop a model production system. As Kabi's project leader Fryklund put it,

It was an exciting but difficult time for the process development people. With one test, we got what we thought was a pure protein just to find out two months later that it was not that pure at all.[87]

Due to changes in analytical methods, the protein purification groups never knew if what they were doing was good enough or not. What they knew about how certain purification techniques should result in a certain level of purity of the protein kept being revised. Their understanding of the world thus had to change, and each improvement in analytical methods gave stronger tools for redesigning and selecting among purification steps.

Analytical methods, like silver staining and HPLC, gave information about the level and type of *E. coli* contaminants in the fermentation broth as well as about variants of the protein. Being able to identify their presence, the purification groups could then develop methods to remove them. According to Olson, who worked under Jones to scale up purification, by the time Genentech submitted clinical data on hGH, purity was down to about ten parts per million; this means that every milligram of hGH had ten nanograms of an *E. coli* contaminant. To put it in perspective, the resulting product from genetic engineering was about 1,000 times purer than that which traditional methods could have identified.

However, the specific purification steps enabling this higher purity were kept trade secrets because

If we've got a way of removing impurities and product variants, we don't want other companies using it free of charge. We don't do R & D for other companies. Trade secrets are usually a special way of handling the process.[88]

---

[87] Fryklund (1992).   [88] Olson (1993a).

Specific knowledge and techniques about purification were thus valuable to the firm. They did not want 'special ways of handling the process' to become public knowledge, not immediately in any case, because that information would help them compete, and disclosing it would reduce their initial advantage.

One of the most immediate challenges for protein purification arose from the fact that the rDNA hGH with an extra methionine was made inside the cell cytoplasm.[89] This was true for both the lac and trp promoters, and so getting to the protein required the breaking apart of the cells (lysate). They could deal with this. A quite unexpected side effect appeared, however, when Genentech switched to the trp promoter in 1980 to increase the level of expression. Previous experiments had shown that normally, when a genetically engineered cell is broken open to extract a protein, the protein is soluble, which means that when the liquid and solid parts of the fermentation cell paste lysis are separated, the protein is with the liquid. Established methods to begin protein purification existed.

The unexpected side-effect of an *E. coli* bacteria's overproducing hGH was that the protein was insoluble, meaning it remained with the solids when separated. This was a new challenge for purification and related to level of expression and scale-up. On a small scale, they did not have to 'kill' the cells to comply with safety regulations, and 'much of the hGH *was soluble*. As protein expression levels were increased and scale was increased, this meant that more of the hGH was insoluble—and it all became insoluble when the cells were 'killed.'[90] Insoluble proteins represented a general challenge for the overproduction of human proteins in genetically modified bacteria. It specifically arose due to commercial criteria.

Moreover, when the hGH protein was insoluble, it was inside what are known as 'inclusion bodies'. The protein is then in a biologically inactive form and cannot be directly used as a pharmaceutical. These proteins 'exist in a reduced, polymeric state which necessitates dissolution and renaturation.'[91] In other words, the firm must first dissolve the solid, then renature and refold the protein into an active form. Doing these many steps entailed loss of yield and increased costs.[92] These inclusion bodies are sturdy entities, and so do give some minor advantages for purification, such as the possibility of using harsher conditions when concentrating the initial fermentation broth.

---

[89] Instead of remaining in the cytoplasm, the protein could have been secreted out of the cell or secreted between the cell membranes.   [90] Jones (1994), emphasis in original.

[91] Ho (1990: 23).

[92] The decrease in yield was due to aggregation, when several (parts of) molecules joined together.

Genentech chose to develop techniques for working with the insoluble hGH proteins, refolding them and such. Kabi, in contrast, chose to work only with the soluble hGH, about 50 per cent of the total in the early 1980s. Kabi's decision simplified purification and reduced the number of steps but could then only use 50 per cent of the hGH made. Kabi thus chose to avoid this challenge by ignoring the insoluble hGH, whereas Genentech incurred the extra cost of first developing and then using a technique to convert the insoluble protein into a usable form. Standard methods were not available for doing so, particularly not on a large scale or according to parameters of commercial use.

Inclusion bodies and the necessity of refolding the protein have proved to be general problems when genetically modified bacteria over-produce a human protein. The challenge was not specific to hGH or to these firms. Despite the general nature of the problem, refolding is not well understood and researchers have had trouble deciding how much standardized procedures can be used versus specific ones for each protein. There is thus a lack of generally available knowledge about this challenge. In contrast, 'a great deal of proprietary information related to practical refolding of proteins has been generated in the private sectors', according to technical articles.[93]

Much information about refolding is thus private, owned by particular firms, and specific to their problems and proteins. For example, Genentech's approach led to a number of patents concerning such techniques, which were also licensed to Kabi under their R & D contract.[94] Property rights relating to refolding techniques have also been involved in the patent dispute between Genentech and Eli Lilly. Genentech suspected that Lilly may have used some of Genentech's patented techniques given to Lilly under the insulin contract in order to solubilize Lilly's version of hGH. Transferring knowledge and techniques to a new product would be a breach of the original R & D contract.[95] Even these techniques are general to the extent that they can be used on similar proteins.

In addition to refolding proteins, another challenge for corporate protein purification was to make sure that the hGH was homogeneous. This implies making sure that only the full protein, properly folded, was in the final solution that was to be formulated as a pharmaceutical. To reach that goal, all aggregates of more than one molecule had to be removed or else split along with all other denatured and 'clipped' variants.

The cell environment is in an active state of metabolism which can result in some oxidation of some amino acids on the protein, proteolytic 'clipping' of certain amino acids resulting in a break in the protein and chemically altering side

---

[93] Ho (1990: 23).   [94] Olson (1993a).   [95] Genentech (1987: 2–3).

chains of amino acids in the protein. The process development scientist is continually battling the degradative forces of nature.[96]

The cell environment is thus continually in a state of flux, attacking and changing the proteins. Such problems become of particular importance to firms working on a large scale because it becomes more difficult to control the physical environment of production.

This instability of the protein in the cell has thus represented a related challenge for the corporate R & D groups. They have had to test different ways of removing the enzyme, or whatever else was degrading the protein, in order to develop what is known as a protease-negative environment. They also had to remove all variants or else re-form those variants back into 'the' desired chemical structure and three dimensional protein. New purification steps and various combinations of steps could be developed and tested to find an efficient one for the specific system. With the development of more and more sensitive analytical methods, it has been possible to identify smaller and smaller differences between 'the' desired protein and similar variants. This has continually redefined the protein in that this finer differentiation imposes new, more precise criteria for distinguishing among them.

In relation to the integrative system, some of the challenges involved in protein purification could be solved with changes to fermentation. Fermentation has a broad impact on protein purification, in that the fermentation process itself can cause a number of variants of the desired protein. One of the best ways of taking care of the problems is to prevent them from happening in the first place, requiring close co-operation between protein purification and fermentation. For example, if the amino acid feed into the fermenter is not correct, then this can result in some amino acid substitutions in the protein.[97] The final purification scheme must then add an extra step to take care of the problem. If the fermentation process is correct, then the purification people have one less problem. Communication and joint problem solving among specialists were, again, necessary to solve challenges.

Even after developing one functioning production system, the corporate researchers and managers could be faced with new challenges. Kabi's first protein purification process was ready in 1982, but there was quite a worry at this time within Kabi about whether their genetically engineered product led to severe side-effects.[98] Keeping in mind that Genentech had got a mild reaction in their preclinical trials, Kabi pursued their toxicology studies on rats in accordance with the standards. The rats seemed fine but had developed some nodules, or lumps, which Kabi interpreted as a sort of 'false preg-

[96] Olson (1993b).   [97] Olson (1993a).   [98] Fhölenhag (1992).

nancy'.[99] However, they had to check it up and asked the experts on birth-control pills and contraceptives, Shering Plough in Berlin, what they thought of these reactions. Shering Plough had never seen anything like it, so Kabi sent it on to a Strasburg-based research group who were experts on cells. They said it was a tumour. Kabi did not agree with this interpretation from basic scientists. 'We were convinced that this was a hormone reaction in rats, so we redid the experiments and took out their ovaries. The [whole] phenomenon was cyclical, ovary-related!'[100] Although Kabi's interpretation of the rats' condition turned out to be true, e.g. that their hGH did not lead to tumours, the possibility that it might do so because a scientific research group offered that hypothesis initially caused concern within the firm.

Thus, even in 1982, people were still asking questions about the safety and usefulness of the new technology. This was after several years of trying to develop genetic engineering knowledge and techniques into commercial uses. What if genetic engineering generated terrible side-effects like tumours? Can we trust the new technology? What if we have spent so many resources on a project which does not work out? Both inside and outside the firms in the early 1980s, proponents had to try to influence opinion to be more positive towards genetic engineering. Actual severe negative reactions would clearly hurt their chances of continuing with the product development.

During this particular incident, Kabi was worried but felt there must be an explanation not related to tumours. This information was, however, extremely sensitive for both firms:

Genentech were in a panic. This episode reflects a cultural difference between Europe and the USA. In fact Swanson threatened to sue us for presenting the data at an FDA meeting. He did not appreciate or understand that concealment of bad results is the very worst thing any company can do![101]

Negative publicity and results could thus endanger the position of firms *vis-à-vis* government agencies and patients, but the information could not be concealed. If it was suppressed, an even larger scandal would erupt, making it even more difficult to launch an alternative explanation (like false pregnancy) of the rat lumps. These particular fears were laid to rest when the parameters of the test were changed, by taking out the rat ovaries. In this case, knowledge generated in the basic scientific environment in relation to medical knowledge would make or break new pharmaceuticals and production methods.

Even though all firms using genetic engineering for similar applications faced similar challenges and even though all firms would benefit

---

[99] This was related to the dual function of hGH as a lactogenic or prolactin-like substance in rats. [100] Quote from Fryklund (1992). Confirmed in Fryklund (1993).
[101] Fryklund (1993).

from common expansion of that knowledge, no one firm wanted to invest the money to develop generally applicable knowledge or to publicize all its specific results. They would have thereby lost their first mover advantages. At the same time, these firms have not been exclusively interested in control over knowledge. Some have attempted to develop more general knowledge for protein purification and analytical methods, among others. One example is when a firm publishes several articles involving different approaches, without divulging which one they use or the specific details of use.

Moreover, in addition to intensive patent protection, some biotech firms have been involved in developing and publishing about industrial standards to spread knowledge about the general challenges faced by industry. A more recent example is the extensive involvement of the British biotech company Celltech in a book called *Protein Purification Methods: A Practical Approach*.[102] This type of book serves as a textbook to train firms' future employees while studying and to provide handbooks for current employees. The books help develop a more general understanding of categories of problems. Developing more information and diffusing it gives benefits to all firms using or potentially using genetic engineering as the basis of production. The information has to be abstracted from the specific local problems that each individual firm faces and from the solutions they guard.

Summary and Conclusions

In the historical material recounted in this chapter, much of the discussion focuses on firms' knowledge-seeking activities to develop new knowledge and techniques for designing and testing functioning production systems. The key to successful commercial implementation of genetic engineering in both Kabi and Genentech has been organizing R & D and information flows to integrate genetic engineering with component technologies such as fermentation, analytical methods, and protein purification. Turning science into functioning technology is challenging.

Genentech and Kabi attempted to develop a commercial trajectory of use while or soon after they carried out and/or funded scientific activities on genetic engineering. Examples include the fact that Genentech notified Kabi that a genetically modified bacteria which could produce hGH was ready in late spring, that is, several months before the published scientific paper. Kabi sent a person to South San Francisco to learn about the modified bacteria, and Genentech was quickly hiring people

---

[102] Harris and Angal (eds. 1989).

with a mix of research and industrial experience. These examples are all from 1979 and illustrate the concurrent nature of corporate knowledge-seeking activities alongside the more basic scientific activities described in the previous chapters.

The reason that these corporate knowledge-seeking activities were concurrent with more basic scientific ones has to do with the different types of challenges requiring solutions in order to compete in the different environments. On the basic scientific side, scientists at both Genentech and the University of California, San Francisco published articles in late 1979 detailing how genetic engineering techniques could produce hGH. These experiments in a loose sense 'proved' that bacteria could make the longer, more complex proteins useful as pharmaceuticals. The Genentech experiment in particular developed useful and practical techniques for controlling nature, which has been argued to reflect their more technological and market-based orientation.

Nevertheless, these two experiments were not designed to answer questions stemming from firms' contexts of use, including the techno-economic environment. The experiments could not, for example, prove that genetically modified bacteria could be grown on a large, commercial scale or that the proteins could be adequately purified from contaminants so as to be acceptable as pharmaceuticals. The firms needed the initial basic scientific activities to identify the possibilities and approaches, but then new challenges arose specific to commercial uses. The firms had to solve such challenges in order to sell the product, because without sales, using genetic engineering to produce pharmaceuticals would be worthless as a strategy to compete in the techno-economic environment.

Designing such a system involved challenges and bottle-necks, requiring that corporate managers decide which specific types of knowledge-seeking activities to focus on at specific times. The corporate managers and researchers faced scientific and technical, economic and political challenges and opportunities, but the focus has been on technological problem-solving. The challenges detailed here would face all agents trying to move into the modern biotech industry in the early 1980s, but are explicitly described in relation to these two firms. Many challenges were provoked by placing the economic and technical demands of industrial-scale biological engineering on scientific-scale genetic engineering techniques. Putting the radical technical change into commercial use required many discrete, incremental steps, and solving each step required additional knowledge-seeking activities.

Each specific challenge was compounded by its interrelations with other technologies, requiring that the firms had to organize knowledge-seeking activities to enable feedback and communication. Initially, the genetically modified bacteria were finicky, leading to problems in fermentation. They died when moved from small, lab scale containers to the large commercial volumes, and when they did grow in large volumes, they produced incorrect variants of hGH and insoluble proteins. Fermentation in turn directly depended on analytical methods and purification techniques.

Some challenges arose from the limits of scientific and technical knowledge, as, for example, when reactions in Genentech's Phase I clinical trials indicated problems. It seemed as if the contaminant was invisible to standard test methods, although it turned out to be a known problem, pyrogens. In fact, Genentech had thought that their rDNA hGH was much purer than pit hGH by those standard tests. Such events focused attention on the necessity of developing more sensitive tests, which meant that more contaminants were 'seen', thereby also requiring changes to fermentation specifications and/or to purification. In these initial genetically engineered pharmaceuticals, challenges were often identified due to the limits of scientific and technical knowledge or in interactions with regulatory agencies. The technical solutions to those challenges in turn intertwined technical and economic considerations so that, for example, adding a purification step involved extra costs of production.

In order both to monitor external information and develop in-house knowledge and techniques for their contexts of use, Kabi and Genentech brought together R & D groups with specialized scientific and engineering knowledge and skills. Their diverse competences were united towards a common goal of identifying, negotiating, and solving such problems and opportunities which arose during the technological innovation process. They were involved in continuous, incremental innovative activities for local, specific technical developments, but their ability to create novelty was based on general and systematized knowledge. That knowledge was partly general, systematic scientific and engineering knowledge and partly related to industrial experience with particular configurations of the production system. Corporate management and researchers need to co-ordinate and feed back information and ideas between different specialists in a way which differs from the constraints of organization in university science. The organizations also differ in incentive structures and controls for keeping researchers on track.

Moreover, making incremental, specific changes for one firm's specific problems sometimes entailed developing more general knowledge about a category of problems. The novelty could be very specific to the firm as well as general. On the one hand, many of the specific challenges—and hence the specific technical solutions in the form of new knowledge, techniques, and equipment—were unique for each firm, even for each alternative set of genetic engineering techniques and biological material or for each new protein. This specificity resulted in firm specific trajectories. On the other hand, these same challenges and solutions sometimes represented general opportunities and challenges for firms trying to produce pharmaceuticals with genetic engineering. There was thus also a general commercial trajectory of use.

These two levels of general and specific information can be related to agents' incentives to innovate and their ability to appropriate benefits. The firms could have different strategies about how to deal with imitation by competitors, or the well-known theoretical problem of 'free riders', when deciding whether or not to invest resources in solving these challenges and deciding whether or not to publicize their findings. All firms would benefit if general solutions were available, but because information diffuses easily without losing its value, all firms also had incentives not to do research but instead get a 'free ride' by using others' solutions. Note, however, that the firms described here were innovators, and therefore, there were few or no other firms whom they could imitate. These firms could instead capture benefits by being first, and innovations required investment in R & D in order to solve the problems identified and take advantage of opportunities. Genentech in particular had incentives to publish in order to be seen as a participant in the scientific community.

Having incentives to engage in innovative activities, the firms then had different strategies about whether or not to make their technical solutions public. Different strategies included publicizing in scientific and engineering journals, giving specific details only to formal government regulatory agencies to gain approval, and/or keeping as many details as possible secret to protect their R & D investment from imitators. The firms often wanted to keep very specific details secret in the short term but would be willing to disclose broad approaches. Sometimes they did so voluntarily, as through publications. Other times, disclosure was less voluntary and/or vaguer. For example, when firms gave technical solutions to government regulatory agencies, the agency sometimes decided in turn that the solution—for example, a new type of analytical method—ought to set an industry-wide standard. By then demanding that the next firm applying for approval have a similar test, the agency gave information that a solution was possible. Knowing that, later firms then knew it could be worth while to invest resources in innovative activity in this area. This is an example of how interactions between agents can direct firms' search activities along certain paths. Common paths in turn rely on common bodies of knowledge within the population of innovating agents.

When addressing the technical challenges detailed in this chapter, Genentech and Kabi generated a diversity of technical solutions in-house, even if solutions were both based on directed in-house R & D and on knowledge and techniques developed elsewhere. Partly through trial-and-error methods, the corporate researchers generated new technical solutions and then tried to determine which alternatives were best for the firm, based mainly on technical and economic criteria. Some of the diversity that corporate R & D generated was truly novel. Some of it represented diversity made by modifying novelty generated in universities according to criteria specific to commercial uses. Moreover, as indicated by the backgrounds of some early Genentech and Kabi employees, the people engaging in R & D often brought experience and training from universities, from other firms, and/or from other similar projects within the same firm. This indicates the collective nature of technological innovation processes, building as it does on common and cumulative bodies of knowledge, techniques, and equipment. Having gained admission to a community through training and experience, the individual could use general knowledge and techniques which could be transmitted and used in many different contexts.

At the same time that firms generated diversity and novelty along a commercially relevant path, there were also incentives within firms to reduce that technical diversity. Again and again, the component technologies were designed, tested, and approved based on criteria such as standardization, reliability, and practicality. These were internal firm selection criteria but generally valid for commercial use. The firms sometimes succeeded in reducing diversity, e.g. in introducing a standard improvement across a number of similar products. At other points, new problems had to be addressed and solved for each new product, for each alternative within genetic engineering techniques, and/or for each component technology.

In short, firms directed their knowledge-seeking activities in relation to existing and expected future selection criteria. At some points, the environment did set boundaries indicating which types of technical solutions should be generated (*ex ante*) or which existing alternatives would be acceptable (*ex post*). At other points, firms acted to circumvent the influence of these factors or tried to modify the selection criteria. For example, just as these first commercial uses were getting under way, the national public contexts for the technology in the United States and in Sweden were being modified. These changes allowed more industrial-scale exploitation. The United States formally regulated only university experiments whereas Sweden initially had rules for university research, but largely due to the pressure of public debate and political parties, the Swedish Parliament voted in national legislation. Moreover, Swedish authorities were willing to bend existing rules a bit for the good of the nation. Once the rules were in place, firms other than early entrants could better judge the risks for the future of developing this radical technology. The later-moving firms then knew approximately what parameters for searches and results could be considered acceptable.

Corporate differences and differences in strategy partly arose from how each firm perceived themselves to fit into an economic system, that is, as a government-owned firm with established products or as a new firm dependent on a more strictly market-based economy.

8

Multiple Uses and Markets for Human Growth Hormone

Introduction

The knowledge-seeking activities detailed in previous chapters have highlighted basic scientific research for genetic engineering techniques as well as its integration into production systems. This chapter examines interdependencies between knowledge-seeking activities and agents setting environmental conditions, here over the definitions of multiple uses of, and markets for, the pharmaceutical human growth hormone. Pituitary hGH was approved to treat a condition called hypopituitary dwarfism, i.e. children who were short as a consequence of not producing enough of this hormone. Recombinant hGH could radically increase supply.

Multiple interpretations of the use of hGH are included in the current analysis of technological innovation processes because uses and markets ultimately work to select products and firms. Selection determines whether or not firms will recuperate their investments in innovative activities, make a profit, generate earnings to invest in new R & D activities, go bankrupt, etc. By the early to mid-1980s, using genetic engineering to make human proteins in bacteria could no longer be termed science fiction, as it had been in the mid-1970s. This context of use had become industrial reality and soon marketable products. The emphasis in this chapter is on the pharmaceutical rather than the technology to produce it, although the two are closely related where changes in one often lead to changes in the other.

When initial production systems integrating genetic engineering had been designed and began functioning, an abundance of supply of hGH was possible. Moving from a situation of scarcity (pit hGH) to one of abundance (rDNA hGH) has been accompanied by negotiations over new uses of the final product, some medically legitimate and some illegitimate. There are also discussions to expand the definitions of the original disease, that is, dwarfism, to include short children within the normal height range. Negotiations over acceptable use are based on the results of medical knowledge-seeking activities about hGH.

Establishing and expanding multiple uses for hGH expands the market, giving firms incentives to fund this type of knowledge-seeking activity. Expanding the market was suddenly possible because genetic engineering would allow firms to obtain control over the source. Bacteria were amenable to control. In contrast, pit hGH faced a number of restrictions on expanding supply, such as the limited number of human pituitary glands available and the amount of hGH which could be extracted from each. With genetic engineering techniques, supply was only limited by uses defined by government regulatory agencies and by economic constraints, particularly how much a firm could sell at a feasible price for legitimate uses.

The first section examines how multiple interpretations of the use of rDNA hGH have been defined in a process of negotiation.[1] A major theme of this section is how needs, uses, and markets were defined and sometimes redefined in relation to medical knowledge, experiments, and tests.

The next section examines a firm-level jump to a new rDNA hGH without the extra methionine (met-less hGH). This involved a new set of genetic engineering techniques, with related changes in production. Genentech developed a functioning technique to cut off the extra methionine in 1983. This change required that corporate managers and researchers make decisions about whether to finance new investments in new knowledge-seeking activities geared to the specifics of these genetic engineering techniques and biological materials. Otherwise they could not switch. It can be said to be a jump to a new trajectory, because of the many changes and basic parameters (model system) which also had to be changed. They had incentives to do so due to both scientific and economic arguments for the superiority of a met-less hGH.

The succeeding section takes a look at negotiations over the definition of quality between rDNA and pit hGH. The latter was initially considered superior because it was natural. Comparisons and evaluation were based on medical scientific knowledge, which was one reason that Kabi's experience and knowledge with pit hGH was considered valuable. The superiority of the 'natural' version over the rDNA was, however, turned on its head in 1985 when doctors discovered a severe medical risk with pit hGH, leading to a ban in many countries. In the countries in which it was banned, the market was suddenly wide open for the rDNA versions. The reactions of producer firms to these events is analysed in relation to their relative positions in developing genetic engineering techniques. This is thus another example of the social definition of selection criteria, here of the market as a whole.

Economic and technical aspects of innovative activities are clearly

---

[1] Legitimate uses are called approved indications. Thus in medical terms, uses of the same drug to treat different diseases are called different indications.

intertwined during different aspects of the innovation process analysed here. The relative success of Genentech and Kabi in relation to the size of the market are discussed at the end of this chapter, in order to indicate the relative success of their innovations.

Multiple Interpretations of Use

Interpretative flexibility about how and why hGH could be used to treat different medical conditions has arisen from different understandings of what hGH can and cannot do in the body. Under conditions of limited supply, treating dwarfism was its only legitimate use.[2]

Production of hGH based on genetic engineering techniques revolutionized this shortage. There was a great expansion in supply, leading in turn to controversies over appropriate uses. The controversies seem to be due to the fact that hGH is involved in metabolic processes of regulation in the body about which medical researchers have theories but do not completely understand. Some of its functions are known whereas others are still hypotheses. In short, the pituitary gland in the brain produces growth hormone, which in turn:

stimulate[s] the liver to produce somatomedins-hormones that are very similar in structure to insulin and that stimulate bones to grow. Children and adolescents produce large quantities of growth hormone, and adults normally produce very little of it.

But researchers believe that the hormone's primary purpose may not be to stimulate growth at all. . . . [its] principal function may be to conserve muscle tissue at the expense of fat tissue during times of stress.[3]

This journalistic summary indicates that medical researchers believe that hGH plays a role in various bodily functions other than growth, but that these roles are still unclear and in doubt. These roles are under negotiation and are hence uncertain.

Because growth hormone possibly has multiple functions in the body, it may be used to treat many other conditions than dwarfism caused by hGH deficiency. Other medical uses cited in the medical literature include retention of muscles in elderly people; as a dietary aid for obese people; to build muscle mass in athletes; as a way to make short 'but normal' children taller; and to treat 'burns or other catabolic conditions, osteoporosis, peptic ulcer disease, or ageing'.[4] In fact, some of these

---

[2] For example, children who produced a 'normal' amount of the hormone but were still short were not supposed to be treated with pituitary hGH, although clinical tests on this condition were to have started in 1985 (Glasbrenner 1986: 582). The trials were stopped due to the 1985 ban of pit hGH.　　　　　　　　　　　　　　　[3] Kolata (1986: 22).
[4] Quote from Underwood (1984: 608).

alternative uses of hGH were mentioned in Genentech's 1979 scientific paper using genetic engineering techniques, specifically the treatment of bone fractures, skin burns, and bleeding ulcers.[5] When carrying out the initial scientific activities involving a genetically modified bacteria, Genentech and Kabi were thus aware that the potential markets for hGH were greater than the existing market for pit hGH (dwarfism).

How, then, should use of this pharmaceutical be understood? The term 'use' could be narrowly defined as patients' use of the pharmaceutical for legitimate purposes, that is, those purposes already approved by government regulatory agencies. This approach obscures, however, the social basis of these markets.

Legitimate uses are here seen as the result of negotiation processes in a locus of interaction between patients, doctors, firms, regulatory agencies, social conventions, and social protests. Negotiation over acceptable conditions is based on scientific research. This process is international because medical knowledge, like basic science, is international and because firms act to establish similar criteria in all their international markets. At the same time, the negotiation process is national because national regulatory agencies are institutions making somewhat different decisions and demanding slightly different tests. This includes establishing criteria to differentiate legitimate from illegitimate uses.

We can first look at the use of hGH to treat dwarfism and short children within the normal height range. When the only supply of hGH was extraction from human pituitary glands, the ever-short supply led to a rationing mentality among doctors and in definitions of the disease. Only those children shown to have unequivocal growth hormone deficiency received treatment. Unequivocal deficiency was fairly easy to spot by administering accepted tests. In this situation, not giving the hormone to one child near the borderline meant that another needy child could receive the treatment. Short supply, leading to a rationing mentality and a strict definition of the disease, hence in turn influenced the definition of medical conditions that doctors believed desirable to treat. The most severe cases could be identified and treated, and questionable or uncertain ones ignored. As discussed earlier, the director of NPA argued in 1979 that 'all patients with diagnosed hyposomatotropism are receiving the hormone . . . "We have no waiting list."'[6] From his perspective, there was no need to develop an alternative way of producing hGH because the strict definition of disease equated the number of potential patients to current patients.

Other medical researchers have argued that the supply of pit hGH only seemed adequate because the criteria for treatment were so very

[5] Goeddel *et al.* (1979: 544).   [6] González (1979: 702).

stringent. Michael Thorner of the University of Virginia Medical School argued in retrospect that when hGH was always in short supply, the idea was to be sure that 'every child who received growth hormone was growth-hormone-deficient, not that every child who was growth-hormone-deficient received treatment'.[7] The difference is quite important in relation to the size of the market. With the advent of plentiful supplies of hGH through genetic engineering-based production, all children who were growth-hormone-deficient could be treated, and supply could still exceed demand. Doctors were then given the real possibility of giving hGH to a larger number of children, including those near the borderline. As a result, doctors/medical researchers had to reconsider their criteria for deciding who should and should not be treated. Doctors were faced with the necessity of developing new, more sensitive medical tests to separate potential patients from non-patients.

The very medical knowledge about hGH thus came under negotiation in the early to mid-1980s when it was thought that supply would soon increase. Medical practitioners began to argue that 'normality' of hGH was not necessarily a static level which could be precisely measured but, instead, that normality included a range of conditions. In a popular account of this range:

[malnourished children] produce excessive amounts of growth hormone, yet they do not grow. Adults, who normally do not make measurable quantities of the hormone, begin producing much more of it when they fast or when they are stressed. Runners, for example, synthesize measurable amounts of growth hormone.[8]

Under certain conditions, people who usually had normal levels produced more, and even within the category 'well-nourished children', no absolute line seemed to exist between normal and deficient. This fuzziness of definition of 'normal' offers possibilities for expanding areas of treatment. That line had to be agreed upon by medical practitioners in relation to social values of height. The medical scientific community could redefine standard levels of normal hormone secretion as well as what constituted a valid medical test. Firms, of course, funded doctors to do such research.

Doctors had existing standard tests to decide which children should be treated with pit hGH, but these criteria came increasingly into question when supply increased. This began when Kabi and Genentech were producing enough of their respective rDNA hGHs to have clinical trials. In November 1983, the (American) National Institute of Child Health and Human Development (part of NIH) held a conference on

---

[7] Kolata (1986: 23).   [8] Ibid. 22.

'the uses and possible abuses of biosynthetic human growth hormone'.[9] The NIH and the community of medical researchers wanted to develop new, adequate criteria to decide whether or not to give treatment to patients on the borderline as well as to air some of the problems they had encountered, or felt likely they would encounter with increasing supply. When this conference was held, Kabi and Genentech did not have approval to sell their products, but they were in clinical testing. The conference attracted about fifty experts, from doctors to regulatory officials to corporate researchers. During the conference, the FDA wanted participants to try to come to agreement about medical uses of genetically engineered hGH and about appropriate testing procedures.

In fact, these conference participants disagreed about many things, indicating the fluidity of scientific knowledge. The discussions mainly centred around using hGH to treat pituitary dwarfism and borderline cases. In relation to that, they disagreed 'about which peak growth hormone values after pharmacologic stimuli, if any, constitute an adequate response'. In other words, they did not agree what test results (peak values) indicated hormone deficiency. They similarly disagreed about which tests under what external conditions were optimal to diagnose the disease.

They disagreed whether and why some children seemed to have 'bioinactive growth hormone'. 'Such patients have growth retardation for which no cause can be found, apparently normal immunoreactive growth hormone secretion, and acceleration of linear growth when given growth hormone.'[10] These patients and their reactions to hGH did not fit with the accepted paradigm of explaining children's failure to grow, and hence did not fit into the accepted idea of treatment. Because these cases did not fit, they indicated that currently accepted tests could not identify all cases where children could potentially benefit. The disagreements clearly indicated that the potential demand to treat short children was much greater than the actual demand expressed under a situation of limited supply of pituitary hGH. It also indicated the fluidity of knowledge, here changing due to expanding possibilities of use and indicating the necessity of developing new test methods.

These conference participants did agree on two things. The first can be seen as recognition of their own ignorance, even when making medical decisions and diagnoses:

It was agreed, however, that the traditionally accepted discriminator of 7 to 8 ng per milliliter is arbitrary and that provocative tests are not always reliable for determining whether insufficient growth hormone is rate-limiting for growth.[11]

---

[9] Underwood (1984).   [10] Underwood (1984: 607).   [11] Ibid. 606.

The medical researchers thus admitted there was little correspondence between their standardized tests for diagnosis and occurrence of the disease. This uncertainty was partially related to the previous short supply, which curtailed the possibility of clinical trials to establish knowledge about such things. Before, even if they had established more sensitive tests to determine more precisely where the border lay, they would not have been so useful because they could not have had enough hormone to treat them. The context of potential use changed, putting pressure on specialists to develop new methods and to change the social criteria for selection of patients.

Secondly, the participants agreed that they needed to educate physicians and the public. They believed that spreading information was the only way to prevent unrealistic expectations about hGH. These unrealistic expectations could lead to severe disappointment and psychological problems in short children who did not respond to hGH treatment, and could fuel the black market trade for illegal uses. In short, expectations of miracles had to be tempered, and uncertainty in diagnosing and treating the diseases be admitted.

Firms have an interest in expanding current legitimate uses by questioning existing tests and standards and by clinical trials on new uses.[12] Increasing the number of patients by redefining and expanding the initial disease would thereby increase demand. In addition to firms' actions, other individuals have placed expectations on the capability of hGH to do things for which it was not intended, that is, illegitimate uses. This includes, for example, weight-lifters using hGH in an attempt to increase muscle mass. From the firms' perspective, more uses translate into larger demand, but at the same time, pharmaceutical firms have an interest in restricting sales to legitimate uses in order to protect their reputations and hence future sales. Firms, government regulatory agencies, and medical researchers thus have a common interest in defining criteria for legitimate uses and controlling illegitimate uses. They define selection criteria for legitimate uses.

The most controversial uses of hGH have included giving it to the elderly and to athletes and making 'normal but short' children taller. Much of the controversy over the use of hGH has centred on whether it is morally, ethically, clinically, and/or legally correct to treat these three conditions.[13] There has been some public debate, in one case leading

---

[12] They can only get approval for a new indication if clinical tests demonstrate the medical value of the product.

[13] Interestingly enough the report of the 1983 conference, analysed above and published in the respected *The New England Journal of Medicine*, brought up many of the same social concerns voiced later in both scientific journals like the *New England Journal of Medicine*, *The Lancet* and in more popular versions such as *The New York Times Magazine*, *Time*, *The Economist* or the news section of *Science*. Respectively, (Underwood 1984), (Grumbach 1988), (*The Lancet* 1992), (Werth 1991), (*Time* 1990), (*The Economist* 1992b), and (Kolata 1986). The scientists were thus addressing many of the concerns which were later presented as critiques in the mass media.

Genentech to temporarily break off a clinical test on short children within the normal range of the height curve.

The largest public controversies over hGH are rooted in philosophical questions concerning tampering with the human body. The basic dispute seems to be whether or not cosmetic changes or improvements can be considered real changes because they do not treat or cure the human body. Simply improving the body through pharmaceuticals is thought unacceptable. This notion of unacceptable tampering is so strongly rooted that it is embodied in law: pharmaceuticals must treat a disease not increase overall physical or psychological health. Neither ageing nor shortness in itself nor insufficient muscles are diseases, and therefore, if firms want to get these uses approved as legitimate, they would have to relate these conditions to a disease.

Medical uncertainty about testing procedures and about where to draw the line to define the disease has been important to the firms, because they could hopefully expand the medically accepted definition of the disease by sponsoring knowledge-seeking activities, clinical tests, conferences, and so forth. For example, similar questions to those mentioned above about appropriate measurements were addressed in a conference sponsored by Genentech in 1986.[14] Obtaining adequate financial resources for such activities could also require creativity. As an illustration, Genentech developed a limited clinical partnership to be able to afford clinical testing of hGH, namely the Genentech Clinical Partners, Ltd. Genentech essentially sold shares in the risk-taking of clinical trials in order to raise short-term money and spread risks. They later bought back the shares.[15] Having the financial resources enabled Genentech to fund the generation of new knowledge and thereby change the interpretations of their product. In doing so, they could fund medical scientific research which would influence selection criteria defining market entry as set by regulatory agencies.

Pharmaceuticals differ from many other technologies in the high degree of negotiation over use between firms, regulatory agencies, and doctors/medical researchers. This social interaction defines the environment and selection criteria. They together define criteria for legitimate treatments based mainly on expanding medical knowledge. In the case of hGH the accepted criteria defining treatment have been increasingly called into question as external conditions change (increased supply). Moreover, when there has been little agreement over basic tests and standards, regulatory control has been weakened, especially over borderline cases.

---

[14] The results of this conference are reported in Underwood (ed. 1988).
[15] *Bioengineering News* (1983: 1). The partnership expected in 1983 to spend 72% of its development budget on clinical testing and only 7% on research to increase yields.

A Market Choice with Technical Implications, 1983

Parallel with the medical science discussions over use which started in the early to mid-1980s, managers and researchers at Kabi and Genentech might have imagined that they had completed the major part of their knowledge-seeking activities to design production systems. New challenges remained, however, when they were faced with the possibility of changing to a new set of genetic engineering techniques.

Researchers at the two firms had solved many of the challenges of developing new, commercially relevant production technologies integrated with genetic engineering. Knowledge-seeking activities to resolve challenges in fermentation, protein purification steps, and analytical methods have been discussed in the previous chapter. Kabi's and Genentech's technical achievements in designing, testing, and choosing a particular configuration of systems would allow the firms to manufacture hGH and compete on the market. The firms had also generated standard, more generalizable knowledge about commercial production of genetically modified bacteria, some of which was published in articles. This process is never finished, however, and the firms have continued to make many incremental improvements to the core and component technologies as long as they have been producing the product.[16]

In 1983, however, Genentech researchers made an improvement to the genetic engineering techniques and biological material which required a larger change. In other words, Genentech and Kabi had to decide whether to continue making incremental improvements within their firm-specific trajectory, or whether to jump to a new set of genetic engineering techniques, following a somewhat different trajectory. Jumping would require investment in new knowledge-seeking activities.

On 25 April 1983, Genentech filed for an American patent for a new technique.[17] In the new bacteria expression system, these researchers used a new signal sequence to direct *E. coli* cells to cut off the extra methionine on hGH by secreting it through the first cell membrane. This improvement enabled them to make hGH with 191 amino acids, like that produced in the body. Under the 1978 R & D contract, Kabi were entitled to any improvements which Genentech made, so both firms had access to these results. Producing hGH without the extra methionine was one of the challenges facing corporate use that had not been solved in the early 1980s.

In 1983 Kabi and Genentech thus faced a technical and economic

---

[16] For example, in 1993, Genentech's fermentation expert Lin said, 'And I'd like to tell you that I am still working on the hGH fermentation process development for higher yield and better quality of hGH. We anticipate new indications and fierce competitions in the market' (Lin 1993b). [17] That was US patent number 4,859,600 (Genentech 1989: 1).

choice. They had two alternative paths to follow, namely ignore the change or use it. A decision had to be made, based on a number of questions. Should they adopt this change in genetic engineering techniques? Was it an advance in technical and/or economic terms? What changes would it entail for the specific production system that each firm had already developed after significant investment in knowledge-seeking activities? Would the improved product, the met-less hGH, give them an advantage on the market? How much resources would have to be invested in new activities to solve the context dependent problems and specific design aspects? These were the general types of questions facing research managers in particular. They could, in fact, already identify clear technical and economic advantages in the new genetic engineering techniques and the 191-amino-acid hGH, but the firms had a difficult choice to make because Genentech and Kabi were already partially locked in to a technological trajectory based on the 192-amino-acid (met) version.

Both Kabi and Genentech had been working on the met hGH for four years when Genentech developed and gained ownership (patent) over this novel technique. The firms had thus invested considerable time and resources in the met hGH. They had invested within the firms to develop a functioning production system, and they had invested in collaboration with doctors and government regulatory agencies to negotiate legitimate uses through clinical testing. Some of the knowledge, techniques, and equipment so developed could be transferred to the met-less version and would be directly useful, but some investment would be lost, worthless. The amount invested in met hGH but which could not be transferred would indicate the degree of positive reinforcement of existing choices about genetic engineering and biological materials. Such positive reinforcement was due to the accumulation of competences within firms, the regulated nature of entry into the market, and the related, systemic technical choices. The question was whether Kabi and Genentech wanted to and could jump to a related but different trajectory for met-less hGH.

In fact, Genentech and Kabi felt they could not just drop the met hGH version until they had developed a functioning production system for the met-less hGH. This might take a couple of years, and during that time, they needed to be able to sell the met hGH. If they chose to develop the met-less variety, each firm would thus have to develop two alternative systems and clinical trials in parallel. In making this choice, one of the main questions that both firms had to answer in 1983 was, Is there room and resources within the firm to develop the met-less version? Can we afford diversity? Each would have to bear the costs of investing resources in knowledge-seeking activities to develop that diversity.

According to persons interviewed, some individuals in each firm thought it would be better to concentrate all the resources on one project, that is, to concentrate on getting the met hGH out on the market. This corporate strategy placed priority on early entrance into the market by concentrating resources. It would select less diversity. Others thought it would be better to divide the firms' resources into two projects because the new met-less alternative was superior. More specifically, if they did not change, any other firm making 191-amino-acid hGH would in the future claim that their version was superior to Kabi's and Genentech's products. It might prove to be so clinically as well, thereby marshalling scientific research to support that claim. That would erode Kabi's and Genentech's future markets. Erosion of market shares was particularly threatening because hGH is a long-term proposition. Children use the medicine for about ten years, and doctors only change brands if there are major problems or major improvements. This long-term lock-in of doctors and patients to the product of a particular firm thus gives advantages to those firms which can quickly move into the market with the highest quality and 'closest to nature' product.

Within Kabi, the project leader Linda Fryklund strongly argued that Kabi ought to pursue the met-less version in parallel, even though the met hGH had been brought so close to market. She was convinced the change was necessary to compete in the market.[18] Within Kabi, resources were made available for more R & D, and deadlines set. This indicates that research management had to judge the extent to which apparently technical changes also entail economic considerations. Genentech was initially more ambivalent but put some resources into the project. Both firms were quite reticent about discussing their decisions publicly, trying to keep their new projects a secret.

Both Genentech and Kabi thus decided to work on the two hGH projects in parallel, and initially worked independently. As indicated above, jumping to a new set of genetic engineering techniques and biological material would require that the firms invest in knowledge-seeking activities to design a new production system. Even though some of the knowledge, techniques, and equipment previously generated, selected, and retained within the firms could be transmitted, the corporate researchers would also have to generate and select new solutions to specific problems. Knowledge and solutions were related to general categories of opportunities and challenges but would again have to be modified for context-dependent use.

One of the first challenges encountered was that fermentation was more difficult. The new bacteria host was more finicky about growing inside the fermenters. As Florell of Kabi put it:

[18] Fhölenhag (1992), Fryklund (1992).

As an aside, I can say that it was really lucky that we started with the first bacteria strain [met] instead of the second [met-less] . . .

The met version was easier from the cultivation point of view. It was easier to reproduce. It didn't go wrong as often. I think that the very hGH [gene] part is more stable. . . . The non-met version was more sensitive; the parameters must be exactly right in certain phases.[19]

The parameters of fermentation thus had to be more carefully controlled because the met-less hGH was more sensitive and hence went 'wrong' more often. The corporate research groups, however, soon developed specific biological conditions for fermentation which were better suited to these finicky bacteria. Precise control and testing were needed to do so. Such difficulties with the fermentation process made these steps more expensive than for met hGH.[20]

The protein purification steps also had to be changed, but these steps could be simplified. Instead of producing the protein within the cytoplasm of the *E. coli* bacteria, Genentech's new technique secreted the hGH in between the two membranes of the cell, into the periplasm. Secretion cut off the signal sequence from hGH and thereby got rid of the extra methionine. This hGH was also soluble and folded correctly. Many of the initial challenges to purification thus disappeared with this major change in the genetic engineering material. Although the bacteria also secreted many other proteins into this periplasm, the firms would no longer have to tear the cells apart to get at the desired protein. A simple water based solution could extract the hGH. The consequence of these changes was that the number of purification steps could be reduced, and so these steps were less difficult in many senses.[21] In contrast to increased cost of fermentation, this worked to reduce costs of production. These two examples indicate the integrated nature of the production process.

On the one hand, Genentech and Kabi benefited from having first developed the met hGH production system. They benefited in that they knew some specifications of engineering and scientific techniques—such as specific parameters and analytical methods—that might be useful for the new system. The firms had already generated, tested, and selected solutions for previous specific problems, but these often represented categories of problems. Discussions among managers and researchers established in-house technical and economic criteria to help select among alternatives. They had also established some common criteria for approval of genetically engineered pharmaceuticals through discussions with various regulatory agencies. Genentech only

[19] Florell (1992).   [20] Lin (1993a).
[21] According to scientists working on protein purification both at Kabi (Holmström 1992, Fhölenhag 1992) and at Genentech (Olson 1993a).

interacted with the American FDA, whereas Kabi interacted with European and Asian agencies as well; the pattern of interactions followed the firms' projected market areas. In short, the firms had learned from being early movers into recombinant hGH and could transfer some experience, competence, and knowledge to the new project.

On the other hand, the general pattern of technological innovation repeated itself with the met-less hGH. New technical challenges were identified, and solutions suggested by the corporate researchers at Genentech and Kabi. Some challenges were specific; others general. These challenges were commercial as well as technical in that different configurations of the production system affected cost of production, and ultimately, selling price and profits. Moreover, having decided to support diversity by developing the two hGHs in parallel, the Kabi R & D group in particular were under enormous pressure to work rapidly to bring the new product to market.

Genentech and Kabi initially worked separately, but in February 1984, Genentech called Kabi and wanted to collaborate. Kabi were interested in co-operation partly because it would speed up their project, and time of entry into the market was essential to them. Moreover, a new person was in charge of the rDNA hGH project at Genentech, William Bennett, and Kabi employees found it easier to communicate with him than had previously been the case.[22]

When Kabi and Genentech started to collaborate in 1984, they were potential rather than actual competitors. They had divided up the rDNA hGH world markets, with Genentech retaining rights to the American and Canadian markets. Kabi intended, however, to continue selling their pit hGH in the United States even after Genentech began selling its rDNA version, making them potential competitors. They had no direct competition over recombinant DNA products, so the two firms had some incentives to co-operate if each could benefit.[23]

They co-operated loosely rather than engaging in a truly joint development project, where each firm would have performed specific subprojects under a unified goal. Their collaboration took more the form of exchange of information about problems, possible solutions, dead end solutions, and so forth.[24] They met once or so annually and had weekly telephone discussions, usually a handful of people crowded around a speaker telephone on each side of the Atlantic discussing problems or

[22] Two Kabi scientists so argued, Fryklund (1992) and Fhölenhag (1992). The Genentech scientist (Bennett 1993a) also thought this co-operation worked well.

[23] They co-operated closely up until Hoffman-LaRoche bought a large percentage of Genentech in 1990 and when Genentech launched the heart-attack drug tPA, which competes with Kabi's streptokinase. Kabi also worked on developing tPA based on genetic engineering but dropped the project. Relations have been quite chilly, but in late autumn 1992, the two firms began discussing new opportunities for co-operation.

[24] Bennett (1993a), Fhölenhag (1992), Fryklund (1993), and Olson (1993a).

ideas. Before the telephone discussions, data was sometimes sent by fax, an emerging technology.

The reason this collaboration was important was that it gave each specialist group someone else with whom to discuss the directions and results of their knowledge-seeking activities. They could discuss new challenges, how to identify problems, what solutions worked and what did not work, try out new ideas which were a bit off the wall, and so forth. In doing so, they would jointly identify some of the contours of their common search space. Communication between the corporate researchers enabled each group to narrow down the broad set of all possible choices to a few alternatives which seemed most likely to function technically at a reasonable price. Firms needed to reduce diversity. Hearing what had and had not worked for others was one way to reduce diversity and fill in the blank spaces on their respective maps without having to do everything themselves. Thus, because of the trial-and-error nature of this type of engineering work, where theoretical models could not replace experimentation in contexts of use, learning from each other's empirical mistakes and successes could accelerate the pace of technical developments.

Communication with the larger community of researchers was largely cut off during this initial R & D phase. Neither firm wanted to disclose publicly that they were working on this new project, or the technical problems encountered. They were keeping their knowledge-seeking activities fairly quiet, even within the broader population of engineers and scientists potentially interested in these questions. Genentech had put in a patent application for the technique to cut off the methionine, indicating to whomever was interested that they had solved that part of the problem, but the firms neither confirmed nor denied rumours about the project.[25] Collaboration between these two firms partially replaced contacts with the larger community.

This meant that contacts with the other firm was the main outside source of ideas and information during certain phases of technical development. Occasionally, university researchers working on process-oriented problems were included in development work but kept under oath of secrecy. For example, Kabi's process R & D group did not want to interact with university researchers in Sweden because of the risk of leakage of information.[26] They were trying to prevent competitors from imitating their techniques and hence being 'free riders'. Instead of risking leaks, Kabi hired a researcher from the Department of Biochemistry and Biochemical Technology at the nearby Royal Institute of Technology on a limited time contract. She worked for a few years on Kabi's hGH production system, under oath of secrecy, before returning to the university.[27]

[25] Hunter (1985: 30), Fryklund (1993).   [26] Fhölenhag (1992).   [27] Enfors (1992).

Kabi found secrecy to be the best way to safeguard details of the process. Genentech was similarly secretive. The generation of new knowledge about specific technical details and even about the existence of major improvements was seen as giving competitive advantage.

The firms did not want to divulge details such as the exact parameters of optimization or the exact order of steps. The value of this knowledge lay in the specifics of translating knowledge into use, which generated economic benefits and entrepreneurial profits. Other knowledge was by its nature more general and often public, and could be distributed through published papers or generalizable problems and solutions taught in textbooks. The firms could contribute to that body of knowledge and still retain secrecy about details. For example, the firms sometimes published four or five different ways of accomplishing the same production engineering task, thereby not divulging which was most effective, or which the firm actually used.[28]

In developing their two relatively similar production systems for met-less hGH, Genentech and Kabi engaged in a process of developing relevant knowledge and techniques. As with the earlier met hGH, search and innovative activities required many employees' specialized knowledge as well as interactions with agents in other organizations. On the one hand, these relations with others were important sources of information and were part of the social process to define selection criteria. On the other hand, many of the specifics of context-dependent knowledge and techniques were generated or known by employees. Most of the equipment, the physical manifestation of production, was rooted inside the firms.

Shaking up hGH Markets in 1985

Despite Swanson's earliest plans to try to get Genentech's recombinant hGH approved by 1982, January 1985 had come and gone without any national regulatory agencies approving either Genentech or Kabi's hGHs. In 1984–5, Kabi were hoping for Swedish approval in 1986 and Genentech for American approval somewhat earlier. The firms were close to commercialization but had faced dead ends and challenges delaying approval, although clinical trials had also been positive. Once approved, they would face competition from pit hGH, which was often

---

[28] Bennett (1993a). Other types of knowledge were owned inside the company, whether legally or organizationally, and were more difficult to transfer. For example, there is knowledge of how to organize activities, or the competences of specific individuals. If a project lacks these, they may be gained by hiring new employees or assigning existing ones with experience to those tasks. Other intangibles, such as organizational skills, are difficult to transfer between firms.

distributed by government agencies free of charge. In addition to price, they had to sell a product based on a radically new technology in a market with a 'natural' alternative.

Interestingly for the firms and their perceptions of markets, the acceptability of genetically engineered hGH was being defined in relation to the human-produced pit hGH. Defining a genetically engineered pharmaceutical product as legitimate was as important as defining legitimate uses for hGH as a pharmaceutical (see second section). Like hGH in general, defining legitimate uses for rDNA versions was a process of negotiation between medical researchers, firms, and government agencies, based on medical knowledge. The firms thus had incentives to promote the superiority of genetic engineering techniques in these negotiations. The two firms differed a bit. As seen by its very name, Genentech—GENetic ENgineering TECHnology—was proud of its genetic engineering proficiency. No one in the firm needed convincing of the superiority of the new technology.

Kabi was a more biological pharmaceutical firm, sensitive to public debate, and less concentrated on the technology *per se*. Kabi was careful in naming its first rDNA hGH to avoid mention of genetic engineering and stress instead its everydayness, namely 'Somatonorm'.[29] Interestingly enough, the name of Kabi's second, met-less, hGH proudly displayed its genetic engineering origins; the brand name is 'Genotropin'. These names were directed towards external agents, such as doctors and patients, and reflected the firms' interpretations of their demands.

Even within Kabi, some employees initially viewed genetically engineered products with suspicion. Many thought that hGH extracted from pituitary glands was the natural, the real stuff and that the rDNA produced version would be second-rate. Marketing people within the company even complained that they would not be able to sell it.[30] Although scientists including the project leader believed in rDNA hGH, others argued that there would be little or no potential demand because a 'natural' alternative existed. Management in the firms also knew, however, that potential demand was greater than existing supply of pit hGH.

The perceived relative superiority of rDNA versus pit hGH changed quite dramatically on 2 April 1985. This changed the market as well. 2 April was the day that the American Food and Drug Administration (FDA) announced that they had found one positive case of a very rare viral infection of the brain called Creuztfeldt-Jakob disease. The person had been treated with pit hGH supplied by NIH in the late 1960s and

---

[29] Somatonorm seems to come from the medical term for this type of hormone, 'Somato(medins)', plus norm(al). The difference between the two brand names was pointed out by Holmström (1992).   [30] Fryklund (1992).

early 1970s.[31] The disease was carried by a 'slow virus', an infective agent which could lie dormant for up to twenty years, and it was thought that contaminated glands had introduced the virus into the hGH solution. This former patient died. A death involving pit hGH thus prompted government regulatory agencies to downgrade radically its perceived quality. This correspondingly opened the market for alternatives. It should be noted that the contaminants in rDNA hGH discussed in previous chapters were marginal compared to this.

The first indication of trouble had come in March 1985 when a Stanford University physician informed the NIH that an autopsy showed that this young man had the disease. The research organization (and research financier) NIH turned the problem over to the government regulatory agency, namely the FDA. The NIH also immediately halted their clinical tests of pituitary hGH which did not involve therapy.

The FDA acted to control this unwanted and dangerous side-effect. It made an announcement about the one positive case on 2 April and then sent corporate employees and NIH and university researchers home to see what could be done to ensure safety—particularly how to test for purity, and how to destroy slow viruses—and set another meeting for a few weeks later. On 19 April the FDA announced to the firms that three more cases had been discovered, although one diagnosis was uncertain.[32] Based on this knowledge, they asked commercial distributors in the USA, which were Kabi and Serono Labs, to withdraw pituitary hGH from the market, but made it clear that if the firms did not, the FDA would. The NIH similarly stopped production.

Later in April, the FDA announced that a new case had been discovered. This time it was in the United Kingdom, with hGH supplied by the Medical Research Council. As this contaminated hGH had come from a somewhat different extraction process, it indicated that slow viruses could be a general problem for tissue extraction. Soon after the FDA took action, similar bans were imposed in Sweden and in a number of European countries, excluding France.[33] The 'natural' hGH from pitui-

---

[31] Fryklund (1992), Hunter (1985), Norman (1985), and Glasbrenner (1986). The NIH ran the National Hormone and Pituitary Program.

[32] One diagnosis was uncertain because no autopsy had been done; that patient had died in February. Another former patient died in April, and the autopsy tentatively confirmed it was Creuztfeld-Jakob.

[33] Authorities in France did not impose a ban on pituitary hGH and did not stop distribution until 1988. A similar attitude prevailed in Japan, one of Kabi's largest markets, which was even slower to stop distribution. There is an interesting comparison in that both France and Japan were also slow about stopping the distribution and testing of blood thought to be affected with the HIV virus. As with the case of HIV-infected blood, albeit on a lesser scale, a number of people in both France and Japan became infected with Creutzfeldt-Jakob disease from contaminated pituitary hGH after 1985. France has been hit the worst, with 24 former patients contracting the disease as of July 1993. See Fryklund (1992), Aldhous (1992: 1571), Carr (1993: 98) and Dickson (1993: 372) about French pituitary hGH in relation to the Creutzfeldt-Jakob cases. See *Nature* (1993), Butler (1993), and Swinbanks (1993) about HIV-infected blood in France and Japan.

tary glands could no longer be argued to be superior to the genetically engineered one, which could not be contaminated with slow viruses.

Kabi prepared to take its brand name Crescormon off all their international markets and made its announcement on 24 April. Not everyone, however, agreed that pituitary hGH should be pulled off the market just because a few former patients had contracted and died from Creuztfeldt-Jakob disease. The medical knowledge and actions of the FDA could be, and were, questioned by agents in both the techno-economic and basic scientific environments. These bans were important for our tale because they closed the market to all firms who had not switched to genetic engineering as the basis of production.

There were many uncertain factors about this decision, one of the most important of which was the purity of the pit hGH that these former patients had received compared to contemporary standards. Before 1977, the pit hGH provided by the NIH was between 25–50 per cent pure, meaning that the remaining 50–75 per cent of the preparation were unknown proteins and contaminants. This was what the patients contracting Creuztfeldt-Jakob disease had received. In contrast, some argued that the pituitary hGH available in 1985 was up to 95 per cent pure.

No evidence could be shown to support the notion that the purification techniques available in 1985 posed a danger of contamination by slow viruses, but the problem was that neither could tests prove that no danger remained. For example, a UCSF medical researcher specializing in this type of virus argued that the NIH had no choice but to halt distribution of pit hGH. In the same article, he argued that there was no evidence that contemporary hGH was contaminated.[34] This time, it was the safety of the pharmaceutical from 'natural sources' like human pituitary glands that was under scrutiny and debate.

The positions and arguments of firms on the question of whether or not it was appropriate to ban pit hGH can be related to their contemporary knowledge-seeking actions to implement genetic engineering. Because Genentech did not supply pit hGH and was one of two firms—along with Eli Lilly—poised to move into the American market with rDNA hGH, a ban on the pituitary version could only be beneficial to them. In fact, immediately after the FDA's withdrawal of pituitary hGH, the FDA gave Genentech an investigative new drug status 'for the time being' for the 150 children who could die without it. However, the majority of children took hGH for dwarfism and could forego treatment for a maximum of six months without sabotaging their final height. They did not immediately get Genentech's product. These six months would, however, be a tight deadline, putting pressure on the FDA to act quickly.

[34] Norman (1985: 1176).

In addition, there were two firms supplying pit hGH to the commercial segment of the American market, for children who had not been receiving it from the NIH. These two firms were Kabi and Serono Laboratories (Massachusetts), a subsidiary of Arès-Serono (Geneva). Both companies sold hGH internationally, and Kabi had about 20 per cent of the American market whereas Serono had about 50 per cent. The two firms reacted oppositely to the FDA's announcement and subsequent ban.

When Kabi had gone home after the first FDA meeting on 2 April to evaluate the different possibilities of testing and destroying slow viruses, they knew that they had an alternative in the form of their rDNA hGH, brand name Somatonorm. Kabi quickly came to the conclusion that they could reduce the probability that pit hGH was contaminated with viruses infected with Creutzfeldt-Jakob disease. However, they could never conclusively say that purification eliminated all such viruses. No test could be definite, and so there would always be a risk involved. Moreover, Kabi thought the necessary changes to reduce the probability of contamination were expensive. Each batch of hGH would have to be tested, and the virus destroyed in two separate ways. Secondly, destroying the virus in two separate ways might destroy some of the hGH, thereby reducing yields. Both of these changes would be costly. In a much later account, Fryklund motivates Kabi's decision with the idea that 'what was unethical in the US was unethical for the rest of the world. Bodies work the same.'[35] Given an alternative at hand, the pit hGH brand name 'Crescormon' was not worth saving.

Nevertheless, Kabi did have to make a difficult decision in that they could have continued selling the pit hGH in a number of countries. It was difficult in that they had to stop distribution immediately and buy back the supplies stockpiled in subsidiaries around the world, ultimately leading to a loss of about 150 million Swedish crowns ($21.4 million dollars). The company as a whole then went from a profit to a loss because Crescormon was their largest product. Even this option was costly, at least in the short run.

In contrast to Kabi, Serono had moved into genetic engineering for hGH much later (starting in 1984) and were not far along with developing a production system, much less clinical testing. Serono Laboratories made the opposite decision about the American market and did not stop distributing its pit hGH until 9 May 1985, when the FDA made a formal request.

Serono argued that its purification methods removed all viruses and felt they should be allowed to continue selling it in the USA and internationally. Serono's director Francesco Pilato maintained that the

[35] Fryklund (1992).

'FDA has no evidence that Serono's product is not safe.'[36] A Serono spokesman similarly said, 'We think the [federal government] acted much too hastily' and also expressed doubts about the very diagnoses of Creutzfeldt-Jakob disease in the patients.[37] It was a difficult diagnosis to make, and perhaps the doctors were wrong. Although Serono employees undoubtedly believed their own interpretations of facts about the safety of their testing methods and product, the fact remains that the firm had no viable alternative. Serono continued selling pit hGH in those countries where it had not been banned, as did, for example, the French firm Sanofi in France.

Serono had only moved into genetic engineering to produce hGH a year earlier. This can be compared with Kabi's six years. In January 1984, Serono signed an agreement with the British biotech company Celltech for an expression system. They were hoping to start clinical tests in late 1985 but were having some technical troubles and challenges. New challenges had arisen because they had chosen to use mammalian cells—rather than bacteria—to produce hGH. Mammalian cells grow much more slowly but were thought to construct the protein more faithfully.[38] In short, Serono's rDNA hGH was considerably further from the market than those of Kabi and Genentech, and Serono thought that their pituitary hGH was worth the cost of saving. The FDA, however, forced them off the American market, as did regulatory agencies in a number of countries afterward.

At the end of October 1985, the FDA approved Genentech's product, called Protropin, for the American market to treat certain kinds of dwarfism. It took almost exactly six months after the first FDA meeting, and six months was the limit for breaking off treatment before it affected the children's final height. Approval took only twenty-three months, about half of the normal approval time.

In connection with approval, the FDA demanded that Genentech design a 'market survey system' in order to gather information about each patient, including, for example, growth rates and side-effects. The FDA saw this as a way to maintain close control. Genentech originally saw this system as an expensive extra burden, but it turned out to be an effective marketing device for convincing doctors of the efficiency and safety of their product.[39] A large body of medical knowledge about the positive effects on other patients was persuasive as a selling argument.

When FDA approval came, Genentech was ready with an offensive marketing strategy. According to an article in *Business Week*, Genentech

---

[36] Hunter (1985: 28).   [37] Norman (1985: 1176)
[38] Celltech (1984: 6–7). Moreover, after the Creutzfeldt-Jakob disease scare, some government agencies questioned whether mammalian cells should be used at all, as they might also be contaminated with slow viruses.   [39] Bennett (1993a).

had been stockpiling the product for almost a year and had plenty to start shipping. Genentech had also developed plans to build a top sales force.

[Genentech] systematically snared top members of the hospital-based forces of such drug companies as Merck, Pfizer, Upjohn, and Eli Lilly, hiring them on a contingency basis. When FDA approval seemed imminent last month [September 1985], Genentech called in the chits.

Boasts President G. Kirk Raab, a 25-year veteran of Abbott Laboratories who joined Genentech last February: 'We've got not just top sales people but elite groups who've been working in academic hospitals and have long-term experience dealing with physicians.'[40]

Genentech wanted to move quickly into the market. They knew that even if the hGH market was wide open with the removal of pit hGH, their product would not completely sell itself. They knew that competitors would soon want to enter the large American market, and there were advantages to being first and capturing market share. In a strategy similar to their hiring experienced production process people, Genentech consciously went after salespersons with relevant experience.

In contrast to Genentech, Kabi had experienced salespersons in-house, who already had established contacts with academic hospitals and specialized physicians. The salespersons were now convinced of the superiority of rDNA hGH. In the longer run, however, Kabi's former marketing strategy based on demand's exceeding supply would have to change to meet the new condition of multiple producers, multiple uses, and the possibility of supply's exceeding demand.

Kabi had expected approval later, not sooner, and had a large international market to cover. When Kabi got approval in their home Swedish market in October 1985 and soon in other countries, they did not have a large enough manufacturing capacity within Sweden to meet demand. They had to find an alternative production site. Kabi once again turned to the government-owned Porton Down in England. After the original R & D contract of December 1980 had run out, Porton Down had run fermentations a second time from 1983 to 1984. This was part of Kabi's R & D work to design a production process, and part of making enough hGH for toxicology and clinical trials. In 1985 Porton Down hoped to become a licensed producer for Kabi, using Kabi's technical specifications, and the two signed a five year contract for manufacturing. Even before that contract lapsed in 1990, however, Kabi had decided that Porton Down's production was too small and too costly. After this contract lapsed, this small percentage of production was discontinued, and all production returned to Sweden.[41] In the mean time, Kabi scaled up its factory outside of Stockholm, leading to new technical challenges to be solved.

[40] Hamilton (1985: 108).   [41] Fryklund (1992), Fhölenhag (1992).

The removal of pit hGH from the American and many European markets in 1985 thus changed attitudes about the desirability and safety of genetically engineered pharmaceuticals. Even 'natural' alternatives extracted from human bodies could be contaminated, and in fact, the genetically engineered version tested much purer. The six-month deadline put pressure on government regulatory agencies to accept the new product. The medical knowledge generated through firms' clinical trials thereby created and legitimized the market, after negotiations over criteria. This negotiation process was about the product as a pharmaceutical, including the strict criteria for safety. Genetic engineering offered an alternative pharmaceutical product which appeared safer than the natural version in 1985, leading to new interpretations of uses and markets.

Monopoly and Competition

In most countries, competition among firms over hGH increased as new entrants into the market began producing in the 1980s and 1990s. The largest single market, the American one, is somewhat different. In 1983, the US Congress passed a law giving firms making 'Orphan Drugs' a seven-year monopoly. The purpose of this federal legislation was to encourage firms to produce pharmaceuticals for small patient groups. The argument was that without exclusive market and monopoly rights, other firms could copy the idea and enter the market. This 'free ride' would thereby reduce incentives for the initial firm to innovate because with that risk of imitation, no one would be willing to invest the substantial R & D expenses necessary to develop a new drug for a small and potentially unprofitable market. With a limited-time monopoly, firms would be encouraged to take risks because the chances of recuperating costs were higher. Genentech received an 'Orphan Drug Status', giving them a seven-year monopoly on the American market along with FDA approval in October 1985.[42]

Although Genentech got a monopoly, the FDA simultaneously expressed a desire for competitors in the market. Dr John Gueriguian, who had called the FDA conference on insulin and human growth hormone made with recombinant DNA back in 1981, clearly stated their position when interviewed by *Chemical Weekly* in 1985:

FDA's Gueriguian insists, though, that the agency has not simply handed over the whole market to Genentech. FDA, he says, has been 'extremely active' in encouraging 'numerous' companies to pursue development of synthetic HGH during the past four years.[43]

[42] *Science* (1985: 523).   [43] Hunter (1985: 30).

The fact that FDA expressly stated its interest in competition may help explain another twist in the American hGH market that happened in 1987.

Genentech had received approval in 1985, but in March 1987 the FDA approved Eli Lilly's genetically engineered hGH for sale. This was thus during Genentech's seven-year monopoly. Moreover, the FDA also gave it Orphan Drug status. What was the difference between the two products that permitted both Orphan Drug status? The difference was the one amino acid, the methionine, still on Genentech's brand name Protropin. Eli Lilly used a bacteria expression system essentially identical to Genentech's, but then cut off the methionine using enzymes. The FDA therefore ruled that Lilly made a different product.

The law on Orphan Drugs was written fairly vaguely, and there was uncertainty both about how the FDA would rule beforehand and why they did so afterward. Genentech was caught by surprise and thought the decision was a violation of the Act and threatened to sue the FDA.[44] This decision seemed particularly unfair to the Genentech researchers, because they had in fact already developed a new production system for a met-less hGH and carried out much of the clinical testing. They were so close. The FDA's decision would exclude Genentech from the met-less hGH market until 1994, although they could and would continue to sell their met hGH. After the Orphan Drug status expired, Genentech replaced Protropin (met hGH) with Nutropin (met-less) in the American market, and both Kabi and Genentech are considering moving into each other's market in the future, when the exclusive market contract expires.

Before the FDA approved Eli Lilly's met-less hGH, Genentech knew they must have been close to submitting material. Genentech knew about their clinical testing, and Kabi had told them around March/April 1987 that Eli Lilly had applied for approval in Sweden, to challenge Kabi's potential monopoly position. Both Lilly and Kabi were approved in Sweden in the spring of 1987. Lilly also had strong incentives to get American approval. They needed American approval because home country approval is necessary to sell internationally, even if it is an informal requirement for doing so. Serono Labs were also close to submitting an application for met-less hGH in the USA. Kabi had urged Genentech to act quickly to get the met-less hGH approved in the USA.

Genentech instead took some extra time, which delayed their FDA application. They decided to make a number of improvements which would make production more efficient but which took time to imple-

---

[44] *Science* reported that Genentech had sued the FDA (Crawford 1987), whereas one of Genentech's current upper management says they only threatened to sue the FDA, but never did (Young 1992).

ment. For example, they further revised the bacteria to increase yield, which thereby reduced the cost of the product but also necessitated changes in related production technologies. Kabi turned down some of these improvements in order to get approval more quickly. Genentech were also slow about sending in the enormous amount of documentation required for new drug approval. Genentech managers felt that time was less urgent than Kabi had suggested, partly because they did not think Eli Lilly had done enough clinical tests with met-less hGH and partly because they never thought the FDA would approve a second hGH. Genentech lost out in that Eli Lilly's got Orphan Drug status. In effect, Genentech and Lilly both got monopoly rights to the same market. The one-amino-acid difference was clinically unimportant for growth.

Genentech have not, however, lost out on sales. The American market was worth around $200 million in 1991 and about $300 million in 1995. Of this, Genentech has had 75 per cent of the market. Genentech sold about $157 million worth of Protropin in 1991; $205 million in 1992; and $216 million of Protropin/Nutropin in 1995.[45] In 1992, Eli Lilly sold $170 of hGH internationally. Thus, despite the fact that Genentech were cut off from developing the improved version, Genentech have been more successful in the American market than Lilly.

The other international markets are more competitive. hGH has been a commercial success as a product and for some early-moving firms. The world-wide market for hGH in 1991 was estimated at $700 million; at $1.96 billion in 1992; and around $1 billion in 1995.[46] There has been an enormous increase in sales since genetic engineering has made increased supply possible. Kabi (subsequently Pharmacia, then UpJohn Pharmacia) have also been successful and hold about 55–60 per cent of the market outside the USA. Kabi sold $243 million (1.7 billion Swedish crowns) in 1992, of which 90 per cent was exported from Sweden.[47] Genentech's first two R & D projects using genetic engineering to make known pharmaceuticals—insulin and human growth hormone—have thus turned out to be enormously successful.

Both the American and international markets have thus turned out to be several times larger than the firms had originally projected in 1978, with the American market soon worth close to $400 million rather than $10 million and the international market worth around $1 billion. The

[45] Data from 1991 and earlier cited in this paragraph and the next are in *Affärsvärlden* (1992: 15), Kabi (1991), Kabi (1992), Lehrman (1993b: 179), and Wallgren (1993: 1). Data in these two paragraphs from 1994/5 are in *Financial Times* (1995: 17) and *Marketletter* (1993). Recombinant DNA insulin has also been hugely successful; in 1992, Eli Lilly sold $526 million while Novo Nordisk sold $824 million (*Marketletter*, 1993).

[46] See previous note for references. 'As a result, 40,000 children put on more than a kilometre in height between them (on average 4cm each)'(*The Economist* 1992b: 81).

[47] Kabi's sales alone constituted about 15 per cent of the total world market for pharmaceuticals made with genetic engineering in 1992.

original calculations of sales, markets, and profits were thus way off due to the expandable nature of multiple uses and markets for this product. The early-moving firms have been rewarded by profits, although Genentech has been rewarded more than Eli Lilly. The firms expect increased competition and lower prices in the future.

Summary and Conclusions

This chapter has concentrated on knowledge-seeking activities directly affecting or creating uses of, and hence markets for, hGH. Much of the focus has been on how firms identified and used technical and economic criteria to direct their activities to conform to existing, and create new, social selection criteria. For pharmaceuticals, selection criteria to enter the market are set by government agencies, based on medical research. Although pharmaceutical markets are created and controlled by government regulatory agencies, their decisions are based on knowledge created in interaction and negotiation between firms, government agencies, and medical researchers, which creates conditions for entry as well as the market. By defining legitimate uses, those uses excluded from the market are illegitimate uses, often obtained through the black market.

The firms had incentives to invest in knowledge-seeking activities to generate legitimate uses of the pharmaceutical. In the best case, medical research would show multiple uses (indications) or else expand the range of uses for existing indications. If approved, these would increase the market for rDNA hGH, which was possible in a situation of expanding supply. In fact, moving from a situation of very restricted to expanding supply has led to new discussions about where boundaries for treatment should lie.

Another important selection criterion was homogeneity and high quality of the product. The firms needed to convince the involved parties that both the product and its production system were standardized, reproducible, and conformed to regulations through more sensitive analytical methods. The firms' generation of novel, legitimate uses of rDNA hGH were thus dependent on their ability to generate medical scientific knowledge and to influence selection criteria defining the market.

In 1983, Genentech and Kabi had to decide whether or not to develop a second version of rDNA hGH, a met-less hGH that was identical to the hGH produced in the human body. Partly based on others' basic scientific research, Genentech modified the general knowledge and techniques to develop this specific technique. Their technique cut off the signal sequence containing the methionine and secreted the protein into the periplasm. Deciding whether or not to change to this new set of genetic engineering techniques was a fairly difficult decision. Genentech and Kabi had already sunk investments into the met hGH, in the form of knowledge-seeking activities, designing production systems, clinical trials, relations with government regulatory agencies, and so forth. Changing to a new set of genetic engineering alternatives would significantly improve the perceived characteristics of the final product but would also entail significant additional R & D activities. A decision had to be made by management.

The sunk investments could have led to a firm-level lock-in to the met hGH. Both firms decided, however, to work on the two projects in parallel. Having made the decision to sustain diversity by developing both versions, Genentech and Kabi knew they ultimately wanted to stop producing the met hGH, and so they had to jump to the met-less trajectory. Initially, they had to work on producing both versions because the new version would take several years of R & D and clinical testing to be ready for sales. They made this decision because in the longer term, the firms wanted a high-quality met-less hGH in order to expand market share. Whether the met-less hGH was actually better clinically or not, its structure was identical to the pituitary hGH, making it more attractive to doctors and patients.

Genentech and Kabi firms initially worked independently, but soon co-operated in exchanging information in order to speed up the innovation process. It gave each group someone to discuss opportunities and problems with in a situation where the firm did not want to divulge information, not even to researchers responding to the basic scientific environment. Information could easily move from those researchers to competing firms.

When Kabi and Genentech developed their respective rDNA hGHs, they assumed it would compete with pituitary hGH, as sold by firms or provided by government sponsored research institutes. Many initially argued that the pituitary hGH was superior. It was 'natural' whereas the rDNA was artificial, produced by a radically new technology. Ability to increase supply with the new technology was not a sufficient marketing argument for those children lucky enough to be receiving pit hGH, although purity could be a good argument. The relative superiority of the two was quickly revised, however, during the mid-1980s. A fatal medical risk with pit hGH (Creutzfeldt-Jakob disease) was uncovered in 1985, leading the United States, Sweden, and many other countries to ban pit hGH. This left the hGH market wide open for those producing with genetic engineering techniques.

The reactions of firms to these bans can be related to their relative positions in developing genetic engineering techniques for production. Genentech was positive and able to step immediately into the American market to supply the neediest children. This was the first pharmaceutical that they produced by themselves, and their sales of hGH rocketed to

$41 million in 1986. Kabi was in a more complicated situation. Pit hGH was already an important product, and taking their brand name Crescormon off all their international markets meant a big financial loss for the firm. At the same time, doing so would be best for the children and favourable for their reputation (an important aspect of the pharmaceutical business), and they had an alternative product in waiting based on a different, low-risk technology. Even for those countries where it was not banned, Kabi destroyed their share of the market by stopping Crescormon sales, hoping, of course, that they would soon fill the vacuum with the rDNA version.

Other firms which had previously made pit hGH but which had not moved into genetic engineering contested the dangers of slow viruses when modern purification techniques were used, and continued selling when and where possible. In contrast, firms previously not selling hGH but interested in entry saw the switch to genetic engineering techniques as an opportunity to move into the market. Government regulatory agencies thus destroyed the market for pit hGH by banning it in many countries, thereby changing the market and putting pressure on themselves to approve shortly thereafter a genetically engineered version (within six months).[48] Associating severe risks with the pituitary hGH dramatically increased the relative superiority of the rDNA hGH.

The new met-less hGH was ready for sale in the mid- to late 1980s. Kabi were particularly successful in quickly jumping to the new trajectory and developing 'Genotropin' to sell internationally, whereas Genentech were somewhat slower, and the FDA shut them out of the met-less segment of the American market in 1987.

Government regulatory agencies could encourage competition or else monopoly over the pharmaceutical. The US Congress had designed a law granting a limited-time monopoly for new pharmaceuticals intended for a small number of patients in order to encourage innovative activities. Genentech was granted such a monopoly on sales of met hGH in 1985. In order to increase competition anyway, the FDA approved the met-less hGH of Genentech's competitor Eli Lilly in 1987. This effectively shut Genentech out of that segment of the market until 1994, but Genentech has successfully competed with their met hGH, then their met-less or natural hGH. They have about 75 per cent of the American market and will consider moving into the international market after the agreement with Kabi expires. Kabi has also been successful internationally, with about 55–60 per cent of the world market, excluding the American market. Competition was thus not

---

[48] The only other rDNA pharmaceutical then approved was insulin. Lilly got US approval for insulin in September 1982.

stopped with the ban of pit hGH in 1985, but competition was thereafter over the rDNA hGH of different producer firms in most countries.

The generation and selection of uses and markets for pharmaceutical hGH has depended on negotiations and interactions particularly among producer firms, medical researchers, and government regulatory agencies. Their interpretations of use and markets have set social selection criteria, defining conditions of entry into the market.

9

Conclusions for Evolutionary Economics

After long reflection, I cannot avoid the conviction that no innate tendency to progressive development exists.[1]

Introduction

This book has described and analysed parallel technological innovation processes which made possible early commercial uses of genetic engineering for pharmaceuticals. The focus here has been on knowledge-seeking activities which led to results which agents could use to generate and select among alternative paths of development. These alternative paths, or trajectories, can be described as general for this type of use of genetic engineering as well as specific for the individual firms. They are general to the extent that most agents pursuing these uses encountered similar opportunities and challenges, and they are specific to the extent that they were unique for each context of use. The decisions and actions of corporate researchers and managers have been described in relation to technological challenges and external agents, such as university scientists and government regulatory agencies.

One reason for writing this book is to examine technological innovation processes, which have a crucial and central role in market competition and economic change. Evolutionary economists argue that new technologies are an important factor determining the long-term viability and growth of an economy as well as the probability that individual firms will successfully compete over time. Partly because diverse firms search for—and find—technological and organizational innovations, some firms will have a better chance of surviving than others. The conditions of market competition will therefore change over time. It is assumed that the diversity of firms' competences, experiences, and decisions matters for their decisions about innovations. No one choice will be a priori most rational and optimal, both because the future is truly uncertain and socially shaped and because firms only know a limited part of the options.

---

[1] Charles Darwin, quoted in Luria *et al.* (1981: 585).

Research questions in this evolutionary economics tradition often centre around firms' strategies, changes in industrial competition, and so forth. Although there are many interesting, alternative ways of examining the interdependencies of firms' strategies, economic change, and technological innovations, this book has shifted the focus to technological innovation processes themselves.

One reason for shifting the focus to technological innovation processes is that evolutionary economists make a fundamental core assumption—namely that technical change is evolutionary. For example, the concluding chapter to the influential collection of articles in *Technical Change and Economic Theory* identifies evolutionary technical change as a common element of all the heterogeneous theoretical approaches presented there. More specifically, the authors agree that 'the creation of technological capabilities involves an evolutionary, endogenous process of change, negotiated and mediated with society at large.'[2] This implies that technological change is the result of firms' activities in interaction with the larger society and that it is often difficult. However, there has been little careful empirical work about the extent to which the assumption holds.

To examine evolutionary innovation, steps have here been taken to integrate an evolutionary economic perspective with some perspectives from sociology, history, and management of technology and innovation. By combining these approaches when analysing technological innovation processes, the emphasis is shifted to the pattern of technological change, to knowledge-seeking activities, and to interactions among innovative agents and their environments.

Linearity or Evolutionary Complexity?

The history of knowledge-seeking activities for rDNA hGH as addressed in Chapters 5 through 7 has been told chronologically. The focus is on those university and corporate researchers who engaged in scientific and technological activities which enabled early commercial uses of genetic engineering. The specific end-point is the ability to manufacture and sell the pharmaceutical human growth hormone (hGH) and to some extent insulin. Indeed, the knowledge-seeking activities of Genentech and Kabi, the two firms detailed in particular here, resulted in viable and competitive production systems and products sold. In between, the process of innovation illustrates many moments of uncertainty, both about the results of knowledge-seeking activities and about future value.

Just as the history of penicillin introduced in Chapter 2 could either be

---

[2] Nelson and Soete (1988: 633).

told as linear progression or as complex interactions among market and government influences and between scientific and technological knowledge, the agents, knowledge-seeking activities, and environments described in this book might also be told either as a linear process or as evolutionary complexity.

On a hasty reading, there appears to be a linear progression from basic scientific research to technology to a marketable product. This seems to be substantiated by the shift of emphasis in the text. Chapter 5 describes knowledge-seeking activities mainly in a basic scientific environment in the 1970s. This was a period when basic scientists contributed to the development of practical genetic engineering techniques and when they engaged in internal scientific, as well as public, debate to influence informal and formal regulation of the technology. Chapters 6 and 7 then shift from scientific research to a description of scientific and technological activities in the late 1970s and 1980s where corporate and university researchers could meet. Some emphasis is on the challenges to R & D of integrating genetic engineering with component technologies in the production systems. Chapter 8 again shifts the emphasis, this time towards knowledge about legitimate uses of the resulting product (hGH) in relation to production and in relations between firms, doctors, and regulatory agencies.

This overly-quick glance of the contents can thus give the impression of an apparent progression in Chapters 5 through 8 from basic science to industrial technology to marketing products. In one sense, this is correct, in that the different time periods exhibit different balances of scientific and technological activities and of market and government influences. The linear-flow model might even be correct in that basic science developed knowledge and techniques that could be used for radically new technology. Developing theoretical arguments about evolutionary innovation has not denied that scientific or technological activities, market or government influences, are more important at different times or to differing degrees. Clearly, different combinations of them, as identified in Figure 3.1, were relatively more important at different points in the innovation processes.

The linear model and explanation, however, misses the point of describing the complex interactions among different agents and among agents and environmental conditions. In fact, a closer examination of the historical material shows that interactions among scientific and technological activities in relation to market and government over time are much more complex and quite different from those implied by the linear model. The process described here could not have been rationally and completely described in advance; it is instead full of visions and disappointments, accusations and praise. Because of this, it implies that managing R & D projects involving radical technologies demands a flexible approach, where goals and evaluations must be made periodically along the way so that, if necessary, it is possible to redirect in-house R & D and access to external knowledge.

The perspective of evolutionary innovation is more specifically explored in the concluding section. The next three sections address issues important for an understanding of how technical and economic aspects are combined in innovation. The issues include questions about the relationships between technological and economic capabilities and about the relationships between firms' decisions and their contacts with others in the environment. These three issues are: (1) firms' competences and perceptions for generating novelty, 2) lock-in and trajectories, and 3) radical versus incremental change.

Firms' Competences and Perceptions to Generate Novelty

The relative importance of firms' competences versus their perceptions of opportunities is discussed here. This is placed in relation to how and why firms generate novelty leading to diversity.

This is an interesting question because, on the one hand, evolutionary economics argues that firms' competences, experiences, and organization limit the types of new technologies that each firm is likely to develop. Based on this perspective and knowing the radical nature of genetic engineering, we might not expect established firms with an alternative technology to develop the radically new. On the other hand, the neo-Schumpeterian perspective also emphasizes the importance of agents' perceptions leading to action. Perceptions can overcome the limits of current competences by identifying new opportunities. Agents have to make decisions about the potential risks and opportunities in the market and about the likelihood that knowledge-seeking activities will lead to results.[3]

The initial perceptions in the 1970s that genetic engineering techniques had commercial potential came from agents most familiar with it, namely scientific researchers. Soon after basic scientists developed practical techniques enabling transfer of DNA between cells, a number of scientists perceived that it should be possible to produce human proteins in bacteria. It was clear to many that this application would interest firms, who could sell the resulting proteins. This was a potential interest, a perception of possible returns. Actually doing so in practice would require additional scientific and technological activities because no one

---

[3] Chapter 2 argues that this generation of novelty in *ex ante* anticipation of environmental conditions is an important difference between biological and socio-economic evolution. The modes of evolution are quite different.

had yet shown that bacteria could express human proteins. Both new knowledge and techniques were needed. Initially, when the perception began to be visible, researchers could not do experiments to prove it because there was an informal moratorium internal to basic science on certain experiments. By the late 1970s, these limits were lifted with the development of formal and/or informal regulations in the public context.

Of all the potential users of genetic engineering as a production method to make insulin and hGH in the late 1970s, only some agents both perceived the economic and technical potential and also acted. The population of potential users included different types of organizations which had been extracting and purifying proteins from tissue. For hGH, this included government financed organizations like the National Pituitary Agency (NPA) as well as firms like Kabi and Serono. There were also commercial firms like Eli Lilly and Novo which supplied insulin.

Government-funded research organizations like the NPA made no attempts to move into genetic engineering for hGH. These organizations did not have the necessary competence to develop this use of genetic engineering, partly because organizations contracted out the extraction to medical researchers. These researchers were interested in the effects of hormones and were not specialists in the scientific fields relevant for genetic engineering. Although they, too, could have bought external competences to access the technology, governments gave direct financing for extraction, and the organizations had few incentives to change technologies. These researchers and organizations were shielded from direct market influence and would not benefit unless they moved to a market environment through, for example, starting a new firm. They saw themselves as performing a service and doing scientific research, not making commercial profits. These organizations simply stopped producing hGH once the pituitary hGH was banned in 1985.

The firms, in contrast, had more incentives to monitor external scientific and technological activities in order to identify novelties which either threatened their business and/or offered new opportunities. Market influences gave firms incentives to try to make a profit, or at least survive. Individuals and firms made different calculations of the technical and economic potential and costs of genetic engineering in a situation characterized by risk and uncertainty. Developing this new technology involved risks, uncertainty, and belief more than it involved rational and optimal calculations of known trade-offs.

There were diverse reactions among existing pharmaceutical firms, and some new biotech firms were also started up. Of firms in this market, by no means all believed in the opportunities of genetic engineering and were willing to invest in knowledge-seeking activities with very uncertain returns. The short-term returns seemed too low. Some firms like Serono and Sanofi continued using only the existing tissue extraction production method. These two firms began developing genetic engineering techniques in 'the mid-1980s, when the potential returns were more visible.

Of the pharmaceutical firms, those that did move in early tended to acquire genetic engineering for existing products. Eli Lilly was interested in the techniques for producing insulin and Kabi in those for hGH. Eli Lilly also moved into hGH, which it had not previously produced but saw as a potentially profitable niche market and sufficiently close in technical matters to production of rDNA insulin. Proteins from the alternative tissue extraction production were, or were projected to be, in short supply, giving firms incentives to explore alternatives.

Although none of these firms had experience or competence with genetic engineering, they did have experience with production of biological products, with the naturally occurring proteins, and with all the complementary aspects, such as marketing regulation. Moreover, they tried to keep their bets open by continuing to improve the proteins coming from tissue extraction.

In contrast, the new competences and budding experience of biotech firms lay with genetic engineering as such. They were therefore interested in a range of potential products which could be produced this way. Genentech's perception and actions focused on carrying out knowledge-seeking activities for other firms based on R & D contracts. As to what they would like to manufacture themselves, the strategy was a pharmaceutical with a specialized market niche which they could relatively easily attack, such as hGH.

The two types of firms thus differed in their previous experience, competences, and organization. These pharmaceutical firms had experience with biological production methods, with handling and purifying proteins, and with scientific, market, and regulatory dimensions of selling. Kabi and Lilly relied on Genentech for genetic engineering techniques to make rDNA hGH and insulin a reality. Kabi, however, immediately set up a subsidiary biotech firm named KabiGen and Lilly expanded in-house R & D into this field. Kabi's knowledge and experience with proteins from tissue extraction was initially seen as a head start for the joint Genentech and Kabi collaboration.

In contrast, Genentech was specifically started to exploit the commercial potential of genetic engineering, and being a new firm, they had no past experience areas, employees, or product markets on which to base new knowledge-seeking activities. To create the R & D department, Genentech hired university scientists able to develop knowledge and techniques for genetic engineering, as well as experienced corporate researchers who might have worked with genetic engineering scientifically but who also had relevant experience with industrial-scale production of other biological substances. Initially, however, it was the scientific reputation of co-founder Boyer and of the first scientists which was important, particularly in order to sell R & D contracts. In addition to high quality research, however, the firm needed to show that the results would be relevant for techno-economic uses. Proving that required many other bodies of knowledge and techniques as well as venture capital experience.

There was thus a close symmetry between the existing firms' markets and the initial application(s) for which they wanted to develop genetic engineering. For existing firms, their accumulated technical and economic knowledge and experience narrowed the uses for which they developed the technology. In contrast, new firms had a profile based on a vision of future use, and what accumulated competence existed depended on that of new employees.

These early commercial uses required that genetic engineering be integrated into production processes. To do so, each firm had to have a strategy and way of implementing decisions. They needed access to persons with the necessary knowledge and experience, either in-house or externally. Strategies included, for example, using current employees, hiring new people, buying research or knowledge from another organization, and so forth. Although like scientific activities, technological activities are dependent on individuals, the firms could bypass some of the problems of individual limitations by organizing larger groups. Firms also have more direct control over how individuals with different specialities should work together towards a common goal.

For knowledge areas seen as vital, Kabi and Genentech strove to develop their competencies in-house even when they had to buy or otherwise access external knowledge to solve an immediate problem. Both types of firms were thus actively developing knowledge and techniques which were seen as vital but missing in-house. They built up competences in-house not for the specific information provided but for the possibility of shaping future knowledge-seeking activities, and these competences were vital when they could be used for improvements and/or for new projects.

Firm's competences and experiences are thus not static, as seen in the active role of firms to develop new ones. Neither do competences explain why of all the established firms, some agents developed novel technologies while others only improved the old. In addition to competences, individuals and the organization must believe that the technical and economic risks and uncertainty of innovation can be overcome and returns captured.

Perception and risk-taking were particularly important for radical technological change. In the 1970s, genetic engineering was still techniques used in the basic scientific environment, and which had been barely proved to function in scientific labs. The degree of novelty was high for all environments, and the technology had not been proved to function or to be reliable for commercial production. Due to uncertainty and different calculations of risks and opportunities, established firms made different perceptions and acted accordingly. Only with the aid of hindsight can we say which bets worked out better or worse. Those firms which waited five or six years were still able to get a product to market only a few years after the early-moving firms, but they have been much less successful in capturing market share.

This argument can best be illustrated by putting firms' perceptions of the risks and profits of genetic engineering in relation to the alternative production techniques available. Some firms decided to improve the existing technologies rather than invest in knowledge-seeking activities for a new and uncertain technology. The history of technology is replete with examples where existing technologies were significantly improved under threat from a new, apparently superior technology which directly competed for function.

An example from the history of insulin can illustrate this argument for genetic engineering. The Danish insulin producer Novo chose in the late 1970s not to move into genetic engineering techniques, partly because they were already working to improve tissue extraction methods. They felt this would be a surer method of making insulin identical to human insulin. Problems in the diffusion of information about the new technology cannot explain why Novo did not move into genetic engineering techniques. Genentech even directly approached Novo about signing an R & D contract for rDNA insulin in the late 1970s, but Novo was not interested. They were simply not convinced about the advantages.

Instead, Novo invested in R & D to further improve their existing production method. Using enzymes, in which Novo has special experience and knowledge, Novo found a way to transform extracted porcine and bovine insulin into insulin identical to human insulin. In 1981, the major pharmaceutical newsletter *Scrip* even argued that Novo were ahead of Lilly in the race to produce semi-synthetic human insulin.[4] Lilly was working on insulin from recombinant DNA techniques. This comparison indicates that *Scrip* made no distinction between the two production sources for 'semi-synthetic human insulin', namely improved tissue extraction and genetic engineering techniques. It was thus not completely obvious, even in the early 1980s, that genetic engineering would turn out to be a superior production method to tissue extraction for existing products. Whether for technical, cost, medical, or marketing reasons, however, Novo later abandoned the tissue extraction approach in favour of genetic engineering techniques.

Moreover, when Novo did acquire genetic engineering techniques for

---

[4] *Scrip* (1981a: 15).

insulin, the events indicate that one biotech firm could have competences and knowledge but still not deliver a functioning technology. In 1981, Novo contracted the Swiss-American biotech firm Biogen for an expression system for insulin.[5] Biogen failed, however, to supply one. Biogen had been started by a famous research scientist (Gilbert) and apparently had all the necessary knowledge, but could not make the scientific techniques work in practice. Their yeast expression system would not express insulin. The Seattle-based biotech firm Zymo Corporation (later ZymoGenetics) succeeded instead in helping Novo express insulin in yeast.[6] Biogen's failure to make the techniques function indicates that knowledge competences alone do not suffice. Techniques and practice are as important as knowledge for technological activities. The requirement that technology function in practice and not just theoretically applies as much to genetic engineering as to machinery.

In integrating genetic engineering and biological production, the firms thus had to interpret information about technical, scientific, and economic possibilities. The firms made decisions about technical alternatives based on the local environments within firms, including both technical competences and market experience. However, their decisions were also partly based on interactions with external agents who could give information about existing environmental conditions or who would shape future conditions. For example, Kabi had much experience with the protein hGH, and extensive contacts with government regulatory agencies, doctors, and so forth. These external agents helped the firm understand and gather regulatory, scientific, and economic information about the product, both the pit and rDNA versions. Choices about, for example, analytical methods were based on responses given by existing external contacts rather than on extensive additional search. Their perceptions of the techno-economic environment helped define the boundaries of a technological trajectory within which to concentrate knowledge-seeking activities. They thus adapted their knowledge-seeking activities to fit their existing niche in the techno-economic environment, partly based on information from external agents.

In contrast, Genentech were interested in and did R & D on many potentially interesting products based on genetic engineering for the R & D contracts. They chose to develop hGH into a product because the market seemed relatively easy to move into and because hGH seemed

---

[5] Lilly was then within months of getting rDNA insulin approved in the USA, whereas the Novo insulin was estimated to be approved within two to four years (*Scrip* 1981b: 5). Interestingly enough, *Scrip*'s source of information, a broker, estimated that recombinant DNA insulin could be sold for 30–50 per cent more than extracted insulin. Increasing the price so much has not been possible in practice.

[6] Gray (1992), Hansen *et al.* (1991: 79). Later, Novo Nordisk bought ZymoGenetics.

a product from which they could learn about the general production challenges for future rDNA products. Genentech also hoped hGH and parallel products could help them develop a model production system, which the firm could use to learn knowledge and techniques applicable to a range of genetically engineered products. hGH would also be a test case to help build up external contacts valuable for pharmaceuticals. This indicates that Genentech had different goals than Kabi, and that these differences led them to emphasize different types of knowledge-seeking activities.

Thus, to initiate knowledge-seeking activities for this use of genetic engineering, firms needed a perception that the technical and economic potential would outweigh the risks. This was a necessary condition. Having or acquiring technical competences and a dose of ingenuity were similarly necessary conditions. Those firms which moved in early faced a high degree of novelty and thereby faced a very uncertain technical and economic future. However, every time their knowledge-seeking activities led to relevant changes in knowledge or to functioning techniques, they gained information which thereby reduced uncertainty about the future technological innovation processes. This information was, however, often valuable to potential imitators as well. The firms further developed internal competences and experience over time in a cumulative process of learning.

Lock-in and Trajectories

Within the economics of technical change, the concept 'lock-in' is often used to refer to competition between two designs, or two competing directions of technical change. An often used example is the competition between the Beta and VHS video standards. One design becomes the dominant technology as the result of a series of decisions and actions. Lock-in is related to the concept of technological trajectories, which means that each change in a series cumulatively builds on the previous one.

Development seems 'locked in' to a path due to positive externalities, not inherent technological superiority. If, for whatever reason, one competing technology becomes more popular than the other, then there are increasing returns from that technology, giving agents incentives to choose it. '[T]he left-behind technology would need to bridge a widening gap if it is to be chosen by adopters at all.'[7] For innovation, this implies that the environment can creatively direct technical change along one path instead of another.

[7] Arthur (1988: 593).

Here, the general concept of lock-in will not be used to analyse a population making choices between two or more competing designs over time. Instead, it is related to firms' choices about specific subsets of genetic engineering techniques and about a commercial versus basic scientific trajectory. This shift has some implications. When the concept is used for populations making choices between two technologies, the focus of analysis is the increased attractiveness of one technology in a situation where more and more people are adopting it. Here, the focus of analysis is whether and why firms stick with one technical alternative and continue making incremental changes to it when an apparently better alternative has been or is being developed elsewhere.

Preceding chapters have argued that these early commercial uses of genetic engineering developed along a different trajectory from that of basic science. The firms' R & D activities stressed improvements which were along the parameters of functioning, reliability, level of expression, purity, ease of use, and so forth, so that the resulting pharmaceutical could compete technically and economically. The basic scientific trajectory, in contrast, continued pushing the frontiers in other directions, in order to develop generalized knowledge about the world. The argument is that the main reason why two separate but interacting trajectories developed is that the two populations of innovators responded to different environmental conditions (see further Chapter 10).

The relationship between knowledge and techniques used for the two trajectories is, however, quite interesting. On the one hand, as agents developed improvements along these two types of trajectories, each developed the technology so that they could use it to compete in their specific environmental conditions. On the other hand, they also shared more general knowledge and techniques. These were more or less available to trained specialists, whatever type of organization they worked in. When university scientists made improvements to genetic engineering techniques or to tests like silver staining, then these activities and results were often of importance for the commercial trajectory. When, in turn, corporate researchers improved analytical methods initially developed in science, many of these improved tools and methods could be reintegrated into use in scientific experiments. Moreover, when the early-moving firms started developing commercial uses in the late 1970s, there were no viable alternatives to *E. coli*. Due mainly to basic scientific activities, the general commercial trajectory for production has since branched out in a number of directions, based on the different cells—*E. coli* bacteria, yeast, mammalian, etc. These uses resemble each other but have different specificities. So, later basic scientific research opened up alternatives such as yeast cells, thereby also opening up more search spaces for late-moving firms.

The differing commercial and basic scientific trajectories were developed from the beginning, even, in this case, when the initial scientific activities and results were in competition with each other. In 1979, both Genentech and the competing UCSF research group engaged in competing knowledge-seeking activities to develop *E. coli* bacteria expression systems for hGH. However, they did so for somewhat different reasons. Genentech was engaged in knowledge-seeking activities to control DNA in order to produce proteins useful to create economic value. UCSF engaged in similar activities but were particularly interested in developing knowledge about how genes and cells work. Their activities were intended to be useful for competing in the basic scientific environment. A major difference was that Genentech's activities developed functioning and practical techniques (synthetic DNA; expression achieved) whereas UCSF's developed knowledge (sequence of gene). Both activities relied, however, on very similar techniques and developed quite similar knowledge. Over time, however, whereas these basic scientists went on to other activities, Genentech as a firm had to concentrate on improving the specific techniques.

Once the firms had made a choice about the set of genetic engineering techniques to develop for a product, they tended to stick with that set. This is particularly true for the general branch of the commercial trajectory, such as *E. coli* bacteria versus yeast but was also true for more specific choices such as strain of cell or promoter. They then tended to make cumulative changes to it, even if the changes themselves could be smaller or more major. They could, however, use different alternative technologies for different products. For a given product, the firms did change to a new, but nearby, trajectory when doing so offered major advantages and if the costs of abandoning the existing one and of developing the new alternative could be recuperated. The technical and economic superiority of a new alternative had to be strongly perceived; otherwise they would be locked into the existing choices.

At the very detailed production level, choices about many technical alternatives had to be made in relation to other choices. For example, the specific choice and sequence of protein purification steps had to be chosen based on the genetic engineering techniques used, parameters for fermentation, and so forth. The development of these component technologies were specifically designed to fulfil technical (functioning) and economic (at a reasonable unit price) goals. This very detailed production level was unique for each firm, and the technical choices previously made constrained the range of alternatives which could be chosen in the next round.

Changes to the genetic engineering techniques and biological materials could involve important changes to the production system and at the firm-level trajectory. It was Genentech who initially had the competences to improve the expression systems, improvements which they gave to Kabi under the R & D contract. Within a year of their first scientific paper on hGH, for example, Genentech changed the signal which told the bacteria to start producing the protein, the promoter. The initial promoter functioned, in the sense that some proteins were expressed, but it was not very efficient, in that yield was too low.

They needed a more effective promoter, not least to produce on the large scale necessary for commercial production and to fulfil the R & D contract bench-marks. Genentech scientists tried out various promoters developed in universities, adapting them for use with the desired insulin, hGH, and other proteins. They then chose the one which gave the best improvement in yield, the trp promoter. Genentech gave this improved expression system to Lilly for insulin and to Kabi for hGH under the respective R & D contracts. Genentech thus used scientific methods and criteria to analyse alternatives developed externally but modified them for their contexts of use, and chose among them based on economic criteria. The new promoter was superior in that it increased yield and thereby reduced unit costs.

Then, in the mid-1980s, Genentech again improved the hGH expression system to secrete the protein into the cell periplasm, and this change enabled them to cut off the extra methionine and produce an hGH identical to natural hGH. Because this improvement came long after the initial decisions to develop genetically based production, Kabi and Genentech had already designed production systems and done clinical testing on the met hGH. Managers then had to choose whether to keep with that product or to abandon it and develop the new met-less hGH. The firms could, however, only abandon the old system after expending additional resources.

Although the met-less hGH was still based on an *E. coli* construction, this change in genetic engineering technique required different parameters in the production system and new clinical testing. Management at both Kabi and Genentech decided to develop the met-less hGH. The firms used knowledge, techniques, and equipment generated, selected, and retained from the met hGH project in order to understand some of the parameters for improvements for the new project. Other parameters were specific to these bacteria and production systems and had to be discovered anew. The change to met-less hGH in 1983 thus required that the firms jump to a somewhat different technical trajectory.

In carrying out knowledge-seeking activities for the met-less hGH, the two firms developed somewhat different firm trajectories and at different speeds. Kabi responded more to the signals in the techno-economic environment and Genentech more to the basic scientific environment. In other words, Kabi emphasized the importance of quick results and thereby gave priority to entry into market whereas Genentech gave priority to doing the job well.[8] Genentech continued making improvements to the genetic engineering techniques and yield, whereas Kabi management decided to be satisfied with what they had and concentrate on clinical tests and government approval.

Partly as a result of Genentech's scientific orientation and partly due to the FDA's wish to encourage competing firms, Genentech could not sell its met-less hGH in the American market from 1987 to 1994, although Genentech could sell their met hGH. Eli Lilly instead got approval for their met-less hGH as an 'orphan drug' just as Genentech had got for met hGH, giving each a special monopoly position for seven years for their respective products. Kabi succeeded in getting their met-less hGH approved in many countries, and phased out the met hGH.

Kabi and Genentech thus tended to stick with small cumulative changes over time. After some challenges had been solved, they used this experience and competences to test only a limited range of diversity. Even when basic scientific results indicated the product could be made in a better way, the firms sometimes decided that changing would require too much investment relative to the expected superiority over the existing, chosen alternative. Firms already using the technology thus had sunk costs to consider, which included not only R & D costs but also expensive clinical testing in the pharmaceutical industry. These firms were only willing to drop their existing choice sets if a new alternative promised great superiority relative to production costs and/or relative to characteristics of the final product. Finding out about and changing to new technologies is thus a difficult process.

In contrast, new firms wanting to move in have been more likely to exploit newer scientific principles and techniques. In practice, this means that early moving firms have continued to use a set of techniques even after the scientific principles of a new and apparently better alternative have been demonstrated (knowledge) and even after other firms have experimented with that alternative (prototype; technology in use).[9] There is thus local adaptation to environmental conditions rather than global optimality.

This proposition of firm lock-in to a chosen trajectory can be further examined by discussing the other firms which tried to produce rDNA hGH. Eli Lilly was the one firm which moved into the technology contemporary with Genentech and Kabi. Lilly had bought rDNA insulin from Genentech and chose an *E. coli* bacteria construction system for hGH which was very similar to Genentech's systems for insulin and

---

[8] The orientation of the two firms was reversed during the earliest stages of development of met hGH. Genentech then pushed time of entrance into market and pre-clinical tests, whereas Kabi stressed gathering medical scientific knowledge.

[9] The extent to which these alternatives are 'better' may be evaluated historically in relation to a specific environment.

hGH—so close, in fact, that Genentech sued Lilly. Like Genentech, Lilly's own corporate R & D group subsequently made incremental improvements which were applicable to several products, including insulin, human growth hormone, and bovine growth hormone. For example, Lilly improved the level of expression of proteins in 1985 and also developed techniques to secrete the protein into the periplasm in 1986.[10] Not only did Lilly work within a set of genetic engineering techniques very similar to Genentech's, Lilly made improvements along a similar trajectory over time.

Other firms which moved into genetic engineering for hGH in the early to mid-1980s could choose from a larger range of techniques developed in the basic scientific environment. For example, Sanofi, a French company, had traditionally supplied the French market with pit hGH. They used scientific results partly from the Pasteur Institute and partly from corporate research to express hGH in *E. coli* bacteria.[11] Novo Nordisk of Denmark also used *E. coli* to make an hGH-precursor molecule but then used enzymes to convert it to met-less hGH. Unlike Genentech's periplasm construction, Novo's technique required two purification procedures.[12] Arès-Serono of Switzerland, and its American subsidiary Serono Labs, made hGH in mammalian cells, based on an R & D contract done by the English biotech firm Celltech.[13] On-going scientific research and results had thus enlarged the search space of technical alternatives from which the later-moving firms could choose.

Having chosen a set of genetic engineering techniques upon which to base industrial production, all these firms tended to become locked in in the sense of making changes along a trajectory. Genentech and Kabi did, however, jump from one trajectory to a very close one when the perceived benefits were greater than the costs or potential losses (market share). Under certain circumstances, such as greatly improved yield through, for example, the trp promoter or making a more exact copy of the desired product (met-less hGH), Kabi and Genentech did invest

---

[10] Based on two published scientific papers indicating that Lilly did research on problems similar to Genentech's Schoner *et al.* (1985: 151) and Hsiung *et al.* (1986: 991).

[11] Both Hunter (1985) and Roskam (1987) mention that Sanofi used scientific research done at the Pasteur Institute whereas *Scrip* (1988: 19) stresses subsequent corporate R & D—and the fact that this was the first French pharmaceutical based on genetic engineering.   [12] Dalbøge *et al.* (1987: 161).

[13] Celltech (1984: 6–7), Celltech (1985: 7), and Celltech (1986: 5). They signed the contract in January 1984 and Serono Laboratories received clearance for clinical tests in the USA in August 1986. Serono had hoped to get its hGH version also approved in the USA, either under the Orphan Drug Act (because their hGH was made in mammalian cells) or through a Congressional change to the Act to allow competition. They were not successful. Delayed introduction was one reason Serono made cut-backs in 1991 (*Scrip* 1991a: 9). BioTechnology General, an American-Israeli biotech firm, also developed genetic engineering for hGH (*Scrip* 1991b: 11).

resources in knowledge-seeking activities in order to be able to switch to a new trajectory.

Because costs sunk in a technological trajectory in the pharmaceutical industry include not only knowledge-seeking activities but also extensive testing and regulatory costs, we can expect that the pharmaceutical industry should exhibit more lock-in than industries where government agencies monitor product and production less intensively.

A final interesting point for evolutionary economic theory is that because agents have the possibility and ability to jump to a new trajectory, agents in socio-economic evolution can correct mistakes by switching to a better alternative. Unlike biological evolution, socio-economic evolution involves learning, stimulus, and more rapid change. In biological evolution, organisms cannot be corrected in this way, because they cannot make conscious decisions to switch one gene for another. Only at the broader level of the population do we find an analogy, where there is a larger gene pool. Because human beings have more flexibility to change their behaviour in socio-economic evolution, the implication is that there may be fewer 'mistakes', dead ends, and less than optimal solutions of evolutionary processes to examine. Agents learn from mistakes and gather more information about strategies which do and do not work in an environment. Nevertheless, the historical material indicates the persistence of technical choices which are somewhat less efficient than those best available globally. There is historical path-dependency within local environments.

Radical versus Incremental Change

Science-based innovations are often seen as those which can lead to radical technical changes, albeit after a lag of many decades. Along with information technology and new materials, genetic engineering is often argued to be such a current radical technology. These science-generated novelties are particularly important because they affect technical and economic parameters for many other technologies and industries. Radical changes are sharply contrasted with small or incremental changes. In the economics of technical change, incremental technical changes are thought to happen all the time in a market economy. Radical changes such as scientific discoveries occur now and again, mainly outside the economic sphere. The question of radical versus incremental change is thus partially related to the question of whether technical change is internal or external to the economic sphere.

This question of radical versus incremental change in technology resembles a similar debate over the rate and magnitude of change in populations in biology. Biological evolutionary theory is subject to a debate about whether changes in populations tend to occur slowly, cumulatively, and possibly continuously over time or whether species and the ecosystem tend to be static for long periods until a major shift occurs and new species suddenly appear. The former corresponds to a common definition of evolution as small changes and the latter to what is known as punctuated equilibrium.[14] The question of the rate and magnitude of change will be discussed in terms of radical versus incremental technological change.

As shown in Figure 3.1, the results of knowledge-seeking activities can be categorized as radical versus incremental along four dimensions. These four correspond to the four poles of the diagram, which are economic, scientific, technological, and government/political. Early commercial uses of genetic engineering to manufacture human growth hormone and insulin have had effects that were radical along all four dimensions.

Economically, these early uses of genetic engineering techniques have had a mixed effect on those firms using it, whether pharmaceutical firms or specialized biotech firms. For Kabi and Genentech, human growth hormone produced in genetically modified bacteria has been the source of significant revenue, and the world market for hGH is around $1 billion. Lilly has been less successful with their rDNA hGH but very successful with rDNA insulin. Some other biotech firms have, of course, gone bankrupt, and even the successful Genentech has largely been bought up by Hoffman-LaRoche. Although genetic engineering techniques have enabled many substitute and novel products to be brought to market, they have not had the explosive effect on industrial and market structures which was assumed in early predictions of the biotech industry.[15] The economic effects have been radically positive only for some products and for some firms.

Scientifically, genetic engineering techniques were radical in giving scientists new tools to make controlled changes to nature. Doing so has enabled scientists further to refine scientific theories about how genes, DNA, and cells function. Throughout the post-World War II investment in biological research, practical techniques for controlling nature have gone hand in hand with understanding and more generalizable knowledge. If scientists had not developed general knowledge and techniques which expanded the frontiers of the known, then firms could not have developed their niche uses either.

Technically, genetic engineering techniques have enabled the practical demonstration of theoretical ideas. They have been the basis of diverse

---

[14] For a recent overview of the debate over punctuated equilibrium by the two researchers who proposed the concept, see Gould and Eldredge (1993).
[15] Walsh (1993: 143–5).

products, production process, and research tools. The technical use described in this book was radical in that firms developed a new and substitute production method for human proteins. However, the most important implication of genetic engineering techniques has been their use as research tools, both to understand and better control nature.

Politically, the development of practical genetic engineering techniques led to debate and subsequent regulation in the public context. Initially in the 1970s, the debate and informal norms were internal to the involved scientific community. Later, when scientists and firms developed viable uses, the debate involved more groups in society, although regulation was set either by scientific bodies or by governmental bodies in collaboration with scientists. A stable public context had to be developed before early commercial uses were feasible.

On the one hand, then, we can argue that genetic engineering techniques have been radical in the economic, scientific, technical, and political dimensions. On the other hand, however, the history of technological innovation processes told in preceding chapters is a history of a series of small steps.

Discrete, incremental steps are visible throughout the material. Individual ingenuity was needed to make each new combination, even though adaptations were based on existing knowledge, techniques, and equipment. For example, existing experience with industrial fermentation was not so helpful the first time the corporate researchers placed the genetically modified bacteria in large tanks: all the bacteria died. Yet, within weeks, the corporate researchers used and adapted the existing body of industrially-specific knowledge to find biological conditions to be able to ferment these new bacteria. Putting together new combinations in turn highlighted new, specific technical challenges to be solved. New challenges required new solutions, which can be represented as incremental changes.

Moreover, an interesting question arises about our perception of whether changes are radical or incremental in relation to diffusion of information. In certain situations, the firms kept their technical changes secret as long as possible. In that this series of incremental changes was not visible until the change was a *fait accompli*, this made the change seem more sudden to observers than to the firms involved. For example, Kabi and Genentech did not tell competitors that they were working on met-less hGH until they started clinical tests, upon which information becomes public. One result of secrecy can thus be to make technical change seem to take more radical jumps than that experienced by innovating agents.

Firms' abilities to access, organize, and direct many complementary bodies of knowledge in order to be able to focus on specific trajectories through incremental searching has been one key message of preceding chapters. This does not deny the creativity and ingenuity involved. In fact, quite the opposite, in that it shows the real challenges of making incremental changes to integrate genetic engineering into production processes and to launch the resulting product. These incremental steps and learning were crucial for modifying the radical potential into a form useful for specific contexts of use. If firms had not made specific investments to utilize radical opportunities and solve challenges, then this radical use would not have come into being.

Socio-Economic Evolution

The technological innovation processes described are argued here to follow an evolutionary pattern of change. One reason why evolutionary theory can be relevant for social science theory about innovations is that evolution gives us a metaphor for thinking about qualitative change. New conditions arise and historical choices, or lock-in, influence later choices. Moreover, at the same time that evolution deals with an aggregate pattern of change, it also highlights the importance of micro-diversity for creating this pattern. The explanation for why an evolutionary pattern of innovation occurs must therefore be sought at a lower level of aggregation than the pattern *per se*. The reasons why agents engage in knowledge-seeking activities in relation to incentives and knowledge must come from a mixture of theoretical approaches to understanding technological change (see further Chapter 10).

Chapter 2 suggested the following four principles as the initial starting-point for defining the pattern of technological change as evolutionary:

1. There are multiple attempts to generate novelty, leading to a diversity of alternatives.
2. The transmission and retention of knowledge, techniques, and behaviour among agents are useful for generating and selecting among technical alternatives.
3. Selection among alternatives is a social process.
4. The assumption of non-optimization, where selection occurs in relation to local environments.

The historical chapters illustrate throughout that the key characteristics of the technological innovation processes have been multiple attempts to develop technology, trial-and-error testing, social selection, and adaptation of search strategies to different environmental conditions. In these multiple attempts to generate novelty and socially shape selection criteria, agents made different bets, based on their previous competences and experiences and based on their expectations about an uncertain future. In other words, at the level of individual firms and organizations, we can identify a diversity of decisions and actions.

Agents' knowledge-seeking activities were carried out in situations of uncertainty, facing competition among alternatives, and uncertain social selection criteria. Three different types of knowledge-seeking activities have been identified as the most important for early commercial uses of genetic engineering. These were: (1) scientific knowledge and techniques for genetic engineering techniques and related biological materials; (2) scientific, technological, and other engineering knowledge for biological productions technologies and for their integration with genetic engineering into a production system; and (3) knowledge about uses of the final product. Within each of these types of knowledge-seeking activities, there are examples of agents, which sometimes competed and sometimes co-operated to develop novelty. Different strategies were necessary under different conditions. As discussed in connection with evolutionary economics, an important assumption underlying heterodox economic explanations of how an economy works is that there is a diversity of firm strategies, competences, and experience. Which mix will prove successful will be determined in the future relative to the local environment.

Evolutionary innovation has been presented as a subcategory of socioeconomic evolution, that is, of human activities involving knowledge. Innovation processes are by definition processes whereby agents seek for different kinds of new knowledge. Agents have been argued to be particularly interested in knowledge about their environment and about which strategies and technologies are likely to be successful. Human knowledge activities rely on a Lamarckian evolutionary mode, which differs from the Darwinian mode found in nature. Learning, stimulus, and acquired characteristics are vital for explaining Lamarckian evolution, hence also for technological innovations.

Chapter 2 identified a number of important differences between biological and socio-economic evolution. Main differences include the importance of human intentionality; the role of learning; and the social nature of knowledge, the environment, and selection criteria. The implication is that the environment cannot be taken as given or as external to organisms. Environments including selection criteria are instead created through social interaction and can therefore be partially internalized in agents' decisions and behaviour. Firms can, for example, carry out tests and do market surveys to try to determine in advance whether their innovation is likely to function technically and to sell. The main pattern of evolutionary innovation as well as some of these differences are discussed below in relation to the historical material. The final Chapter 10, however, more specifically addresses how this pattern is generated through interactions among agents, environments, and knowledge-seeking activities.

The first principle of the pattern is multiple attempts to generate novelty, leading to diversity. Technical change may then seem 'wasteful' because different approaches to the same problem are tried, even though we know that only a few will be implemented. (It is assumed for the moment that agents have incentives to generate novelty for different environments.)

Multiple knowledge-seeking activities can be identified either as the result of multiple agents each trying out one alternative or of the same agent trying out multiple alternatives. Both situations may occur simultaneously, so that competing agents each engage in multiple but similar knowledge-generating activities and test multiple alternatives. In both cases, the agents test multiple alternatives according to their perceptions of environmental conditions, thereby enabling greater diversity and faster testing.

This novelty and diversity is evident in the historical material, in the three types of relevant knowledge mentioned above—genetic engineering, its integration into production, and its use. Chapters 5 and 6 detailed the activities of a limited number of scientific groups carrying out similar rDNA experiments on insulin and hGH in the mid- to late 1970s. Three groups succeeded with genetic engineering for insulin—University of California, San Francisco (UCSF), Harvard University, and Genentech—and two with hGH—UCSF and Genentech. Each had somewhat different approaches, including orientation of expected results. This diversity is evident despite the fact that UCSF and Genentech in particular relied to some extent on the same individuals and/or individuals who had previously collaborated (Boyer; Seeburg; other UCSF post-docs). There were also, however, new individuals and organizations involved (City of Hope; Goeddel). There are thus forces at work encouraging diversity, despite shared starting points for the knowledge-seeking activities.

As to the integration of genetic engineering into production, the R & D effort to do so occurred mainly within firms, as described in Chapter 7 and parts of Chapter 8. Integration involved new opportunities and new challenges, which the firms had to solve. Solutions often involved very specific problems created by the particular configuration of component technologies. Each firm generated, tested, and chose among existing as well as newly developed alternatives for each part. Even though corporate researchers at Kabi and at Genentech closely co-operated during some periods and used essentially identical genetically modified bacteria, the two did things somewhat differently. For example, Genentech quickly developed new, very sensitive analytical tests for contaminants whereas Kabi initially used the existing tests, which were considered of a high enough standard.

There were also multiple attempts to generate knowledge about medical uses for the final product hGH. Multiple uses, hence markets, were developed. Some of the uses were already known, such as dwarfism, but were extended by giving hGH to children who were short but still within the average height range. Other uses were novel compared to previous practice, such as burns or retention of muscle mass. Exploring these expanded and multiple uses was possible because genetic engineering greatly increased the supply relative to tissue extraction. These uses were generated by medical scientists, through the questioning of existing medical knowledge and testing procedures. Different interpretations of the relative superiority of pit versus rDNA hGH were also generated through clinical tests, more sensitive analytical methods, and through unexpected side effects in former pit hGH patients (Creutzfeldt-Jakob disease).

Moreover, the generation of novelty can often not be separated from selection processes in socio-economic evolution. This has to do with human intentionality, including perceptions and actions to influence the environment. This proximity can be seen throughout the book, particularly when agents internalize selection criteria. By approximating environmental conditions while generating and testing alternatives, they can generate alternatives which are better adapted than would be the case if they were randomly generated. For example, the firms used extensive testing procedures throughout the innovation process to reproduce expected conditions of use.

So, in that agents often have a purpose in their behaviour, they adapt their knowledge-seeking activities and novelty generated to fit their perceptions of the environment. This statement assumes a degree of purposive human behaviour and the ability to perceive and internalize some aspects of environmental conditions. The relationships between agents, activities, and the four environments are discussed in more detail in the next chapter.

The second principle of evolutionary innovation is that the transmission and retention of knowledge, skills, and behaviour are useful for generating and selecting among alternatives. Here, transmission and retention are concerned with elements which enable agents to pursue knowledge-seeking activities in various directions. It is argued that there is a common body of knowledge and know-how which is used by individual researchers, whether doing scientific or technological activities and whether under market or government influence. Some of that knowledge is widely available whereas other parts are only accessible to specialists. Some is very specific to categories of innovations, like specific challenges of production.

A common body of knowledge, techniques, and behaviour which is transferred in the community of innovators should be visible through the limited range of alternatives generated. Diversity should not be random but constrained. Limited diversity has to do with agents' intentionality but also the fact that new combinations are made out of the old.[16] For example, despite important differences, the approaches and techniques used at UCSF and Genentech or at Genentech and Kabi were quite similar. At certain points, their activities even followed similar trajectories. Because of intentionality and because of the importance of learning and experience, agents neither search for nor develop random novel knowledge.

Although searching is not random, the agents are nevertheless uncertain about the outcome of search activities. Searching is blind, in the dark. This uncertainty is one reason why diversity is valuable. One might think multiple attempts and approaches are a waste, but this is also a way to test different alternatives. The problem is that although diversity can be a strength, it is also expensive. For radical changes, which alternatives will function technically at a reasonable cost is usually difficult to predict in advance. During the development of technologies, people also tend to imagine new, unexpected uses or opportunities.

An important question for managers is therefore whether one agent can afford to fund and access diversity or whether they have to make a bet on one alternative. For example, Eli Lilly attempted to fund or license all three initial basic scientific techniques relevant for rDNA insulin, whereas Kabi could only afford an R & D contract with Genentech. Even in Lilly's case, they financed scientific activities outside the firm but also built up their own competences.

An important question for policy-makers interested in aiding a new field is how to facilitate communication about dead ends and opportunities. As illustrated in the collaboration between Kabi and Genentech over met hGH, the firms were torn between keeping information secret in order to get an advantage over competitors and diffusing information in order to identify fruitful search spaces. These two firms solved the conflict by confining information-sharing to the collaborator. Sharing valuable secrets about both dead ends and opportunities would help the population as a whole. For example, sharing information would help a national industry compete with firms from other countries, if the national firms could accrue first-mover advantages before the information became generally known. More of the population could then be in a virtuous search space, where they would help each other. The problem

---

[16] In relation to technological innovation processes, transmission and retention both enable but also limit the creation of novelty and diversity in a population.

for policy-makers is how to balance incentives to innovate with the diffusion of information.

As to selection, this is the result of a social process. Markets are obviously crucial for innovations but there are other dimensions as well, such as gaining access to technological and scientific activities. Selection criteria in an environment are thus not wholly determined in advance. Environments are changing and created through interaction, and therefore selection criteria depend on the dynamics of social institutional change. Social dimensions identified as important here include economic, technological, scientific, and political, as analysed in the next chapter.

The principle about adaptation to local environments can be illustrated by indicating how the demands which firms place on new technology differ from those of basic scientists. At all stages, these firms demanded more rigorously that knowledge be translatable into practice and that equipment and techniques function reliably. Doing so requires knowledge-seeking activities quite simply because new technologies often do not function so reliably. They must be adapted for use, made to function more reliably, which leads to costs in production as well as in R & D to generate solutions. Moreover, for genetically engineered pharmaceuticals, the techniques and production systems not only had to function technically but also at a cost, yield, purity, and so forth that could allow the final products to compete on a market. These were new challenges to be solved which differ greatly from those encountered in the basic scientific environment. These challenges require firms to invest in R & D to generate and select local, particular technical solutions relevant for their own challenges. The next chapter explicitly examines how knowledge, institutions, and agents coevolved during the parallel technological innovation processes.

10

Conclusions for Science and Technology

Introduction

This chapter draws some conclusions about science and technology based on the theoretical and empirical discussions in previous chapters. Both scientific and technological activities involve searching for new knowledge and techniques, but it has been proposed that scientific activities are generally about understanding the world whereas technological activities are generally about controlling nature for human purposes. Either type of activity can, however, be carried out under either market or government influence. For example, scientific activities can be financed and expected to give economic advantage, however uncertain and distant it may be.

One advantage of this conceptual framework is that it no longer makes assumptions about which type of activity is carried out at which type of organization. Researchers at different types of organizations—universities, firms, and so forth—are instead assumed to choose which type of knowledge-seeking activities to engage in, and they can make different choices at different points. For example, a university researcher can first compete in the basic scientific environment through scientific activities and then later start a biotech firm to sell scientific-economic knowledge which is perceived to have value in the techno-economic environment. This has been a common pattern in the modern biotech business, where basic researchers start biotech firms to sell R & D contracts to established firms. This perspective thus separates agents and knowledge-seeking activities from the socially constructed environments.

This chapter first addresses how and why agents engage in scientific and technological activities in response to the four environments by analysing the historical material about genetic engineering for human growth hormone and insulin. The focus is on agents, environments, and knowledge-seeking activities from the 1970s and 1980s. The next section discusses cross-stimulus of scientific and technological activities, or interactions in the development of the two bodies of knowledge. This contributes to debates about the similarities and differences among science and technology. The chapter then ends with a discussion of the social nature of selection and concluding remarks about this book.

Agents, Environments, and Knowledge-Seeking Activities

This section addresses the question of whether the agents described in this book engaged in knowledge-seeking activities in response to environmental conditions. Four environments were defined in Chapter 3 as giving incentives for knowledge-seeking activities—the basic scientific, the techno-economic, the scientific-economic, and the techno-government. Each environment consists of informal institutions, incentive structures, and other socially constructed selection criteria which influence the direction of agents' search activities. In addition to these four, the public context has been defined as consisting of debate, informal norms, and formal regulation about the technology and/or final product. It is the larger context which sets parameters for what types of knowledge-seeking activities and results are generally considered acceptable.[1]

Instead of analysing the environments one by one, this section chronologically analyses the main events in preceding empirical chapters. It will indicate how and why agents responded to the incentive structures and informal institutions of various environments. Generally, the agents tended to look for novelty which fitted their perceptions of the environment, although the results could be quite different from those expected. Because learning is a cumulative process, new challenges arose which could not be foreseen. These challenges and opportunities only became evident as different types of knowledge and techniques were integrated into the firms' contexts of use.

The starting-point for these early commercial uses of genetic engineering was the development of relatively practical techniques in the early 1970s. Of particular relevance here, Professors Stephen Cohen and Robert Boyer, working at, respectively, Stanford University and UCSF, developed the recombinant DNA technique, although many other basic researchers were working on complementary approaches. Those who developed such knowledge and techniques did so in reference to the internal basic scientific environment in order to publish papers, compete for future research grants, and so forth. Researchers in these scientific fields had traditionally had little or no contacts with industry or other economic influence. They instead competed for positions within the academic world and for government funding which was distributed by other scientists. These researchers were engaged in scientific activ-

---

[1] It is not an environment in the sense defined here, because it does not give agents specific incentives to engage in knowledge-seeking activities.

ities mainly at universities, and they oriented their search to fit the incentive structure (rewards and punishments) of that environment.

In competing to achieve results, they developed both scientific knowledge as well as practical techniques for carrying out experiments and verifying knowledge. Knowledge and techniques for manipulating DNA were thus developed hand in hand over a long time period in this community. Recombinant DNA techniques were, however, radical in giving practical control.

With the development of practical and relatively simple techniques, it was apparent to many basic scientists that genetic engineering could be used for various purposes, both destructive and beneficial. They could also be used to create economic value. Due to the radical implications of possible uses of the technology, however, there arose an internal scientific debate about the risks of genetic engineering, leading to an international, temporary moratorium on certain experiments. Scientists then set guidelines for certain experiments, particularly in the Berg letter, the Berg committee, and finally, in the discussions at the 1975 Asilomar meeting and the publishing of guidelines in *Science*. Scientists based the guidelines on research intended to identify risks as well as acceptable categories of safety precautions. The moratorium and guidelines were voluntary but enforced through strong informal norms.

This informal moratorium was lifted in the mid-1970s, and the initial guidelines were used to develop more formal regulation. In the United States, the National Institutes of Health, the major medical research council and research institute, published guidelines in 1976 based on the Asilomar conference. The Swedish research councils similarly initiated a Genetic Manipulation Advisory Committee, although industrial representatives also participated. The scientists' own debate and decisions about guidelines thus strongly influenced regulation of the technology.

Although the commercial potential of genetic engineering to produce pharmaceuticals was apparent to some, this vision was a long way from reality in the mid- to late 1970s. Even the vision seemed like science fiction to many. In addition to practical difficulties, a question of direct interest to pharmaceutical firms had not been answered. Before investing in developing the new technology, they needed to know whether bacteria could express human proteins in general, particularly the longer proteins relevant as pharmaceuticals. Although genes could now be transferred, experiments had not confirmed that these techniques would work in practice to get bacteria faithfully to reproduce human proteins. Doing so would require a combination of scientific and technological activities. A particularly interesting characteristic of biotechnology is that knowledge-seeking activities to answer such questions were considered relevant for both basic scientists and firms.

By the mid- to late 1970s, genetic engineering thus offered agents a potential way to compete in the techno-economic and scientific-economic environments as well as the basic scientific one. They could reap benefits from the scientific and technological activities of recombinant DNA techniques. Partly in response to these potential benefits (incentives), some scientists who had previously worked within the basic scientific environment reoriented some activities towards economic potential. This reorientation started in the United States but later spread (to a lesser degree) to scientists in other countries.

The most immediate strategy apparent in this book is the creation of the dedicated biotech firm Genentech in 1975–6 as a combination of venture capital (Swanson) and basic science (Boyer). Once biotech firms like Genentech had been started, they also created a demand for other scientists versed in genetic engineering, either directly through employment or more indirectly through consulting.

From the start of this reorientation towards combined basic scientific and economic goals, scientists trained in fields relevant for genetic engineering could choose from a number of different strategies. This book identifies the following strategies to exploit some of the economic potential of genetic engineering:

1. Stay at a university but engage in multiple activities, where some are directed towards the basic scientific environment and others towards one of the economic environments. This was possible when similar and/or complementary activities had both scientific and technological dimensions due to the radical novelty of techniques. Examples include the research on insulin and hGH by Boyer's (Genentech) and Goodman's (UCSF) respective groups. The results led both to scientific papers and to patentable techniques. Similar experiments could therefore be used to develop scientific knowledge as well as to develop techniques to control nature.

2. Start a dedicated biotech firm to exploit the economic potential of the new technology. Examples include Genentech as well as the large number of biotech firms started by senior researchers from UCSF and elsewhere in the early 1980s and onwards. The researchers who started these firms did not necessarily leave their university. Instead, many senior scientists remained at a university and divided their time between university and firm. These biotech firms in turn hired other scientists.

3. Move from an organization responding mainly to one type of environment to an organization responding mainly to the other. Such moves have generally been from universities to specialized biotech firms or to pharmaceutical firms expanding into these fields. Examples include Kleid, Goeddel, Seeburg, and UCSF post-docs starting work at Genentech.[2]

[2] More recently, some corporate researchers have moved back to universities or else have left the first generation biotech firms to start up new biotech firms in newer fields. Goeddel, for example, left Genentech to start a new biotech firm.

Individuals could thus either move physically to organizations mostly oriented to this new environment, or divide their knowledge-seeking activities so that some were towards one environment and some towards the other. This duality of activities is visible in this book, in that scientists at universities and at firms sometimes competed and sometimes co-operated.

As noted, one key question for both basic science and commercial uses of genetic engineering in the mid- to late 1970s was actual expression of human proteins in bacteria. A number of competing university groups engaged in research to answer related questions, but it was university research supported by Genentech which first indicated it was possible in practice. This was the somatostatin research results of December 1977. Boyer and others of Genentech/UCSF carried out this research in collaboration with researchers at the national medical centre City of Hope. This Genentech result for the somatostatin experiment is parti-cularly interesting because it was used to influence the basic scientific and scientific-economic environments as well as the American public context.

The public context was in the process of being shaped in 1977, this time by agents other than scientists. The American public debate over genetic engineering had got underway in a hostile tone, and the US Congress were attempting to impose stricter federal regulation. The national public context would take over regulation from scientists themselves and would more strictly define which types of activities were acceptable. Having decided that this public debate was exaggerat-ing the risks of the technology, these scientists changed tactics. They began to argue that scientific results would offer great benefits to the public, particularly in the medical fields. In particular, this project at UCSF, funded by Genentech, had results showing that the human protein somatostatin could be expressed in bacteria. This, scientists argued, indicated the great potential medical benefits of the technology and the necessity of allowing continued scientific research. No new federal guidelines were imposed.

This was also one of the first times when some scientists indicated more publicly that their activities had moved towards the scientific-economic environment. Their research was financed by a biotech firm, with the underlying understanding that although these activities were scientific, they were also technological. Techniques to control genes, including those enabling protein expression, were crucial for future commercial uses. The newspapers and magazine articles creating the public debate were, however, less clear about the multiple purposes. They rarely if ever simultaneously identified the researchers with both universities and biotech firms; depending on the angle, only one type of organization or the other was mentioned.

This new pattern—for scientific researchers in these fields—of individuals and organizations responding to economic influences also led to changes in the informal institutions. There were implications in the basic scientific environment and the creation of norms for the scientific-economic environment. The first contacts between basic scientists and firms in the USA led to some perceived conflicts of interest and attempts were made to implement clearer rules for interactions. Examples discussed in Chapter 6 include UCSF's Senate hearing about Genentech's relationships with the university and the Pajaro Dunes meeting. The latter brought together firms and the most prestigious research universities in order to discuss the general norms for interactions among universities and firms. In both cases, they discussed new patterns of interaction, or informal institutions regulating interaction. Soon thereafter, the informal institutions of the basic scientific environment more specifically allowed, even encouraged, the university scientists to have more extensive contacts with firms and even to respond directly to the techno-economic environment.

Another consequence of the somatostatin experiment was that the nascent firm Genentech gained scientific prestige which concurrently advertised that they were willing to direct scientific activities in commercial directions. Scientific activities were necessary to address these questions because all experiments to get the bacteria to achieve expression were challenging and required new knowledge and techniques. Partly based on the somatostatin results, Kabi contacted Genentech in late 1978 about hGH and signed an R & D contract in 1978. Eli Lilly also funded similar research at UCSF for hGH and insulin and then later signed an R & D contract for insulin with Genentech. The advantage of biotech firms like Genentech was that they could develop practical and reliable techniques as well as complementary knowledge in order to succeed with commercial developments.

In the long run, Genentech's management saw that genetic engineering went hand in hand with activities involving other types of knowledge. Their vision was that the firm's long term survival would depend on moving more directly into the techno-economic environment. This is reflected by the fact that Genentech's strategy from the beginning was to move into pharmaceutical production and not just sell R & D contracts involving genetic engineering. To fulfil these multiple goals, the organization had to engage in various types of activities. Genentech started by developing its basic scientific potential much more than established firms, but soon hired specialists with other types of competences, such as fermentation, purification, and analytical methods. The same organization, whether university or firm, could thus respond to different environments simultaneously with different sets of knowledge-seeking activities.

In exceptional cases of radical science-based change, the same knowledge-seeking activities could generate novelty relevant to more than one environment. These scientific activities could be made relevant for economic goals, whether more immediately (additional R & D contracts for Genentech) or in the longer-term future (products sold). To produce pharmaceuticals, additional techniques and knowledge had to be developed before the vision could be realized in practice. Even Genentech's early scientific activities however, were, oriented towards commercial use, as illustrated by the comparison of Genentech and UCSF regarding hGH in 1979. The Genentech results were more relevant than UCSF's to engaging in additional technological activities to create economic value. Thus, even when carried out parallel in time and in general orientation, similar knowledge-seeking activities could still be adapted towards different environmental conditions.

Those firms wishing to move into commercial uses early on had to find a way to access the necessary knowledge and techniques. Initially, this required funding knowledge-seeking activities or else licensing very new discoveries. The firm could engage researchers inside the firm (requiring the development of new competence areas) or else contract out the activities to external agents, whether firms or universities. The strategies of these early-moving firms to support or gain access to scientific research directed towards commercial uses included:

1. Giving direct financial support to basic scientists working at universities. Examples include Eli Lilly's support of Baxter and Goodman for research involving insulin and hGH, and Genentech's support of Boyer and City of Hope for insulin and hGH. This strategy involves much uncertainty about what will be developed, partly because the research is basic, and hence involves major unknown factors, and partly because the firm has little control over the scientists and the experiments. It may, however, be the only way to access certain information and monitor future developments.

2. Hiring basic scientists to carry out scientific activities within the firm. Genentech hired, for example, the university scientists Kleid, Goeddel, and Yansura, and Lilly set up a new department with relevant knowledge and techniques. Instead of placing these basic scientists in-house, the firm can also start a specialized biotech firm, as when Kabi and the Swedish government started KabiGen. These activities are sometimes relevant for more than one environment. The firms should carry out (basic) scientific activities in-house when it is necessary for being able to monitor (and understand) external research. In addition, doing research in-house can be seen as an admission ticket to being considered a member of the larger scientific community. The firm then contributes as well as draws upon the generally available knowledge.

3. Contacting a dedicated biotech firm to carry out research applicable to a specific commercial goal. These firms have special knowledge and techniques which may not be available in-house in a larger firm. Examples include Kabi contracting Genentech to make hGH in bacteria, and Lilly contracting Genentech to make insulin in bacteria. This also results in a sort of dual-use activity, which might also be relevant to the basic scientific environment. It involves less uncertainty than funding university scientists, because the R & D contracts specify that they will develop practical techniques which are relevant for firms' contexts of use such as level of expression.

4. Buying the right to use the results of previous scientific research by, for example, licensing patents. Examples here include Eli Lilly's attempts to buy Gilbert's patents on insulin techniques (which were sold to Biogen), and Lilly's payment for patent rights held by UCSF and by Genentech. The results already exist, so the firm has some idea of what information and techniques it is buying, but it will often have only a vague idea of the economic value.

The common element in the above four firm strategies is an attempt to gain direct access to the results of activities which could be relevant to the techno-economic environment. The examples given all relate to genetic engineering as the basis of a new production method. The uncertainty in the late 1970s was high because it was not clear what results would be forthcoming, or their technical and economic relevance for the firms. Managers thus had to decide between the risks of losing the money invested and the possibility of high but uncertain future returns. As described in Chapters 5 and 6, knowledge-seeking activities relevant to producing human proteins were oriented towards developing knowledge and techniques of genetic engineering.

From there onward in this book, activities only for genetic engineering in the basic scientific environment are no longer discussed. Instead, the focus is on early commercial uses, and there is therefore a shift to how and why the firms engaged in activities to integrate genetic engineering with biological production systems and to create markets.

Having accessed genetic engineering techniques either in-house or externally, the firms concentrated on using genetically engineered bacteria as the basis of production. Integrating the new and existing technologies and bodies of knowledge sparked new challenges for the specific uses, whose solutions required significant investment in focused and specific knowledge-seeking activities. The firms had to spend much money on R & D to make the process work so that the desired protein(s) could be sold.

In this R & D, Kabi and Genentech reacted to their interpretations of economic criteria for pharmaceutical sales. R & D decisions had to take the different aspects of the integrated production system into account, such as identifying challenges requiring solutions. Firms' internalization of the environment thereby affected the type of solutions they generated as well as which selection criteria were internalized through testing. For example, the yield of pure proteins was initially low largely because the initial set of genetic engineering techniques was not very efficient in getting the bacteria to express proteins. If the firms had kept that level of yield, then the costs of production and hence the selling price for hGH would have been too high. Yield was therefore one of the most important challenges to be solved, both specifically for these products and generally for genetically engineered proteins. The firms therefore had to invest in R & D to try to increase the yield of proteins made in bacteria.

Activities to improve the protein yield initially focused on changing the chosen set of genetic engineering techniques. Genentech had the special competence to do so by trying out different alternative bits of the puzzle, mainly developed in universities. Changing the promoter (start signal) turned out to be particularly effective in increasing yield. When testing these different alternatives, Genentech tried to develop model systems which could be applied to their various products. The way of making changes and the changes themselves were intended to be standardized, because this would reduce costs of additional R & D. Models are thus a way of reducing diversity to a subset which is likely to work. The general corporate goals of reasonable yield, standardization of techniques, high purity, and so forth were based on expected economic and regulatory conditions.

Changes in the specific set of genetic engineering techniques and biological material or in one component technology usually required changes elsewhere as well. Most such changes entailed new challenges for R & D, where solutions also had to be adapted to the specific conditions of use. The amino-acid feed in the fermentation phase, for example, had to be calibrated to the specifics of the bacteria strain and also affected protein purification, making it more or less difficult. Research within different specialist bodies of knowledge and techniques could often offer different solutions to the challenges. Improving yield, for example, could not only be achieved by changing the genetic engineering but also by developing more sensitive parameters for fermentation and by improving the protein purification steps. There had to be decisions about how much improvement could be achieved by making various changes. Doing so also required feedback and communication inside the firms to keep the different specialist research groups heading in the same direction.

In fact, these component technologies and underlying bodies of knowledge were so important that Kabi could contribute even initially in the 1970s to the collaboration with Genentech. In other words, Kabi was not just the recipient of the results of the R & D contract. Initially in 1979, Genentech and Kabi researchers worked together in California to ferment (grow) the genetically modified bacteria, but the resulting solution was then sent to Sweden for analysis and purification. Kabi already had competence and experience in these areas due to their existing product, pit hGH. Before long, however, Genentech built up their competences in these areas by hiring experienced individuals, and Kabi also built up competence in areas relating to genetic engineering, albeit in a separate biotech firm. Thus each firm had identified certain bodies of knowledge and techniques which were crucial for their survival. In the short term, they could rely on others (co-operation; external contracts) but in the longer term, they had decided these areas needed to be represented in-house. They stopped collaborating as well.

The division of labour between Kabi and Genentech can also be related to the public contexts. During 1979 and 1980, the two national public contexts influenced the parameters for research somewhat differently for the two firms. In the USA, the debate had become more positive about the scientific and economic potential of the technology, and restrictions relaxed. In Sweden, public debate arrived somewhat later than the USA and arrived about the time Kabi began grappling with the first experiments. Initially the firm had no permit, then no labs to grow the bacteria; they were instead working with Genentech in California. As in the United States, the Swedish debate over genetic engineering was polarized into opponents and proponents. Partly for political reasons, the Swedish government called for a temporary moratorium on industrial activities. Kabi then shifted some experiments to England, not least because no labs meeting safety specifications were available in Sweden. The Swedish government and Parliament subsequently constructed more formal government regulations for the technology (replacing the scientists' committee), although Sweden followed America's lead in incorporating much of the regulation of genetic engineering into existing laws. These changes to regulation in the public context clearly limited the direction of search and innovative activities considered acceptable. At the same time, however, having stable boundaries assured firms that they knew what would be considered acceptable, and could therefore get on with their business.

In these cases of genetically engineered proteins used as pharmaceuticals, public debate and formal regulation set standards not only for genetic engineering but also for the resulting product. Firms in both countries had to take these regulatory conditions into account when directing knowledge-seeking activities. In other words, research managers had to make decisions about the specific characteristics of the product and market when deciding about R & D. For example, a high yield of proteins had to be correlated with purity because very high purity is a condition for government approval of pharmaceuticals. Firms therefore had to invest resources to solve technical challenges such as impurities arising in the production process (contaminants; variants). Solving such challenges was particularly dependent upon devising more sensitive tests and analytical methods. As these tests and methods became more sensitive and could 'see' more impurities, it became obvious that changes also had to be made to protein purification steps or fermentation parameters. Discussions were necessary to identify what the common challenges were.

As the market for rDNA hGH did not yet exist during this period—although the market for pituitary hGH did—the firms had to make assumptions about the desirable trade-offs between quality and quantity. How much would potential patients and health services be willing to pay, at what quantity and quality? Firms had to make assumptions about conditions in the techno-economic environment, and they made such bets directly dependent both on medical research for hGH and on R & D involving the production process. Better analytical methods were also needed to convince both patients/doctors and regulatory agents that the pharmaceutical product could be used safely. Because genetic engineering represented a novel source of supply, the innovating producer firms engaged in extensive discussions with government regulatory agencies and doctors. In these cases, doctors were not only a professional group representing users but also a group developing scientific knowledge about the efficiency and use of the product.

Doctors have the power to change the boundaries of acceptable uses by, for example, indicating the efficacy of a substance in treating a new condition or in expanding the boundaries for treatment of a known indication. By changing the boundaries, medical researchers increased the potential demand for the product. Changing the boundaries of medical knowledge directly affected market demand when it either expanded the potential group for one use (short but not hGH-deficient children) and/or discovered new uses (retaining muscle mass in the elderly; Turner's syndrome). The firms have therefore had incentives to invest in medical scientific research. On the fringes of the accepted market, a black market for illegal uses (athletes) also sprung up when these users perceived a potential, although medically questionable, benefit from the product. Firms, medical researchers, and government regulatory agencies had a common interest in defining legitimate uses and in patrolling uses and abuses.

This book has shown that environmental conditions shaped the directions of agents' search activities. Solving different challenges could involve scientific and/or technological activities, depending on the current state of knowledge and techniques. The two were often dependent upon each other, so that developing new knowledge required more practical techniques or more sensitive analytical methods. Moreover, agents in one environment often monitored and/or financed knowledge-seeking activities in another, to make general knowledge and techniques applicable to their uses. The contexts of use discussed were mostly commercial, entailing both general and very specific challenges.

Cross-Stimulus of Scientific and Technological Activities

Cross-stimulus means that scientific and technological activities mutually influence each other. Cross-stimulus refers to significant interactions and influences between the two types of knowledge-seeking activities, which is evident throughout the historical chapters of this book. Some technological activities are relevant for science—such as analytical methods—whereas other corporate improvements are too incremental to be of interest in basic science, such as which specific promoter is used by a firm.

There are various reasons why cross-stimulus is possible. One is that both types of activities draw upon common bodies of knowledge and techniques, albeit with different degrees of access even for specialists. The more specialized something is, the fewer there are who understand it. Another reason is that both scientific and technological activities can lead to the development of more general or more specific knowledge and techniques. The more general something is, the more there are who are likely to be interested in it for different reasons.

The history told in this book emphasizes interactions among agents engaging in various scientific and technological activities. These early commercial uses of genetic engineering involved both scientific and technological activities, and it is clear that using basic scientific knowledge and techniques for early commercial uses was usually not easy. It often involved significant challenges and necessitated the development of a different kind of knowledge and techniques. Scientific techniques and knowledge could form the starting-point from which new, commercially relevant activities could be developed. Knowledge-seeking activities relevant for these cases have been classified as involving: (1) genetic engineering techniques, (2) integration of genetic engineering and production systems, and (3) medical knowledge about uses of hGH. However, these new activities had to be specifically oriented in directions relevant for the scientific-economic and techno-economic environments.

Knowledge and techniques relevant for these three types of knowledge-seeking activities could be general for both scientific and technological activities. For example, once university scientists had improved SDS gels through silver staining, their results were available to the community of interested practitioners and could be used for various purposes (generalizable). These initial methods however, were, impractical for corporate goals. If corporate researchers wanted to use silver staining to analyse proteins, then they had to make many additional improvements and changes to make them more reliable, easier to use, and so forth. Those changes could in turn be reincorporated by university scientists (some of whom worked on similar improvements). There could thus develop a general body of knowledge and techniques available to trained researchers in different environments.

Knowledge and techniques relevant for both scientific and technological activities involving rDNA hGH can be classified as more or less available. Some have been shown to be very specialized and only available to a few specialists, whereas other parts are more generally available. Note, however, that the extent to which knowledge is general or specialized within the community of practitioners will change over time. Recombinant DNA techniques were highly specialized and only practised by some scientists in the 1970s but have become increasingly available to a larger number of researchers. The extent to which knowledge and techniques are specialized or more generally available within the community can thus change over time. Its diffusion depends to a large extent on what is taught to new practitioners, either in formal training situations or through experience in firms. When this general body of knowledge does not suffice for solving challenges, then firms have to engage in knowledge-seeking activities which are useful in their local contexts of use. These may nevertheless result in more general solutions of interest to others.

Through the transfer of knowledge, techniques, behaviour, and individuals, the knowledge search activities (and their results) in one environment have been shown to change agents' abilities to engage in search activities in another. Firms can be influenced by basic science and vice versa. As an example, basic scientists can be influenced by firms when they take a firm's very specific problems with growing genetically modified cells in fermenting tanks as the basis of developing model systems useful for understanding general principles.

The cross-stimulus may be based on knowledge and techniques which have been known for a while in the other environment, or which are quite recent. Agents in one environment can perceive the economic and technical potential, or relevance, of knowledge and techniques which are just being established in another environment. When they do perceive such potential, then the agents can choose whether to wait and see what happens or to invest resources to develop that idea or technique further. The relevant comparison here is between those established firms which waited to see how genetic engineering would be developed before moving in the 1980s and the firms described here who actively searched for relevant developments by the late 1970s.

Due to the economic incentive of potential profits, some individuals and firms saw the possibility of developing genetic engineering to make human proteins for sale in the techno-economic environment as soon as the techniques were possible on lab scale in the mid- to late 1970s. Their interest in functioning techniques coincided with the interests of some contemporary basic scientists, who were dependent upon these new techniques for controlling genes and cells in order to develop theoretical knowledge. The ability of basic scientists to do things in practice and to use new knowledge to do new things was one feature which made this basic scientific research attractive to firms. The environments converged in giving incentives for very similar activities at a point when there was a high level of uncertainty and risks involved.

The firms then played a particularly important role in translating what they perceived to be economically possible (market signals) and scientifically possible into functioning technology. Once rudimentary genetic engineering techniques were available for the firms' specific purposes in 1979, then these firms shifted their R & D emphasis to integrating genetic engineering techniques and biological material within a controlled biological production system. As shown in this book, the firms translated scientific knowledge and lab techniques into practical, usable production systems that made a marketable product.

Translating knowledge into practice through the intermediary of technological activities was not, however, a simple proposition. Sometimes it was relatively simple, but sometimes it was quite challenging. Accumulated knowledge, techniques, and equipment formed the starting-point for additional R & D, but how the translation would actually be achieved was often not evident. Instead, a variety of approaches and alternatives were tested, and often, several variants functioned. The firms had to choose among them based on both economic and technological criteria. Firms thus initially faced uncertainty about which technical alternative(s) would function more efficiently technically and economically and which would become dominant in the future. (These two conditions of efficiency and dominance are not necessarily synonymous because an inferior technology can become dominant.) Firms had to make decisions based on their expectations of future selection criteria.

For existing firms, these early uses of genetic engineering required mastery over different scientific knowledge and different organizational and distributional channels for obtaining the raw materials, and posed new problems relating to scale-up, purification, and production. The new technology represented a break with former skills and knowledge for those firms like Kabi which had previously extracted hGH from tissue. They faced a technological discontinuity which could destroy firm competences. Biotechnology thus threatened to make certain knowledge obsolete.

Existing pharmaceutical firms reacted, however, and although the technology changed, both existing pharmaceutical and new biotech firms could compete. Researchers and organizations active in biologically-based pharmaceutical production and R & D could acquire new knowledge and skills. They could compete with new, specialized firms which sold specialized research and which sometimes entered the market for pharmaceuticals. An important reason why there has been room for both types of firms is that the pharmaceutical industry has no single core technology which could be directly threatened by this change. Instead, there are multiple technologies whose integration is important. Genetic engineering required major changes and acquisition of new knowledge, but this new technology is put into the context of other bodies of knowledge and techniques.

For managers, an important implication of cross-stimulus of scientific and technological activities is that those firms involved in science-based innovation need to monitor and carry out knowledge-seeking activities within more than one environment. Genentech's activities as documented here include activities which were considered relevant within the basic scientific, the scientific-economic, and the techno-economic environments. This is true to a lesser extent for the established firms, although each type of firm actively developed in-house competence and experience in crucial fields.

A particularly interesting contribution of this book has to do with the analysis of the integration of genetic engineering with biological production. Both the problems of integration and the importance of these bodies of scientific and technological knowledge and techniques have been neglected. Too much of the analysis of biotechnology only emphasizes molecular biology.

Shifting the perspective in this way has allowed us to see the challenges and creativity of the other fields of science and technology which have contributed to commercial uses. Integrating the new and the old has required the development of a whole body of knowledge and techniques which were general for these commercial uses. Nevertheless, many of these challenges arose because the firm suddenly found local and very specific problems having to do with their particular configuration of the system, such as amino-acid feed or where in the cell the proteins were made. Many specific challenges, such as the low yield of hGH or contaminants 'invisible' to contemporary testing methods, were then identified as representing general categories of problems. The knowledge and techniques were different from those developed in basic science because they had to take into account the specific criteria which interested firms. Some of the challenges encountered by both corporate and university researchers—such as the problems of insoluble proteins and inclusion bodies when bacteria overproduce human proteins—in turn stimulated new scientific research on questions which were particularly important to the firms. There has thus been significant cross-stimulus.

Developing commercially relevant genetic engineering techniques and integrating them into production systems for hGH and insulin thus involved both scientific and technological activities. The two types of activities were concurrently important and stimulated each other. Interaction has increased the diversity of knowledge and techniques which can be used to generate additional novelty. We can therefore say that diversity within each specific environment is increased, compared to a situation of isolated activities in each environment. Overlap enlarges the agents' search spaces. It helps provoke additional questions and solutions, which are sometimes relevant in more than one environment. This may help explain the potential of genetic engineering for productivity gains and for creating new sectors.

Selection as a Social Process

A final discussion relevant for coevolution in scientific and technological activities is the extent to which selection processes are social. Chapter 2 argued that the social nature of selection processes was one of the major differences between biological and socio-economic evolution. Socio-economic selection criteria are created through interactions. This is one of the main reasons why it is so important to try to understand how selection criteria are created in different environments and how they influence agents' knowledge-seeking activities. This social basis of selection has been illustrated in different ways in this book.

First, the definition of environments relies on the idea that agents belong to a community of practitioners when engaging in knowledge-seeking activities. These are practitioners of scientific and/or technological activities although they may work at different types of organizations. Their communality lies in their shared, specialized bodies of knowledge and techniques, but they also often share norms. Sometimes these communities can set the informal institutions and incentive structures defining what is relevant and rewarded in an environment; sometimes these criteria are defined in interactions with non-researchers, such as with managers and others in firms. Individual decisions and actions are positioned and evaluated relative to a social context.

Secondly, acting in response to different environments means directing search activities towards different audiences and towards different reward and punishment structures. To draw on an earlier example, a firm can 'engage in scientific activities', and the results can be of relevance within the basic scientific environment. Nevertheless, the firm will go bankrupt if it only does basic scientific activities unless it is funded by government research grants (and evaluated scientifically). If the main force influencing survival is market allocation, then this firm will have trouble in the long run because of the difficulties of using scientific activities to create economic value. Even if they sell the knowledge and techniques to others, they must translate them into a usable form, which may no longer involve basic science. The difficulties of this translation as described in this book differ from the common understanding that biotech is science-based.

The difficulties have to do with the uncertain and long-term character of scientific activities to understand the world. Therefore, when a firm engages in scientific activities, these may not be of immediate economic interest, in the sense that they might not be saleable, but they had better be of some longer-term economic interest. Longer-term interest can include, for example, building up the knowledge foundation for an existing or future product; building up competences within the firm which make later knowledge-seeking activities possible; and/or being seen as a participating member of the research community in order more easily to access others' research of potential interest.

The fact that selection depends on social processes also leads to a number of additional research questions. For example, even though market forces (supply/demand) are important, one implication is that even market selection should be analysed more thoroughly as a social process. In this book, for example, medical knowledge about the product was necessary to get government approval to sell at all. Another implication is that selection criteria cannot be fully determined in advance. For this reason, a hypothesis that agents try to maximize returns according to known selection criteria cannot be supported. The implications of this perspective for understanding technical and economic change should be further explored.

There are also important questions about how and why the generation of novelty is so closely related to selection in human knowledge processes. It has been argued that agents interpret environmental conditions when and while they generate novelty. This implies that during innovation processes, agents must internalize some conditions into the innovation process. For technological activities, this is done particularly through testing and through the development of models or other generalizable knowledge and techniques. Internalizing environmental conditions means that the firm narrows the range of diversity to a subset considered favourable or most valuable. This argument could be further explored through, for example, analysing whether and why some firms can select a more fruitful range of diversity than others.

As to whether economic or technological criteria are most important for innovation, this book illustrates how agents try to interpret them in tandem. Successful innovations are a combination of economic and technical aspects. For example, firms try to estimate what the conditions of sale and demand are likely to be before actually developing and selling a product. In connection with that, management must make decisions about the trade-offs between, for example, performance and price. However, they can also try to change the current trade-offs by increasing quality at the same price. Another alternative is to try to change environmental conditions if they are apparently unfavourable, as when negative public debate threatened to stop research involving genetic engineering.

Agents, however, are working under conditions of uncertainty about future selection criteria and about the results of their knowledge-seeking activities. They will therefore be more or less successful in interpreting those conditions a priori. For example, it is not surprising that Genentech and Kabi were not the only firms in the world which recognized the economic and technical potential of genetic engineering for pharmaceuticals in the 1970s. Nor is it surprising that some pharmaceutical firms decided not to invest in genetic engineering because they felt the risks and uncertainties to be too great. Firms made diverse calculations of risks and possibilities in a situation of uncertainty. Those firms which did develop early commercial uses of genetic engineering still made different decisions about how to access the necessary knowledge and how to proceed with actualizing their visions. Analysis of both firm-level and economic performance must therefore be based on firms' diversity of knowledge, experience, and strategy, and how their choices corresponded to economic and political conditions. The process of evolutionary innovation rests on social interaction as well as on individual decisions.

Concluding Remarks

The theoretical perspective of evolutionary innovation has provoked a number of research questions about economic and technological change in market economies. The analysis of evolutionary innovation unifies market incentives and institutional structures for understanding agents' decisions and behaviour when engaging in knowledge-seeking activities. By so doing, the book will hopefully provoke further reflections and discussions not only about technological innovation processes but also about the implications of an evolutionary and institutional approach for analysing such phenomena.

The contributions of this book lie in uniting empirical and theoretical domains of enquiry in order to address questions about science-based, also known as high-tech, innovation processes. The book presents original empirical material about genetic engineering and biotechnology and an analysis of how technological innovation processes occur. The current approach has implications for our understanding of the world around us and for additional research.

The conclusions to be drawn should therefore interest readers with a more practical orientation, such as R & D managers, researchers, and policy-makers in the fields of science, technology, and industry, as well as readers with a more theoretical interest in technological change. The latter category includes researchers and students from a variety of disciplines, such as economics of technical change, history of science and technology, management of technology, and sociology of technology. If nothing else, the past thirty years of research on science, technology, and innovation has indicated that technological change is a complex social phenomenon. It does not neatly fit into any one discipline or field of activity. Conclusions drawn on the basis of a multi-disciplinary approach can therefore contribute to discussions among a broad range of readers.

The benefits of this multi-disciplinary approach to science-based technology can therefore be as valid for researchers working specifically on technical change as for practitioners directly influencing technical change in firms and government agencies. An example of the latter case can clarify the argument. Let us assume that management in a firm accepts the idea that the development of technological knowledge includes both R & D activity for specific goals and R & D activity to keep up with new knowledge elsewhere but with no apparent return. In this case, the corporate R & D management can see the necessity of having search activities which apparently do not give returns to investment but which still give benefits in the realm of technological knowledge, such as giving absorptive capacity for identifying new options.

It also indicates that high-tech, or science-based, innovation processes in particular involve extended interaction and communication among researchers in different organizations such as universities and firms. This book clearly shows that researchers located in different types of organizations may be doing similar research for similar or different purposes and may be doing related but quite different research. There should be further analysis of how and why researchers at the different types of organizations communicate and how such shared knowledge can be encouraged through policy.

Multi-disciplinarity, the very core of this book, in itself indicates interesting directions for future research. Having chosen a research problem, it is possible truly to integrate different disciplines. Integration means that the specific questions asked, the methodology used, and the theoretical and conceptual discussions referred to come from more than one scientific discipline.

The current book addresses questions and conceptual issues about technical novelty in firms and economies as raised in the economics of technological change.[3] It draws upon historical methodology and upon discussions in history and in sociology of technology about the cognitive dimensions of science and of technology and engineering. Finally, it develops the notion of coevolution of knowledge, institutions, and agents through an analysis integrating economic, sociological, and techno-scientific factors as modes of explanation of change.

One conclusion to be drawn is, therefore, that an approach which truly integrates economic, sociological, and historical approaches is a fruitful way to address research questions about technological innovation processes. The key to doing so is to select limited research questions dealing with complex issues which can be addressed in parallel. Such an approach is not always necessary or beneficial. There are many times when it is enough to compare parallel theoretical and empirical discussions. Nevertheless, multi-disciplinarity at the very core of analysis can open new perspectives and address existing questions in new ways. Like technological innovation processes, this process involves many dead ends and problems, new challenges and opportunities which do not exist but must instead be created and solutions proposed.

[3] It is important to restate that this heterodox tradition within evolutionary and institutional economics and economic history differs quite substantially from neo-classical economics, not least in its similarity to other social sciences in the conceptualization of individual action relative to context.

References

Abbott, Alison (1992), 'Biotechnology Loses Another Battle in Germany', *Nature* 360: 6403, 402.

Åberg, Bertil (1982), *Tillräckligt säkert. Kring införandet av en ny teknik i Sverige— hybrid DNA* (Stockholm: ALBA).

——and Sirvell, Kerstin (1978), 'Förbud skapar utländskt beroende', *Dagens Nyheter* (3 Feb.), 2.

——(1979), 'Svensk industri behöver DNA' *Svenska Dagbladet* (27 Oct.), 3.

Affärsvärlden (1992), 'Tillväxthormon säljer bäst', *Affärsvärlden* 37, 15.

Aharonowitz, Yair and Cohen, Gerald (1981), 'The Microbiological Production of Pharmaceuticals', *Scientific American* 245: 3, 106–18.

Åkerman, Nordal (1977a), 'Vilken rätt har forskning att vara fri?' *Dagens Nyheter* (14 June), 4.

——(1977b), 'Det gäller själva överlevandet', *Dagens Nyheter* (19 July), 4.

——(1977c), 'Stoppa högrisklaboratoriet!', *Dagens Nyheter* (19 Nov.), 2.

——(1978), 'Forskningen och djävulsdoktrinen', *Dagens Nyheter* (30 Jan.), 2.

Aldhous, Peter (1992), 'French Officials Panic over Rare Brain Disease Outbreak', *Science* 258: 4 Dec., 1571–2.

Andersen, Esben Sloth (1994), *Evolutionary Economics: Post-Schumpeterian Contributions* (London: Pinter Publishers).

Andersson, Birgit (1990), 'Smugglande professor gjorde gentekniken lönsam', *Ny Teknik* 16, 12.

Andreopoulos, Spyros (1980), 'Gene Cloning by Press Conference', *The New England Journal of Medicine* 302: 13, 743–6.

Archibugi, Daniele, and Pianta, Mario (1992), *The Technological Specialization of Advanced Countries* (Dordrecht, Netherlands: Kluwer).

Arrow, Kenneth (1962), 'Economic Welfare and the Allocation of Resources for Invention', in *The Rate and Direction of Inventive Activity: Economic and Social Factors* (Princeton, N.J.: Princeton University Press), 609–25.

Arthur, Brian (1988), 'Competing Technologies: An Overview', in Dosi, Giovanni *et al.* (eds.), *Technical Change and Economic Theory* (London: Pinter Publishers).

Bader, Michael (1978), 'Funds from Medical Institute. Biochemistry Split over Hughes Issue', *UCSF Synapse* (Dec.), 1, 4, 5.

Basalla, George (1988), *The Evolution of Technology* (Cambridge: Cambridge University Press).

Benfell, Carol (1980), 'Millions Riding on U.C. Battle with Drug Firms over Interferon', *San Francisco Chronicle* (18 Sept.).

Benner, Susan (1981), 'Genentech: Life under a Microscope. Wall Street and the Media Study Bob Swanson's Every Move', *Inc* (May), 62–8.

Berg, Paul; Baltimore, David; Boyer, Herbert; Cohen, Stanley; Davis, Ronald; Hogness, David; *et al.* (1974), 'Potential Biohazards of Recombinant DNA Molecules', *Science* 185: 26 July, 303.

———Brenner, Sydney; Roblin, Richard III; and Singer, Maxine (1975), 'Asilomar Conference on Recombinant DNA Molecules', *Science* 188: 6 June, 991–4.

Bernal, John D. (1967), *The Social Function of Science* (Cambridge, Mass.: MIT Press).

Bijker, Wiebe; Hughes, Thomas; and Pinch, Trevor (1987) (eds.), *The Social Construction of Technological Systems: New Directions in the Sociology and History of Technology* (Cambridge, Mass.: MIT Press).

Bioengineering News (1983), 'Genentech Partnership Closes: A Detailed Look', 4: 2, 1.

Blume, Stuart S. (1992), *Insight and Industry: On the Dynamics of Technological Change in Medicine* (Cambridge, Mass.: MIT Press).

Boman, Hans (1979), 'Kabi och Hybrid-DNA-forskningen: Här är mer papper på bordet', *Dagens Nyheter* (23 Aug.), 2.

Bud, Robert (1993), *The Uses of Life: A History of Biotechnology* (Cambridge: Cambridge University Press).

Bush, Vannevar (1945), *Science: The Endless Frontier. A Report to the President on Postwar Scientific Research* (Washington, DC).

Business Week (1977), 'A Commercial Debut for DNA Technology' (12 Dec.), 128–9.

Butler, Declan (1993), 'French Appeal Court Sends Allain to Jail', *Nature* 364: 22 July, 269.

Campbell, Donald T. (1987), 'Blind Variation and Selective Retention in Creative Thought as in other Knowledge Processes', in Radnitzky, Gerard, and Bartley, W. W. III (eds.), *Evolutionary Epistemology, Rationality, and the Sociology of Knowledge* (La Salle, Ill.: Open Court).

Carlsson, Bo (1995) (ed.), *Technological Systems and Economic Performance: The Case of Factory Automation* (Dordrech Netherlands: Kluwer).

Carr, Kimberly (1993), 'Creutzfeldt-Jakob Verdict May Prompt New Claims', *Nature* 366: 11 Nov., 98.

Celltech (1984), Annual Report.

———(1985), Annual Report.

———(1986), Annual Report.

Christensen, Kathryn (1980), 'Gene Splicers Develop a Product: New Breed of Scientist–Tycoons', *Wall Street Journal* (24 Nov.), 1, 27.

Clark, Norman (1987), 'Similarities and Differences between Scientific and Technological Paradigms', *Futures* 19: 1, 26–42.

Clarke, Adele and Fujimura, Joan (1992) (eds.), *The Right Tools for the Job: At Work in Twentieth-Century Life Sciences* (Princeton, N.J.: Princeton University Press).

Clayton, Shirley (1986), 'Covering Operating Expenses with Operating Revenues', in *Biotech 86: At the Crossroad* (Arthur Young High Technology Group), 63–7.

Cohen, Stephen (1982), 'The Stanford DNA Cloning Patent', in Whelan, William, and Black, Sandra (eds.), *From Genetic Experimentation to Biotechnology: The Critical Transition* (New York: John Wiley and Sons).

Cohen, Wesley and Levinthal, Daniel (1989), 'Innovation and Learning: The Two Faces of R & D', *The Economic Journal* 99: Sept., 569–96.

Cohn, Victor (1977), 'An Artifical Gene Makes Exact Copy of Brain Hormone', *Washington Post* (3 Nov.), A9.

Constant, Edward W. II (1980), *The Origins of the Turbojet Revolution* (Baltimore: Johns Hopkins University Press).

———(1984), 'Communities in Hierarchies: Structure in the Practice of Science and Technology', in Laudan, Rachael (ed.), *The Nature of Technological Knowledge: Are Models of Scientific Change Relevant?* (Dordrecht, Netherlands: Reidel).

Coombs, Rod; Saviotti, Paolo; and Walsh, Vivien (1987), *Economics and Technological Change* (London: Macmillan Education).

Crawford, Mark (1987), 'Genentech Sues FDA on Growth Hormone', *Science* 235: 20 Mar., 1454–5.

Crick, Francis (1974), 'The Double Helix: a Personal View', *Nature* 248, 766–9.

Culliton, Barbara J. (1981), 'Biomedical Research Enters the Marketplace', *The New England Journal of Medicine* 304: 20, 1195–201.

———(1982a). 'Pajaro Dunes: The Search for Consensus', *Science* 216: 9 Apr., 155–8.

———(1982b). 'The Hoechst Department at Mass General', *Science* 216: 11 June, 1200–3.

Cyert, Richard and March, James (1963), *A Behavioral Theory of the Firm* (Englewood Cliffs, NJ: Prentice-Hall).

Dagens Nyheter (1979), 'Kritik i Stockholm mot Kabis planer: Riskfylld forskning mitt i stan' and 'Behövs för gen-forskning: Risklaboratorium byggs mitt i Stockolm' (15 Aug.), 1, 11.

Dalbøge, Henrik; Dahl, Hans-Henrik M.; Pedersen, John; Hansen, Jørli W.; and Christensen, Thorkild (1987), 'A Novel Enzymatic Method for Production of Authetic hGH from an *Escherichia coli*-Produced hGH-Precursor', *Bio/Technology* 5: Feb., 161–4.

Dasgupta, Partha and David, Paul (1987), 'Information Disclosure and the Economics of Science and Technology', in Feiwel, George R. (ed.), *Arrow and the Ascent of Modern Economic Theory* (New York: Macmillan Press).

David, Paul (1986), 'Understanding the Economics of QWERTY: The Necessity of History', in Parker, William (ed.), *Economic History and the Modern Economist* (Oxford: Basil Blackwell).

DeBresson, Chris (1987), 'The Evolutionary Paradigm and the Economics of Technical Change', *Journal of Economic Issues* 21: 2, 751–62.

Dickson, David (1979), 'Recombinant DNA Research: Private Actions Raise Public Eyebrows', *Nature* 278: 5 Apr., 494–5.

———(1993), 'Malpractice Denied', *Nature* 364: 29 Jul., 372.

Dosi, Giovanni (1984), *Technical Change and Industrial Transformation* (New York: Macmillan).

———(1988), 'Sources, Procedures and Microeconomic Effects of Innovation' *Journal of Economic Literature* 26: 3 (Sept.), 1120–71.

———Freeman, Christopher; Nelson, Richard; Silverberg, Gerald; and Soete, Luc (1988) (eds.), *Technical Change and Economic Theory* (London: Pinter Publishers).

———Pavitt, Keith; and Soete, Luc (1990), *The Economics of Technical Change and International Trade* (London: Harvester Wheatsheaf).

DsU (1978), *Hybrid-DNA tekniken under kontroll*. Utbildningsdepartementet, Nr. 11 (written by Bertil Wennergren) (Stockholm: LiberFörlag).

Durham, William (1991), *Coevolution: Geneses, Culture, and Human Diversity* (Stanford, Calif.: Stanford University Press).

The Economist (1992a), 'Tests of the Truth', 325: 7785, 92–3.

——(1992b), 'The Long and the Short of it', 324: 7767, 81–2.

Edquist, Charles and McKelvey, Maureen (forthcoming), 'The Swedish Paradox: High R & D Intensity Without High Tech Products', in Nielsen, Klaus, and Johnson, Björn (eds.), *Evolution of Institutions, Organizations, and Technology* (Aldershot: Edward Elgar).

Ehrling, Guy (1979a), 'KabiGen bygger högrisklaboratorium i innerstan', *Dagens Nyheter* (15 Aug.), 2.

——(1979b), 'Lägg papperen på bordet', *Dagens Nyheter* (23 Aug.), 2.

——and Ekengard, Inger (1980), *Genetisk ingenjörskonst: tjuvkoppling eller genväg?* (Stockholm: LTs förlag).

Faulkner, Wendy (1994), 'Conceptualizing Knowledge Used in Innovation: A Second Look at the Science–Technology Distinction and Industrial Innovation', *Science, Technology, & Human Values* 19: 4, 425–58.

——and Senker, Jacqueline (1994), *Knowledge Frontiers: Public Sector Research and Industrial Innovation in Biotechnology, Engineering Ceramics, and Parallel Computing* (Oxford: Clarendon Press).

Financial Times (1995), 'Eli Lilly and Genentech Settle Dispute' (6 Jan.), 17.

Foray, Dominique and Freeman, Christopher (1993) (eds.), *Technology and the Wealth of Nations: The Dynamics of Constructed Advantage* (London: Pinter Publishers).

Forecasting and Assessment in Science and Technology (FAST 1982), *Biotechnology in Europe*. Commission of the European Communities. No. 59 Dechema (Frankfurt-am-Main: European Federation of Biotechnology).

Freeman, Christopher (1982), *Economics of Industrial Innovation* (London: Pinter Publishers).

Friedman, Milton (1953), *Essays in Positive Economics* (Chicago: University of Chicago Press).

Genetic Engineering News (1981), 'Side Effects Seen in HGH Trial' (Mar./Apr.), 1, 7.

Gerholm, Tor Ragnar (1977), 'Är forskningen verkligen fri?', *Dagens Nyheter* (22 June), 4.

Gibbons, Michael; Limoges, Camille; Howotny, Helga; Schwartzman, Simon; Scott, Peter; and Trow, Martin (1994), *The New Production of Knowledge: The Dynamics of Science and Research in Contemporary Societies*, (London: Sage Publications).

Glasbrenner, Kimberly (1986), 'Technology Spurt Resolves Growth Hormone Problem, Ends Shortage', *Journal of the American Medical Association* 255: 5, 581–7.

Goeddel, David; Heyneker Herbert; Hozumi Toyohara; Arentzen Rene; Itakura Keiichi ; Yansura Daniel; *et al.* (1979), 'Direct Expression in *Escherichia coli* of a DNA Sequence Coding for Human Growth Hormone', *Nature* 281: 18 Oct. 544–8.

González, Elizabeth Rasche (1979), 'Teams Vie in Synthetic Production of Human Growth Hormone', *Journal of the American Medical Association* 242: 8, 701–2.

Gould, Stephen Jay (1980), *The Panda's Thumb: More Reflections in Natural History* (New York: W. W. Norton and Co.).

304   *References*

Gould, Stephen Jay (1987), 'The Panda's Thumb of Technology', *Natural History* 1: Jan., 14–23.

———and Eldredge, Niles (1993), 'Punctuated Equilibrium comes of Age' *Nature* 366: 18 Nov., 223–7.

Green, Kenneth (1992), 'Creating Demand for Biotechnology: Shaping Technologies and Markets', in Coombs, Rod; Saviotti, Paola; and Walsh, Vivian (eds.), *Technological Change and Company Strategies: Economic and Sociological Perspectives* (London: Harcourt Brace Jovanovich).

Grumbach, Melvin M. (1988), 'Growth Hormone Therapy and the Short End of the Stick', *The New England Journal of Medicine* 319: 4, 238–41.

Gueriguian, John L.; Miller, Henry; Gregoire, A. T.; Schaffenburg, Carlos; and Sobel, Solomon (1981) (eds.), *Insulins, Growth Hormone, and Recombinant DNA Technology* (New York: Raven Press).

Hamilton, Joan (1985), 'Genentech Gets a Shot at the Big Time', *Business Week* (28 Oct.), 108.

Hall, Stephen S. (1988), *Invisible Frontiers: The Race to Synthesize a Human Gene* (London: Sidgwick & Jackson).

Hamrin, Harald (1977), 'Gud vet vilka monster ni har i era provrör', *Dagens Nyheter* (6 Mar.), 23.

Hannon, Norm (1977), 'Cashing in on DNA Research', *San Francisco Tribune* (4 Dec.), 1.

Hansen, Annegrethe; Hansen, Niels; and Pedersen, Jørgen Lindgaard (1991), *Forskning og udvikling i dansk bioteknologi* Projekt Pegasus (Copenhagen: TeknologiNævet).

Harris, E. L. V. and Angal, S. (1989) (eds.), *Protein Purification Methods: A Practical Approach* (Oxford: IRL Press).

Harvey, C.; Olson K.; deCzekala, A; and Nussbaum, A, (1975), 'Construction of a Double-Stranded Deoxyribonucleotide Sequence of 45 Base Pairs Designed to Code for S-Peptide 2–14 of Bovine Ribonuclease A', *Nucleic Acids Research* 2, 2007–20.

Hippel, Eric von (1988), *The Sources of Innovation* (Oxford: Oxford University Press).

Ho, Sa V. (1990), 'Strategies for Large-Scale Protein Purification', in Landisch, Michael; Willson, Richard; Painton, Chih-duen; and Builder, Stuart (eds.), *Protein Purification: From Molecular Mechanisms to Large-Scale Processes* (Washington, DC: ACS).

Hobby, Gladys (1985), *Penicillin: Meeting the Challenge* (New Haven, Conn.: Yale University Press).

Hodgson, Geoffrey (1988), *Economics and Institutions: A Manifest for a Modern Institutional Economics* (Cambridge: Polity Press).

———(1989), 'Institutional Economic Theory: The Old versus the New', *Review of Political Economy* 1: 3, 249–69.

———(1993), *Economics and Evolution: Bringing Life Back into Economics* (Cambridge: Polity Press).

Holmberg, Bo (1977), 'Fri forskning förutsätter ansvarskännade forskare', *Dagens Nyheter* (13 July), 4.

Hsiung, Hansen; Mayne, Nancy; and Becker, Gerald (1986), 'High-Level Expression, Efficient Secretion and Folding of Human Growth Hormone in *Escherichia coli*', *Bio/Technology* 4: Nov. 1986, 991–5.

Hull, David L. (1988), *Science as a Process: An Evolutionary Account of the Social and Conceptual Development of Science* (Chicago: University of Chicago Press).

Hunter, David (1985), 'The Race for Synthetic Human Growth Hormone', *Chemical Weekly* (10 July), 28, 30, 32.

Itakura, Keiichi; Hirose, Tadaaki; Crea, Roberto; Riggs, Arthur; Heyneker, Herbert; Bolivar, Francisco; *et al.* (1977), 'Expression of *Escherichia coli* of a Chemically Synthesized Gene for the Hormone Somatostatin', *Science* 198: 9 Dec., 1056–63.

Judson, Horace (1979), *The Eighth Day of Creation* (New York: Simon and Schuster).

KabiVitrum (1991), Annual Report.

——(1992), Annual Report.

Kahn, Patricia (1992), 'Germany's Gene Law Begins to Bite', *Science* 255: 31 Jan., 524, 526.

Kenney, Martin (1986), *Biotechnology: The University-Industrial Complex* (New Haven, Conn.: Yale University Press).

Kline, Stephen, and Rosenberg, Nathan (1986), 'An Overview of Innovation', in Landau, Ralph, and Rosenberg, Nathan (eds.), *The Positive Sum Strategy: Harnessing Technology for Economic Growth* (Washington, DC: National Academy Press).

Kolata, Gina (1986), 'New Growth Industry in Human Growth Hormone?', *Science* 234: 3 Oct., 22–4.

Koncessionsnämnden för miljöskydd (KNM) (1980a). BESLUT Nr. 141/80, 1980-07-04, Dnr. 502-10/80. Aktbil. 35. Sökande: KabiGen AB. Saken: Ansökan om tillstånd att bedriva forskning med hybrid-DNA-teknik (Stockholm: Miljödepartementet). 11 pages.

——(1980b). BESLUT Nr. 223/80, 1980-12-09, Dnr. 502-146/80. Aktbil. 26. Sökande: KabiVitrum AB. Saken: Ansökan om tillstånd att bedriva utvecklingsarbete med hybrid-DNA-material (Stockholm: Miljödepartementet). 14 pages.

——(1980c). BESLUT Nr. 224/80, 1980-12-09, Dnr. 502-10/80. Aktbil. 72. Sökande: KabiGen AB. Saken: Ansökan om utvidgat tillstånd att bedriva forskning med hybrid-DNA-teknik (Stockholm: Miljödepartementet). 12 pages.

Krimsky, Sheldon (1982), *Genetic Alchemy: The Social History of the Recombinant DNA Controversy* (Cambridge, Mass.: MIT Press).

——Ennis, James G.; and Weissman, Robert (1991), 'Academic-Corporate Ties in Biotechnology: A Quantitative Study', *Science, Technology, & Human Values* 16: 3, 275–87.

Kuhn, Thomas (1970), *The Structure of Scientific Revolutions*, 2nd edn. (Chicago: University of Chicago Press).

Laage-Hellman, Jens (1986), *Bioteknisk FoU i Sverige—forskningvolym, forskningsinriktningar och samarbetsmönster: En studie av det biotekniska FoU-nätverket 1979–1985.* STU-Info 536–1986 (Stockholm: STU).

Landisch, Michael; Willson, Richard; Painton, Chih-duen; and Builder, Stuart (1990) (eds.), *Protein Purification: From Molecular Mechanisms to Large-Scale Processes* (Washington, DC: ACS).

The Lancet (1992), 'Too Tall?' 339: 8 Feb., 339–40.

Lambert, Bo (1977), 'Forskning kan ej styras', *Dagens Nyheter* (5 July), 4.

Langlois, Richard, and Everett, Michael (1994), 'What is Evolutionary Economics?', in Magnusson, Lars (ed.), *Evolutionary and Neo-Schumpeterian Approaches to Economics* (Boston: Kluwer).

Latour, Bruno (1983), 'Give Me a Laboratory and I Will Raise the World', in Knorr-Cetina, Karin, and Mulkay, Michael (eds.), *Science Observed: Perspectives on the Social Studies of Science* (London: Sage).

Laudan, Rachael (1984) (ed.), *The Nature of Technological Knowledge: Are Models of Scientific Change Relevant?* (Dordrecht, Netherlands: Reidel).

Layton, Edwin (1976), 'Technology as Knowledge', *Technology and Culture* 15: 1, 31–41.

Lehrman, Sally (1993a), 'Stanford Seeks Life after Cohen-Boyer Patent Expires', *Nature* 363: 17 June, 574.

——(1993b), 'Challenge to Growth Hormone Trial', *Nature* 364: 15 July, 179.

Lerner, Terry (1981), 'Genentech HGH Goes on Trial', *Genetic Engineering News* (Nov./Dec.), 18.

Levin, Richard; Klevorick, Alvin; Nelson, Richard; and Winter, Sidney (1987), 'Appropriating the Returns from Industrial Research & Development', *Brookings Papers on Economic Activity 3* (Washington, DC: The Brookings Institution).

Lewin, Roger (1978), 'Profile of a Genetic Engineer', *New Scientist* (28 Sept.), 924–6.

Lewontin, R. C. (1992), 'The Dream of the Human Genome', *New York Review of Books* 39: 10, 31–9.

LO/TCO (1982), *Bioteknik—Vår sköna nya värld?* (Stockholm: Tidens förlag).

Lundvall, Bengt-Åke (1988), 'Innovation as an Interactive Process: From User-Producer Interaction to the National System of Innovation', in Dosi, Giovanni et al. (eds.), *Technical Change and Economic Theory* (London: Pinter Publishers).

——(1992) (ed.), *National Systems of Innovation: Towards a Theory of Innovation and Interactive Learning* (London: Pinter Publishers).

Luria, Salvador E.; Gould, Stephen Jay; and Singer, Sam (1981), *A View of Life* (Menlo Park, Calif.: Benjamin/Cummings Publishing Co.).

Läkemedelsindustriföreningen (LIF) (1990), *Fakta 1990* (Läkemedels-industriföreningen (LIF) och Representant föreningen för utländska farmaceutiska industrier. Stockholm: LIF).

McKelvey, Maureen (1991), 'How do National Systems of Innovation Differ? A Critical Analysis of Porter, Freeman, Lundvall and Nelson', in Hodgson, G., and Screpanti, E. (eds.), *Rethinking Economics: Markets, Technology and Economic Evolution* (Aldershot: Edward Elgar Publishing).

——(1992), 'How Evolution Became Male. Or, it is not a Dog Eat Dog World', *European Association for Evolutionary Political Economy Newsletter* 7: Jan., 6.

——(1993a), 'Japanese Institutions Supporting Innovation', in Sjöstrand, Sven-Erik (ed.), *Institutional Development and Change: Theory and Empirical Findings* (New York: Sharpe).

——(1993b), 'Technologies Embedded in Nations? Genetic Engineering and Technological Change in National Systems of Innovation', *The Journal of Socio-Economics* 22: 4, 353–77.

——(1994a), 'National Systems of Innovation', in Tool, Marc; Samuels, Warren; and Hodgson, Geoffrey (eds), *The Elgar Companion to Institutional and Evolutionary Economics* (Aldershot: Edward Elgar Publishing).

——(1994b), *Evolutionary Innovation: Early Industrial Uses of Genetic Engineering*. Ph.D. dissertation (Linköping, Sweden: Linköping University: Department of Technology and Social Change).

——(1995a), 'Evolutionary Systems of Innovation', in Edquist, Charles (ed.), *Systems of Innovation: Conceptual and Theoretical Aspects*.

MacKenzie, Donald, and Wajcman, Judy (1985) (eds.), *The Social Shaping of Technology: How the Refrigerator got its Hum* (Philadelphia: Open University Press).

Marketletter (1993), 'Rapid Growth for World Endocrines' (25 Oct.).

Martial, Joseph; Hallewell, Robert; Baxter, John; and Goodman, Howard (1979), 'Human Growth Hormone: Complementary DNA Cloning and Expression in Bacteria', *Science* 205: 10 Aug., 602–7.

Medical World News (1977), 'Gene-Splicing Factory Set to Produce Hormone' (26 Dec.), 17–18.

——(1979) 'Rival Claims Staked over Gene-spliced Growth Hormone' (6 Aug.), 20–1, 24.

Merton, Robert (1942), *Social Theory and Social Structure* (New York: The Free Press).

Miozzari, Giuseppe (1981), 'Strategies for Obtaining Expression of Peptide Hormones in *E. Coli*', in Gueriguian *et al.* (eds.), *Insulins, Growth Hormone, and Recombinant DNA Technology* (New York: Raven Press).

Mirowski, Philip (1989), *More Heat than Light: Economics as Social Physics, Physics as Nature's Economics* (Cambridge: Cambridge University Press).

Mowery, David, and Rosenberg, Nathan (1982), 'The Influence of Market Demand upon Innovation: A Critical Review of some Recent Empirical Studies', in Rosenberg, Nathan, *Inside the Black Box: Technology and Economics* (Cambridge: Cambridge University Press).

Mulkay, Michael (1977), 'Sociology of the Scientific Research Community' in Spiegel-Rösing, Ina, and Price, Derek de Solla (eds.) *Science, Technology and Society* (London: Sage Press).

National Institutes of Health (NIH 1975), *Research Awards Index*, vol. 2, Fiscal Year 1975. DHEW Publication No. (NIH) 78-200. US Department of Health, Education and Welfare, Public Health Services (Bethesda, Md.: NIH, Division of Research Grants).

——(NIH 1976a), *Research Awards Index*, vol. 2, Fiscal Year 1976. DHEW Publication No. (NIH) 78-200. US Department of Health, Education and Welfare, Public Health Services. (Bethesda, Md.: NIH, Division of Research Grants).

——(NIH 1976b), *Recombinant DNA Research Guidelines*, 7 July, 1976 (Bethesda, Maryland: NIH).

——(NIH 1977), *Research Awards Index*, vol. 2, Fiscal Year 1977. DHEW Publication No. (NIH) 78-200. US Department of Health, Education and Welfare, Public Health Services (Bethesda, Md.: NIH, Division of Research Grants).

——(NIH 1978), *Research Awards Index*, vol. 2, Fiscal Year 1978. DHEW Publication No. (NIH) 78-200. US Department of Health, Education and Welfare, Public Health Services (Bethesda, Maryland: NIH, Division of Research Grants).

National Institutes of Health (NIH 1979), *Research Awards Index*, vol. 2, Fiscal Year 1979. DHEW Publication No. (NIH) 78-200. US Department of Health, Education and Welfare, Public Health Services (Bethesda, Md.: NIH, Division of Research Grants).

Nature (1993), 'Justice Unevenly Spread in Paris', 364: 22 July, 267.

Nelson, Richard (1959), 'The Simple Economics of Basic Scientific Research', *The Journal of Political Economy* 67, 297–306.

——(1987), *Understanding Technical Change as an Evolutionary Process* (Amsterdam: Elsevier Science Publishers).

——(1988), 'Institutions Supporting Technical Change in the United States' in Dosi, Giovanni *et al.* (eds.), *Technical Change and Economic Theory* (London: Pinter Publishers).

——(1990), 'Capitalism as an Engine of Progress', *Research Policy* 19, 193–214.

——(1993) (ed.), *National Systems of Innovation: Case Studies* (Oxford: Oxford University Press).

——(1994), 'The Role of Firm Difference in an Evolutionary Theory of Technical Advance', in Magnusson, L. (ed.), *Evolutionary and Neo-Schumpeterian Approaches to Economics* (Boston: Kluwer).

——and Soete, Luc (1988), 'Policy Conclusions' in Dosi, Giovanni *et al.* (eds.), *Technical Change and Economic Theory* (London: Pinter Publishers).

——and Winter, Sidney (1974), 'Neoclassical versus Evolutionary Theories of Economic Growth: Critique and Prospectus' *Economic Journal* 84, 886–905.

————(1982), *An Evolutionary Theory of Economic Change* (Cambridge, Mass.: Belknap Press).

The New England Journal of Medicine (1980), Letters to Editor in Response to Andreopoulos (1980) 303: 28 Aug., 531–2.

New Scientist (1981), 'Genetic Engineers Make Growth Drug that Works' (22 Oct.), 238.

Nilsson, Göran B. (1973), 'Om det fortfarande behovet av källkritik: Jämte några reflexioner över midsommaren 1941', *Historisk tidskrift* 1, 173–211.

Norgren, Lennart (1989), *Kunskapsöverföring från universitetet till företag: En studie av forskningsbetydelse för de svenska läkemedelsföretagens produktlanseringar 1945-1984*. Ph.D. dissertation (Stockholm: Allmänna Förlaget).

Norman, Colin (1985), 'Virus Scare Halts Hormone Research', *Science* 228: 7 June, 1176–7.

Nossal, Gustav (1985), *Reshaping Life: Key Issues in Genetic Engineering* (Melbourne: Melbourne University Press).

——and Coppel, Ross (1989), *Reshaping Life: Key Issues in Genetic Engineering*, 2nd edn. (Melbourne: Melbourne University Press).

Office of Technology Assessment (OTA 1984), *Commercial Biotechnology: An International Analysis* (Washington DC: US Congress, OTA, OTA-BA-218).

Olson, Kenneth; Fenno, James; Lin, Norman; Harkins, Richard; Snider, C.; Kohr, W. H.; *et al.* (1981), 'Purified Human Growth Hormone from *E. coli* is Biologically Active', *Nature* 293: 1 Oct., 408–11.

Orsenigo, Luigi (1989), *The Emergence of Biotechnology: Institutions and Markets in Industrial Innovation* (London: Pinter Publishers).

Pavitt, Keith (1984), 'Sectoral Patterns of Technical Change: Towards a Taxonomy and a Theory', *Research Policy* 13, 343–73.

———(1991a), 'Key Characteristics of the Large Innovating Firm', *British Journal of Management* 2, 41–50.

———(1991b), 'What Makes Basic Research Economically Useful?' *Research Policy* 20: 2, 109–19.

Penrose, Edith (1952), 'Biological Analogies in the Theory of the Firm', *American Economic Review* 42, 211–40.

Petit, Charles (1977a), 'The Bold Entrepreneurs of Genetic Engineering' *San Francisco Chronicle* (12 Dec.), 2.

———(1977b), 'A Triumph In Genetic Engineering', *San Francisco Chronicle* (2 Dec.), 1, 22.

Pfund, Nancy, and Hofstadter, Laura (1981), 'Biomedical Innovation and the Press', *The Journal of Communication* 31: 2, 138–54.

Philipson, Lennart (1977a), 'Lita på vårt samhällsansvar', *Dagens Nyheter* (28 Nov.), 2.

Piller, Charles, and Yamamoto, Keith (1988), *Gene Wars: Military Control over the New Genetic Technologies* (New York: Beech Tree Books).

Price, Derek de Solla (1963), *Little Science, Big Science* (New York: Columbia University Press).

Rapp, Östen (1977), 'Det onda med det goda', *Dagens Nyheter* (2 June), 4.

Robbins-Roth, Cynthia (1991), 'Who's Who in Biotech', *Upside* 3: 6, 22–37, 84, 86–7.

Root-Bernstein, Robert Scott (1989), *Discovering* (Cambridge, Mass.: Harvard University Press).

Rosenberg, Nathan (1976), *Perspectives on Technology* (Cambridge: Cambridge University Press).

———(1982), *Inside the Black Box: Technology and Economics* (Cambridge: Cambridge University Press).

———(1990), 'Why do Firms do Basic Research (with their own Money)?', *Research Policy* 19: 2, 165–74.

———Landau, Ralph, and Mowery, David (1992) (eds.), *Technology and the Wealth of Nations* (Stanford Calif.: Stanford University Press).

Roskam, Willem (1987), 'La production industrielle de l'hormone de croissance', *La Recherche* 188, 646–56.

Ross, Michael (1981), 'Production of Medically Important Polypeptides using Recombinant DNA Technology', in Gueriguian *et al.* (eds.), *Insulins, Growth Hormone, and Recombinant DNA Technology* (New York: Raven Press).

Sahal, Dieter (1981), 'Alternative Conceptions of Technology', *Research Policy* 10, 2–24.

San Francisco Chronicle (1977), '"Astonishing" Report on Gene Research' (3 Nov.), 3.

Saviotti, Paolo, and Metcalfe, Stan (1991) (eds.), *Evolutionary Theories of Economic and Technological Change: Present Status and Future Prospects* (Reading: Harwood Academic).

Scherer, Frederic (1984), *Innovation and Growth: Schumpeterian Perspectives* (Cambridge, Mass.: MIT Press).

Schmookler, Jacob (1966), *Invention and Economic Growth* (Cambridge, Mass.: MIT Press).

Schoner, Ronald G.; Ellis, Lee F.; and Schoner, Brigitte E. (1985), 'Isolation and

Purification of Protein Granules from *Escherichia coli* Cells Overproducing Bovine Growth Hormone', *Bio/Technology* (Feb. 1985), 151–4.

Schumpeter, Joseph (1968), *The Theory of Economic Development* (Cambridge, Mass.: Harvard University Press).

Science (1978), 'Gene-Splicing Rules: Another Round of Debate', 199: 6 Jan., 30–1.

——(1985), 'Gene-Spliced Hormone for Growth Approved', *Science* 230: 1 Nov., 523.

——(1990), 'Data Sharing: A Declining Ethic?', 'Genome Project: An Experiment in Sharing', 'Agencies, Journals Set Some Rules', 'Geneva on the Beltway', and 'The Great Clone Giveaway', 248: 25 May, 952–8.

Science News (1977), 'Rat Insulin Gene Spliced into Bacteria', 111: 28 May, 340–1.

Scrip (1979), 'Swedish Center Party Urges Halt to KabiGen's Recombinant DNA Research Lab', 440: 21 Nov., 3.

——(1981a), 'Volunteer Studies Establish Safefy and Efficacy of Novo's Human Insulin', 579: 6 Apr., 15.

——(1981b), 'Novo's Strength in Insulin Market', 635: 19 Oct., 5.

——(1988), 'Somatropin Approved in France', 1327: 20 July, 19.

——(1991a), 'Serono Lay-offs, Human Growth Hormone (hGH) action' 1658: 9 Nov., 9.

——(1991b), 'Bio-Technology General Corporation (BTGC) in 1990', 1638: 31 July, 11.

Seeburg, Peter; Shine, John; Martial, Joseph; Baxter, John; and Goodman, Howard (1977), 'Nucleotide Sequence and Amplification in Bacteria of Structural Gene for Rat Growth Hormone' *Science* 270: 8 Dec., 486–93.

————————Ivarie, R. D.; Morris, J. A.; Ullrich, Axel; *et al.* (1978), 'Synthesis of Growth Hormone by Bacteria', *Science* 276: 21/28 Dec., 795–8.

Sharp, Margaret (1991), 'Pharmaceuticals and Biotechnology: Perspectives for the European Industry', in Freeman, Christopher; Sharp, Margaret; and Walker, William (eds.), *Technology and the Future of Europe: Global Competition and the Environment in the 1990s* (London: Pinter Publishers).

Shine, John; Seeburg, Peter; Martial, Joseph; Baxter, John; and Goodman, Howard (1977), 'Construction and Analysis of Recombinant DNA for Human Chorionic Somatomammotropin', *Science* 270: 8 Dec., 494–9.

Simon, Herbert (1957), *Administrative Behavior: A Study of Decision-Making Processes in Administrative Organization*, 2nd edn. (New York: Free Press).

Singer, Maxine, and Soll, Dieter (1973), 'Guidelines for DNA Hybrid Molecules', *Science* 181: 21 Sept., 1114.

Skottner, A.; Forsman, A.; Fhölenhag, K.; Helleberg, A.; Löfberg, E.; Fryklund, L.; *et al.* (1981), 'Human Growth Hormone Produced by *E. coli*: A Preliminary Study of Effects on Hypophysectomized Rats', in Gueriguian *et al.* (eds.), *Insulins, Growth Hormone, and Recombinant DNA Technology* (New York: Raven Press).

Statens offentliga utredningar (SOU) (1984), *Genetisk integritet.* Betänkande av genetikkommitten 1984: 88 (Stockholm: Allmänna Förlaget).

——(1992), *Genteknik—en utmaning.* Betänkande av genteknikberedningen (Stockholm: Allmänna Förlaget).

Staudenmaier, John M. (1985), *Technology's Storytellers: Reweaving the Human Fabric* (Cambridge, Mass.: MIT Press).

Stebbing, N.; Olson K.; Lin N.; Harkins R. N.; Snider C.; Ross M.; *et al.* (1981), 'Biological Comparison of Natural and Recombinant DNA-Derived Polypeptides', in Gueriguian *et al.* (eds.), *Insulins, Growth Hormone, and Recombinant DNA Technology* (New York: Raven Press).

Steinmueller, W. Edward (1994), 'Basic Research and Industrial Innovation', in Dodgson, Mark and Rothwell, Roy (eds.), *The Handbook of Industrial Innovation* (Aldershot: Edward Elgar).

Stockton, William (1980), 'On the Brink of Altering Life', *New York Times Magazine* (17 Feb.), 17–19, 62–4, 76–8.

Styrelsen för Teknisk Utveckling (STU) och Delegationen för hybrid-DNA-frågor (1982), *Etik och Genteknik*, STU-information nr. 304-1982 (Stockholm: STU).

Svenska Farmaceutisk Tidskrift (1980), 'KabiVitrum sluter avtal med det engelska hälsovårdsdepartementet', 84: 15, 623.

Swanson, Robert (1986a), 'People Make Decisions as Owners', in *Biotech 86: At the Crossroad* (Arthur Young High Technology Group), 58–62.

——(1986b), 'Entrepreneurship and Innovation: Biotechnology', in Landau, Ralph, and Rosenberg, Nathan (eds.), *The Positive Sum Strategy: Harnessing Technology for Economic Growth* (Washington, DC: National Academy Press).

Swinbanks, David (1993), 'American Witnesses Testify in Japan about AIDS Risks', *Nature* 364: 15 July, 181.

Tatum, Edward (1959), 'A Case History of Biological Research', *Science* 129: 26 June, 1711–15.

Time (1990), 'A Chance to Be Taller' (8 Jan.), 70.

Tushman, Michael, and Anderson, Philip (1986), 'Technological Discontinuities and Organizational Environments', *Administrative Science Quarterly* 31, 439–65.

Tyson, Laura D'Andrea (1992), *Who's Bashing Whom? Trade Conflict in High-Technology Industries* (Washington, DC: Institute for International Economics).

Ullrich, Axel; Shine, John; Chirgwin, John; Pictet, Raymond; Tischer, Edmund; Rutter, William; *et al.* (1977), 'Rat Insulin Genes: Construction of Plasmids Containing the Coding Sequences', *Science* 196: 13 June, 1313–19.

Underwood, Louis (1984), 'Report of the Conference on Uses and Possible Abuses of Biosynthetic Human Growth Hormone', *The New England Journal of Medicine* 311: 9, 606–8.

——(1988) (ed.), *Human Growth Hormone: Progress and Challenges* (New York: Marcel Dekker, Inc.).

Uppsala Nya Tidningen (1977), 'Medicinpristagarnas arbeten möjliggör studiet av livsviktiga organs funktioner' (14 Oct.), 10.

Utterback, James M., and Abernathy, William J. (1975), 'A Dynamic Model of Product and Process Innovation', *Omega* 3: 6, 639–56.

Vincenti, Walter G. (1990), *What Engineers Know and How they Know it: Analytical Studies from Aeronautical History* (Baltimore: Johns Hopkins Press).

Wade, Nicholas (1980), 'What's Happening at Genentech', *San Francisco Chronicle* (14 Nov.), 31, 34.

Walgate, Robert (1980), 'Genetic Engineering: Hormone Growth', *Nature* 288: 11 Dec., 528.

Wallgren, Jacques (1993), 'Läkemedelsjätten måste växa', *Dagens Nyheter* (8 Mar.), C: 1, 2.

Walsh, Vivien (1993), 'Demand, Public Markets and Innovation in Biotechnology', *Science and Public Policy* 20: 3, 138–56.

Watson, James (1968), *The Double Helix: A Personal Account of the Discovery of the Structure of DNA* (New York: Mentor).

——(1986), 'From Understanding to Manipulating DNA', in Landau, Ralph, and Rosenberg, Nathan (eds.), *The Positive Sum Strategy: Harnessing Technology for Economic Growth* (Washington, DC: National Academy Press).

Werth, Barry (1991), 'How Short is Too Short? Marketing Human Growth Hormone', *The New York Times Magazine* (16 June) sect. 6, 14–17, 28–9.

Wieslander, Lars (1977), 'Vem ska bestämma?', *Dagens Nyheter* (16 June), 4.

Witt, Ulrich (1991), 'Reflections on the Present State of Evolutionary Economic Theory', in Hodgson, G., and Screpanti, E. (eds.), *Rethinking Economics: Markets, Technology and Economic Evolution* (Aldershot: Edward Elgar Publishing).

Wright, Susan (1978), 'DNA: Let the Public Choose', *Nature* 275: 12 Oct., 468.

——(1986), 'Recombinant DNA Technology and its Social Transformation, 1972–1982', *Osiris* (2nd ser.) 2, 303–60.

Yamamoto, Keith (1982), 'Faculty Members as Corporate Officers: Does Cost Outweigh Benefit?', in Whelan, William, and Black, Sandra (eds.), *From Genetic Experimentation to Biotechnology—The Critical Transition* (New York: John Wiley and Sons).

Yoxen, Edward (1987), *The Impact of Biotechnology on Living and Working Conditions* (Shankill, Ireland: Loughlinstown House).

Archival and Unpublished Material

Genentech (1981), press release about vaccine against foot-and-mouth virus (South San Francisco).

——(1987), *Amended Complaint* to the US District Court, Northern District of California, Case No. C-87 5643 TEH.

——(1989),'Recombinant Procaryotic Cell Containing Correctly Processed Human Growth Hormone', US Patent No. 4,859,600. Patent dated 22 Aug. 1989.

Glass, Laurel E. (1979a), Vice-Chairperson, UCSF Academic Senate. Letter to Sheldon Wolff, Chair, Committee on Rules and Jurisdication. (Dated 11 Jan., 1979.)

——(1979b). Chairperson, UCSF San Francisco Division, Academic Senate. Letter from Glass, to Michela Reichman, Director, News Services and Publications. (Dated 2 Oct., 1979).

McKelvey, Maureen (1995a), 'Technological Discontinuities in Genetic Engineering in Pharmaceuticals? Firm Jumps and Lock-in in Systems of Innovation', paper presented at the European Conference on Management of Technology, Aston Univ., Birmingham, 3–5 July 1995.

Philipson, Lennart (1977b), transcript of interviews with Professor Charles Weiner. Recombinant DNA History Collection (MC 100), Institute Archives and Special Collections, MIT Libraries, Cambridge, Mass.

Reichman, Michela (1979), Director of UCSF News Services/Publications. A Press release about human growth hormone (Dated 9 July, 1979).

Rosén, Carl-Gustaf (1991), Referat av 'Bioteknik -Fakta och Visioner', Konferens i Stockholm den 26 November 1991 på inbjudan av Delegationen för hybrid-DNA-frågor, NUTEK och Stiftelsen Bioteknisk Forskning.

Styrelsen för Teknisk Utveckling (STU) (1979), Handlingar för 1979/80, Behovsområdet 'Livsmedelsteknik'.

United States Department of Agriculture (USDA 1981), 'Block Announces Production of Foot and Mouth Disease Vaccine', press release (USDA News Center).

Wolff, Sheldon (1979), 'Report of Committee on Rules and Jurisdiction', mimeo (undated). UCSF, the Library, Special Collections. Archival Collection News Services, Records, 1976–86. Archives number AR 86–7, Series II, Recombinant DNA, folder 94.

Interviews and Personal Communication

Andreopoulos, Spyros (1992), Director of the News Bureau, Stanford University Medical Center. Interview with author, 2 April Palo Alto-Stanford University, Calif.

Bennett, William (1993a), Staff Scientist and Director, Recovery Process R & D, Genentech. Interview with author on 13 January in South San Francisco, Calif.
———(1993b), letter to author dated 18 Oct. (South San Francisco).

Bower, Sandra (1992), Corporate Communications, Eli Lilly and Company, letter to author dated 6 Mar.

Brunius, Gustaf (1992a), Associate Professor. Delegationen för Hybrid-DNA-frågor. telephone interview with author, 4 Mar.
———(1992b), telephone interview with author, 8 Dec.

Chirgwin, John M. (1993), Associate Professor of Medicine, the University of Texas Health Science Center; formerly post-doc under Professor Rutter, UCSF, in the late 1970s, letter to author dated 6 July (San Antonio).

Danielsson, Gunnar (1992), Previously Chairman of the 'Arbetarskydsstyrelesen'; retired. Telephone interview with author, 15 Dec.

Enfors, Sven-Olof (1992), Professor, Institutionen för biokemi och biokemisk teknologi. Interview with author, 1 Dec., Stockholm.

Florell, Cirl (1992), '1:e laboratorieingenjör', Fermentation Development, Kabi, Stockholm; retired. Interview with author, 19 Oct., (Stockholm).
———(1993), letter to author dated 13 Nov., (Sunbyberg, Sweden).

Fhölenhag, Karin (1992), Kabi Pharmacia, Stockholm. Interview with author, 19 Oct., (Stockholm).

Fryklund, Linda (1992), Director of R & D Peptide Hormones, Kabi, Stockholm; previously Department Head of the Recip Hormone Laboratory and Head of

Growth Factors Research at KabiVitrum. Interview with author, 25 Nov., (Stockholm).

———(1993), letter to author dated 18 Nov., (Stockholm).

Goeddel, David (1993), Vice President of Research, Tularik; Previously Genentech Scientist. Letter to author dated 27 Oct., (South San Francisco).

Gray, Charles (1992), Scientific Affairs Manager, ZymoGenetics. Interview with author, 29 Mar., (Seattle).

Holmström, Björn (1992), Fermentation, Peptide-Hormone R & D, Kabi Pharmacia, Stockholm. Interview with author, 7 Oct., (Stockholm).

———(1994), letter to author dated 8 Feb., (Stockholm).

Jones, Andrew (1993), Protein Chemist, R & D, Genentech. Interview with author, 18 Jan., (South San Francisco).

———(1994), letter to author no date (received Jan. 1994) (South San Francisco).

Kleid, Dennis (1993), Legal Department, Genentech. Interview with author, 18 Jan., (South San Francisco).

———(1994), letter to author dated 14 Jan., (South San Francisco).

Lin, Norm (1993a), Senior Scientist, Cell Culture & Fermentation R & D, Genentech. Interview with author, 11 Jan., (South San Francisco).

———(1993b), letter to author. Dated 19 Oct., (South San Francisco).

af Malmborg, Charlotte (1992), previous position 'Handläggare på livsmedelsteknik', Styrelsen för Teknisk Utveckling. Interview with author, 27 Oct., (Stockholm).

———(1993), letter to author dated 25 Nov., (Sundbyberg, Sweden).

McKelvey, Maureen (1992b), letter to Sandra Bower, Corporate Communications, Eli Lilly and Co., dated 16 Oct., (Linköping, Sweden).

Messer, Barb (1992), Genentech, Library Manager. Letter to author dated 9 Dec.

Olson, Kenneth (1993a), Recovery Process R & D, Genentech. Interview with author on 13 Jan., (South San Francisco).

———(1993b), letter to author dated 12 Dec., (South San Francisco).

Pettersson, Ulf (1992), Professor, Department of Medical Genetics, Uppsala University, Uppsala, Sweden. Interview with author on 27 Oct., (Uppsala).

Raines, Stephen (1992), Legal Department, Genentech. Letter to author dated 10 Dec., (South San Francisco).

———(1993), interview with author, 13 Jan., (South San Francisco).

Reichard, Peter (1993), Professor Emeritus, Biochemical Department, Karolinska Institute, Stockhom. Letter to author dated 21 June, (Stockholm).

Ross, Barbara (1992), Corporate Communications, Genentech. Letter to author dated 15 Dec., (South San Francisco).

Sievertsson, Hans (1992), Vice-president for R & D, Kabi Pharmacia, Uppsala. Interview with author on 2 Dec., (Uppsala).

———(1993), letter to author dated 19 June, (Uppsala).

Wieslander, Lars (1992), Associate Professor in Molecular Genetics, Karolinska Institute, Stockholm. Telephone interview with author, 18 Nov.

Yamamoto, Keith (1992), Professor at the Department of Biochemistry and Biophysics, UCSF. Interview with author, 30 Mar., (San Francisco).

Yansura, Daniel (1992), Senior Research Associate, Department of Cell Genetics,

Genentech, South San Francisco, California. Interview with author on 1 Apr., (South San Francisco).

———(1993a), interview with author, 18 Jan., (South San Francisco).

———(1993b), letter to author dated 19 Nov., (South San Francisco).

Young, William (1992), Vice President of Manufacturing and Process Sciences, Genentech. Interview with author, 1 Apr., (South San Francisco).

Index